From Logic Programming to Prolog

From Logic Programming to Prolog

Krzysztof R. Apt
Stichting Mathematisch Centrum

PRENTICE HALL
London New York Toronto Sydney Tokyo Singapore
Madrid Mexico City Munich Paris

First published 1997 by
Prentice Hall Europe
Campus 400, Maylands Avenue
Hemel Hempstead
Hertfordshire, HP2 7EZ
A division of
Simon & Schuster International Group

Printed and bound in Great Britain by
Redwood Books, Trowbridge, Wiltshire

Library of Congress Cataloging-in-Publication Data

Apt, Krzysztof, 1949–
    From logic programming to Prolog / Krzysztof R. Apt
      p.   cm. — (Prentice-Hall international series in computer
science)
    Includes bibliographical references and index.
    ISBN 0-13-230368-X
    1. Logic programming.   2. Prolog (Computer program language)
I. Title. II. Series.
QA76.63.A67   1996
005.13'3—dc20   96-9779
                                     CIP

British Library Cataloguing-in-Publication Data

A catalogue record for this book is available from the British Library

ISBN 0-13-230368-X

1 2 3 4 5 01 00 99 98 97

To Alma, Daniel and Ruth

Contents

List of Figures

List of Programs

Preface

Prolog is some twenty years old and so is logic programming. However, they were developed separately and these two developments never really merged. In particular, the books on Prolog place an emphasis on the explanation of various language features and concentrate on teaching the programming style and techniques. In contrast, the books on logic programming deal with the theoretical foundations of the subject and place an emphasis on the mathematical theory of the underlying concepts. As a result of these separate developments, verification of Prolog programs fell somewhere in the middle and did not receive the attention it deserved.

Many Prolog programs are much simpler and shorter than their counterparts written in imperative programming languages. But for practically every Prolog program there exists a fine line separating the queries which yield correct results from the queries which "go wrong". So program verification is as important for Prolog as for other programming languages.

The aim of this book is to introduce the foundations of logic programming and elements of Prolog, and show how the former can be applied to reason about the latter. To make the book also appropriate for teaching Prolog, a separate chapter on advanced features of Prolog is included.

Due to its structure the book makes it possible to teach in the same course, in an integrated way, both logic programming and Prolog. It is appropriate for the senior undergraduate and for the graduate courses. In fact, we used it for both of them.

Throughout the theoretical chapters some basic mathematical ability is needed to follow the arguments. We assume from the reader familiarity with mathematical induction, but not much more. The presentation is self-contained and in particular, all the notions used are precisely explained and often illustrated by examples.

It is useful to mention that very few results about the theory of logic programming are needed to reason about the considered subset of Prolog. On the other hand, these results have to be augmented by additional ones that are established while dealing with specific program properties, like the termination or absence of run-time errors.

Each of these program properties can be dealt with by applying one or two specific results tailored to this property. The usefulness of these methods is demonstrated by several examples.

We confined our presentation to a basic core of the theory of logic programming and only a simple subset of Prolog is treated in a formal way. This allowed us to keep the book limited in size and consequently appropriate for a one semester course. Such a course naturally breaks down into three components:

- theory of logic programming,
- programming in Prolog,
- verification of Prolog programs.

Each of these topics is of importance in its own right and in fact the book is organized so that the first two can be studied independently. But studying these three subjects together shows that they form a meaningful whole.

Acknowledgements

Various chapters of this book are based on a joint work I carried out during the last five years with a number of colleagues. I would like to take this opportunity and thank them for this fruitful cooperation.

In particular, Chapter 6 is based on a joint work with Dino Pedreschi, Chapter 7 on a joint work with Alessandro Pellegrini and Chapter 10 profited from papers written jointly with Sandro Etalle and Elena Marchiori. Further, in Chapters 5 and 11 I used some concepts from a joint work with Frank Teusink, in Chapters 6, 8 and 10 I incorporated some results from a joint paper with Ingrid Luitjes and in Chapters 8 and 10 I drew on some results from a joint work with Maurizio Gabbrielli and Dino Pedreschi.

Speaking about joint work — this book was started as a joint project with Kees Doets in 1991, the aim of which was to write a comprehensive book on the resolution method, logic programming and formal aspects of Prolog. However, soon it turned out that, in contrast to me, Kees was able to shut off from all other tasks and concentrate solely on the book writing.

Noticing the growing disproportion (to my disadvantage) between my part and that of Kees I finally took up the courage and suggested to Kees that he publishes his part as a separate book. And so it happened — see Doets [Doe94] on page 17 for the outcome. I heartily recommend this book to those who would like to study various aspects of logic programming theory omitted from this text, like computability and foundations of logic programming with negation. I would like to thank Kees here for numerous discussions we had on the subject of logic programming from which I greatly profited.

Further, several people took the trouble to read and comment on this book in different stages of its writing and provided me with valuable criticism. These are anonymous referees, Annalisa Bossi, Livio Colussi, Włodek Drabent, Nissim Francez, Zoe Goey, Andrew Jones, Witek Marek and Dino Pedreschi. I also benefited from useful discussions with Marianne Kalsbeek, Katuscia Palamidessi and Andrea Schaerf. Frank Teusink kindly designed most of the figures for me and students of my courses helped me to polish the material.

Finally, I would like to thank the staff of Prentice Hall, in particular Jacqueline Harbor, for the efficient and professional handling of all the stages of the production of this book.

Chapter 1

Introduction

1.1 Background

Logic programming is a simple, yet powerful formalism suitable for programming and for knowledge representation. It was introduced in 1974 by R. Kowalski. Logic programming grew out of an earlier work on automated theorem proving based on the resolution method. The major difference is that logic programming can be used not only for proving but also for computing. In fact, logic programming offers a new programming paradigm, which was originally realized in Prolog, a programming language introduced in the early 1970s by a group led by A. Colmerauer. Since then the logic programming paradigm has inspired a design of new programming languages which have been successfully used to tackle various computationally complex problems.

The simplicity of the logic programming framework attracted to this area many researchers with interest in theoretical foundations. A rigorous mathematical framework for logic programming can be built by applying methods and techniques of mathematical logic. In many cases these methods have to be fine-tuned and appropriately modified to be useful in logic programming. It should be added here that some basic concepts of logic programming, like unification, were developed earlier by computer scientists working in the field of automated reasoning.

But there have been also many challenges for those inclined in more practical aspects of computer science. Efficient implementation of Prolog and its extensions, development of appropriate programming methodology and techniques, that aim at better understanding of the logic programming paradigm and, finally, design of various successors and/or improvements of Prolog turned out to be an exciting and highly non-trivial field calling for new solutions and fresh insights.

Prolog was originally designed as a programming language for natural language processing. But it soon turned out that other natural applications for the logic programming paradigm exist. This accounts for its widespread popularity. Current applications of logic programming involve such diverse areas as molecular biology, design of VLSI systems, representation of legislation and option trading. These applications exploit the fact that knowledge about certain domains can be conveniently written down as facts and rules which can be directly translated into Prolog programs.

These three aspects of logic programming — theory, programming and applications — grew together and often influenced each other. This versatility of logic programming makes it an attractive subject to study and an interesting field to work in.

1.2 Declarative Programming

Logic programming allows us to write programs and compute using them. There are two natural interpretations of a logic program. The first one, called a *declarative interpretation*, is concerned with the question *what* is being computed, whereas the second one, called a *procedural interpretation*, explains *how* the computation takes place. Informally, we can say that declarative interpretation is concerned with the *meaning*, whereas procedural interpretation is concerned with the *method*.

These two interpretations are closely related to each other. The first interpretation helps us to better understand the second and explains why logic programming supports *declarative programming*. Loosely speaking, declarative programming can be described as follows. *Specifications*, when written in an appropriate format, can be used as a *program*. Then the desired conclusions follow *logically* from the program. To compute these conclusions some *computation mechanism* is available.

Now "thinking" declaratively is in general much easier than "thinking" procedurally. So declarative programs are often simpler to understand and to develop. In fact, in some situations the specification of a problem in the appropriate format already forms the algorithmic solution to the problem. In other words, declarative programming makes it possible to write executable specifications. It should be added however, that in practise the programs obtained in this way are often inefficient, so this approach to programming has to be coupled with appropriate use of program transformations and various optimization techniques.

Moreover, declarative programming reduces the issue of correctness of programs to an analysis of the program from the logical point of view. In this analysis the computation mechanism can be completely disregarded. This is an important reduction which significantly simplifies the task of program verification.

This dual interpretation of logic programs also accounts for the double use of logic programming — as a formalism for programming and for knowledge representation, and explains the importance of logic programming in the field of artificial intelligence.

1.3   Logic Programming Paradigm

To get a better understanding of the logic programming paradigm let us consider now three simple examples of Prolog programs. They will illustrate various aspects of programming in Prolog. They are chosen to be simplistic on purpose.

Example 1 Consider a problem of setting up a database of flight connections. The idea is to be able to answer various simple questions, like "is there a direct flight from A to B", "can I fly from C to D", "what are the possible destinations I can reach from E", etc. Of course, at the end of this century one can fly practically from every large city to every other one, but think for a moment about the beginnings of civil aviation or about the connections of only one company, say Busy World Airlines.

To make things simple, suppose that there are only a couple of direct flights, which we shall list as follows:

```
direct(amsterdam, seattle).
direct(amsterdam, paramaribo).
direct(seattle, anchorage).
direct(anchorage, fairbanks).
```

To deal with possibly indirect flights, let us first agree that there are two possibilities. The first one is to fly directly, which we write as

```
connection(X, Y)  ←  direct(X, Y).
```

which is to be read as "there is a connection from X to Y if there is a direct flight from X to Y". Here X and Y are variables. In Prolog they are written starting with an upper case letter. (Here and elsewhere in the book we use the logic programming symbol " ← " instead of Prolog's ":-").

The second possibility is to fly indirectly. So such a connection involves first a direct flight to a third place followed by a possibly indirect flight from there to the final destination. We shall write it as follows:

```
connection(X, Y)  ←  direct(X, Z), connection(Z, Y).
```

which is to be read as "there is a connection from X to Y if there is a direct flight from X to Z and a connection from Z to Y". We call the above two expression *rules*. In this way we summarized the problem. Now we would like to answer the above mentioned questions. To this end we should write the corresponding program(s) and run it on specific inputs. But the program is already written — the above six formal lines form a Prolog program. We can now run it with the queries of interest. So we have (what follows is an actual listing of Prolog output):

"is there a flight from Amsterdam to Fairbanks?"

```
| ?- connection(amsterdam, fairbanks).
```

yes

"where can one fly to from Seattle?"

```
| ?- connection(seattle, X).
```

```
X = anchorage ;
```

```
X = fairbanks ;
```

no

(Here ";" is a request typed by the user to get more solutions.)

"can one fly somewhere from Fairbanks?"

```
| ?-  connection(fairbanks, X).
```

no

etc.

   This example shows two aspects of Prolog. First, the same program can be used
to compute answers to different problems (or queries). Second, a program can
be used much like a database. However, in a usual database all the facts about
connections would be stored, whereas here they are computed from more basic
facts by means of rules. The databases in which the knowledge is stored in the
form of both facts and rules is called a deductive database. Thus, Prolog allows us
to model query processing in deductive databases.

Example 2 Consider the problem of finding all elements which appear in two given
lists. In what follows we denote a list of elements $a_1, \ldots, a_n$ by $[a_1, \ldots, a_n]$. Such a
list can be alternatively written as $[a_1 | [a_2 \ldots, a_n]]$; a_1 is called the head of $[a_1, \ldots, a_n]$
and $[a_2, \ldots, a_n]$ the tail of $[a_1, \ldots, a_n]$. So for example, 1 is the head of $[1, 2, 3, 4, 5]$,
whereas $[2, 3, 4, 5]$ is the tail of $[1, 2, 3, 4, 5]$, and we have $[1, 2, 3, 4, 5] = [1 | [2, 3, 4, 5]]$.

   First we need to define when an element X is a member of the list. Two cases
arise. If X is the head, then the answer is positive. Otherwise we need to check if
X is a member of the tail. This translates into the following rules that define the
member relation:

```
member(X, [X | List]).
member(X, [Y | List])  ←  member(X, List).
```

   The solution to our problem is now straightforward: we just introduce the rule
which defines the desired relation:

```
member_both(X, L1, L2)  ←  member(X, L1), member(X, L2).
```

which is to be read as — how else? — X is a member of both L1 and L2 if it is a member of L1 and a member of L2. In such a way we obtained a Prolog program which solves the problem. We can now use it for computing. For example, we have

```
| ?- member_both(X, [1,2,3], [2,3,4,5]).
```

```
X = 2 ;
```

```
X = 3 ;
```

```
no
```

Note that a solution of the analogous problem in the imperative programming style requires a double loop. For example, in Pascal we need to write something like

program members_both;
const $m = 100$;
$\qquad n = 200$;
type $A = \mathbf{array}[1..m]$ **of** *integer*;
$\qquad B = \mathbf{array}[1..n]$ **of** *integer*;
$\qquad C = \mathbf{array}[1..n]$ **of** *integer*;
var $a : A$;
$\qquad b : B$;
$\qquad c : C$;
$\qquad l : integer$;
procedure $members(a : A;\ b : B;\ \mathbf{var}\ c : C,\ \mathbf{var}\ l : integer)$;
$\quad$ **var** $i : 1..m$;
$\qquad\quad j : 1..n$;
$\qquad\quad k : 1..n$;
$\quad$ **begin**
$\quad k := 1$;
$\quad$ **for** $i := 1$ **to** m **do**
$\qquad$ **for** $j := 1$ **to** n **do**
$\qquad\quad$ **if** $a[i] = b[j]$ **then**
$\qquad\quad$ **begin**
$\qquad\qquad c[k] := a[i];\ k := k + 1$
$\qquad\quad$ **end**;
$\quad l := k - 1$
$\quad$ **end**;
begin
$\ \ldots$
$members(a, b, c, l)$;

. . .

end.

Here the original lists are stored in the arrays $a[1..m]$ and $b[1..n]$ and the outcome is computed in the segment $[1..l]$ of the array $c[1..n]$. In addition to the above three arrays two constants and four integer variables are also used.

This example shows that the searching mechanism does not need to be explicitly specified in Prolog — it is implicitly given. In the last rule the variable X implicitly generates all elements of the first list, which are then tested for membership in the second list. But this is the procedural interpretation of the program and it was not needed to design it. In fact we obtained the program by referring to its declarative interpretation.

In contrast to the Pascal solution, the Prolog solution can be used in a number of ways, for example for testing

```
| ?- member_both(2, [1,2,3], [2,3,4,5]).
```

yes

or even for instantiating an element of a list:

```
| ?- member_both(2, [1,2,3], [X,3,4,5]).
```

X = 2

Finally, in Pascal the length of the arrays has to be known in advance. So the above piece of Pascal program had to be preceded by an initialization of the constants m, n to some values fixed in advance, here 100 and 200. So in principle for every pair of lengths a different program needs to be written. To be able to deal with lists of arbitrary lengths arrays cannot be used and one has to construct the lists dynamically by means of pointers.

Example 3 Consider the following puzzle from Brandreth [Bra85, page 22]:

> **Strange Squares**. The square of 45 is 2025. If we split this in two, we get 20 and 25. 20 plus 25 is 45 — the number we started with.
> Find two other numbers with four-digit squares that exhibit the same peculiarity.

To solve it using Prolog we just write down the definition of the number the square of which is "strange" according to the above description. For clarity, we also include the second argument which stands for the square of the number in question.

```
sol(N, Z) ←
    between(10, 99, N),
    Z is N*N,
    Z ≥ 1000,
    Z // 100 + Z mod 100 =:= N.
```

Here "*" stands for multiplication, "//" for integer division, "mod" for the reminder of the integer division and "=:=" for Prolog's equality. In turn "is" is Prolog's counterpart of the assignment statement which evaluates the right-hand side and assigns the value of it to the variable on the left-hand side. So for example

```
| ?- X is 2*3.
```

```
X = 6
```

Finally, `between(X, Y, Z)` is a relation which holds if `Z` is an integer between the integers `X` and `Y`, i.e. if $X \leq Z \leq Y$ holds. It is used here to successively generate all integers between 10 and 99. For certain reasons we postpone the definition of `between` to Section 1.4.

Now, to solve the puzzle, we just need to run the query `sol(N, Z)`:

```
| ?- sol(N, Z).
```

```
N = 45,
Z = 2025 ;
```

```
N = 55,
Z = 3025 ;
```

```
N = 99,
Z = 9801 ;
```

```
no
```

The above program is very simple. Note that all what was needed was to describe the problem. This declarative interpretation turned out to be sufficient for obtaining the desired program. Procedurally, this program performs quite a laborious computation: for every natural number between 10 and 99 it tests whether it is a possible solution to the problem. As in the case of the other two programs we can use it not only for computing but also for testing or for a mixture of both:

```
| ?- sol(55, 3025).
```

```
yes
```

```
| ?- sol(55, Z).
```

```
Z = 3025
```

```
yes
```

```
| ?- sol(44, Z).
```

```
no
```

We have seen so far three examples of Prolog programs. In general, a Prolog program is a sequence of facts, like `direct(amsterdam, seattle)` and rules, like `member(X, [Y | List])` ← `member(X, List)`. These facts and rules define *relations*. Both the order of the facts and rules in the program and the order of elements in rules bodies matter from the computation point of view.

The computation starts by posing a query, like `sol(N, Z)`. A query can be seen as a request to find values for the query variables for which the query holds. As we have seen, each program can be used with various queries.

So programming in Prolog boils down to writing definitions of relations in a specific, restricted syntax.

1.4   Shortcomings of Prolog

The programs exhibited in the previous section and many other Prolog programs are concise, versatile and elegant. So naturally, Prolog was advertised by some as the programming language in which programming is reduced to the writing of self-explanatory specifications. This view is in our opinion incorrect and misleading.

It is undoubtedly true that many Prolog programs are strikingly elegant and straightforward to write. This explains its widespread use and remarkable popularity. However, one should also bear in mind that a naive use of Prolog can easily lead to unexpected difficulties and undesired behaviour. More specifically

  (i) almost every Prolog program can be used in a wrong way,
 (ii) arithmetic in Prolog is quite clumsy and its use can easily lead to problems,
(iii) some Prolog programs can be hopelessly inefficient.

Let us discuss these statements one by one.

Re: (i) (a) **Termination.** Suppose that to the program from Example 1 we add the seemingly innocent fact

```
direct(seattle, seattle).
```

(Think about some scenic flights above the town.) Then if this fact is added at the end of the program, the query `connection(seattle, X)` produces repeatedly all the answers:

```
| ?- connection(seattle, X).
```

```
X = anchorage ;
```

```
X = seattle ;

X = fairbanks ;

X = anchorage ;

etc.
```

If on the other hand this fact is added at the beginning of the program, then the following puzzling behaviour results:

```
| ?- connection(seattle, X).

X = seattle ;

X = anchorage ;

X = seattle ;

X = anchorage ;

etc.
```

So the answer `X = fairbanks` is never produced.

Further, consider now the situation when the order of the rules defining the `connection` relation is reversed. Then when the fact `direct(seattle, seattle)` is added at the beginning of the program, the execution of the above query continues forever, and when this fact is added at the end of the program, repeatedly only one answer is produced:

```
| ?- connection(seattle, X).

X = fairbanks ;

X = fairbanks ;

etc.
```

This shows that it is easy to end up with non-terminating computations.

(b) **The Occur-check Problem**. Consider now the program from Example 2. If we run it with the query `member(X, [f(X),X])` which checks whether the variable X occurs in the list consisting of two terms, `f(X)` and X, then instead of yielding a positive answer, the execution unexpectedly continues forever and produces the following interrupted listing:

```
| ?- member(X, [f(X), X]).


X = f(f(f(f(f(f(f(f(f(f(f(f(f(f(f(f(f(f(f(f(f(f(f(f(f(f(f(f(f(f(f(f(f(f(
...
```

In Prolog variables are assigned values by means of the unification algorithm. The reason for the above abnormal behaviour is an omission of the so-called occur-check test from this algorithm.

Re: (ii) Arithmetic. In the program from Example 3 we omitted the definition of the `between` relation. Conforming to the declarative character of logic programming we would expect that this relation is defined by the rule

$$\texttt{between(X, Y, Z)} \leftarrow \texttt{X} \leq \texttt{Z, Z} \leq \texttt{Y}.$$

Unfortunately, this definition is appropriate only for a very limited use of the `between` relation, namely for the calls of the form `between(s, t, u)` where s,t,u are integers. With this use of the `between` relation in Example 3 only queries of the form `sol(n, z)`, where n is an integer, can be computed and the queries of the form `sol(N, Z)` lead to an error. The reason is that the relation $\leq$ can be used only when both of its arguments evaluate to numbers, and when one of its arguments is a variable an error arises.

It turns out that instead of something remotely resembling the above rule we actually need the following program:

```
between(X, Y, Z) ← X ≤ Y, Z is X.
between(X, Y, Z) ← X < Y, X1 is X+1, between(X1, Y, Z).
```

This small program is disappointingly complicated. Without going into the details let us just explain that if X $\leq$ Y, then the value of X is assigned to Z, and if additionally X < Y then the procedure is called recursively with X incremented by 1. This increment of X necessitates an introduction of a fresh variable, here X1. The name X1 is chosen to indicate that it is related to the variable X.

This program is not easy to understand, among others because of the use of another variable, X1, and due to the elaborated procedure used to generate the appropriate values. Moreover, it is still easy to end up with an error if one uses the relation `between` with wrong arguments:

```
| ?- between(X, X+10, Z).
{INSTANTIATION ERROR: in expression}
```

This error is again caused by the fact that the arithmetic comparison relations require arguments that evaluate to numbers. This shows that arithmetic in Prolog is not simple to use.

In contrast, in Pascal the integers between the integers x and y are generated by the **for** loop:

for $i := x$ **to** y **do** ...

which looks like a simpler solution.

Re: (iii) **Inefficiency**. Declarative programming allows us to write programs which are easy to understand and develop. In fact, they are executable specifications. But this way of programming does not take into account the efficiency. And indeed it is very easy to end up with Prolog programs which are hopelessly inefficient. A good example is the following definition of sorting of a list of numbers:

```
sorted(List, Out) ← permutation(List, Out), ordered(Out).
```

Here `permutation` is a relation that generates all permutations of a list and `ordered` is a relation that tests whether a list of numbers is ordered. We omit here their definitions. Declaratively, this rule has an obvious meaning: to sort a list `List` it suffices to find a permutation `Out` of it which is ordered. Procedurally, this rule successively generates all permutations of `List` until one is found which is ordered. This results in a hopelessly inefficient behaviour. In the worst case one can end up generating all the permutations of a list before terminating with the desired result.

The inefficiency of the above program has of course been well recognized in the logic programming community and in fact this program is routinely used as a computing intensive benchmark program aimed at comparing the efficiency of various implementations.

It is easy to generate other examples of inefficient Prolog programs by simply translating some definitions into programs. These examples show that in order to write efficient programs in Prolog it is not in general sufficient to "think" declaratively. Some understanding of the underlying procedural interpretation is needed.

1.5   Theoretical Foundations of Logic Programming

This understanding can be acquired by a systematic study of the underlying computational mechanism of Prolog. This mechanism for a "pure" subset of Prolog can be precisely explained and clarified by means of the basic notions of logic programming. These concepts are unification, logic programs and queries, the SLD-resolution and semantics. Their study is of independent interest.

Unification is a basic mechanism by means of which values are assigned in logic programming to variables. Logic programs and queries are counterparts of the Prolog programs and Prolog queries that were informally introduced in Section 1.3. The SLD-resolution is a proof method built upon the unification that allows us to prove queries from a program in a constructive way. "Constructive" means here that the values for the variables are in effect computed. For example, if we pose the query (see Example 1 in Section 1.3) `connection(seattle, X)` which formalizes the question "is there any city to which there is a connection from Seattle?", then the answer is not "yes" but a constructive one, like "`X = fairbanks`".

Finally, to properly understand the meaning of the SLD-resolution, semantics for logic programs and queries is introduced. The relationships between the proof theory and semantics are clarified by means of so-called soundness and completeness results.

This is, in a nutshell, the background on logic programming which will be needed to understand the procedural and declarative interpretation of Prolog programs considered here.

1.6 Program Verification

The usual way of explaining that a program is correct is that it meets its specifications. This statement has a clear intention but is somewhat imprecise so we shall be more specific in the sequel.

Correctness of programs is important, both from the point of view of software reliability and from the point of view of software development. Program verification is the formal activity whose aim is to ensure correctness of programs. It has a history spanning a quarter of a century. To quote from our previous book:

> The origins of [...] program verification can be traced back to Turing [Tur49], but the first constructive effort should be attributed to Floyd [Flo67], where proving correctness of flowchart programs by means of assertions was proposed. This method was subsequently presented in a syntax-directed manner in Hoare [Hoa69], where an axiomatic proof method was proposed to verify simple **while**-programs. Hoare's approach received a great deal of attention, and many Hoare-style proof systems dealing with various programming constructs have been proposed since then.

> (Apt and Olderog [AO91, page 11])

Most of the effort concerning program verification was devoted to imperative programs. When studying such programs one attempts to establish at least the following program properties.

- Termination.
  For example, a sorting program should terminate.
- Partial correctness.
  For example, upon termination of a sorting program, the computed output should be sorted.
- Absence of run-time errors.
  These errors depend on the programming language under consideration. In imperative programs violation of the array bounds and division by zero are typical examples.

Declarative programming is usually considered to be a remedy for program verification. The reason is that it allows us to narrow the gap between the specifications and the final program. This makes the task of proving program correctness simpler and less error prone.

However, programming languages supporting declarative programming usually do not score well on efficiency and expressiveness, and consequently they have to be fine-tuned to cope with these additional needs. This often creates a mismatch which is either ignored or deemed as irrelevant. In particular Prolog, or even its subset usually called pure Prolog, differs from logic programming in many small, but important aspects. They have to do with efficiency, need for better expressiveness and ease of programming.

We conclude that the need for program verification does not disappear in the case of declarative programs. In the case of Prolog the problems mentioned in Section 1.4 have to be taken care of very much in the same way as in the case of imperative programs.

1.7   Prolog and Program Verification

Because of the differences between Prolog and logic programming the theory of logic programs cannot be directly applied to reason about Prolog programs. As a result, to properly understand Prolog programs this theory has to be appropriately modified and revised.

We mentioned at the end of Section 1.4 that in order to write efficient Prolog programs some understanding of its procedural interpretation is necessary. However, for simplicity, while reasoning about Prolog programs it is much more preferable to rely on a declarative interpretation.

Unfortunately, due to several "non-declarative" features of Prolog, such a declarative interpretation is, to say the least, problematic. To cope with this problem we determine a small, but expressive subset of Prolog and show that for programs written in this subset it is possible to reason about their correctness by a combination of syntactic analysis and declarative interpretation.

In our approach we deal with all program properties mentioned in the previous section. Thus we study:

- Termination.
  Now it means that the program under consideration should terminate for the *appropriate* queries.
- Partial correctness.
  Now it means that the program under consideration should deliver correct answers for the *appropriate* queries.
- Absence of run-time errors.
  In the case of Prolog these are:

    − absence of the occur-check problem,

    − absence of errors in presence of arithmetic expressions.

The resulting framework is simple to use and readily applicable to many of the well-known Prolog programs. Moreover, several aspects of the proposed methods can be automated.

We believe that this possibility of rigorously verifying a substantial collection of Prolog programs is of interest both from the practical and from the theoretical point of view.

1.8   Structure of the Book

Let us discuss now briefly the contents of this book. You are at this stage almost done with **Chapter 1**.

The theoretical framework of logic programming is explained in **Chapters 2– 4**. In logic programming values are assigned to variables by means of certain substitutions, called *most general unifiers*. The process of computing most general unifiers is called *unification*. In **Chapter 2** we discuss in detail the concepts needed to understand unification and study two well-known algorithms that compute them.

Then in **Chapter 3** we define the syntax of logic programs and explain how one can compute using them. To this end we introduce the resolution method, called *SLD-resolution*, define the basic concepts of *SLD-derivations* and *SLD-trees* and provide a study of their fundamental properties.

This computational interpretation of logic programs is called *procedural interpretation*. It explains *how* logic programs compute. This interpretation is needed both to understand properly the foundations of logic programming and to explain the computation mechanism of Prolog.

To understand the *meaning* of logic programs, we define in **Chapter 4** their semantics. This interpretation of logic programs is called *declarative interpretation*. It explains *what* logic programs compute. The declarative interpretation abstracts from the details of the computation process and focuses on the semantic relationship between the studied notions.

The claim that logic programming supports declarative programming refers to the ability of using the declarative interpretation instead of the procedural interpretation when developing logic programs and analyzing their behaviour. In Chapter 4 we prove the fundamental results which link these two interpretations of logic programs, namely the *Soundness Theorem* and *Completeness Theorem*.

Thanks to its procedural interpretation logic programming can be used as a programming language. However, to make it a viable tool for programming, the problems of efficiency and of ease of programming have to be adequately addressed. Prolog is a programming language based on logic programming in which these two objectives were adequately met. Prolog goes far beyond logic programming in that it offers several built-in facilities most of which cannot be explained within the framework of logic programming.

The aim of **Chapter 5** is to provide an introduction to programming in a subset of Prolog which corresponds with logic programming. We call this subset "pure Prolog". We found it convenient to explain the essence of programming in pure Prolog by dividing the presentation according to the domains over which computing takes place. So, we successfully deal with finite domains and then *numerals, lists, complex domains*, by which we mean domains built from some constants by means of arbitrary function symbols and, finally, *binary trees*. We also summarize the relevant aspects of programming in pure Prolog.

Chapters 6–8 are devoted to a study of formal properties of pure Prolog programs. To this end we use the theoretical results concerning logic programming established in Chapters 2–4. These results have now to be coupled with additional theoretical results that deal with specific program properties. In **Chapter 6** we study termination of pure Prolog programs. More specifically, by termination we mean here finiteness of all possible derivations starting in the initial query. This notion of termination does not depend on the ordering of the clauses in the program. We show the usefulness of the proposed method by applying it successfully to programs studied in Chapter 5.

In **Chapter 7** we study another aspect of correctness of pure Prolog programs — absence of the occur-check problem. To this end we analyze the unification process more closely. The program analysis is based on various syntactic properties that involve so-called *modes*. Informally, modes indicate which argument positions of a relation symbol should be viewed as an input and which as an output.

We introduce here two syntactic program classes which involve modes and for each of them establish the absence of the occur-check problem. For some programs and queries the occur-check problem cannot be avoided. To deal with this difficulty we propose here program transformations which allow us to insert so-called occur-checks in the program and the query under consideration.

Next, in **Chapter 8** we deal with partial correctness, that is the property that a program under consideration delivers correct answers for the queries of relevance. As pure Prolog programs can yield several answers, partial correctness can be interpreted either as the task of determining the form of the answers to a query (such as that all possible answers to the query `member_both(X, [1,2,3], [2,3,4,5])`. are contained in the set $\{X = 2, X = 3\}$), or as the task of computing all of these answers (such as that $X = 2$ and $X = 3$ are precisely all the possible answers to the query `member_both(X, [1,2,3], [2,3,4,5])`).

We consider in detail both of these interpretations and provide methods that allow us to deal with them. To this end we introduce *assertions* and use them to establish the desired program properties. In addition, we identify here yet another program property, *absence of failures* and propose a method allowing us to deal with it.

After this study of verification of pure Prolog programs, in **Chapter 9** we consider a larger subset of Prolog which allows us to deal with arithmetic. This is achieved by adding to the programming language of Chapter 5 Prolog's *arithmetic comparison relations* and the *arithmetic evaluator* "`is`".

We follow here the style of presentation of Chapter 5 and present programs written in this subset that deal successively with complex domains which now involve *integers, lists of integers* and *binary search trees*, a subclass of the binary trees studied in Chapter 5 which remain properly "balanced".

In **Chapter 10** we return to program verification by considering now programs written in Prolog's subset, which is considered in Chapter 9. We show here that after a simple modification the methods introduced in Chapters 6–8 can be also applied to pure Prolog programs with arithmetic. One new aspect of program correctness is the possibility of run-time errors due to the presence of arithmetic relations. To deal with it we introduce the notion of *types*.

Finally, in **Chapter 11** we discuss various more advanced features of Prolog and explain their meaning. These are *cut*, the facilities that allow us to collect all solutions to a query, that is *findall, bagof* and *setof*, subsequently *meta-variables, negation*, several built-ins that allow us to inspect, compare and decompose terms, like *functor* and *arg*, the built-ins that allow us to inspect and modify the programs, like *clause, assert* and *retract*, and the input/output facilities. We also illustrate their use by presenting various Prolog programs that deal with *sets, directed graphs*, non-monotonic reasoning, unification and interpreters for the subsets of Prolog considered in Chapters 5 and 9.

Sections marked with an asterisk ("*") can be omitted at the first reading.

1.9   Further Reading

For the reader interested in pursuing matters further we would like to suggest the following books.

- For a further study of Prolog: Bratko [Bra86] and Sterling and Shapiro [SS86].
- For a further study of the foundations of logic programming: Doets [Doe94] and various survey articles in Bruynooghe *et al.* [BDHM94].
- For an alternative approach to the foundations of logic programming and Prolog's verification, based on the use of the attribute grammars: Deransart and Małuszyński [DM93].
- For a different approach to the subject in which stress is put on development of Prolog programs from specification instead of on program's verification: Deville [Dev90].
- For a more informal and more comprehensive treatment of the logic programming paradigm: Nilsson and Małuszyński [NM95].

Finally, the presentation of the subject is self-contained and as precise as possible. More than 170 exercises and more than sixty Prolog programs should help the reader to test her/his understanding of the text.

1.10   References

[AO91]   K.R. Apt and E.-R. Olderog. *Verification of Sequential and Concurrent Programs*. Texts and Monographs in Computer Science, Springer-Verlag, New York, 1991.

[BDHM94] M. Bruynooghe, S. Debray, M. Hermenegildo, and M. Maher, editors. *The Journal of Logic Programming, Special Issue: Ten Years of Logic Programming*. North-Holland, Amsterdam, 1994.

[Bra85]   G. Brandreth. *Everyman's Classic Puzzles*. J.M. Dent & Sons Ltd, Melbourne, 1985.

[Bra86]   I. Bratko. *PROLOG Programming for Artificial Intelligence*. International Computer Science Series. Addison-Wesley, Reading, MA, 1986.

[Dev90]   Y. Deville. *Logic Programming. Systematic Program Development*. International Series in Logic Programming. Addison-Wesley, Reading, MA, 1990.

[Doe94]   H. C. Doets. *From Logic to Logic Programming*. The MIT Press, Cambridge, MA, 1994.

[DM93]   P. Deransart and J. Małuszyński. *A Grammatical View of Logic Programming*. The MIT Press, Cambridge, MA, 1993.

[Flo67]   R. Floyd. Assigning meaning to programs. In J.T. Schwartz, editor, *Proceedings of Symposium on Applied Mathematics 19, Mathematical Aspects of Computer Science*, pages 19–32. American Mathematical Society, New York, 1967.

[Hoa69]   C.A.R. Hoare. An axiomatic basis for computer programming. *Communications of the ACM*, 12:576–580, 583, 1969.

[NM95]   U. Nilsson and J. Małuszyński. *Logic, Programming and Prolog*. Wiley, New York, second edition, 1995.

[SS86]   L. Sterling and E. Shapiro. *The Art of Prolog*. MIT Press, Cambridge, MA, 1986.

[Tur49]   A.M. Turing. On checking a large routine. *Report of a Conference on High Speed Automatic Calculating Machines*, pages 67–69, 1949. University Mathematics Laboratory, Cambridge, 1949. (See also: F.L. Morris and C.B. Jones. An early program proof by Alan Turing, *Annals of the History of Computing*, 6:139–143, 1984.)

Chapter 2

Unification

In logic programming variables represent unknown values, very much like in mathematics. The values assigned to variables are terms (expressions). These values are assigned by means of certain substitutions, called most general unifiers. The process of computing most general unifiers is called unification. So unification forms a basic mechanism by means of which logic programs compute. This chapter provides an introduction to its study.

The use of unification to assign values to variables forms a distinguishing feature of logic programming and is one of the main differences between logic programming and other programming styles. Unification was defined in Robinson [Rob65] in the context of automated theorem proving. Its use for computing is due to Kowalski [Kow74]. Since the seminal paper of Robinson several unification algorithms were presented. To provide some insight into their nature we present here two of the most known unification algorithms.

We begin by defining in the next section a language of terms. Then in Section 2.2 we introduce the substitutions and prove some basic properties of them. Next, in Section 2.3 we define the unifiers and most general unifiers (mgus), and in Section 2.4 prove correctness of a non-deterministic version of Robinson's unification algorithm. By specializing this algorithm we obtain in Section 2.5 the classical Robinson's unification algorithm. In Section 2.6 we study another well-known unification algorithm, due to Martelli and Montanari. Finally, in Section 2.7, we analyze various useful properties of mgus. We end this and every other chapter by concluding remarks, bibliographic remarks and a list of references.

2.1 Terms

There exists a regrettable notational discrepancy between Prolog and logic programming. In Prolog variable names start with an upper case letter whereas logic programming follows in this respect mathematical logic tradition, so variables are denoted by the lower case letters $x, y, z, u, \ldots$, possibly with subscripts.

In this book we use logic programming to study Prolog programs, so we face a notational problem. In what follows we shall adhere to Prolog's notation while presenting Prolog programs but when studying these programs from a formal view we shall shift to the logic programming notation. This will not cause confusion because no entities within logic programs are denoted by upper case letters.

In this book we shall introduce logic programs gradually. In this chapter we shall deal only with a small language, which we call a *language of terms*. It allows us to discuss substitutions and unification. It consists of an alphabet and all terms defined over it.

An *alphabet* consists of the following disjoint classes of symbols:

- *variables*,
- *function symbols*,
- *parentheses*, which are: (and),
- *comma*, that is: , .

We assume that the set of variables is infinite and fixed. In contrast, the set of function symbols may vary and in particular may be empty. Each language of terms is thus determined by its function symbols.

Each function symbol has a fixed *arity*, that is the number of arguments associated with it. 0-ary function symbols are called

- *constants*, and are denoted by $a, b, c, d, \ldots$.

Throughout the book we denote function symbols of positive arity by $f, g, h, k, l, \ldots$. Sometimes, one assumes that function symbols have positive arity and constants are introduced as a separate class of symbols. The approach we take here is slightly more convenient.

Terms are defined inductively as follows:

- a variable is a term,
- if f is an n-ary function symbol and $t_1, \ldots, t_n$ are terms, then $f(t_1, \ldots, t_n)$ is a term.

In particular every constant is a term. Terms are denoted by $s, t, u, w, \ldots$. A term with no variables is called *ground*. By $Var(t)$ we denote the set of variables occurring in t. By a *subterm* of a term s we mean a substring of s which is again a term. If w is a subterm of s, then we say that w *occurs* in s. In general, there can be several occurrences of a given subterm in a term — take for example $f(x)$ and $g(f(x), f(x))$.

By definition, every term is a subterm of itself. Not surprisingly, a subterm s of a term t is called *proper* if $s \neq t$.

2.2   Substitutions

Substitutions bind variables to terms. They are the only means of assigning values to variables within the logic programming framework. The relevant substitutions are automatically generated during the computation process, so — in contrast to the imperative programming — the assignment of values to variables takes place implicitly.

More precisely, consider now a fixed language of terms. A *substitution* is a finite mapping from variables to terms which assigns to each variable x in its domain a term t different from x. We write it as

$$\{x_1/t_1, \ldots, x_n/t_n\}$$

where

- $x_1, \ldots, x_n$ are different variables,
- $t_1, \ldots, t_n$ are terms,
- for $i \in [1, n]$, $x_i \neq t_i$.

Informally, it is to be read the variables $x_1, \ldots, x_n$ are *bound* to $t_1, \ldots, t_n$, respectively. A pair x_i/t_i is called a *binding*. When $n = 0$, the mapping becomes the empty mapping. The resulting substitution is then called *empty substitution* and is denoted by ϵ.

Consider a substitution $\theta = \{x_1/t_1, \ldots, x_n/t_n\}$. If all $t_1, \ldots, t_n$ are ground, then θ is called *ground*, and if all $t_1, \ldots, t_n$ are variables, then θ is called a *pure variable substitution*. If θ is a 1-1 and onto mapping from its domain to itself, then θ is called a *renaming*. In other words, a substitution θ is a renaming if it is a permutation of the variables from its domain. For example $\{x/y, y/z, z/x\}$ is a renaming. In addition, the empty substitution ϵ is a renaming.

Further, we denote by $Dom(\theta)$ the set of variables $\{x_1, \ldots, x_n\}$, by $Range(\theta)$ the set of terms $\{t_1, \ldots, t_n\}$, and by $Ran(\theta)$ the set of variables appearing in $t_1, \ldots, t_n$. Then we define $Var(\theta) = Dom(\theta) \cup Ran(\theta)$. Given a set of variables V we denote by $\theta|V$ the substitution obtained from θ by restricting its domain to V.

We now define the result of *applying a substitution θ to a term s*, written as $s\theta$, as the result of the *simultaneous* replacement of each occurrence in s of a variable from $Dom(\theta)$ by the corresponding term in $Range(\theta)$.

Example 2.1 Consider a language allowing us to build arithmetic expressions in prefix form. It contains two binary function symbols, "+" and "·" and infinitely many constants: 0, 1, ... Then $s = +(\cdot(x, 7), \cdot(4, y))$ is a term and for the substitution $\theta = \{x/0, y/+(z, 2)\}$ we have

$$s\theta = +(\cdot(0, 7), \cdot(4, +(z, 2))).$$

$\square$

Exercise 1

(i) Prove that $s\theta$ can be equivalently defined by structural induction as follows:

- for a variable x, if $x \in Dom(\theta)$, then $x\theta := \theta(x)$,

- for a variable x, if $x \notin Dom(\theta)$, then $x\theta := x$,

- $f(t_1, \ldots, t_n)\theta := f(t_1\theta, \ldots, t_n\theta)$.

In particular, if c is a constant, then $c\theta := c$.

(ii) Give an example showing that without the restriction to the simultaneous replacement these two definitions of $s\theta$ do not need to coincide.

(iii) Prove that $\theta = \gamma$ iff $x\theta = x\gamma$ for all variables x. $\square$

The term $s\theta$ is called an *instance* of s. An instance is called *ground* if it contains no variables. If θ is a renaming, then $s\theta$ is called a *variant* of s. Finally, s is called *more general than t* if t is an instance of s.

Example 2.2

(i) $f(y, x)$ is a variant of $f(x, y)$, since $f(y, x) = f(x, y)\{x/y, y/x\}$.

(ii) $f(x, y')$ is a variant of $f(x, y)$, since $f(x, y') = f(x, y)\{y/y', y'/y\}$. Note that the binding y'/y had to be added to make the substitution a renaming.

(iii) $f(x, x)$ is not a variant of $f(x, y)$. Indeed, suppose otherwise. Then $f(x, x) = f(x, y)\theta$ for a renaming θ, so $y/x \in \theta$; hence for some variable z different than x we have $x/z \in \theta$. Thus $f(x, y)\theta = f(z, x)$. Contradiction. $\square$

Next, we define the *composition* of substitutions θ and η, written as $\theta\eta$, as follows. We put for a variable x

$$(\theta\eta)(x) := (x\theta)\eta.$$

In other words, $\theta\eta$ assigns to a variable x the term obtained by applying the substitution η to the term $x\theta$. Clearly, for $x \notin Dom(\theta) \cup Dom(\eta)$ we have $(\theta\eta)(x) = x$, so $\theta\eta$ is a finite mapping from variables to terms, i.e. it uniquely identifies a substitution.

Exercise 2 Prove that for any substitution θ we have $\theta\epsilon = \epsilon\theta = \theta$. $\square$

The following lemma provides an alternative definition of composition of substitutions which makes it easier to compute it.

Lemma 2.3 (Composition) Consider two substitutions, $\theta := \{x_1/t_1, \ldots, x_n/t_n\}$ and $\eta := \{y_1/s_1, \ldots, y_m/s_m\}$. The composition $\theta\eta$ equals the result of the following procedure:

- remove from the sequence

$$x_1/t_1\eta, \ldots, x_n/t_n\eta, y_1/s_1, \ldots, y_m/s_m$$

the bindings $x_i/t_i\eta$ for which $x_i = t_i\eta$ and the bindings y_j/s_j for which $y_j \in \{x_1, \ldots, x_n\}$,
- form from the resulting sequence of bindings a substitution. $\square$

For example, we can now easily check that for $\theta = \{u/z, x/3, y/f(x,1)\}$ and $\eta = \{x/4, z/u\}$ we have $\theta\eta = \{x/3, y/f(4,1), z/u\}$.

Exercise 3
(i) Prove the Composition Lemma 2.3.

(ii) Prove that for every renaming θ there exists exactly one substitution θ^{-1} such that $\theta\theta^{-1} = \theta^{-1}\theta = \epsilon$. Prove that θ^{-1} is also a renaming.

(iii) Prove that if $\theta\eta = \epsilon$, then θ and η are renamings. $\square$

The next lemma shows that when writing a sequence of substitutions the parentheses can be omitted.

Lemma 2.4 (Associativity)

(i) $(s\theta)\eta = s(\theta\eta)$.
(ii) $(\theta\eta)\gamma = \theta(\eta\gamma)$.

Proof.
(i) By a straightforward induction on the structure of s, using Exercise 1(i).

(ii) For a variable x we have

$$x(\theta\eta)\gamma$$
$$= \quad \{\text{definition of composition of substitutions}\}$$
$$(x\theta\eta)\gamma$$
$$= \quad \{\text{(i) with } s := x\}$$
$$((x\theta)\eta)\gamma$$
$$= \quad \{\text{(i) with } s := x\theta, \theta := \eta, \eta = \gamma\}$$
$$x\theta(\eta\gamma),$$

which proves the claim. $\square$

Thus the composition of substitutions is associative. So when writing a sequence of substitutions the parentheses can be omitted. Finally, the following result clarifies the concept of a variant.

Lemma 2.5 (Variant)

(i) s is a variant of t iff s is an instance of t and t is an instance of s.

(ii) If s is a variant of t, then $s = t\theta$, for some renaming θ such that
$$Var(\theta) \subseteq Var(s) \cup Var(t).$$

Proof.

(i) ($\Rightarrow$) For some renaming θ we have $s = t\theta$. Take θ^{-1} (see Exercise 3). Then $t = t\theta\theta^{-1} = s\theta^{-1}$.

($\Leftarrow$) We begin with the following observation, where we say that a function f *has no fixpoints* if for all x in its domain $f(x) \neq x$.

Claim 1 Every finite 1-1 mapping f from A onto B can be extended to a permutation g of $A \cup B$. Moreover, if f has no fixpoints, then it can be extended to a g with no fixpoints.

Proof. The sets A and B have the same number of elements, hence so do $B - A$ and $A - B$. Let h be a 1-1 mapping from $B - A$ onto $A - B$. Define now g as the extension of f by h. Then g is a permutation of $A \cup B$. Moreover, h has no fixpoints, so the second conclusion follows, as well. $\square$

For some θ and η we have $s = t\theta$ and $t = s\eta$. Thus $t = t\theta\eta$. Consequently, for $x, y \in Var(t)$, if $x \neq y$, then $x\theta\eta \neq y\theta\eta$, so $x\theta \neq y\theta$. Moreover, for $x \in Var(t)$ we have $x\theta\eta = x$, so $x\theta$ is a variable because $x\theta\eta$ is. We can assume that $Dom(\theta) \subseteq Var(t)$, so we proved that θ is a 1-1, pure variable substitution.

Now by Claim 1 θ can be extended to a renaming γ such that $Dom(\gamma) = Var(\theta)$. If we now prove

$$Var(t) \cap Dom(\gamma) \subseteq Dom(\theta), \tag{2.1}$$

then we get $t\gamma = t\theta$, that is $s = t\gamma$, so s is a variant of t.

To prove (2.1) note that for $x \in Var(t) - Dom(\theta)$ we have $x = x\theta\eta = x\eta$, so $x \notin Dom(\eta)$. This implies that $x \notin Ran(\theta)$, since otherwise for some $y \in Var(t)$, $y \neq x$ we would have $y/x \in \theta$ and $y\theta\eta = y$, so $x \in Dom(\eta)$ would hold, which is a contradiction. So we proved that $(Var(t) - Dom(\theta)) \cap Ran(\theta) = \emptyset$, that is (2.1), since $Dom(\gamma) = Var(\theta)$.

(ii) It suffices to note that for γ constructed in (i) we have

$$Var(\gamma) = Var(\theta) \subseteq Var(s) \cup Var(t).$$

$\square$

The notions of an (ground) instance, variant and the notation $Var(\dots)$ were defined here only for terms. However, it is clear that they can be defined without any difference for *arbitrary* strings of symbols in a given language, not necessarily terms. In particular, the Associativity Lemma 2.4(i) and Variant Lemma 2.5 hold for arbitrary strings. In the sequel, we shall use these notions, the notation and the results for other syntactic constructs of interest.

Finally, let us remark that often a different definition of renaming is used — see the exercise below. The definition used here seems to be more convenient because it allows us to talk about renamings independently of the term to be renamed. Consequently, one can use it in other contexts, for example when relating substitutions in the next section.

Exercise 4 A substitution $\theta := \{x_1/t_1, ..., x_n/t_n\}$ is called a *renaming for a term s* if

- $t_1, \ldots, t_n$ are different variables (θ is a pure variable 1-1 substitution),

- $\{x_1, \ldots, x_n\} \subseteq Var(s)$ (θ only affects variables of s),

- $(Var(s) - \{x_1, \ldots, x_n\}) \cap \{t_1, \ldots, t_n\} = \emptyset$ (θ does not introduce variables which occur in s but are not in the domain of θ).

Prove that terms s and t are variants iff there exists a renaming θ for s such that $t = s\theta$.

$\square$

2.3   Unifiers

We already mentioned at the beginning of this chapter that unification is a fundamental concept that is crucial for logic programming.

Informally, unification is the process of making terms identical by means of certain substitutions. For example, the terms $f(a, y, z)$ and $f(x, b, z)$, with a, b constants and x, y, z variables, can be made identical by applying to them the substitution $\{x/a, y/b\}$: both sides then become $f(a, b, z)$. But the substitution $\{x/a, y/b, z/a\}$ also makes these two terms identical. Such substitutions are called unifiers. The first unifier is preferable because it is "more general" — the second one is a "special case" of the first one. More precisely, the first unifier is a *most general unifier* of $f(a, y, z)$ and $f(x, b, z)$ while $\{x/a, y/b, z/a\}$ is not.

We begin the formal presentation with the following definition needed to define the notion of a most general unifier.

Definition 2.6 Let θ and τ be substitutions. We say that θ is *more general than* τ if for some substitution η we have $\tau = \theta\eta$.
$\square$

Thus θ is more general than τ if τ can be obtained from θ by applying to it some substitution η. Since η can be chosen to be the empty substitution ϵ, we conclude that every substitution is more general than itself.

This definition is more subtle than it seems.

Example 2.7
(i) As expected, the substitution $\{x/y\}$ is more general than $\{x/a, y/a\}$, because $\{x/y\}\{y/a\} = \{x/a, y/a\}$.

(ii) However, unexpectedly, $\{x/y\}$ is *not* more general than $\{x/a\}$, because if for some substitution η, $x/a \in \{x/y\}\eta$, then $y/a \in \eta$ and thus $y \in Dom(\{x/y\}\eta)$.

(iii) Similarly $\{x/f(y,z)\}$ is not more general than $\{x/f(a,a)\}$, where y and z are distinct variables (though possibly one of them is equal to x). Indeed, suppose otherwise. Then for some γ we have $\{x/f(y,z)\}\gamma = \{x/f(a,a)\}$. Thus γ contains the bindings y/a and z/a and at least one of them is not a binding for x, so $Dom(\{x/f(y,z)\}\gamma) \neq Dom(\{x/f(a,a)\})$ which gives a contradiction.

We shall see in the next two chapters that this observation is of importance for the theory of logic programming. $\qquad\square$

The following lemma is a counterpart of the Variant Lemma 2.5(i).

Lemma 2.8 (Renaming) θ is more general than η and η is more general than θ iff for some renaming γ such that $Var(\gamma) \subseteq Var(\theta) \cup Var(\eta)$ we have $\eta = \theta\gamma$.

Proof. ($\Rightarrow$) Let t be a term such that $Var(t) = Var(\theta) \cup Var(\eta)$. (In the degenerated case when the considered language of terms contains no function symbols of arity bigger than 1 such a term need not exist. In such a case extend the language by a binary function symbol and carry out the reasoning in this extended language.)

By the assumption $t\eta$ is an instance of $t\theta$ and $t\theta$ is an instance of $t\eta$, so by the Variant Lemma 2.5(i) for some renaming γ we have $t\eta = t\theta\gamma$. By the Variant Lemma 2.5(ii) and the choice of t we can assume that $Var(\gamma) \subseteq Var(\theta) \cup Var(\eta)$, so $Var(\theta\gamma) \subseteq Var(t)$ and $Var(\eta) \subseteq Var(t)$. Consequently $\eta = \theta\gamma$.

($\Leftarrow$) Take γ^{-1} (see Exercise 3). Then $\eta\gamma^{-1} = \theta\gamma\gamma^{-1} = \theta$. $\qquad\square$

The following notion is the key concept of this chapter.

Definition 2.9

- θ is called a *unifier* of s and t if $s\theta = t\theta$. If a unifier of s and t exists, we say that s and t are *unifiable*.
- θ is called a *most general unifier* (*mgu* in short) of s and t if it is a unifier of s and t that is more general than all unifiers of s and t.
- An mgu θ of s and t is called *strong* if for all unifiers η of s and t we have $\eta = \theta\eta$. $\qquad\square$

Intuitively, an mgu is a substitution which makes two terms equal but which does it in a "most general way", without unnecessary bindings. So θ is an mgu if for every unifier η for some substitution γ we have $\eta = \theta\gamma$. An mgu θ is strong if for every unifier η, the substitution γ for which $\eta = \theta\gamma$ holds can be always chosen to be η itself. All mgus produced by the algorithms presented in this chapter always satisfy this additional property.

Example 2.10

(i) Consider the terms $f(g(x,a),z)$ and $f(y,b)$. Then $\{x/c, y/g(c,a), z/b\}$ is one of their unifiers and so is $\{y/g(x,a), z/b\}$ which is more general than the first one, since $\{x/c, y/g(c,a), z/b\} = \{y/g(x,a), z/b\}\{x/c\}$.

Actually, one can show that $\{y/g(x,a), z/b\}$ is an mgu of $f(g(x,a), z)$ and $f(y,b)$, in fact a strong one. In particular, we have

$$\{x/c, y/g(c,a), z/b\} = \{y/g(x,a), z/b\}\{x/c, y/g(c,a), z/b\}.$$

(ii) Consider the terms $f(g(x,a), z)$ and $f(g(x,b), b)$. They are not unifiable, since for no substitution θ we have $a\theta = b\theta$.

(iii) Finally consider the terms $g(x,a)$ and $g(f(x),a)$. They are not unifiable either because for any substitution θ the term $x\theta$ is a proper subterm of $f(x)\theta$. $\quad\square$

The problem of deciding whether two terms are unifiable is called the *unification problem*. This problem is solved by providing an algorithm that terminates with failure if the terms are not unifiable and that otherwise produces one of their most general unifiers, in fact a strong one.

In general, two terms may be not unifiable for two reasons. The first one is exemplified by Example 2.10(ii) above which shows that two constants (or, more generally, two terms starting with a different function symbol) cannot unify. The second one is exemplified by (iii) above which shows that x and $f(x)$ (or more generally, x and a term different from x but in which x occurs) cannot unify. Each possibility can occur at some "inner level" of the considered two terms.

These two possibilities for failure are present in all unification algorithms. The second of them is called the *occur-check* failure. We shall discuss it in more detail at the end of Section 2.6, after presenting unification algorithms. We present here two such algorithms. To prove their correctness the following simple lemma will be needed.

Lemma 2.11 (Binding) For a variable x and a term t, $x\theta = t\theta$ iff $\theta = \{x/t\}\theta$.

Proof. First, note that $x\{x/t\}\theta = t\theta$, so $x\theta = t\theta$ iff $x\theta = x\{x/t\}\theta$. Moreover, for $y \neq x$ we have $y\{x/t\} = y$, so $y\theta = y\{x/t\}\theta$. Thus $x\theta = x\{x/t\}\theta$ iff $\theta = \{x/t\}\theta$. $\quad\square$

Exercise 5

(i) Find two terms s and t such that s is an instance of t but s and t are not unifiable.

(ii) Prove that if s is an instance of t then s unifies with a variant of t. $\quad\square$

2.4　* The Nondeterministic Robinson Algorithm

The first unification algorithm is due to Robinson [Rob65]. We start by presenting its nondeterministic version given in Fitting [Fit90]. Robinson's algorithm operates on so-called disagreement pairs. To define them it is convenient to view terms as augmented trees.

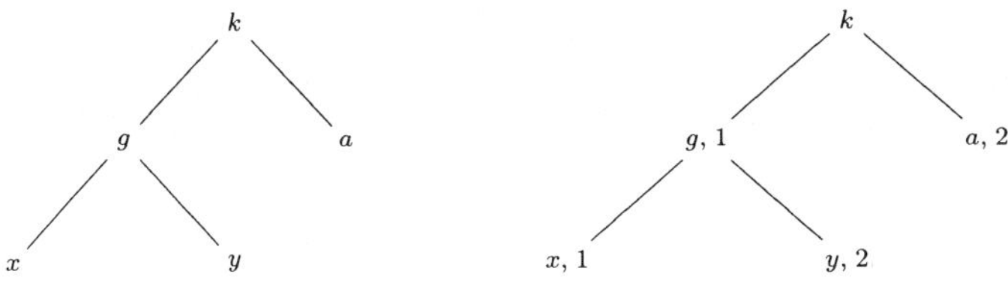

Figure 2.1 Terms as trees

Such trees are defined inductively. First, we associate with each term a tree. The tree associated with a variable x has just one node, labelled by x itself. The tree associated with $f(t_1, \ldots, t_n)$ is obtained by attaching the trees associated with $t_1, \ldots, t_n$, in that order, under the root labelled by f. In particular, the tree associated with a constant c has one node, labelled by c itself.

Given such a tree associated with a term, we then obtain an *augmented tree* by augmenting each node different from the root with the positive natural number indicating which child it is of its parent. For example, the tree associated with the term $k(g(x, y), a)$ is displayed in the left part of Figure 2.1, and the corresponding augmented tree is displayed in the right part of Figure 2.1.

Now, given an occurrence of a term w in a term s, by the *access path* of w we denote the sequence of nodes leading from the root of the augmented tree associated with s down to and including the root of the augmented subtree associated with w. For example, $\langle k \rangle, \langle g, 1 \rangle, \langle y, 2 \rangle$ is the access path of the subterm y of the term $k(g(x, y), a)$.

Consider an occurrence of a term w in a term s and an occurrence of a term u in a term t. We call w, u a *disagreement pair* if their access paths differ only in the label of the last node. For example, $y, h(u)$ is a disagreement pair of $k(g(x, y), a)$ and $k(g(x, h(u)), h(b))$, because — as we just noted — the access path of y in $k(g(x, y), a)$ is $\langle k \rangle, \langle g, 1 \rangle, \langle y, 2 \rangle$, whereas the access path of $h(u)$ in $k(g(x, h(u)), h(b))$ is $\langle k \rangle, \langle g, 1 \rangle, \langle h, 2 \rangle$. The corresponding augmented trees are displayed in Figure 2.2. The differing labels of the discussed disagreement pair are framed. They form the roots of the terms forming the disagreement pair.

Finally, we call a pair of terms *simple* if one of them is a variable that does not occur in the other term. Given a simple pair of terms w, u we say that the substitution $\{x/v\}$ is *determined* by w, u if $\{x, v\} = \{w, u\}$. Note that if both w and u are variables, then two substitutions are determined by w, u.

The following lemma clarifies the role played by the disagreement pairs.

Lemma 2.12 (Disagreement) Let w, u be a disagreement pair of s and t.

(i) Every unifier of s and t is also a unifier of w and u.

(ii) If the pair w, u is simple, then w and u are unifiable. In fact, every substitution determined by w, u is a strong mgu of w and u.

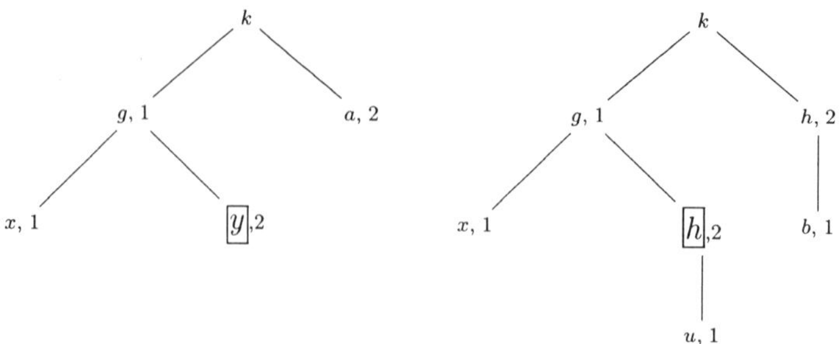

Figure 2.2 A disagreement pair

(iii) If the pair w, u is not simple, then w and u are not unifiable.

Proof.
(i) Every unifier of s and t also unifies every pair of subterms of s and t with the same access path.

(ii) If x does not occur in t, then $x\{x/t\} = t\{x/t\}$. The rest follows by the Binding Lemma 2.11.

(iii) If neither w nor u is a variable, then clearly w and u are not unifiable, because by the definition of the disagreement pair they start with a different symbol. If one of w and u, say w, is a variable that occurs in the other term, u (that is, we are dealing with the occur-check failure), then for no θ we have $w\theta = u\theta$, because $w\theta$ is then a proper subterm of $u\theta$. $\qquad\square$

Thus for disagreement pairs we know how to solve the unification problem. The following algorithm attempts to construct an mgu of two terms by repeatedly searching for the disagreement pairs. This mgu is constructed by composing the substitutions determined by the successively chosen disagreement pairs.

THE NONDETERMINISTIC ROBINSON ALGORITHM

set θ to ϵ;
while $s\theta \neq t\theta$ **do**
nondeterministically choose from $s\theta$ and $t\theta$ a disagreement pair w, u and perform the associated actions.

(1) w, u is a simple pair	*let γ be a substitution determined by w, u;* *set θ to $\theta\gamma$,*
(2) w, u is not a simple pair	*halt with failure.*

od

Thus the algorithm terminates when $s\theta = t\theta$ or when failure arises. We now prove the correctness of this algorithm. More specifically, we prove the following theorem.

Theorem 2.13 (Unification 1) The nondeterministic Robinson algorithm always terminates. If the original pair of terms s and t has a unifier, then the algorithm successfully terminates and produces a strong mgu θ of this pair and otherwise it terminates with failure.

Proof. We establish three claims.

Claim 1 The algorithm always terminates.

Proof. Let $\gamma = \{x/v\}$ be a substitution used in action (1). Then prior to this execution of action (1) x occurs in $s\theta, t\theta$, but it does not occur in $s\theta\gamma, t\theta\gamma$, because it does not occur in v. In addition, all variables that occur in $s\theta\gamma, t\theta\gamma$ occur in $s\theta, t\theta$, as well. So action (1) reduces the number of variables that occur in $s\theta, t\theta$. This implies termination. $\qquad\square$

We call a statement an *invariant* of a **while** loop if it holds each time the body of the **while** loop is to be traversed.

Suppose now that η is a unifier of s and t. We then establish the following invariant of the algorithm:

$$(\text{inv}) \quad \eta = \theta\eta.$$

First, this statement clearly holds upon initialization of θ. Suppose it holds prior to an execution of action (1). Then by the Disagreement Lemma 2.12(i) we have $w\eta = u\eta$, where w, u is the pair considered in action (1). By the Disagreement Lemma 2.12(ii) we have $\eta = \gamma\eta$ where γ is the substitution used in action (1). Thus $\eta = \theta\gamma\eta$. So (inv) holds upon termination of action (1).

We can now prove the remaining two claims.

Claim 2 If the algorithm successfully terminates, then the produced θ is a strong mgu of s and t.

Proof. Suppose the algorithm successfully terminates. Then upon termination the **while** loop condition does not hold, that is $s\theta = t\theta$ holds. Hence θ is a unifier of s and t. Moreover, for every unifier η of s and t the invariant (inv) holds upon termination, as well. So θ is indeed a strong mgu of s and t. $\qquad\square$

Claim 3 If the algorithm terminates with failure, then s and t are not unifiable.

Proof. Suppose by contradiction that s and t are unifiable, say by a unifier η. Then (inv) is an invariant of the algorithm. Let w, u be the disagreement pair whose choice led to failure. Prior to this choice the invariant (inv) holds, so η is a unifier of $s\theta$ and $t\theta$. By the Disagreement Lemma 2.12(i) and (iii) applied to the disagreement pair w, u of the terms $s\theta, t\theta$ the pair w, u is simple which gives a contradiction. $\qquad\square$

The above three claims imply the desired conclusion. $\qquad\square$

2.5   * Robinson's Algorithm

The above algorithm can be made more efficient by searching for the disagreement pairs in a particular order. The most natural order is the one which coincides with the simple textual scanning of a term from left to right. When this order is used the customary representation of a term as a string of symbols, instead of the tree representation used before, is sufficient for the formulation of the algorithm.

The textual scanning of two terms for the first disagreement pair now locates the first from left disagreement pair. An important observation is that after applying a substitution determined by the so located disagreement pair to the considered pair of terms, the obtained pair of terms coincides on all symbols to the left of the located disagreement pair. Thus the first disagreement pair of the new pair of terms lies textually to the right of the one previously considered. These observations lead to the following algorithm which employs a variable θ ranging over substitutions and two pointers to perform the textual scanning of two terms.

ROBINSON'S ALGORITHM

set θ to ϵ;
set the pointers to the first symbols of $s\theta$ and $t\theta$;
while $s\theta \neq t\theta$ **do**
advance simultaneously the pointers to the right until a pair of different symbols in $s\theta$ and $t\theta$ is found;
determine the pair of terms w and u whose leading symbols are the ones identified and perform the associated actions.

(1) w, u is a simple pair   *let γ be a substitution determined by w, u;*
                                     set θ to $\theta\gamma$,
(2) w, u is not a simple pair   *halt with failure.*

od

As before, the algorithm terminates when $s\theta = t\theta$ or when failure arises. The correctness of this algorithm is a direct consequence of the correctness of the non-deterministic Robinson algorithm and of the above discussion. To illustrate the operation of this algorithm consider the following example.

Example 2.14 To enhance readability, in all considered pairs of terms we underline the first from left pair of different symbols.

(i) Take the following pair of terms:

$$k(\underline{z}, f(x, b, z)) \text{ and } k(\underline{h}(x), f(g(a), y, z)). \tag{2.2}$$

Scanning them we locate the first disagreement pair, which is $z, h(x)$. This pair determines the substitution $\{z/h(x)\}$. Applying it to each of the original terms we obtain a new pair of terms, namely

$$k(h(x), f(\underline{x}, b, h(x))) \text{ and } k(h(x), f(\underline{g}(a), y, h(x))).$$

The next located disagreement pair is $x, g(a)$ which determines the substitution $\{x/g(a)\}$. Applying this substitution to the last pair of terms we obtain a new pair of terms:

$$k(h(g(a)), f(g(a), \underline{b}, h(g(a)))) \text{ and } k(h(g(a)), f(g(a), \underline{y}, h(g(a)))).$$

The next located disagreement pair is b, y which determines the substitution $\{y/b\}$. Applying it to the last pair of terms we obtain the pair

$$k(h(g(a)), f(g(a), b, h(g(a)))) \text{ and } k(h(g(a)), f(g(a), b, h(g(a))))$$

of identical terms.

Now, composing the successively found substitutions we obtain

$$\{z/h(x)\}\{x/g(a)\}\{y/b\} = \{z/h(g(a)), x/g(a), y/b\}$$

which by Theorem 2.13 is an mgu of the pair (2.2).

(ii) Take the following pair of terms:

$$k(\underline{z}, f(x, b, z)) \text{ and } k(\underline{h}(x), f(g(z), y, z)). \tag{2.3}$$

The only difference between this pair and the pair (2.2) is in the argument of the function symbol g. The first disagreement pair is as before, namely $z, h(x)$. This pair determines the substitution $\{z/h(x)\}$. Applying it to the terms we obtain a new pair, namely

$$k(h(x), f(\underline{x}, b, h(x))) \text{ and } k(h(x), f(\underline{g}(h(x)), y, h(x))).$$

The next located disagreement pair is $x, g(h(x))$. This pair is not simple, so by Theorem 2.13 we conclude that the pair (2.3) has no unifier. $\qquad\square$

2.6   The Martelli–Montanari Algorithm

The second unification algorithm we present is due to Martelli and Montanari [MM82]. Instead of unifying two terms, we solve an apparently more general problem of unifying finite sets of pairs of terms, written as a set of equations

$$\{s_1 = t_1, ..., s_n = t_n\}.$$

The algorithm operates on such finite sets of equations. Therefore we first adjust our terminology. First, we define the result of applying a substitution to a set of equations by

$$\{s_1 = t_1, ..., s_n = t_n\}\theta := \{s_1\theta = t_1\theta, ..., s_n\theta = t_n\theta\}.$$

θ is called a *unifier* of the set of equations $\{s_1 = t_1, ..., s_n = t_n\}$ if

$$s_1\theta = t_1\theta, \ldots, s_n\theta = t_n\theta.$$

Thus the singleton set of equations $\{s = t\}$ has the same unifiers as the terms s and t. A unifier θ of a set of equations E is called a *most general unifier* (in short *mgu*) of E if it is more general than all unifiers of E and is called a *strong* mgu of E if for all unifiers η of E we have $\eta = \theta\eta$.

Two sets of equations are called *equivalent* if they have the same set of unifiers. A set of equations is called *solved* if it is of the form $\{x_1 = t_1, ..., x_n = t_n\}$ where the x_is are distinct variables and none of them occurs in a term t_j. The interest in solved sets of equations is revealed by the following lemma.

Lemma 2.15 (Solved Form) If $E := \{x_1 = t_1, ..., x_n = t_n\}$ is solved, then the substitution $\theta := \{x_1/t_1, ..., x_n/t_n\}$ is a strong mgu of E.

Proof. First note that θ is a unifier of E. Indeed, for $i \in [1, n]$ we have $x_i\theta = t_i$ and moreover $t_i\theta = t_i$, since by assumption no x_j occurs in t_i.

Next, suppose η is a unifier of E. Then for $i \in [1, n]$ we have $x_i\eta = t_i\eta = x_i\theta\eta$ because $t_i = x_i\theta$ and for $x \notin \{x_1, ..., x_n\}$ we have $x\eta = x\theta\eta$ because $x = x\theta$. Thus $\eta = \theta\eta$. $\qquad\square$

We call θ the *unifier determined by* E. To find an *mgu* of a set of equations it thus suffices to transform it into an equivalent one which is solved. The following algorithm does it if this is possible and otherwise halts with failure.

Martelli–Montanari Algorithm

Nondeterministically choose from the set of equations an equation of a form below and perform the associated action.

(1) $f(s_1, ..., s_n) = f(t_1, ..., t_n)$ *replace by the equations*
     $s_1 = t_1, ..., s_n = t_n$,

(2) $f(s_1, ..., s_n) = g(t_1, ..., t_m)$ where $f \neq g$ *halt with failure,*

(3) $x = x$ *delete the equation,*

(4) $t = x$ where t is not a variable   *replace by the equation $x = t$,*

(5) $x = t$ where $x \notin Var(t)$ *perform the substitution $\{x/t\}$*
     and x occurs elsewhere   *on all other equations*

(6) $x = t$ where $x \in Var(t)$ and $x \neq t$ *halt with failure.*

The algorithm terminates when no action can be performed or when failure arises. Note that action (1) includes the case $c = c$ for every constant c which leads to deletion of such an equation. In addition, action (2) includes the case of two different constants.

To use this algorithm for unifying two terms s, t we activate it with the singleton set $\{s = t\}$.

To prove termination of this algorithm it is useful to use well-founded orderings. Let us recall first the relevant definitions.

A *relation R on a set $\mathcal{A}$* is a subset of the Cartesian product $\mathcal{A} \times \mathcal{A}$. A relation R on a set $\mathcal{A}$ is called *reflexive* if $(a, a) \in R$ for all $a \in \mathcal{A}$, it is called *irreflexive* if for no $a \in \mathcal{A}$ $(a, a) \in R$, it is called *antisymmetric* if for all $a, b \in \mathcal{A}$ whenever $(a, b) \in R$ and $(b, a) \in R$ then $a = b$ and it is called *transitive*, if for all $a, b, c \in \mathcal{A}$ whenever $(a, b) \in R$ and $(b, c) \in R$, then also $(a, c) \in R$.

A *partial ordering* is a pair $(\mathcal{A}, \sqsubseteq)$ consisting of a set $\mathcal{A}$ and a reflexive, antisymmetric and transitive relation $\sqsubseteq$ on $\mathcal{A}$. For example, the relation $\leq$ on integers is a partial ordering.

Finally, we introduce two concepts that will be needed only in Chapter 6. The *transitive closure* of a relation R on a set $\mathcal{A}$ is the smallest transitive relation on $\mathcal{A}$ that contains R as a subset. The *transitive, reflexive closure* is defined in an analogous way.

Let $(\mathcal{A}, \sqsubset)$ be an *irreflexive partial ordering*, that is let $\mathcal{A}$ be a set and $\sqsubset$ an irreflexive transitive relation on $\mathcal{A}$. We then say that $\sqsubset$ is a *well-founded ordering on $\mathcal{A}$* if there is no infinite descending chain

$$\ldots \sqsubset a_2 \sqsubset a_1 \sqsubset a_0$$

of elements $a_i \in \mathcal{A}$.

For example, the relation $<$ on natural numbers is an irreflexive partial ordering that is well-founded, while the relation $<$ on integers is an irreflexive partial ordering that is not well-founded.

In what follows we shall need a specific well-founded ordering, called the *lexicographic ordering* $\prec_n$ ($n \geq 1$), defined on the n-tuples of natural numbers. The relation $\prec_n$ is defined by induction on n, where we set $\prec_1$ to the relation $<$ on natural numbers and put for $n \geq 1$

$$(a_1, \ldots, a_{n+1}) \prec_{n+1} (b_1, \ldots, b_{n+1})$$

iff

$$(a_1, \ldots, a_n) \prec_n (b_1, \ldots, b_n)$$
$$\text{or} \quad (a_1, \ldots, a_n) = (b_1, \ldots, b_n) \text{ and } a_{n+1} < b_{n+1}.$$

In particular we have

$$(a_1, a_2, a_3) \prec_3 (b_1, b_2, b_3)$$

iff

$$a_1 < b_1$$
$$\text{or} \quad a_1 = b_1 \text{ and } a_2 < b_2$$
$$\text{or} \quad a_1 = b_1 \text{ and } a_2 = b_2 \text{ and } a_3 < b_3.$$

Exercise 6 Prove that for $n \geq 1$, $\prec_n$ is indeed a well-founded ordering on the set of n-tuples of natural numbers. $\square$

Theorem 2.16 (Unification 2) The Martelli–Montanari algorithm always terminates. If the original set of equations E has a unifier, then the algorithm successfully terminates and produces a solved set of equations determining a strong mgu of E and otherwise it terminates with failure.

Proof. We establish four claims.

Claim 1 The algorithm always terminates.

Proof. In contrast to Robinson's algorithm, the proof of termination is a bit more involved.

Given a set of equations E, we call a variable x *solved in E* if for some term t we have $x = t \in E$ and this is the only occurrence of x in E. We call a variable *unsolved* if it is not solved.

With each set of equations E we now associate the following three functions:

$$
\begin{array}{lll}
uns(E) & - & \text{the number of variables in } E \text{ that are unsolved,} \\
lfun(E) & - & \text{the total number of occurrences of function symbols} \\
& & \text{on the left-hand side of an equation in } E, \\
card(E) & - & \text{the number of equations in } E.
\end{array}
$$

We claim that each successful action of the algorithm reduces the triple of natural numbers

$$(uns(E), lfun(E), card(E))$$

in the lexicographic ordering $\prec_3$.

Indeed, no action turns a solved variable into an unsolved one, so $uns(E)$ never increases. Further, action (1) decreases $lfun(E)$ by 1, action (3) does not change $lfun(E)$ and decreases $card(E)$ by 1, action (4) decreases $lfun(E)$ by at least 1 and action (5) reduces $uns(E)$ by 1.

The termination is now the consequence of the well-foundedness of $\prec_3$. $\qquad\square$

Claim 2 Each action replaces the set of equations by an equivalent one.

Proof. The claim holds for action (1) because for all θ we have $f(s_1, ..., s_n)\theta = f(t_1, ..., t_n)\theta$ iff for $i \in [1, n]$ it holds that $s_i\theta = t_i\theta$. For actions (3) and (4) the claim is obvious.

For action (5) consider two sets of equations $E \cup \{x = t\}$ and $E\{x/t\} \cup \{x = t\}$, where $E\{x/t\}$ denotes the set obtained from E by applying to each of its equations the substitution $\{x/t\}$.

Then

$$
\begin{array}{ll}
& \theta \text{ is a unifier of } E \cup \{x = t\} \\
\text{iff} & \theta \text{ is a unifier of } E \text{ and } x\theta = t\theta \\
\text{iff} & \{\text{Binding Lemma 2.11}\} \\
& \{x/t\}\theta \text{ is a unifier of } E \text{ and } x\theta = t\theta \\
\text{iff} & \theta \text{ is a unifier of } E\{x/t\} \text{ and } x\theta = t\theta \\
\text{iff} & \theta \text{ is a unifier of } E\{x/t\} \cup \{x = t\}.
\end{array}
$$

$$\qquad\square$$

Claim 3 If the algorithm successfully terminates, then the final set of equations is solved.

Proof. If the algorithm successfully terminates, then the actions (1), (2) and (4) do not apply, so the left-hand side of every final equation is a variable. Moreover, actions (3), (5) and (6) do not apply, so these variables are distinct and none of them occurs on the right-hand side of an equation. $\qquad\square$

Claim 4 If the algorithm terminates with failure, then the set of equations at the moment of failure does not have a unifier.

Proof. If the failure results by action (2), then the selected equation $f(s_1, ..., s_n) = g(t_1, ..., t_m)$ is an element of the current set of equations and for no θ we have $f(s_1, ..., s_n)\theta = g(t_1, ..., t_m)\theta$.

If the failure results by action (6), then the equation $x = t$ is an element of the current set of equations and for no θ we have $x\theta = t\theta$, because $x\theta$ is a proper subterm of $t\theta$. $\qquad\square$

These four claims and the Solved Form Lemma 2.15 imply the desired conclusion. $\qquad\square$

To illustrate the operation of this algorithm reconsider the pairs of terms analyzed in Example 2.14.

Example 2.17
(i) Consider the set

$$\{k(z, f(x, b, z)) = k(h(x), f(g(a), y, z))\} \tag{2.4}$$

associated with the pair of terms $k(z, f(x, b, z))$ and $k(h(x), f(g(a), y, z))$. Action (1) applies and yields

$$\{z = h(x), f(x, b, z) = f(g(a), y, z)\}.$$

Choosing the second equation again action (1) applies and yields

$$\{z = h(x), x = g(a), b = y, z = z\}.$$

Choosing the third equation action (4) applies and yields

$$\{z = h(x), x = g(a), y = b, z = z\}.$$

Now, choosing the last equation action (3) applies and yields

$$\{z = h(x), x = g(a), y = b\}.$$

Finally, choosing the second equation action (5) applies and yields

$$\{z = h(g(a)), x = g(a), y = b\}.$$

At this stage no action applies, so by the Unification 2 Theorem 2.16 the substitution $\{z/h(g(a)), x/g(a), y/b\}$ is an mgu of (2.4).

Thus the same mgu was produced here as by Robinson's algorithm in Example 2.14(i).

(ii) Consider the set

$$\{k(z, f(x, b, z)) = k(h(x), f(g(z), y, z))\} \tag{2.5}$$

associated with the pair of terms $k(z, f(x, b, z))$ and $k(h(x), f(g(z), y, z))$. Let us try to repeat the choices made in (i). By action (1) we get the set

$$\{z = h(x), f(x, b, z) = f(g(z), y, z)\}.$$

Next, choosing the second equation action (1) applies again and yields

$$\{z = h(x), x = g(z), b = y, z = z\}.$$

Choosing the third equation action (4) applies and yields

$$\{z = h(x), x = g(z), y = b, z = z\}.$$

Now, choosing the fourth equation action (3) applies and yields

$$\{z = h(x), x = g(z), y = b\}.$$

Finally, choosing the second equation action (5) applies and yields

$$\{z = h(g(z)), x = g(z), y = b\}.$$

But now choosing the first equation action (6) applies and a failure arises. By the Unification 2 Theorem 2.16 the set (2.5) has no unifier. $\square$

Exercise 7 Prove that every mgu produced by Robinson's algorithm can also be produced by the Martelli–Montanari algorithm.
Hint. Treat the equations as a sequence instead of as a set. Always choose the first equation from the left to which an action applies. $\square$

Exercise 8 Find a set of equations for which the Martelli–Montanari algorithm yields two different mgus. $\square$

The test "x does not occur in t" in action (5) is called the *occur-check*. This test is also present in other unification algorithms, though in a less conspicuous form. In Robinson's algorithm it is a part of the test whether a pair of terms is simple.

In most Prolog implementations for efficiency reasons the occur-check is omitted. By omitting the occur-check in action (5) and deleting action (6) from the Martelli–Montanari algorithm we are still left with two options depending on whether the substitution $\{x/t\}$ is performed in t itself. If it is, then divergence can result, because x occurs in t implies that x occurs in $t\{x/t\}$. If it is not, then an incorrect result can be produced, as in the case of the single equation $x = f(x)$ which yields the substitution $\{x/f(x)\}$. None of these alternatives is desirable. In practise the second option is chosen.

In Chapter 7 we shall study under which conditions the occur-check can be safely omitted.

2.7   Properties of Mgus

We conclude this chapter by studying various properties of most general unifiers. When the substitutions θ and η are such that for a renaming γ we have $\eta = \theta\gamma$, we say that θ and η are *equivalent*. We shall see that all mgus of two terms s and t are equivalent. Still, a number of properties will allow us to distinguish between different mgus.

Recall from Definition 2.9 that an mgu θ is strong if for all unifiers η we have $\eta = \theta\eta$. The unification algorithms we considered all produced strong mgus. We now provide a simple criterion allowing us to decide whether an mgu is indeed strong.

Definition 2.18 A substitution θ is called *idempotent* if $\theta\theta = \theta$. $\square$

Theorem 2.19 (Idempotence) An mgu is strong iff it is idempotent.

Proof. Suppose θ is a strong mgu. In particular, θ is a unifier, so by the definition of a strong mgu we have $\theta = \theta\theta$. So θ is idempotent.

Conversely, suppose θ is an idempotent mgu and let η be a unifier. Then for some γ we have $\eta = \theta\gamma$. But by the idempotence of θ we have $\theta\gamma = \theta\theta\gamma = \theta\eta$. So θ is strong. $\square$

The following observation allows us easily to check when a substitution is idempotent.

Lemma 2.20 (Idempotence) A substitution θ is idempotent iff

$$Dom(\theta) \cap Ran(\theta) = \emptyset.$$

$\square$

For example, using it we can immediately check that $\{x/u, z/f(u,v), y/v\}$ is idempotent whereas $\{x/u, z/f(u,v), v/y\}$ is not.

Exercise 9
(i) Prove Lemma 2.20.

(ii) Prove that idempotent substitutions are not closed under composition.

(iii) Suppose that θ and η are idempotent substitutions such that $Dom(\theta) \cap Ran(\eta) = \emptyset$. Prove that $\theta\eta$ is idempotent.

(iv) Prove that $Var(s\theta) \cap Dom(\theta) = \emptyset$ when θ is idempotent. $\square$

It is worthwhile to note that not all mgus are idempotent and consequently not all mgus are strong. Indeed, take two identical terms. Then the substitution $\{x/y, y/x\}$ is an mgu, but it is not idempotent, because $\{x/y, y/x\}\{x/y, y/x\} = \epsilon$.

To better understand the role played by the idempotent or, equivalently, strong mgus, we introduce the following natural notion.

Definition 2.21 A unifier θ of s and t is called *relevant* if $Var(\theta) \subseteq Var(s) \cup Var(t)$. $\qquad\square$

Thus a relevant unifier neither uses nor introduces any "new" variables. A simple inspection of the actions performed shows that all mgus produced by the nondeterministic Robinson algorithm, Robinson's algorithm and by the Martelli–Montanari algorithm are relevant. This observation is used in the proof of the following result which shows why the idempotent mgus are of interest.

Theorem 2.22 (Relevance) Every idempotent mgu is relevant.

Proof. First we prove that for arbitrary substitutions θ and η

$$Var(\theta) \subseteq Var(\eta) \cup Var(\theta\eta) \tag{2.6}$$

by establishing

$$Dom(\theta) - Dom(\theta\eta) \subseteq Ran(\eta) \tag{2.7}$$

and

$$Ran(\theta) - Dom(\eta) \subseteq Ran(\theta\eta). \tag{2.8}$$

To prove (2.7) take $x \in Dom(\theta) - Dom(\theta\eta)$. Then for some $t \neq x$ we have $x\theta = t$ and $t\eta = x$. So t is a variable and $x \in Ran(\eta)$.

To prove (2.8) take $x \in Ran(\theta) - Dom(\eta)$. Then for some y and t we have $y/t \in \theta, y \neq t, x \in Var(t)$ and $x \in Var(t\eta)$. Now, if $y = t\eta$, then t is a variable and $t/y \in \eta$. But then $x = t$, since $x \in Var(t)$, so $x \in Dom(\eta)$. Contradiction. Thus $y \neq t\eta$, i.e. $y/t\eta \in \theta\eta$ and consequently $x \in Ran(\theta\eta)$.

Now let θ be an idempotent mgu of two terms s and t and η a unifier of s and t. By the Idempotence Theorem 2.19 θ is strong, so $\eta = \theta\eta$ and by (2.6) we obtain

$$Var(\theta) \subseteq Var(\eta).$$

Choose now for η an mgu of s and t produced by, say, Robinson's algorithm. Then η is relevant, so θ is relevant, as well. $\qquad\square$

On the other hand, not all relevant mgus are idempotent. Indeed, the substitution $\{x/y, y/x\}$ is a relevant mgu of the identical terms $k(x,y)$ and $k(x,y)$ but, as we already noted, it is not idempotent. Moreover, not all mgus are relevant. Indeed, take two identical ground terms and their mgu $\{x/y, y/x\}$.

As not all mgus are strong, the unification algorithms we considered do not generate all mgus of a pair of two terms or, more generally, of a set of equations E. The following lemma allows us to cope with this peculiarity.

Lemma 2.23 (Equivalence) Let θ_1 be an mgu of a set of equations E. Then for every substitution θ_2, θ_2 is an mgu of E iff $\theta_2 = \theta_1\gamma$ for some renaming γ such that $Var(\gamma) \subseteq Var(\theta_1) \cup Var(\theta_2)$.

Proof. By the definition of an mgu and the Renaming Lemma 2.8. $\square$

Finally, the following lemma allows us to search for mgus in an iterative fashion.

Lemma 2.24 (Iteration) Let E_1, E_2 be two sets of equations. Suppose that θ_1 is an mgu of E_1 and θ_2 is an mgu of $E_2\theta_1$. Then $\theta_1\theta_2$ is an mgu of $E_1 \cup E_2$. Moreover, if $E_1 \cup E_2$ is unifiable then an mgu θ_1 of E_1 exists and for any mgu θ_1 of E_1 an mgu θ_2 of $E_2\theta_1$ exists, as well.

Proof. If e is an equation of E_1, then it is unified by θ_1, so *a fortiori* by $\theta_1\theta_2$. If e is an equation of E_2, then $e\theta_1$ is an equation of $E_2\theta_1$. Thus $e\theta_1$ is unified by θ_2 and consequently e is unified by $\theta_1\theta_2$. This proves that $\theta_1\theta_2$ is a unifier of $E_1 \cup E_2$.

Now let η be a unifier of $E_1 \cup E_2$. By the choice of θ_1 there exists a substitution λ_1 such that $\eta = \theta_1\lambda_1$. Thus λ_1 is a unifier of $(E_1 \cup E_2)\theta_1$ and *a fortiori* of $E_2\theta_1$. By the choice of θ_2 for some λ_2 we have $\lambda_1 = \theta_2\lambda_2$. Thus $\eta = \theta_1\lambda_1 = \theta_1\theta_2\lambda_2$. This proves that $\theta_1\theta_2$ is an mgu of $E_1 \cup E_2$.

Finally, note that if $E_1 \cup E_2$ is unifiable, then *a fortiori* E_1 is unifiable. Let θ_1 be an mgu of E_1. The previously inferred existence of λ_1 implies that $E_2\theta_1$ is unifiable, so θ_2 exists. $\square$

Exercise 10 Prove the claim corresponding to the Iteration Lemma 2.24 with "mgu" everywhere replaced by "relevant mgu". $\square$

As a consequence we obtain the following conclusion which will be needed in the next chapter.

Corollary 2.25 (Switching) Let E_1, E_2 be two sets of equations. Suppose that θ_1 is an mgu of E_1 and θ_2 is an mgu of $E_2\theta_1$. Then E_2 is unifiable and for every mgu θ_1' of E_2 there exists an mgu θ_2' of $E_1\theta_1'$ such that

$$\theta_1'\theta_2' = \theta_1\theta_2.$$

Moreover, θ_2' can be so chosen that $Var(\theta_2') \subseteq Var(E_1) \cup Var(\theta_1') \cup Var(\theta_1\theta_2)$.

Proof. By the Iteration Lemma 2.24 $\theta_1\theta_2$ is an mgu of $E_1 \cup E_2$. So *a fortiori* E_2 is unifiable. Let θ_1' be an mgu of E_2. Again by the Iteration Lemma 2.24 there exists an mgu γ of $E_1\theta_1'$. Choose γ relevant, so that

$$Var(\gamma) \subseteq Var(E_1) \cup Var(\theta_1').$$

For the third time by the Iteration Lemma 2.24 $\theta_1'\gamma$ is an mgu of $E_1 \cup E_2$. By the Equivalence Lemma 2.23 for some renaming η such that

$$Var(\eta) \subseteq Var(\theta_1'\gamma) \cup Var(\theta_1\theta_2)$$

we have $\theta_1'\gamma\eta = \theta_1\theta_2$ and, again by the Equivalence Lemma 2.23, $\theta_2' := \gamma\eta$ is an mgu of $E_1\theta_1'$. Now $\theta_1'\theta_2' = \theta_1\theta_2$ and

$$Var(\theta_2') \subseteq Var(\gamma) \cup Var(\eta) \subseteq Var(E_1) \cup Var(\theta_1') \cup Var(\theta_1\theta_2).$$

$\square$

This corollary shows that the order of searching for mgus in an iterative fashion can be reversed.

Exercise 11 The concept of a unifier generalizes in an obvious way to finite sets of terms. Let $\mathcal{T}$ be a finite set of terms. Prove that there exists a pair of terms s, t such that for all substitutions θ we have θ is a unifier of $\mathcal{T}$ iff θ is a unifier of s and t. $\square$

2.8   Concluding Remarks

In this chapter we studied substitutions and most general unifiers in detail. The concept of a substitution in spite of its simplicity is more subtle than it seems and is a source of a number of common errors.

For example, the procedure discussed in the Composition Lemma 2.3 is usually formulated in a simpler way:

> remove from the set $\{x_1/t_1\eta, \ldots, x_n/t_n\eta, y_1/s_1, \ldots, y_m/s_m\}$ the bindings $x_i/t_i\eta$ for which $x_i = t_i\eta$ and the bindings y_j/s_j for which $y_j \in \{x_1, \ldots, x_n\}$,

and its outcome is taken as the definition of the composition $\theta\eta$. Unfortunately, as pointed out to us by N. Francez (private communication) this "simplification" is incorrect. The problem is that the bindings $x_1/t_1\eta, \ldots, x_n/t_n\eta, y_1/s_1, \ldots, y_m/s_m$ do not need to be pairwise different. So when the set notation is used, the removal of the bindings of the form y_j/s_j can have an undesired effect of removing an identical binding of the form $x_i/t_i\eta$. For example, according to the above simplification $\{x/y\}\{y/3, x/3\}$ equals $\{y/3\}$, whereas the procedure of the Composition Lemma 2.3 yields the correct result $\{x/3, y/3\}$.

We also noted in Example 2.7 that the relation "more general than" between two substitutions is quite subtle and is in some cases counterintuitive.

In this chapter we presented two nondeterministic unification algorithms. The fact that these algorithms are nondeterministic allows us to specialize them in various ways. In particular a specialization of the first one yielded Robinson's unification algorithm. However, all three algorithms are inefficient, as for some inputs they can take an exponential time to compute their mgu.

A standard example is the following pair of two terms, where $n > 0$: $f(x_1, \ldots, x_n)$ and $f(g(x_0, x_0), \ldots, g(x_{n-1}, x_{n-1}))$. Define now inductively a sequence of terms $t_1, \ldots, t_n$ as follows:

$$t_1 := g(x_0, x_0),$$

$$t_{i+1} := g(t_i, t_i).$$

It is easy to check that $\{x_1/t_1, \ldots, x_n/t_n\}$ is then a mgu of the above two terms. However, a simple proof by induction shows that each t_i has more than 2^i symbols.

This shows that the total number of symbols in any mgu of the above two terms is exponential in their size. As the representation of terms as strings or as augmented trees is common to all three unification algorithms presented in this chapter, we conclude that each of these algorithms runs in exponential time.

Note that the mgu of the above two terms can be computed using n actions of the Martelli–Montanari algorithm. This shows that the number of actions used in an execution of the Martelli–Montanari algorithm is not the right measure of the time complexity of this algorithm.

More efficient unification algorithms avoid explicit presentations of the most general unifiers and rely on different internal representation of terms.

2.9   Bibliographic Remarks

The unification problem was introduced and solved by Robinson [Rob65] who recognized its importance for automated theorem proving. The unification problem also appeared implicitly in the PhD thesis of Herbrand in 1930 (see [Her71, page 148]) in the context of solving term equations, but in an informal way and without proofs. The Martelli–Montanari algorithm presented in Section 2.6 is based upon Herbrand's original algorithm.

Eder [Ede85] provides a systematic account of the properties of substitutions and unifiers. Lassez *et al.* [LMM88] give a tutorial presentation of various basic results on unification. Properties of idempotent substitutions and unifiers are extensively studied in Palamidessi [Pal90]. Efficient unification algorithms are presented in Paterson and Wegman [PW78] and Martelli and Montanari [MM82]. A thorough analysis of the time complexity of various unification algorithms is carried out in Albert *et al.* [ACF93]. For a recent survey on unification see Baader and Siekmann [BS94].

The Relevance Theorem 2.22 has been discovered independently by a number of researchers. The proof given here is a modification of the one due to C. Palamidessi (unpublished). Robinson [Rob92] provides an interesting account of the history of the unification algorithms.

2.10   Summary

In this chapter we studied the unification problem. To this end we introduced the basic concepts, namely

- terms,
- substitutions,
- renamings,

- unifiers,
- most general unifiers (in short mgus),

and proved their elementary properties. Then we studied in detail three unification algorithms:

- the nondeterministic Robinson algorithm,
- Robinson's algorithm,
- the Martelli–Montanari algorithm,

and proved various properties of mgus. In particular, we considered

- idempotent mgus,
- relevant mgus.

2.11   References

[ACF93]   L. Albert, R. Casas, and F. Fages. Average case analysis of unification algorithms. *Theoretical Computer Science*, 113(1, 24):3–34, 1993.

[BS94]   F. Baader and J.H. Siekmann. Unification Theory. In D.M. Gabbay, C.J. Hogger, and J.A. Robinson, editors, *Handbook of Logic in Artificial Intelligence and Logic Programming Vol. 2, Deduction Methodologies*, pages 41–125. Oxford University Press, Oxford, 1994.

[Ede85]   E. Eder. Properties of substitutions and unifications. *Journal of Symbolic Computation*, 1:31–46, 1985.

[Fit90]   M. Fitting. *First-Order Logic and Automated Theorem Proving*. Texts and Monographs in Computer Science. Springer-Verlag, New York, 1990.

[Her71]   J. Herbrand. *Logical Writings*. Reidel, Dordrecht, 1971. W.D. Goldfarb, editor.

[Kow74]   R.A. Kowalski. Predicate logic as a programming language. In J. L. Rosenfeld, editor, *Information Processing '74*, pages 569–574. North-Holland, Amsterdam, 1974.

[LMM88]   J.-L. Lassez, M. J. Maher, and K. Marriott. Unification Revisited. In J. Minker, editor, *Foundations of Deductive Databases and Logic Programming*, pages 587–625. Morgan Kaufmann, Los Altos, CA, 1988.

[MM82]   A. Martelli and U. Montanari. An efficient unification algorithm. *ACM Transactions on Programming Languages and Systems*, 4:258–282, 1982.

[Pal90]   C. Palamidessi. Algebraic properties of idempotent substitutions. In *Proceedings of the 17th International Colloquium on Automata, Languages and Programming*, Warwick, England, 1990. Full version available as Technical Report TR-33/89, Dipartimento di Informatica, Università di Pisa.

[PW78]   M.S. Paterson and M.N. Wegman. Linear unification. *Journal of Computer and System Sciences*, 16(2):158–167, 1978.

[Rob65]   J.A. Robinson. A machine-oriented logic based on the resolution principle. *Journal of the ACM*, 12(1):23–41, 1965.

[Rob92]   J.A. Robinson. Logic and logic programming. *Communications of the ACM*, 35(3):40–65, 1992.

Chapter 3

Logic Programs: Procedural Interpretation

After this tour of unification we move on to the main topic of this book: logic programs. We begin by defining their syntax. Logic programs compute by means of the resolution method, called SLD-resolution. Unification forms a basic ingredient of this resolution method which explains why we have dealt with it first.

This computational interpretation of logic programs is called *procedural interpretation*. It explains *how* logic programs compute. The detailed knowledge of this interpretation is needed both to understand properly the foundations of logic programming and to explain the computation mechanism of Prolog.

At the end of Section 1.4, we have already said that the grasp of the procedural interpretation is crucial for a proper understanding of Prolog. While Prolog differs from logic programming, it can be naturally introduced by defining the computation mechanism of logic programs first and then by explaining the differences.

This process has the additional advantage of clarifying certain design decisions (like the choice of the search mechanism and the omission of the occur-check in the unification algorithm) and of shedding light on the resulting dangers (like the possibility of divergence or the occur-check problem).

In the next section we begin by extending the language of terms, originally defined in Section 2.1, to the language of programs. This brings us to the definition of programs and queries. In Section 3.2 we define the SLD-derivations. These are computations used to compute answers to a query.

In Section 3.3 we compare this computation process with computing in the imperative and functional programming style. This allows us to understand better the specific aspects of the logic programming style. Then in Section 3.4 we study properties of resultants, which are syntactic constructs that allow us to explain what is proved after each step of the SLD-derivations. The results obtained are used in Section 3.5 to prove the fundamental properties of the SLD-derivations, like similarity w.r.t. renaming and lifting. In Section 3.6 we consider what additional properties hold when we restrict the choice of the mgus in the SLD-derivations.

Next, in Section 3.7, we study selection rules. The results obtained are applied in the subsequent section, 3.8, to the study of SLD-trees — natural search spaces arising in the study of the SLD-resolution.

The properties of SLD-derivations and SLD-trees established in this chapter shed light on the computation process used in logic programming and help to understand better the differences between logic programming and Prolog.

3.1   Queries and Programs

We extend now the language of terms to the *language of programs*. First, we add to the alphabet

- *relation symbols* denoted by $p, q, r, \ldots$,
- *reversed implication*, that is: $\leftarrow$.

As in the case of function symbols, we assume that the class of relation symbols may vary. In addition, we assume that each relation symbol has a fixed arity associated with it. When the arity is 0, the relation symbol is usually called a *propositional symbol*.

Next, we define atoms, queries, clauses and programs as follows:

- if p is an n-ary relation symbol and $t_1, \ldots, t_n$ are terms then $p(t_1, \ldots, t_n)$ is an *atom*,
- a *query* is a finite sequence of atoms,
- a *clause* is a construct of the form $H \leftarrow \mathbf{B}$, where H is an atom and $\mathbf{B}$ is a query; H is called its *head* and $\mathbf{B}$ its *body*,
- a *program* is a finite set of clauses.

In mathematical logic it is customary to write $H \leftarrow \mathbf{B}$ as $\mathbf{B} \rightarrow H$. The use of reversed implication is motivated by the procedural interpretation according to which for $H := p(\mathbf{s})$ the clause $H \leftarrow \mathbf{B}$ is viewed as part of the declaration of the relation p.

For further analysis we also introduce the following notion:

- a *resultant* is a construct of the form $\mathbf{A} \leftarrow \mathbf{B}$, where $\mathbf{A}$ and $\mathbf{B}$ are queries.

Atoms are denoted by $A, B, C, H, \ldots$, queries by $Q, \mathbf{A}, \mathbf{B}, \mathbf{C}, \ldots$, clauses by $c, d, \ldots$, resultants by R and programs by P. The empty query is denoted by $\Box$. When $\mathbf{B}$ is empty, $H \leftarrow \mathbf{B}$ is written $H \leftarrow$ and is called a *unit clause*.

This use of the upper case letters should not cause confusion with the use of upper case letters for variables in Prolog programs. In fact, in Prolog programs we shall rather use upper case letters from the end of the alphabet. From the context it will be always clear to what syntactic entity we refer to.

Another regrettable, terminological difference between logic programming and Prolog is that the word "atom" has a completely different meaning in the context of

Prolog. Namely, in Prolog, an *atom* denotes any non-numeric constant. Throughout this book only the logic programming meaning of "atom" will be used.

For the reader familiar with the basics of first-order logic the following explanation can be useful. Intuitively, a query $A_1, \ldots, A_n$ is to be interpreted as the formula

$$\exists x_1 \ldots \exists x_k (A_1 \wedge \ldots \wedge A_n),$$

where $x_1, \ldots, x_k$ are the variables which occur in $A_1, \ldots, A_n$. From the computational point of view the query $A_1, \ldots, A_n$ should be viewed as a request for finding values for the variables $x_1, \ldots, x_k$ such that the conjunction $A_1 \wedge \ldots \wedge A_n$ becomes true. The empty query $\square$ stands for the empty conjunction so it is considered true.

In turn, a clause $H \leftarrow B_1, \ldots, B_n$ is to be interpreted as the implication

$$\forall x_1 \ldots \forall x_k (B_1 \wedge \ldots \wedge B_n \rightarrow H),$$

where $x_1, \ldots, x_k$ are the variables which occur in $H \leftarrow B_1, \ldots, B_n$. The reverse implication can thus be read as "if" and "," as "and". From the computational point of view the clause should be interpreted as a statement "to prove H prove $B_1, \ldots, B_n$". The order in which $B_1, \ldots, B_n$ are to be proved is of importance and will be discussed later.

Finally, a resultant $A_1, \ldots, A_m \leftarrow B_1, \ldots, B_n$ is to be interpreted as the implication

$$\forall x_1 \ldots \forall x_k (B_1 \wedge \ldots \wedge B_n \rightarrow A_1 \wedge \ldots \wedge A_m),$$

where $x_1, \ldots, x_k$ are the variables which occur in $A_1, \ldots, A_m \leftarrow B_1, \ldots, B_n$.

Resultants should not be confused with the sequents of sequent calculi and with clauses considered in automated theorem proving which — apart of the direction of the implication — have the same syntax but a different interpretation.

One last point. When considering a program we assume that it is defined in a specific language. It is tempting to choose for this language the language *determined by the program*, that is the one whose function and relation symbols are those occurring in the program. However, we wish to be more flexible and assume that the language of a program is *an* extension of the language determined by the program in the above sense. In this extension some new function and relation symbols can appear. They can be then used in the queries posed to the program. We shall see later that this choice is much more natural when studying properties of logic and Prolog programs.

3.2   SLD-derivations

Informally, the computation process within the logic programming framework can be explained as follows. A program P can be viewed as a set of axioms and a query

Q as a request to find an instance $Q\theta$ of it which follows from P. A successful computation yields such a θ and can be viewed as a proof of $Q\theta$ from P.

Such a computation is constructed as a sequence of "basic" steps. Each basic step consists of a selection of an atom A in the current query and of a clause $H \leftarrow \mathbf{B}$ in the program. If A unifies with H, then the next query is obtained by replacing A by the clause body $\mathbf{B}$ and by applying to the outcome an mgu of A and H. The computation terminates successfully when the empty query is produced. θ is then the composition of the mgus used.

Thus logic programs compute through a combination of two mechanisms — replacement and unification. To understand better various fine points of this computation process let us concentrate first on replacement in the absence of variables. So assume for a moment that no variables occur in the queries and the program.

Take a program P and consider a non-empty query $\mathbf{A}, B, \mathbf{C}$ and a clause $B \leftarrow \mathbf{B}$ of P. Then the query $\mathbf{A}, \mathbf{B}, \mathbf{C}$ is the result of replacing the indicated occurrence of B in $\mathbf{A}, B, \mathbf{C}$ by $\mathbf{B}$ and is called a *resolvent* of $\mathbf{A}, B, \mathbf{C}$ and $B \leftarrow \mathbf{B}$. B is called the *selected atom* of $\mathbf{A}, B, \mathbf{C}$. We write then $\mathbf{A}, B, \mathbf{C} \Longrightarrow \mathbf{A}, \mathbf{B}, \mathbf{C}$.

Iterating this replacement process we obtain a sequence of resolvents which is called a *derivation*. A derivation can be finite or infinite. If its last query is empty then we speak of a *successful derivation* of the original query Q. We can then say that we proved the query Q from the program P. If the selected atom H in the last query is such that no clause in P has H as its head, then we speak of a *failed derivation*.

Example 3.1 Consider the program *SUMMER* that consists of the following clauses:

$$happy \;\leftarrow\; summer,\; warm,$$
$$warm \;\leftarrow\; sunny,$$
$$warm \;\leftarrow\; summer,$$
$$summer \;\leftarrow\; .$$

Here *summer, warm* and *sunny* are 0-ary relation symbols, that is propositional symbols.

Then the sequence of queries

$$happy \Longrightarrow \underline{summer}, warm \Longrightarrow warm \Longrightarrow summer \Longrightarrow \square$$

is a successful derivation of the query *happy* and

$$happy \Longrightarrow summer, \underline{warm} \Longrightarrow summer, \underline{sunny}$$

is a failed derivation of *happy*. When a choice arises the selected atoms in the resolvents are underlined. $\square$

An important aspect of logic programs is that they can be used not only to *prove* but also to *compute*. We now explain this process by extending the above discussion to the case of queries and programs which can contain variables.

First, we extend unification from terms to atoms. This extension is immediate: just treat the relation symbols as if they were function symbols and use any of the previous unification algorithms!

Next, we define the notion of a resolvent, to be precise an *SLD-resolvent*. We explain the origin of the abbreviation "SLD" after Definition 3.4.

Definition 3.2 Consider a non-empty query $\mathbf{A}, B, \mathbf{C}$ and a clause c. Let $H \leftarrow \mathbf{B}$ be a variant of c variable disjoint with $\mathbf{A}, B, \mathbf{C}$. Suppose that B and H unify. Let θ be an mgu of B and H.

Then $(\mathbf{A}, \mathbf{B}, \mathbf{C})\theta$ is called an *SLD-resolvent* of $\mathbf{A}, B, \mathbf{C}$ and c *w.r.t.* B, *with an mgu* θ. B is called the *selected atom* of $\mathbf{A}, B, \mathbf{C}$. We write then

$$\mathbf{A}, B, \mathbf{C} \overset{\theta}{\underset{c}{\Longrightarrow}} (\mathbf{A}, \mathbf{B}, \mathbf{C})\theta$$

and call it an *SLD-derivation step*. $H \leftarrow \mathbf{B}$ is called its *input clause*. If the clause c is irrelevant we drop a reference to it. $\square$

Note that the SLD-resolvent was built using a specific variant of the clause instead of the clause itself. Thanks to it the definition of the SLD-resolvent does not depend on the accidental choice of variables in the clause. The following example illustrates this point.

Example 3.3 Take the query $Q := p(x)$ and the clause $c := p(f(y)) \leftarrow$. Then the empty query is an SLD-resolvent of Q and c. The same is the case for $c := p(f(x)) \leftarrow$ even though the atoms $p(x)$ and $p(f(x))$ do not unify. $\square$

We can present an SLD-derivation step in the form of a rule:

$$\frac{\mathbf{A}, B, \mathbf{C} \qquad H \leftarrow \mathbf{B}}{(\mathbf{A}, \mathbf{B}, \mathbf{C})\theta}$$

where $\mathbf{A}, B, \mathbf{C}$ and $H \leftarrow \mathbf{B}$ are variable disjoint, θ is an mgu of B and H and $H \leftarrow \mathbf{B}$ is a variant of c.

Thus a resolvent of a non-empty query and a clause is obtained by the following successive steps.

- **Selection**: select an atom in the query,
- **Renaming**: rename (if necessary) the clause,
- **Instantiation**: instantiate the query and the clause by an mgu of the selected atom and the head of the clause,
- **Replacement**: replace the instance of the selected atom by the instance of the body of the clause.

So the above definition of a resolvent is a generalization of the variable-free case where the resolvents were constructed solely by means of a replacement.

By iterating SLD-derivation steps we obtain an SLD-derivation. In order to obtain most general answers to the original query some syntactic restrictions need to be imposed on the mgus and the input clauses used. Their impact is discussed in Section 3.4. The formal definition is as follows.

Definition 3.4 A maximal sequence $Q_0 \overset{\theta_1}{\underset{c_1}{\Longrightarrow}} Q_1 \cdots Q_n \overset{\theta_{n+1}}{\underset{c_{n+1}}{\Longrightarrow}} Q_{n+1} \cdots$ of SLD-derivation steps is called an *SLD-derivation of* $P \cup \{Q_0\}$ if

- $Q_0, \ldots, Q_{n+1}, \ldots$ are queries, each empty or with one atom selected in it,
- $\theta_1, \ldots, \theta_{n+1}, \ldots$ are substitutions,
- $c_1, \ldots, c_{n+1}, \ldots$ are clauses of P,

and for every step the following condition holds:

- **Standardization apart**: the input clause employed is variable disjoint from the initial query Q_0 and from the substitutions and the input clauses used at earlier steps. More formally:

$$Var(c_i') \cap \left(Var(Q_0) \cup \bigcup_{j=1}^{i-1} (Var(\theta_j) \cup Var(c_j')) \right) = \emptyset$$

for $i \geq 1$, where c_i' is the input clause used in the step $Q_{i-1} \overset{\theta_i}{\underset{c_i}{\Longrightarrow}} Q_i$.

If the program is clear from the context, we speak of an *SLD-derivation of Q_0* and if the clauses $c_1, \ldots, c_{n+1}, \ldots$ are irrelevant we drop the reference to them. $\square$

We now see that the concept of a derivation explained for programs and queries with no variables is a special case of an SLD-derivation.

SLD-resolution stands for *S*election rule driven *L*inear resolution for *D*efinite clauses. Linearity means that each resolvent depends only on the previous one, so that derivations become sequences. Definite clauses are clauses in our terminology.

Intuitively, at each step of an SLD-derivation the variables of the input clauses should be "fresh". A simple way to achieve this is (assuming that no subscripted variables occur in the initial query) by adding the subscript "$_i$" to the variables of the program clause used at step i.

Two more definitions will be helpful.

Definition 3.5

- A clause is called *applicable to* an atom if a variant of its head unifies with the atom.
- The *length* of an SLD-derivation is the number of SLD-derivation steps used in it. So an SLD-derivation of length 0 consists of a single query Q such that either Q is empty or no clause of the program is applicable to its selected atom. $\square$

SLD-derivations can be of finite or infinite length. The finite ones are of special interest.

Definition 3.6 Consider a finite SLD-derivation $\xi := Q_0 \overset{\theta_1}{\Longrightarrow} Q_1 \cdots \overset{\theta_n}{\Longrightarrow} Q_n$ of a query $Q := Q_0$.

- ξ is called *successful* if $Q_n = \square$. The restriction $(\theta_1 \ldots \theta_n) \mid Var(Q)$ of the composition $\theta_1 \cdots \theta_n$ to the variables of Q is called then a *computed answer substitution* (*c.a.s.* in short) of Q and $Q\theta_1 \ldots \theta_n$ is called a *computed instance* of Q.

- ξ is called *failed* if Q_n is non-empty and no clause of P is applicable to the selected atom of Q_n. $\qquad\qquad\qquad\qquad\qquad\qquad\qquad\qquad\square$

Thus a computed answer substitution of Q is the restriction to the variables of Q of the composition of the successive mgus employed in a successful SLD-derivation. It should be viewed as a result computed by the query Q. Given a successful SLD-derivation ξ of Q with a c.a.s. θ we should view $Q\theta$ as the statement proved by ξ. Thus the c.a.s. provides the values for the variables of the query Q for which Q becomes true. We justify this statement in the next chapter once semantics of logic programs is introduced.

Note that the definition of a failed SLD-derivation presupposes that the selection of an (occurrence of an) atom in the query is the first step in computing a resolvent.

After this string of definitions let us consider an example to clarify the introduced notions.

Example 3.7 Consider terms built out of the constant 0 ("zero") by means of the unary function symbol s ("successor"). We call such terms *numerals*. The following program SUM computes the addition of two numerals:

$$
\begin{aligned}
&1.\quad sum(x,0,x) \leftarrow , \\
&2.\quad sum(x,s(y),s(z)) \leftarrow sum(x,y,z).
\end{aligned}
$$

In the SLD-derivations considered below the input clauses at the level i are obtained from the program clauses by adding the subscript "i" to all its variables which were used earlier in the derivation. In this way the standardization apart condition is satisfied.

The following is a successful SLD-derivation of the query $sum(s(s(0)), s(s(0)), z)$:

$$
sum(s(s(0)), s(s(0)), z) \overset{\theta_1}{\underset{2}{\Longrightarrow}} sum(s(s(0)), s(0), z_1) \overset{\theta_2}{\underset{2}{\Longrightarrow}} sum(s(s(0)), 0, z_2) \overset{\theta_3}{\underset{1}{\Longrightarrow}} \square,
$$

$$(3.1)$$

where
$$
\begin{aligned}
\theta_1 &= \{x/s(s(0)), y/s(0), z/s(z_1)\}, \\
\theta_2 &= \{x_2/s(s(0)), y_2/0, z_1/s(z_2)\}, \\
\theta_3 &= \{x_3/s(s(0)), z_2/s(s(0))\}.
\end{aligned}
$$
The corresponding computed answer substitution is

$$
\theta_1\theta_2\theta_3 \mid \{z\} = \{z/s(z_1)\}\{z_1/s(z_2)\}\{z_2/s(s(0))\} \mid \{z\} = \{z/s(s(s(s(0))))\}.
$$

More informally, we found a value for z for which $sum(s^2(0),\ s^2(0), z)$ holds, namely $s^4(0)$. The intermediate values of z generated in this SLD-derivation are $s(z_1)$, $s^2(z_2)$ and $s^4(0)$.

Now consider the query $sum(x, y, z)$. Repeatedly using clause 2 we obtain the following infinite SLD-derivation:

$$sum(x, y, z) \overset{\theta_1}{\underset{2}{\Longrightarrow}} sum(x_1, y_1, z_1) \overset{\theta_2}{\underset{2}{\Longrightarrow}} sum(x_2, y_2, z_2) \ldots \qquad (3.2)$$

where
$$\theta_1 = \{x/x_1, y/s(y_1), z/s(z_1)\},$$
$$\theta_2 = \{x_1/x_2, y_1/s(y_2), z_1/s(z_2)\},$$
$$\ldots \qquad \qquad \qquad \qquad \qquad \qquad \square$$

Exercise 12 Exhibit two successful SLD-derivations of the query $sum(s(x), y, s(s(0)))$ which yield the c.a.s.s $\{x/0, y/s(0)\}$ and $\{x/s(0), y/0\}$. $\qquad \square$

3.3 Comparison with other Programming Styles

After this explanation of the computation process in logic programming let us compare it with computations in the imperative and functional programming style. In imperative programming languages values are assigned to variables by means of the assignment command $x := t$. It is tempting to identify the effect of the assignment $x := t$ with the substitution $\{x/t\}$, especially when one is familiar with the axiom $\{\phi\{x/t\}\}\ x := t\ \{\phi\}$ of Hoare [Hoa69] describing the effect of the assignment in terms of pre- and post-assertions.

This identification allows us to model adequately the effect of some sequences of assignments. For example $x := 3; y := z$ corresponds to the substitution $\{x/3\}\{y/z\}$, i.e. $\{x/3, y/z\}$. However, it fails to model the effect of other sequences, like $x := 3; x := x + 1$. The problem is that after applying the first substitution $\{x/3\}$ the variable x "disappears" and so it cannot be any more incremented by 1. In other words, the first assignment is *destructive* and consequently its effect cannot be adequately modelled by a substitution.

So how is this problem solved in logic programming? Well, as we have already learned, the value of a variable, say x, is computed by means of a sequence of substitutions, say $\theta_1, \ldots, \theta_n$, which successively generate the intermediate values $x\theta_1 \ldots \theta_i$ (where $i \in [1, n]$) of x. Thus these intermediate values of x form a "monotonic" sequence of increasingly more instantiated terms. The final result is an instance of all the intermediate values. In general, the intermediate values of all variables (the "store") form a monotonic w.r.t. the "more general than relation" sequence of substitutions.

This is in sharp contrast with imperative programming languages in which the sequence of intermediate values of variables does not need to admit any regularity. So computing in logic programs is essentially different from computing in imperative programming languages and there is no direct counterpart in it of the concepts like destructive assignment or incrementing a value.

In contrast, the comparison with the functional programming style reveals certain similarities. Assume for a moment from the reader basic knowledge of term rewriting systems which form a basis for most functional programming languages. The above program *SUM* from Example 3.7 can be represented in a similar way as a term rewriting system:

1. *sum(x,0)* $\rightarrow$ *x*,
2. *sum(x,s(y))* $\rightarrow$ *s(sum(x,y))*,

where *sum* is now a function symbol.

Then the following computation (called *reduction sequence* in the term rewriting systems terminology) for the term $sum(s(s(0)), s(s(0)))$ yields the "same" result, namely $s(s(s(s(0))))$:

$$sum(s(s(0)), s(s(0))) \rightarrow s(sum(s(s(0)), s(0))) \rightarrow s(s(sum(s(s(0)), 0))) \rightarrow$$

$$s(s(s(s(0)))).$$

However, unlike the above term rewriting system, the logic program *SUM* can also be used to compute answers to more complex queries like $sum(s(x), y, s(s(0)))$ or to compute a difference of two numerals, say u, v, by means of the query $sum(z, u, v)$.

In conclusion, programming in logic programming differs in a significant way from computing in other programming styles.

3.4 Resultants

To facilitate a systematic study of SLD-derivations we now associate resultants with the SLD-derivations steps and SLD-derivations and prove some results about them. Consider an SLD-derivation step $Q \overset{\theta}{\Longrightarrow} Q_1$. It is useful to reflect what has actually been proved after performing this step. The answer can be given in terms of the resultants: $Q\theta \leftarrow Q_1$. We shall justify this statement in the next chapter, when studying soundness of the SLD-resolution. This motivates the following definition.

Definition 3.8

- Given an SLD-derivation step $Q \overset{\theta}{\Longrightarrow} Q_1$ we call $Q\theta \leftarrow Q_1$ *the resultant associated with* it.
- Consider a resultant $Q \leftarrow \mathbf{A}, B, \mathbf{C}$ and a clause c. Let $H \leftarrow \mathbf{B}$ be a variant of c variable disjoint with $Q \leftarrow \mathbf{A}, B, \mathbf{C}$ and θ an mgu of B and H. Then $(Q \leftarrow \mathbf{A}, \mathbf{B}, \mathbf{C})\theta$ is called an *SLD-resolvent* of $Q \leftarrow \mathbf{A}, B, \mathbf{C}$ and c w.r.t. B, *with an mgu* θ. B is called the *selected atom* of $Q \leftarrow \mathbf{A}, B, \mathbf{C}$.
  We write then $(Q \leftarrow \mathbf{A}, B, \mathbf{C}) \overset{\theta}{\underset{c}{\Longrightarrow}} (Q \leftarrow \mathbf{A}, \mathbf{B}, \mathbf{C})\theta$ and call it an *SLD-resultant step*. $H \leftarrow \mathbf{B}$ is called its *input clause*. If the clause c is irrelevant we drop a reference to it. $\square$

Next, we associate resultants with an SLD-derivation.

Definition 3.9 Consider an SLD-derivation

$$Q_0 \overset{\theta_1}{\underset{c_1}{\Longrightarrow}} Q_1 \cdots Q_n \overset{\theta_{n+1}}{\underset{c_{n+1}}{\Longrightarrow}} Q_{n+1} \cdots \tag{3.3}$$

Let for $i \geq 0$

$$R_i := Q_0\theta_1\ldots\theta_i \leftarrow Q_i.$$

We call R_i the *resultant of level i* of the SLD-derivation (3.3). $\square$

Example 3.10 Reconsider the SLD-derivation (3.1) of Example 3.7. It has the following four resultants:

of level 0: $sum(s(s(0)), s(s(0)), z) \leftarrow sum(s(s(0)), s(s(0)), z),$

of level 1: $sum(s(s(0)), s(s(0)), s(z_1)) \leftarrow sum(s(s(0)), s(0), z_1),$

of level 2: $sum(s(s(0)), s(s(0)), s(s(z_2))) \leftarrow sum(s(s(0)), 0, z_2),$

of level 3: $sum(s(s(0)), s(s(0)), s(s(s((0))))) \leftarrow \square.$ $\square$

Exercise 13 Compute the resultants of the SLD-derivation (3.2) considered in Example 3.7. $\square$

In particular, $R_0 = Q_0 \leftarrow Q_0$, R_1 coincides with the resultant associated with the SLD-derivation step $Q_0 \overset{\theta_1}{\Longrightarrow} Q_1$ and if $Q_n = \square$, then $R_n = Q_0\theta_1\ldots\theta_n \leftarrow \square$. Intuitively, the resultant R_i describes what is proved after i SLD-derivation steps by maintaining the effect of the mgus used so far on the original query Q_0. Originally, the tautology $Q_0 \leftarrow Q_0$ holds, and if $Q_n = \square$, then $Q_0\theta_1\ldots\theta_n$ is proved.

When proving formal properties of SLD-derivations if is often more convenient to work with the resultants associated with them. The following lemma is then helpful. It provides some insight into the role played by the standardization apart condition of Definition 3.4.

Lemma 3.11 (Disjointness) Consider an SLD-derivation of $P \cup \{Q\}$ with the sequence $d_1, \ldots, d_{n+1}, \ldots$ of input clauses used and with the sequence $R_0, \ldots, R_n, \ldots$ of resultants associated with it. Then for $i \geq 0$

$$Var(R_i) \cap Var(d_{i+1}) = \emptyset.$$

Proof. It suffices to prove by induction on i that

$$Var(R_i) \subseteq Var(Q) \cup \bigcup_{j=1}^{i} (Var(\theta_j) \cup Var(d_j)), \tag{3.4}$$

where $\theta_1, \ldots, \theta_n, \ldots$ are the substitutions used. The claim then follows by standardization apart.

Base. $i = 0$. Obvious.

Induction step. Suppose (3.4) holds for some $i \geq 0$. Note that if $R_i =$

$Q' \leftarrow \mathbf{A}, B, \mathbf{C}$ where B is the selected atom, and $d_{i+1} = H \leftarrow \mathbf{B}$, then $R_{i+1} = (Q' \leftarrow \mathbf{A}, \mathbf{B}, \mathbf{C})\theta_{i+1}$. Thus

$$
\begin{aligned}
& Var(R_{i+1}) \\
\subseteq \quad & Var(R_i) \cup Var(\theta_{i+1}) \cup Var(d_{i+1}) \\
\subseteq \quad & \{\text{induction hypothesis (3.4)}\} \\
& Var(Q) \cup \bigcup_{j=1}^{i+1} (Var(\theta_j) \cup Var(d_j)).
\end{aligned}
$$

$\square$

Exercise 14 Show that one can strengthen the claim of the Disjointness Lemma 3.11 to

$$Var(R_j) \cap Var(d_{i+1}) = \emptyset,$$

where $i \geq j \geq 0$. $\square$

In fact, for the theory of SLD-resolution it is sufficient to use the conclusion of the Disjointness Lemma 3.11 instead of the standardization apart condition. This strengthens somewhat the results but makes the presentation more technical, so we did not adopt this alternative.

The above result allows us to associate with the SLD-derivation (3.3) a derivation of resultants

$$R_0 \xrightarrow[c_1]{\theta_1} R_1 \cdots R_n \xrightarrow[c_{n+1}]{\theta_{n+1}} R_{n+1} \cdots$$

In this derivation each resultant R_{i+1} is obtained from its predecessor R_i by an SLD-resultant step $R_i \xrightarrow[c_{i+1}]{\theta_{i+1}} R_{i+1}$ in a way analogous to the corresponding SLD-derivation step $Q_i \xrightarrow[c_{i+1}]{\theta_{i+1}} Q_{i+1}$ of the SLD-derivation (3.3), that is by selecting in the antecedent Q_i of R_i the same atom as in Q_i, and by using the same input clause and the same mgu. Note that the Disjointness Lemma 3.11 ensures that for $i \geq 0$ indeed $R_i \xrightarrow[c_{i+1}]{\theta_{i+1}} R_{i+1}$.

Finally, we prove the following technical result which shows that, if the atoms are selected in the same positions, the property of being an instance of "propagates" through the derivation of resultants.

Lemma 3.12 (Propagation) Suppose that $R \xrightarrow[c]{\theta} R_1$ and $R' \xrightarrow[c]{\theta'} R'_1$ are two SLD-resultant steps such that

- R is an instance of R',
- in R and R' atoms in the same positions are selected.

Then R_1 is an instance of R'_1.

Note that in each step the *same* clause is used.

Proof. The proof is quite straightforward, though the details are a bit tedious. Let c_1 and c_1' be the corresponding input clauses employed to construct the resultants R_1 and R_1'. By assumption c_1 is a variant of c_1' and

$$Var(R) \cap Var(c_1) = Var(R') \cap Var(c_1') = \emptyset. \tag{3.5}$$

Assume for a moment that also

$$Var(R') \cap Var(c_1) = Var(R) \cap Var(c_1') = \emptyset. \tag{3.6}$$

For some η with $Var(\eta) \subseteq Var(R, R')$ we have $R = R'\eta$ and for some γ with $Var(\gamma) \subseteq Var(c_1, c_1')$ we have $c_1 = c_1'\gamma$. Let

$$R := Q \leftarrow \mathbf{A}, B, \mathbf{C},$$

$$R' := Q' \leftarrow \mathbf{A}', B', \mathbf{C}',$$

$$c_1 := H \leftarrow \mathbf{B},$$

$$c_1' := H' \leftarrow \mathbf{B}'.$$

Then

$$R_1 = (Q \leftarrow \mathbf{A}, \mathbf{B}, \mathbf{C})\theta,$$

$$R_1' = (Q' \leftarrow \mathbf{A}', \mathbf{B}', \mathbf{C}')\theta'.$$

By (3.5) and (3.6) $Var(\eta) \cap Var(\gamma) = \emptyset$, so $\eta \cup \gamma$, the union of η and γ, is well-defined. Moreover,

$$(Q' \leftarrow \mathbf{A}', \mathbf{B}', \mathbf{C}')(\eta \cup \gamma) = Q'\eta \leftarrow \mathbf{A}'\eta, \mathbf{B}'\gamma, \mathbf{C}'\eta = Q \leftarrow \mathbf{A}, \mathbf{B}, \mathbf{C},$$

so

$$R_1 = (Q' \leftarrow \mathbf{A}', \mathbf{B}', \mathbf{C}')(\eta \cup \gamma)\theta. \tag{3.7}$$

But, also by (3.5) and (3.6),

$$B'(\eta \cup \gamma) = B'\eta = B,$$

$$H'(\eta \cup \gamma) = H'\gamma = H,$$

so $(\eta \cup \gamma)\theta$ is a unifier of B' and H'. By the definition of an mgu, for some δ we have $(\eta \cup \gamma)\theta = \theta'\delta$. Hence by (3.7) $R_1 = R_1'\delta$, i.e. R_1 is an instance of R_1', so we obtain the desired conclusion ... under the assumption of (3.6).

For a general case take a variant R'' of R such that

$$Var(R'') \cap Var(c_1, c_1') = \emptyset$$

and then a variant c_1'' of c such that

$$Var(c_1'') \cap Var(R, R', R'') = \emptyset.$$

Then the SLD-resolvent R_1'' of R'' and c exists with the input clause c_1'' and with the atom selected in the same position as in R. By the above reasoning used twice R_1 is an instance of R_1'' and R_1'' is an instance of R_1'. $\square$

This lemma will be used in the proofs of all theorems dealing with the SLD-derivations established in the forthcoming sections. Note that the following conclusion is now immediate.

Corollary 3.13 (Propagation) Suppose that $Q \overset{\theta}{\underset{c}{\Longrightarrow}} Q_1$ and $Q' \overset{\theta'}{\underset{c}{\Longrightarrow}} Q_1'$ are two SLD-derivation steps such that

- Q is an instance of Q',
- in Q and Q' atoms in the same positions are selected.

Then Q_1 is an instance of Q_1'. $\square$

Exercise 15
(i) Prove the Propagation Corollary 3.13.

(ii) Consider two SLD-derivation steps which differ only in the choice of the variants of the input clause. Prove that the resulting SLD-resolvents are variants of each other. $\square$

Exercise 16 Analyze the proof of the Propagation Lemma 3.12 and show that its conclusion also holds when the first SLD-resultant step is of the form $R \overset{\theta}{\underset{d}{\Longrightarrow}} R_1$, where d is an instance of c. $\square$

3.5   Properties of SLD-derivations

According to the definition of an SLD-derivation the following four choices are made in each SLD-derivation step:

(A) choice of the selected atom in the considered query,
(B) choice of the program clause applicable to the selected atom,
(C) choice of the renaming of the program clause used,
(D) choice of the mgu.

We discuss now the consequences of these choices. We begin by considering (C) and (D). To this end we first prove some results allowing us to relate the SLD-derivations.

The next definition allows us to compare SLD-derivations of queries related by the "an instance of" relation.

Definition 3.14 Consider an SLD-derivation

$$\xi := Q_0 \underset{c_1}{\overset{\theta_1}{\Longrightarrow}} Q_1 \cdots Q_n \underset{c_{n+1}}{\overset{\theta_{n+1}}{\Longrightarrow}} Q_{n+1} \cdots$$

We say that the SLD-derivation

$$\xi' := Q_0' \underset{c_1}{\overset{\theta_1'}{\Longrightarrow}} Q_1' \cdots Q_n' \underset{c_{n+1}}{\overset{\theta_{n+1}'}{\Longrightarrow}} Q_{n+1}' \cdots$$

is a *lift* of ξ if

- ξ is of the same or smaller length than ξ',
- Q_0 is an instance of Q_0',
- for $i \geq 0$, in Q_i and Q_i' atoms in the same positions are selected. $\qquad \square$

Note that this definition is meaningful because in both SLD-derivations the sequence of clauses is the same, so for $i \geq 0$, Q_i and Q_i' have the same number of atoms.

Example 3.15 Consider the SLD-derivation (3.1) of Example 3.7 and the following successful SLD-derivation:

$$sum(x, y, z) \overset{\theta_1}{\underset{2}{\Longrightarrow}} sum(x_1, y_1, z_1) \overset{\theta_2}{\underset{2}{\Longrightarrow}} sum(x_2, y_2, z_2) \overset{\theta_3}{\underset{1}{\Longrightarrow}} \square \qquad (3.8)$$

where $\theta_3 = \{x_2/x, y_2/0, z_2/x\}$. Note that (3.8) is a lift of the SLD-derivation (3.1), since

- (3.1) and (3.8) are of the same length,
- $sum(s(s(0)), s(s(0)), z)$ is an instance of $sum(x, y, z)$,
- in both SLD-derivations at each step the same clauses are used and atoms in the same positions are selected.

In addition, observe that the SLD-derivation (3.2) is not a lift of the SLD-derivation (3.1), because at the third step different clauses are used. $\qquad \square$

The following important result shows that in lifts the property of being an instance of "propagates" through the derivation.

Theorem 3.16 (Instance) Consider an SLD-derivation ξ and its lift ξ'. Then for $i \geq 0$, if the resultant R_i of level i of ξ exists, then so does the resultant R_i' of level i of ξ' and R_i is an instance of R_i'.

Proof. It suffices to consider the corresponding derivations of resultants. The claim then follows by induction on i using the definition of a lift and the Propagation Lemma 3.12. $\qquad \square$

We now apply the Instance Theorem 3.16 to a study of SLD-derivations of queries which are variants of each other.

Definition 3.17 Consider two SLD-derivations:

$$\xi := Q_0 \overset{\theta_1}{\underset{c_1}{\Longrightarrow}} Q_1 \cdots Q_n \overset{\theta_{n+1}}{\underset{c_{n+1}}{\Longrightarrow}} Q_{n+1} \cdots$$

and

$$\xi' := Q_0' \overset{\theta_1'}{\underset{c_1}{\Longrightarrow}} Q_1' \cdots Q_n' \overset{\theta_{n+1}'}{\underset{c_{n+1}}{\Longrightarrow}} Q_{n+1}' \cdots.$$

We say that ξ and ξ' are *similar* if

- ξ and ξ' are of the same length,
- Q_0 and Q_0' are variants of each other,
- for $i \geq 0$, in Q_i and Q_i' atoms in the same positions are selected. $\qquad\square$

As in the case of a lift this definition is meaningful because in both SLD-derivations the sequence of the clauses used is the same. Thus two SLD-derivations are similar if

- their initial queries are variants of each other,
- they have the same length,
- for every SLD-derivation step

  - the input clauses employed are variants of each other,

  - atoms in the same positions are selected. $\qquad\square$

The following results relate similar SLD-derivations.

Theorem 3.18 (Variant) Consider two similar SLD-derivations. Then for $i \geq 0$ their resultants of level i are variants of each other.

Proof. Similar SLD-derivations are lifts of each other so it suffices to use the Instance Theorem 3.16 twice and apply the Variant Lemma 2.5. $\qquad\square$

Corollary 3.19 (Variant) Consider two similar successful SLD-derivations of Q with c.a.s.s θ and η. Then $Q\theta$ and $Q\eta$ are variants of each other.

Proof. By the Variant Theorem 3.18 applied to the final resultants of these SLD-derivations. $\qquad\square$

This corollary shows that choices (C) and (D) defined at the beginning of this section have no influence — modulo renaming — on the statement proved by a successful SLD-derivation of a query Q.

We conclude this section by proving existence of lifts. We begin with a study of lifts of SLD-derivation steps.

Definition 3.20 Consider an SLD-derivation step $Q \overset{\theta}{\underset{c}{\Longrightarrow}} Q_1$. We say that the SLD-derivation step $Q' \overset{\theta'}{\underset{c}{\Longrightarrow}} Q_1'$ is a *lift* of $Q \overset{\theta}{\underset{c}{\Longrightarrow}} Q_1$ if

- Q is an instance of Q',
- in Q and Q' atoms in the same positions are selected,
- Q_1 is an instance of Q_1'. $\qquad\square$

The following diagram illustrates this situation:

$$
\begin{array}{ccc}
Q' & \overset{\theta'}{\underset{c}{\Longrightarrow}} & Q_1' \\
\downarrow & & \downarrow \\
Q & \overset{\theta}{\underset{c}{\Longrightarrow}} & Q_1,
\end{array}
$$

where the vertical arrow $\downarrow$ indicates the "is more general than" relation. Note that in each step the same clause is used.

Lemma 3.21 (One Step Lifting) Consider an SLD-derivation step $Q\eta \overset{\theta}{\underset{c}{\Longrightarrow}} Q_1$ and a variant c' of c, variable disjoint with Q. Then for some θ' and Q_1',

- $Q \overset{\theta'}{\underset{c}{\Longrightarrow}} Q_1'$, where c' is the input clause used,
- $Q \overset{\theta'}{\underset{c}{\Longrightarrow}} Q_1'$ is a lift of $Q\eta \overset{\theta}{\underset{c}{\Longrightarrow}} Q_1$.

Proof. First we establish the following observation.

Claim 1 Suppose that the atoms A and H are variable disjoint and unify. Then A also unifies with any variant H' of H variable disjoint with A.

Proof. For some γ, such that $Dom(\gamma) \subseteq Var(H')$, we have $H = H'\gamma$. Let θ be a unifier of A and H. Then

$$A\gamma\theta = A\theta = H\theta = H'\gamma\theta,$$

so A and H' unify. $\qquad\square$

Now let c_1 be a variant of c variable disjoint with $Q, Q\eta$ and $Dom(\eta)$. By Claim 1

$$Q\eta \overset{\theta_1}{\underset{c}{\Longrightarrow}} Q_2$$

for some θ_1 and Q_2, where c_1 is the input clause used. Moreover, the same atom $A\eta$ is selected in $Q\eta$, both in the original and in the above SLD-derivation step.

Let H be the head of c_1. Note that A and H unify, since by the choice of c_1 we have $A\eta\theta_1 = H\theta_1$ and $H = H\eta$. Hence

$$Q \overset{\theta_2}{\underset{c}{\Longrightarrow}} Q_3$$

for some θ_2 and Q_3, where c_1 is the input clause used and A is the selected atom. Again by Claim 1

$$Q \overset{\theta'}{\underset{c}{\Longrightarrow}} Q_1'$$

for some θ' and Q_1', where c' is the input clause used and A is the selected atom. Moreover, by the Propagation Corollary 3.13 $Q \overset{\theta'}{\underset{c}{\Longrightarrow}} Q_1'$ is a lift of $Q\eta \overset{\theta}{\underset{c}{\Longrightarrow}} Q_1$, which concludes the proof. $\qquad\square$

Now we generalize this result to the case of SLD-derivations.

Theorem 3.22 (Lifting) For every SLD-derivation ξ of $P \cup \{Q\eta\}$ there exists an SLD-derivation of $P \cup \{Q\}$ which is a lift of ξ.

Proof. The required SLD-derivation can be constructed by repeatedly using the One Step Lifting Lemma 3.21. □

Exercise 17 Consider a more general notion of a lift according to which the clauses of the original SLD-derivation are respective instances of the clauses of the lift. Prove a strengthening of the above theorem which employs this more general notion of a lift. *Hint.* Use Exercise 16. □

Exercise 18 Give an example of a finite SLD-derivation whose lift is infinite. □

This brings us to the following conclusion.

Corollary 3.23 (Lifting) For every successful SLD-derivation ξ of $P \cup \{Q\eta\}$ with c.a.s. θ there exists a successful SLD-derivation ξ' of $P \cup \{Q\}$ with c.a.s. θ' such that

- ξ' is a lift of ξ of the same length as ξ,
- $Q\theta'$ is more general than $Q\eta\theta$.

Proof. It suffices to use the Lifting Theorem 3.22 to obtain a lift ξ' of ξ and to apply the Instance Theorem 3.16 to ξ, ξ' and the final resultant of ξ. □

3.6   * SLD-derivations with Idempotent Mgus

In Section 2.7 we observed that the mgus produced by the nondeterministic Robinson algorithm and by the Martelli–Montanari algorithm are always relevant. This fact leads to a natural restriction in the definition of the SLD-derivations in that all the mgus used are relevant.

Can we then prove additional properties of SLD-derivations? This question is of interest not only for the foundations of the SLD-resolution but also for the study of Prolog. The reason is that the unification algorithms used in practically all Prolog implementations are based on some modification of the nondeterministic Robinson algorithm or of the Martelli–Montanari algorithm.

The answer to this question is affirmative. Consider the following property of successful SLD-derivations. Here and below we assume that the composition of substitutions binds stronger than the restriction "$| \; Var(X)$" of a substitution.

Definition 3.24 Let ξ be a successful SLD-derivation of a query Q with the c.a.s. θ. Suppose that $Q \stackrel{\theta_1}{\Longrightarrow} Q'$ is the first step of ξ and τ is the c.a.s. of the suffix of ξ starting at Q'. We say that ξ enjoys the *composition property* if

$$\theta = \theta_1 \tau \mid Var(Q).$$

□

Informally, a successful SLD-derivation enjoys the composition property if its c.a.s. can be built in a "step-wise" fashion, by using the first mgu and the c.a.s. of the remainder of the SLD-derivation.

Theorem 3.25 (Composition) Let ξ be a successful SLD-derivation in which all the mgus used are relevant. Then ξ enjoys the composition property.

Proof. We say that a variable x is *released* at the SLD-derivation step $Q \stackrel{\theta}{\Longrightarrow} Q'$ if $x \in Var(Q\theta) - Var(Q')$. In other words, x is released at an SLD-derivation step if x occurs in the conclusion but not in the premise of the resultant $Q\theta \leftarrow Q'$ associated with it.

Claim 1 No variable released at the first step of ξ occurs in mgus used in later steps.

Proof. Suppose that x is released at the first step of ξ, $Q_0 \stackrel{\theta_1}{\Longrightarrow} Q_1$. Let d_1 be the first input clause used. Then $x \in Var(Q_0\theta_1)$ and θ_1 is relevant, so $Var(\theta_1) \subseteq Var(Q_0) \cup Var(d_1)$. Hence $x \in Var(Q_0) \cup Var(d_1)$. By the standardization apart x does not occur in the input clauses used in later steps.

But, due to the relevance of the mgus, the variables occurring in the mgus used in later steps occur either in Q_1 or in the input clauses used in these later steps. So the claim follows. $\square$

Let $\xi := Q_0 \stackrel{\theta_1}{\Longrightarrow} Q_1 \cdots \stackrel{\theta_n}{\Longrightarrow} \square$. We need to prove that

$$\theta_1\ldots\theta_n \mid Var(Q_0) = \theta_1(\theta_2\ldots\theta_n \mid Var(Q_1)) \mid Var(Q_0).$$

Suppose otherwise. Then a variable $x \in Var(Q_0)$ exists such that $x\theta_1\ldots\theta_n \neq x\theta_1(\theta_2\ldots\theta_n \mid Var(Q_1))$. Then a variable $y \in Var(x\theta_1)$ exists such that $y\theta_2\ldots\theta_n \neq y(\theta_2\ldots\theta_n \mid Var(Q_1))$. Thus $y \notin Var(Q_1)$, and $y(\theta_2\ldots\theta_n \mid Var(Q_1)) = y$. So $y \in Var(Q_0\theta_1) - Var(Q_1)$, that is y is released at the first SLD-derivation step. But then, by Claim 1, $y \notin Dom(\theta_2) \cup \ldots \cup Dom(\theta_n)$, hence $y\theta_2\ldots\theta_n = y$. Therefore, $y = y\theta_2\ldots\theta_n \neq y(\theta_2\ldots\theta_n \mid Var(Q_1)) = y$, which is a contradiction. $\square$

The following example shows that the Composition Theorem 3.25 does not hold when non-relevant mgus are used.

Example 3.26 Take the program $P := \{p(x_1) \leftarrow , q(x_2) \leftarrow \}$ and the query $Q := p(x), q(z)$ and consider the following SLD-derivation of $P \cup \{Q\}$:

$$\xi := Q \stackrel{\theta_1}{\Longrightarrow} q(z) \stackrel{\theta_2}{\Longrightarrow} \square,$$

where
$$\theta_1 = \{x/x_1\}\{x_1/y, y/x_1\} = \{x/y, x_1/y, y/x_1\},$$
$$\theta_2 = \{z/x_2\}\{x_2/y, y/x_2\} = \{z/y, x_2/y, y/x_2\}.$$
Here the c.a.s. of the query $q(z)$ is $\{z/y\}$ and $\theta_1\{z/y\} \mid Var(Q) = \{x/y, z/y\}$, which is not a c.a.s. of Q. $\square$

Note that by the Relevance Theorem 2.22 the Composition Theorem 3.25 applies when all the mgus are idempotent. In this case another property also holds.

Theorem 3.27 (Idempotent c.a.s.) Consider an SLD-derivation

$$\xi := Q_0 \overset{\theta_1}{\underset{c_1}{\Longrightarrow}} Q_1 \cdots Q_n \overset{\theta_{n+1}}{\underset{c_{n+1}}{\Longrightarrow}} Q_{n+1} \cdots$$

with the sequence $d_1, \ldots, d_{n+1}, \ldots$ of input clauses used, such that each θ_i $(i \geq 1)$ is idempotent. Then for $i \geq 1$, $\theta_1 \ldots \theta_i$ is idempotent. In particular, if ξ is successful, then its c.a.s. is idempotent.

Proof. We prove the claim by induction together with the statement that for $i \geq 1$

$$Var(Q_i) \subseteq Var(Q_0 \theta_1 \ldots \theta_i) \cup \bigcup_{j=1}^{i} (Var(d_j \theta_1 \ldots \theta_i)). \tag{3.9}$$

First note that by the Relevance Theorem 2.22 each θ_i is a relevant mgu, so for $i \geq 1$,

$$Var(Q_i) \subseteq Var(Q_{i-1}\theta_i) \cup Var(d_i \theta_i). \tag{3.10}$$

So the induction base holds. For the induction step in the proof (3.9) notice that

$$Var(Q_{i+1})$$
$$\subseteq \quad \{(3.10)\}$$
$$Var(Q_i \theta_{i+1}) \cup Var(d_{i+1}\theta_{i+1})$$
$$\subseteq \quad \{\text{induction hypothesis (3.9)}\}$$
$$Var(Q_0 \theta_1 \ldots \theta_{i+1}) \cup \bigcup_{j=1}^{i} Var(d_j \theta_1 \ldots \theta_{i+1}) \cup Var(d_{i+1}\theta_{i+1})$$
$$= \quad \{ Var(\theta_1 \ldots \theta_i) \cap Var(d_{i+1}) = \emptyset \text{ by the standardization apart}\}$$
$$Var(Q_0 \theta_1 \ldots \theta_{i+1}) \cup \bigcup_{j=1}^{i+1} Var(d_j \theta_1 \ldots \theta_{i+1}).$$

By the induction hypothesis $\theta_1 \ldots \theta_i$ is idempotent, so by Exercise 9(iv), the second induction hypothesis (3.9) and the standardization apart

$$Dom(\theta_1 \ldots \theta_i) \cap (Var(Q_i) \cup Var(d_{i+1})) = \emptyset.$$

But by the relevance of θ_{i+1}, $Ran(\theta_{i+1}) \subseteq Var(Q_i) \cup Var(d_{i+1})$, so $Dom(\theta_1 \ldots \theta_i) \cap Ran(\theta_{i+1}) = \emptyset$. Hence $\theta_1 \ldots \theta_{i+1}$ is idempotent by virtue of Exercise 9(iii). $\square$

It is legitimate to ask why we did not require in the definition of an SLD-derivation that the mgus used are all relevant or all idempotent. Then we would have at our disposal one or both of the theorems just established. The reason is that in this case another, very natural, property of SLD-derivations ceases to hold.

Recall from Definition 3.5 that $Q\theta$, where θ is a c.a.s. for Q, is called a computed instance of Q.

Note 3.28 (Closure) For every selection rule the computed instances of every query are closed under renaming.

Proof. Consider a computed instance Q' of a query Q. Let η be a renaming and θ_n the last mgu used in a successful SLD-derivation of Q of which Q' is the computed instance. By the Equivalence Lemma 2.23 $\theta_n \eta$ is an mgu (of the same two atoms), as well. Now using in the last step of the original SLD-derivation $\theta_n \eta$ instead of θ_n we obtain a successful SLD-derivation via the same selection rule of which $Q'\eta$ is the computed instance. $\qquad\square$

Now suppose that only relevant (respectively only idempotent) mgus are used and consider the program $P := \{p(f(y)) \leftarrow\}$ and $Q := p(x)$. Then the only computed instances of Q are of the form $p(f(z))$, where $z \neq x$. But $p(f(x))$ is a variant of $p(f(z))$, so we conclude that when we restrict our attention to relevant (respectively idempotent) mgus, then the Closure Note 3.28 does not hold any more.

Exercise 19 In Apt [Apt90] a different definition of SLD-derivation is used. It is assumed there that all mgus used are relevant and the standardization apart condition is formulated as follows:

> the input clause employed is variable disjoint from the initial query Q_0 and from the input clauses used at earlier steps.

(i) Prove then that the standardization apart condition used here holds.

(ii) Prove the Disjointness Lemma 3.11 and Exercise 14 for the case of this alternative definition. $\qquad\square$

3.7 Selection Rules

Let us discuss now the impact of choice (A) of Section 3.5, of the selection of an atom in a query. It is in general dependent on the whole "history" of the derivation up to the current resolvent. This motivates the following definition.

Definition 3.29

- Let *INIT* stand for the set of initial fragments of SLD-derivations in which the last query is non-empty. By a *selection rule* $\mathcal{R}$ we mean a function which, when applied to an element of *INIT* yields an occurrence of an atom in its last query.
- Given a selection rule $\mathcal{R}$, we say that an SLD-derivation ξ is *via* $\mathcal{R}$ if all choices of the selected atoms in ξ are performed according to $\mathcal{R}$. That is, for each initial fragment $\xi^<$ of ξ ending with a non-empty query Q, $\mathcal{R}(\xi^<)$ is the selected atom of Q. $\qquad\square$

Such a general definition of the selection rule allows us to select different atoms in resolvents that happen to occur more than once in the SLD-derivation, that is in identical resolvents with different "histories".

Example 3.30 Consider the selection rule $\mathcal{LR}$ that chooses the leftmost atom at even SLD-derivation steps and the rightmost atom at odd SLD-derivation steps. It is easy to define $\mathcal{LR}$ formally.

Now let $P := \{A \leftarrow A\}$ and $Q := A, A$. Then

$$A, \underline{A} \Longrightarrow \underline{A}, A \Longrightarrow \ldots$$

is an SLD-derivation; the selected atoms are underlined. Note that $\mathcal{LR}$ chooses here atoms at different positions in the same SLD-resolvents. $\qquad\square$

The following simple observation reveals the desired generality of the definition of the selection rule.

Note 3.31 (Selection) Every SLD-derivation is via a selection rule. $\qquad\square$

Exercise 20
(i) Prove the Selection Note 3.31.

(ii) Usually the following definition of a selection rule is used: it is a function which given a non-empty query selects from it an occurrence of an atom. Give an example of an SLD-derivation which is not via any selection rule in this sense. $\qquad\square$

The most natural selection rule is the *leftmost selection rule* according to which always the leftmost atom is chosen in a query. This is the rule used in Prolog. The result below shows that given a query Q, for each selection rule $\mathcal{R}$ the set of c.a.s.s of the successful SLD-derivations of Q via $\mathcal{R}$ is the same.

First we establish the following auxiliary result which is of independent interest.

Lemma 3.32 (Switching) Consider a query Q_n with two different atoms A_1 and A_2. Suppose that

$$\xi := Q_0 \xrightarrow[c_1]{\theta_1} Q_1 \cdots Q_n \xrightarrow[c_{n+1}]{\theta_{n+1}} Q_{n+1} \xrightarrow[c_{n+2}]{\theta_{n+2}} Q_{n+2} \cdots$$

is an SLD-derivation where

- A_1 is the selected atom of Q_n,
- $A_2\theta_{n+1}$ is the selected atom of Q_{n+1}.

Then for some Q'_{n+1}, θ'_{n+1} and θ'_{n+2}

- $\theta'_{n+1}\theta'_{n+2} = \theta_{n+1}\theta_{n+2}$,
- there exists an SLD-derivation

$$\xi' := Q_0 \xrightarrow[c_1]{\theta_1} Q_1 \cdots Q_n \xrightarrow[c_{n+2}]{\theta'_{n+1}} Q'_{n+1} \xrightarrow[c_{n+1}]{\theta'_{n+2}} Q_{n+2} \cdots$$

where

  $-$ ξ and ξ' coincide up to the resolvent Q_n,

  $-$ A_2 is the selected atom of Q_n,

  $-$ $A_1\theta'_{n+1}$ is the selected atom of Q'_{n+1},

  $-$ ξ and ξ' coincide after the resolvent Q_{n+2}.

Informally, this lemma says that two SLD-derivation steps can be switched provided that in the second step an instance of an "old" atom is selected. When referring to this lemma we shall say that the $(n+1)$-th and $(n+2)$-th steps in ξ "can be switched".

Proof. We intend to apply the Switching Corollary 2.25 of Chapter 2. Below, for two atoms $A := p(s_1, \ldots, s_n)$ and $H := p(t_1, \ldots, t_n)$ with the same relation symbol we denote by $A = H$ the set of term equations $\{s_1 = t_1, \ldots, s_n = t_n\}$. Let now $H_1 \leftarrow \mathbf{B}_1$ be the input clause used in the SLD-derivation step $Q_n \overset{\theta_{n+1}}{\underset{c_{n+1}}{\Longrightarrow}} Q_{n+1}$ and $H_2 \leftarrow \mathbf{B}_2$ the input clause used in the SLD-derivation step $Q_{n+1} \overset{\theta_{n+2}}{\underset{c_{n+2}}{\Longrightarrow}} Q_{n+2}$.

Then θ_{n+1} is an mgu of $A_1 = H_1$ and θ_{n+2} is an mgu of $A_2\theta_{n+1} = H_2$. But by the standardization apart $H_2\theta_{n+1} = H_2$, so θ_{n+2} is an mgu of $(A_2 = H_2)\theta_{n+1}$.

By the Switching Corollary 2.25 and the Unification 1 Theorem 2.13 there exists a relevant mgu θ'_{n+1} of $A_2 = H_2$ and an mgu θ'_{n+2} of $(A_1 = H_1)\theta'_{n+1}$ such that

$$\theta'_{n+1}\theta'_{n+2} = \theta_{n+1}\theta_{n+2} \tag{3.11}$$

and

$$Var(\theta'_{n+2}) \subseteq Var(\theta_{n+1}\theta_{n+2}) \cup Var(A_1 = H_1) \cup Var(A_2 = H_2). \tag{3.12}$$

But by the standardization apart $H_1\theta'_{n+1} = H_1$, so θ'_{n+2} is an mgu of $A_1\theta'_{n+1} = H_1$.
Moreover, by the Disjointness Lemma 3.11 and the standardization apart

$$Var(H_1 \leftarrow \mathbf{B}_1) \cap (Var(Q_n) \cup Var(H_2 \leftarrow \mathbf{B}_2)) = \emptyset,$$

so by the relevance of θ'_{n+1}

$$Var(H_1 \leftarrow \mathbf{B}_1) \cap Var(\theta'_{n+1}) = \emptyset. \tag{3.13}$$

Suppose now that

$$Q_n := \mathbf{A}, A_1, \mathbf{B}, A_2, \mathbf{C}$$

where without loss of generality we assumed that A_1 occurs in Q_n before A_2. Let

$$Q'_{n+1} := (\mathbf{A}, A_1, \mathbf{B}, \mathbf{B_2}, \mathbf{C})\theta'_{n+1}.$$

Note that by Exercise 14 $Var(H_2 \leftarrow \mathbf{B}_2) \cap Var(Q_n) = \emptyset$. So

$$Q_n \overset{\theta'_{n+1}}{\underset{c_{n+2}}{\Longrightarrow}} Q'_{n+1},$$

where $H_2 \leftarrow \mathbf{B_2}$ is the input clause used. Furthermore,

$$
\begin{aligned}
&Q_{n+2} \\
=\quad &\{\text{definition of an SLD-resolvent}\} \\
&(\mathbf{A}, \mathbf{B_1}, \mathbf{B})\theta_{n+1}\theta_{n+2}, \mathbf{B_2}\theta_{n+2}, \mathbf{C}\theta_{n+1}\theta_{n+2} \\
=\quad &\{ Var(H_2 \leftarrow \mathbf{B_2}) \cap Var(\theta_{n+1}) = \emptyset \text{ by standardization apart}\} \\
&(\mathbf{A}, \mathbf{B_1}, \mathbf{B}, \mathbf{B_2}, \mathbf{C})\theta_{n+1}\theta_{n+2} \\
=\quad &\{(3.11)\} \\
&(\mathbf{A}, \mathbf{B_1}, \mathbf{B}, \mathbf{B_2}, \mathbf{C})\theta'_{n+1}\theta'_{n+2} \\
=\quad &\{(3.13)\} \\
&\mathbf{A}\theta'_{n+1}\theta'_{n+2}, \mathbf{B_1}\theta'_{n+2}, (\mathbf{B}, \mathbf{B_2}, \mathbf{C})\theta'_{n+1}\theta'_{n+2},
\end{aligned}
$$

so

$$
Q'_{n+1} \xrightarrow[c_{n+1}]{\theta'_{n+2}} Q_{n+2},
$$

where $H_1 \leftarrow \mathbf{B_1}$ is the input clause used. This shows that

$$
Q_0 \xrightarrow[c_1]{\theta_1} Q_1 \cdots Q_n \xrightarrow[c_{n+2}]{\theta'_{n+1}} Q'_{n+1} \xrightarrow[c_{n+1}]{\theta'_{n+2}} Q_{n+2} \cdots
$$

is indeed an SLD-derivation, as (3.11), (3.12), (3.13) and Exercise 14 ensure that the standardization apart condition is satisfied. $\qquad\square$

Exercise 21 The last step of the above proof is more subtle than it seems. Complete the proof by showing that

$$
Var(\theta'_{n+2}) \subseteq Var(\theta_{n+1}) \cup Var(\theta_{n+2}) \cup Var(Q_n) \cup Var(H_1) \cup Var(H_2).
$$

$\qquad\square$

Exercise 22 Formulate a special case of the Switching Lemma 3.32 which applies to the SLD-derivations via the leftmost selection rule. $\qquad\square$

We can now prove the desired result.

Theorem 3.33 (Independence) For every successful SLD-derivation ξ of $P \cup \{Q\}$ and a selection rule $\mathcal{R}$ there exists a successful SLD-derivation ξ' of $P \cup \{Q\}$ via $\mathcal{R}$ such that

- the c.a.s.s of ξ and ξ' are the same,
- ξ and ξ' are of the same length.

Proof. Call two SLD-derivations of $P \cup \{Q\}$ *equivalent* if

- they have the same length,
- they are both successful,
- their c.a.s.s are equal.

Let

$$\xi := Q_0 \overset{\theta_1}{\Longrightarrow} Q_1 \cdots \overset{\theta_n}{\Longrightarrow} Q_n,$$

where $Q_n = \square$. Consider the least i such that in Q_i the atom selected in ξ differs from the atom A selected by $\mathcal{R}$. ξ is successful, so for some $j > 0$ the instance $A\theta_{i+1}\ldots\theta_{i+j}$ of A is the selected atom of Q_{i+j}. If such an i does not exist (that is, if ξ is via $\mathcal{R}$), then we let $i := n$ and $j := 0$.

Intuitively, i is the first place where ξ "deviates" from the selection rule $\mathcal{R}$ and j is the "delay" of ξ w.r.t. $\mathcal{R}$. Informally, the following diagram illustrates the situation:

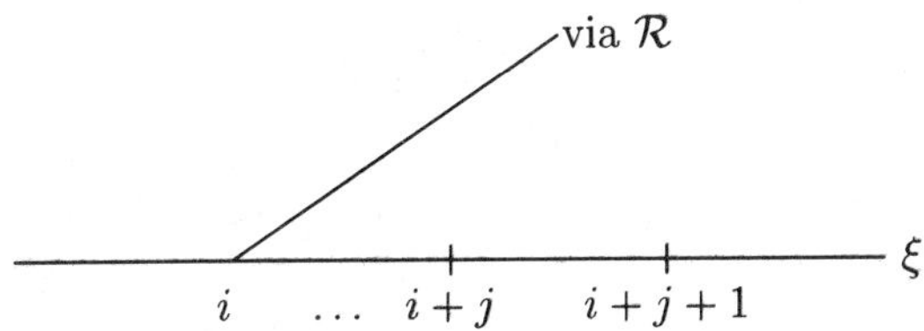

We call $(n - i, j)$ a *deviate-delay pair of ξ w.r.t.* $\mathcal{R}$. We now prove the claim by induction on the lexicographic ordering $\prec_2$ on the deviate-delay pairs (see Section 2.6 for the definition of $\prec_2$). If the deviate-delay pair of ξ w.r.t. $\mathcal{R}$ is of the form $(0, 0)$, then ξ is via $\mathcal{R}$.

Otherwise, by the Switching Lemma 3.32 the $(i + j)$-th and $(i + j + 1)$-th steps in ξ can be switched yielding an equivalent SLD-derivation ξ' of $P \cup \{Q\}$. The deviate-delay pair of ξ' w.r.t. $\mathcal{R}$ is either $(n - i, j - 1)$ if $j > 1$ or $(n - (i + 1), k)$ for some $k \geq 0$ if $j = 1$, so in both cases it is $\prec_2 (n - i, j)$. By the induction hypothesis ξ' is equivalent to an SLD-derivation of $P \cup \{Q\}$ via $\mathcal{R}$ and, consequently, so is ξ.
$\square$

Exercise 23 Find the counterexamples to the following claims:

(i) For every infinite SLD-derivation of $P \cup \{Q\}$ and a selection rule $\mathcal{R}$ there exists an infinite SLD-derivation of $P \cup \{Q\}$ via $\mathcal{R}$.
(ii) For every failed SLD-derivation of $P \cup \{Q\}$ and a selection rule $\mathcal{R}$ there exists a failed SLD-derivation of $P \cup \{Q\}$ via $\mathcal{R}$.
$\square$

3.8   SLD-trees

Finally, let us discuss the impact of choice (B) of Section 3.5, that is the choice of the program clause applicable to the selected atom. Assume that choice (A) is given by means of a selection rule $\mathcal{R}$.

When searching for a successful derivation of a query, SLD-derivations are constructed with the aim of generating the empty query. The totality of these derivations forms a *search space*. One way of organizing this search space is by dividing

SLD-derivations into categories according to the selection rule used. This brings us to the concept of an SLD-tree.

Essentially, an SLD-tree for $P \cup \{Q\}$ via a selection rule $\mathcal{R}$ groups all SLD-derivations of $P \cup \{Q\}$ via $\mathcal{R}$, though for the reasons explained in Section 3.5 choices (C) and (D) which are defined there are discarded. The formal definition is as follows.

Definition 3.34 An *SLD-tree for $P \cup \{Q\}$ via* a selection rule $\mathcal{R}$ is a tree such that

- its branches are SLD-derivations of $P \cup \{Q\}$ via $\mathcal{R}$,
- every node Q with selected atom A has exactly one descendant for every clause c from P which is applicable to A. This descendant is a resolvent of Q and c w.r.t. A. $\hspace{1em}\square$

Definition 3.35

- We call an SLD-tree *successful* if it contains the empty query.
- We call an SLD-tree *finitely failed* if it is finite and not successful. $\hspace{1em}\square$

In other words, an SLD-tree is successful if a branch of it is a successful SLD-derivation and an SLD-tree is finitely failed if all its branches are failed SLD-derivations.

The SLD-trees for a given query can differ in size and form.

Example 3.36 Consider the following program *PATH*:

1. $path(x,z) \;\leftarrow\; arc(x,y),\; path(y,z),$
2. $path(x,x) \;\leftarrow\;,$
3. $arc(b,c) \;\leftarrow\;.$

A possible interpretation of the relations *arc* and *path* is as follows: $arc(x,y)$ holds if there is an arc from x to y and $path(x,y)$ holds if there is a path from x to y. Figures 3.1 and 3.2 depict two SLD-trees for $PATH \cup \{path(x,c)\}$.

The selected atoms are put in bold and used clauses and performed substitutions are indicated. Thus the first SLD-tree is via the leftmost selection rule, whereas the second SLD-tree is via the rightmost selection rule (the rightmost atom is always selected). As in Example 3.7 the input clauses at level i are obtained from the program clauses by adding the subscript "i" to all its variables which were used earlier in the derivation. Note that the first tree is finite while the second one is infinite. However, both trees are successful. Actually, in both trees the same c.a.s.s, namely $\{x/b\}$ and $\{x/c\}$, are generated. $\hspace{1em}\square$

Informally, an SLD-tree via the leftmost selection rule corresponds to Prolog's search space. In order to find the computed answer substitutions to the original query, this tree is traversed by means of a so-called depth-first search which will be explained in Section 5.1.

For example, the tree of Figure 3.1 corresponds to Prolog's search space and $\{x/b\}$ and $\{x/c\}$ are the answers to the query $path(x,c)$ generated by Prolog.

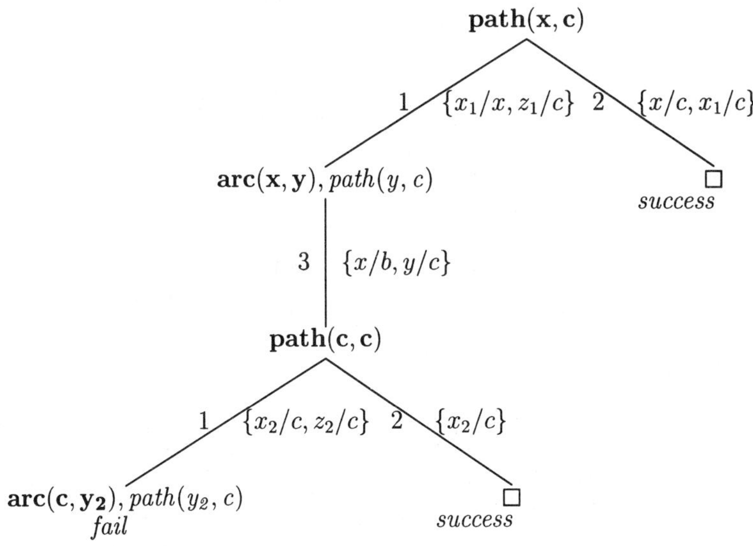

Figure 3.1 An SLD-tree

Exercise 24 Reconsider the *SUMMER* program considered in Example 3.1. Draw the SLD-trees for *SUMMER* $\cup$ {*happy*} via the leftmost selection rule and via the rightmost selection rule. $\quad\square$

Note that it is not the case that all SLD-derivations of $P \cup \{Q\}$ via a selection rule $\mathcal{R}$ are present as branches in every SLD-tree for $P \cup \{Q\}$ via $\mathcal{R}$. Still, the results of the previous sections imply a limited property of this kind.

In Definition 3.17 we defined when two SLD-derivations are similar. In an analogous way we can define when two initial fragments of SLD-derivations are similar.

Definition 3.37 We call a selection rule $\mathcal{R}$ *variant independent* if in all initial fragments of SLD-derivations which are similar, $\mathcal{R}$ chooses the atom in the same position in the last query. $\quad\square$

For example, the leftmost selection rule is variant independent. However, a selection rule which chooses the leftmost atom if the last query contains the variable x and otherwise the rightmost atom, is not variant independent. Indeed, take the program $\{p(y) \leftarrow p(y)\}$, the query $p(x), q(x)$ and its two SLD-resolvents $p(x), q(x)$ and $p(y), q(y)$. Then in the first query the first atom is chosen and in the second query the second one.

Clearly every SLD-derivation is via a variant independent selection rule, because we can extend the fragment of the selection rule employed in an appropriate way.

Exercise 25 Prove that every SLD-tree is via a variant independent selection rule. $\quad\square$

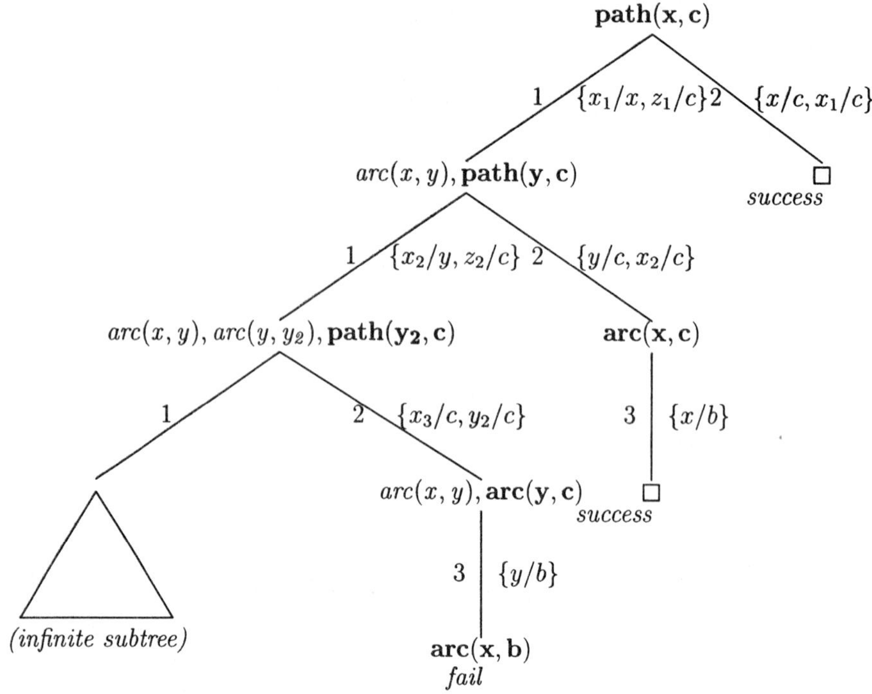

Figure 3.2 Another SLD-tree

Theorem 3.38 (Branch) Consider an SLD-tree $\mathcal{T}$ for $P \cup \{Q\}$ via a variant independent selection rule $\mathcal{R}$. Then every SLD-derivation of $P \cup \{Q\}$ via $\mathcal{R}$ is similar to a branch of $\mathcal{T}$. $\square$

Exercise 26 Prove the Branch Theorem 3.38. $\square$

Using the example of a non-variant independent selection rule given above it is easy to see that the Branch Theorem 3.38 does not hold for arbitrary selection rules. We now obtain the following conclusion exemplified by Figures 3.1 and 3.2.

Corollary 3.39 (Independence) If an SLD-tree for $P \cup \{Q\}$ is successful, then all SLD-trees for $P \cup \{Q\}$ are successful.

Proof. Consider a successful SLD-derivation of $P \cup \{Q\}$ and take an SLD-tree $\mathcal{T}$. By Exercise 25 $\mathcal{T}$ is via a variant independent selection rule $\mathcal{R}$. By the Independence Theorem 3.33 there exists a successful SLD-derivation ξ via $\mathcal{R}$. By the Branch Theorem 3.38 ξ is similar to a branch of $\mathcal{T}$, so $\mathcal{T}$ is successful. $\square$

Exercise 27 Fix a selection rule $\mathcal{R}$. Prove that for every SLD-derivation ξ via $\mathcal{R}$ there exists an SLD-tree via $\mathcal{R}$ with ξ as a branch. $\square$

3.9 Concluding Remarks

In this chapter we considered various properties of SLD-derivations. The precise treatment of these properties is quite tedious and prone to errors. For example the following version of the Lifting Corollary (usually termed "Lifting Lemma") is often claimed:

> For every successful SLD-derivation of $P \cup \{Q\eta\}$ with the mgus $\theta_1, \ldots, \theta_n$ used there exists a successful SLD-derivation of $P \cup \{Q\}$ of the same length with the mgus $\theta'_1, \ldots, \theta'_n$ used, such that $\theta'_1 \ldots \theta'_n$ is more general than $\eta\theta_1 \ldots \theta_n$.

Unfortunately, as noticed by Ko and Nadel [KN91], this version is incorrect. Indeed, let x, y be distinct variables and consider the program $P := \{p(x) \leftarrow \}$, the query $Q := p(f(y))$ and the substitution $\eta := \{y/f(x)\}$. Then $Q\eta = p(f(f(x)))$. Take $p(y) \leftarrow$ as the (first) input clause and $\{y/f(f(x))\}$ as the mgu of $p(y)$ and $p(f(f(x)))$.

Every (first) input clause in an SLD-derivation of $P \cup \{Q\}$ is of the form $p(z) \leftarrow$, where z is a variable distinct from y. By the Equivalence Lemma 2.23 any mgu of $p(z)$ and $p(f(y))$ is of the form $\{z/f(y)\}\gamma$, where γ is a renaming. So in every successful SLD-derivation of $P \cup \{Q\}$, for a variable z distinct from y and a renaming γ, $\{z/f(y)\}\gamma$ is the only mgu used.

Suppose now that $\{z/f(y)\}\gamma$ is more general than the substitution $\eta\{y/f(f(x))\}$, that is $\{y/f(x)\}$. Then for some δ we have $\{z/f(y)\}\gamma\delta = \{y/f(x)\}$, so z and y coincide, which is a contradiction.

On the other hand, the established properties of SLD-derivations are quite natural and pretty intuitive. Let us illustrate them on the examples of the already introduced programs.

Consider first the *SUM* program from Example 3.7 and reconsider the query $sum(s(s(0)), s(s(0)), z)$. In Example 3.7 we noted that there exists a successful SLD-derivation of $sum(s(s(0)), s(s(0)), z)$ with the c.a.s. $\{z/s(s(s(s(0))))\}$. Then $sum(s(s(0)), s(s(0)), s(s(s(s(0)))))$ is the computed instance of the query $sum(s(s(0)), s(s(0)), z)$ produced by this SLD-derivation. By the Variant Corollary 3.19 the computed answer substitution $\{z/s(s(s(s(0))))\}$ of $sum(s(s(0)), s(s(0)), z)$ does not depend on the choice of variables in the input clauses.

By applying the Lifting Corollary 3.23 we further conclude that any query more general than $sum(s(s(0)), s(s(0)), z)$ also admits a successful SLD-derivation. Moreover, we can require that in such a successful SLD-derivation at every SLD-derivation step the same clauses are used. The obtained c.a.s. is such that the resulting computed instance is more general than the computed instance produced by the original SLD-derivation: $sum(s(s(0)), s(s(0)), s(s(s(s(0)))))$. So for example the query $sum(x, s(s(0)), z)$ admits a c.a.s. θ such that $sum(x, s(s(0)), z)\theta$ is more general than $sum(s(s(0)), s(s(0)), s(s(s(s(0)))))$.

To illustrate the use of the results of Sections 3.7 and 3.8 let us consider now the program *PATH* from Example 3.36 and the query $path(x, c)$. We already noted that there exists a successful SLD-derivation of $path(x, c)$ via the leftmost selection rule (see Figure 3.1). In fact, the SLD-tree of Figure 3.1 shows that there exist at least two c.a.s.s for this query: $\{x/b\}$ and $\{x/c\}$. As the leftmost selection rule is variant independent, by the Branch Theorem 3.38 we conclude that no other c.a.s.s for this query exist.

Further, the Independence Theorem 3.33 tells us that each of these c.a.s.s can be also obtained when we use another selection rule. Moreover, we can require that the corresponding SLD-derivations are of the same lengths as the original ones. Note that the lengths of the successful SLD-derivations in the SLD-trees of Figures 3.1 and 3.2 are the same, namely 1 and 3. This fact is not a coincidence but an instance of a more general phenomenon directly derivable from the Independence Theorem 3.33 combined with the Branch Theorem 3.38.

3.10 Bibliographic Remarks

The concepts of unification, standardization apart and lifting were introduced in Robinson [Rob65] in a different, but related, framework of the resolution method. SLD-resolution was originally formulated in Kowalski [Kow74] as a special case of SL-resolution of Kowalski and Kuehner [KK71]. Our account of it differs from the usual one in that we use here queries and successful derivations instead of goals and refutations. (A goal is an expression of the form $\leftarrow Q$, where Q is a query; in this context $\leftarrow$ should be seen as negation.) This makes the exposition more intuitive, but the link with the usual resolution method becomes somewhat weaker.

The abbreviation "SLD" was first used in Apt and van Emden [AvE82], where the notion of an SLD-tree was also formally introduced and Example 3.36 provided. SLD-trees were informally used in Clark [Cla79] where they were called evaluation trees.

The selection rule was originally defined as in Exercise 20, as a function from queries to atoms. Our formulation follows the suggestion of Shepherdson [She84, page 62]. The notion of a resultant and Variant Theorem 3.18 are due to Lloyd and Shepherdson [LS91]. The proof of the Variant Theorem given here differs from the original one. Gabbrielli *et al.* [GLM96] established various properties of resultants.

Shepherdson [She94] discusses in detail various versions of standardization apart used in the definitions of an SLD-derivation. The notion of standardization apart used here necessitates an extensive renaming of the variables of the program clauses used. In Doets [Doe93] and in a more didactic form in Doets [Doe94], a more general account of SLD-resolution is developed that clarifies exactly which variables need to be renamed to retain most general answers.

Our presentation of lifts and the results about them are inspired by Doets [Doe93] where a stronger version of the Lifting Theorem 3.22 is given. The Composition Theorem 3.25 is from Apt and Doets [AD94]. The Switching Lemma 3.32 and the Independence Theorem 3.33 are due to Lloyd [Llo84], where slightly weaker versions were established.

The discussion at the end of Section 3.2 does not provide an adequate picture of the relation between computing in logic programming and imperative programming languages, because there is a way to relate the computations in the latter style to logic programming. This was done in van Emden [vE76] where it was shown that flowchart programs can be simulated by logic programs which generate the same results by means of "backward" computations. In particular the effect of the program $x := 3$; $x := x + 1$ can be simulated by the substitution $\{x/x + 1\}\{x/3\}$ which reverses the order of the assignment statements.

3.11 Summary

In this chapter we studied SLD-resolution. First, we fixed the syntax by defining

- queries,
- programs,
- resultants.

Then we introduced the notions of

- an SLD-resolvent,
- an SLD-derivation

and proved various properties of SLD-derivations. Finally, we defined

- selection rules,
- SLD-trees

and proved various properties of SLD-trees.

3.12 References

[AD94] K. R. Apt and H. C. Doets. A new definition of SLDNF-resolution. *Journal of Logic Programming*, 18(2):177–190, 1994.

[Apt90] K. R. Apt. Logic programming. In J. van Leeuwen, editor, *Handbook of Theoretical Computer Science*, pages 493–574. Vol. B, Elsevier, Amsterdam, 1990.

[AvE82] K.R. Apt and M.H. van Emden. Contributions to the theory of logic programming. *Journal of the ACM*, 29(3):841–862, 1982.

[Cla79] K. L. Clark. Predicate logic as a computational formalism. Res. Report DOC 79/59, Imperial College, Department of Computing, London, 1979.

[Doe93] H. C. Doets. Levationis laus. *Journal of Logic and Computation*, 3(5):487–516, 1993.

[Doe94]   H. C. Doets. *From Logic to Logic Programming*. The MIT Press, Cambridge, MA, 1994.

[GLM96]   M. Gabbrielli, G. Levi, and M.C. Meo. Resultants semantics for Prolog. *Journal of Logic and Computation*, 6(4):491–521, 1996.

[Hoa69]   C.A.R. Hoare. An axiomatic basis for computer programming. *Communications of the ACM*, 12:576–580, 583, 1969.

[KK71]   R.A. Kowalski and D. Kuehner. Linear resolution with selection function. *Artificial Intelligence*, 2:227–260, 1971.

[KN91]   H.-P. Ko and M. Nadel. Substitution and refutation revisited. In K. Furukawa, editor, *Proceedings of the 1991 International Conference on Logic Programming*, pages 679–692. MIT Press, Cambridge, MA, 1991.

[Kow74]   R.A. Kowalski. Predicate logic as a programming language. In J. L. Rosenfeld, editor, *Information Processing '74*, pages 569–574. North-Holland, Amsterdam, 1974.

[Llo84]   J. W. Lloyd. *Foundations of Logic Programming*. Springer-Verlag, Berlin, 1984.

[LS91]   J.W. Lloyd and J.C. Shepherdson. Partial evaluation in logic programming. *Journal of Logic Programming*, 11:217–242, 1991.

[Rob65]   J.A. Robinson. A machine-oriented logic based on the resolution principle. *Journal of the ACM*, 12(1):23–41, 1965.

[She84]   J. C. Shepherdson. Negation as failure: a comparison of Clark's completed data base Reiter's closed world assumption. *Journal of Logic Programming*, 1(1):51–79, 1984.

[She94]   J. C. Shepherdson. The role of standardising apart in logic programming. *Theoretical Computer Science*, 129:143–166, 1994.

[vE76]   M.H. van Emden. Verification conditions as programs. In S. Michaelson and R. Milner, editors, *Automata, Languages and Programming*, pages 99–119. Edinburgh University Press, Edinburgh, 1976.

Chapter 4

Logic Programs: Declarative Interpretation

To understand the *meaning* of logic programs, we now define their semantics. This interpretation of logic programs explains *what* logic programs compute, in contrast to the procedural interpretation which, as already noted in Chapter 3, explains *how* logic programs compute. It is called *declarative interpretation*. So the declarative interpretation abstracts from the details of the computation process and focuses on the semantic relationship between the studied notions.

The claim that logic programming supports declarative programming refers to the ability of using the declarative interpretation instead of the procedural interpretation when developing logic programs and analyzing their behaviour. As already mentioned in Section 1.2, this reduction considerably simplifies the task of program verification.

Let us now explain the structure of this chapter. In the next section we define algebras, which allow us to assign a meaning (or semantics) to terms. Then, in Section 4.2 we extend algebras to interpretations, which allow us to assign a meaning to programs, resultants and queries. In Section 4.3 we relate the procedural and declarative interpretation of logic programs by proving the soundness of the SLD-resolution. This result shows that the computed answer substitutions are correct answer substitutions or in other words that the results computed by the successful SLD-derivations semantically follow from the given program.

To prove a converse result we introduce first in Section 4.4 term interpretations. The appropriate form of the completeness of SLD-resolution is then proved in Section 4.5. In Section 4.6 we return to the term models and discuss the least term models. To prove various characterizations of these models we establish first in Section 4.7 the basic results on fixpoints. The appropriate characterization results are then proved in Section 4.8.

In Section 4.9 we introduce another natural (and in fact more often studied) class of interpretations of logic programs — so-called Herbrand interpretations and provide in Section 4.10 various characterizations of the least Herbrand models, analogous to those of the least term models.

The least term models and the least Herbrand models form two possible declarative interpretations of a logic program. In Section 4.11 we compare these two interpretations and show that under a natural condition they are isomorphic.

4.1   Algebras

We begin by defining the meaning of terms. An *algebra* (sometimes called a *pre-interpretation*) J for a language of terms L consists of:

- a non-empty set D, called the *domain* of J,
- an assignment to each n-ary function symbol f in L of a mapping f_J from D^n to D.

In particular, to each constant c in L an element c_J of D is assigned.

We now assign to terms elements of the domain of an algebra. We do this by using the notion of a state. A *state over the domain D* is a mapping assigning each variable an element from D. Given now a state σ over D, we extend its domain to all terms, that is we assign a term t an element $\sigma(t)$ from D, proceeding by induction as follows:

- $\sigma(f(t_1,\ldots,t_n)) = f_J(\sigma(t_1),\ldots,\sigma(t_n))$.

So $\sigma(f(t_1,\ldots,t_n))$ is the result of applying the mapping f_J to the sequence of values (already) associated by σ with the terms $t_1,\ldots,t_n$. Observe that for a constant c, we have $\sigma(c) = c_J$, so $\sigma(c)$ does not depend on σ.

Exercise 28 Prove that for a ground term t, $\sigma(t)$ has the same value for all σ. $\square$

Example 4.1 Consider the language allowing us to build arithmetic expressions in the prefix form introduced in Example 2.1. It contains two binary function symbols, "+" and "$\cdot$" and infinitely many constants: 0, 1, ... We provide two algebras for it.

(i) First, consider the standard algebra for this language which consists of the domain of natural numbers, assignment of the natural number i to each constant i, assignment of the addition function on natural numbers to the function symbol "+" and assignment of the multiplication function on natural numbers to the function symbol "$\cdot$".

(ii) Another, less expected but still perfectly correct, algebra for this language consists of the domain of real numbers, assignment of the real number $i\pi$ to each constant i, assignment of the multiplication function on real numbers to the function symbol "+" and assignment of the addition function on real numbers to the function symbol "$\cdot$".

The second algebra was chosen to show that the symbols of the language used do not determine their meaning, so + does not need to mean "plus", etc. $\square$

4.2   Interpretations

Next, we define the meaning of queries, resultants and clauses. To this end we introduce the notion of an *interpretation* I for a language L of programs. It consists of an algebra J with a domain D for the language of terms defined by L extended by

- an assignment, to each n-ary relation symbol p in L, of a subset p_I, of D^n.

We then say that I is *based on* J and denote for uniformity the mapping f_J by f_I. D is considered to be the domain of I, as well.

Example 4.2 Let us extend now the language of terms considered in Example 4.1 by a binary relation $<$. We provide two interpretations for this language of programs.

(i) First, we extend the algebra of Example 4.1(i) by assigning to $<$ the set $\{(a,b) \mid a \text{ and } b \text{ are natural numbers such that } a < b\}$.

(ii) As another interpretation consider the extension of the algebra of Example 4.1(ii) according to which the set $\{(a,a) \mid a \text{ is a real number}\}$ is assigned to $<$.

$\qquad\qquad\qquad\qquad\qquad\qquad\qquad\qquad\qquad\qquad\qquad\qquad\qquad\qquad\qquad\qquad$ $\Box$

From now on we fix a language $\mathcal{L}$ of programs. By an *expression* we mean an atom, query, resultant or a clause defined in $\mathcal{L}$.

We now define a relation $I \models_\sigma E$ between an interpretation I for $\mathcal{L}$, a state σ over the domain of I and an expression E. Intuitively, $I \models_\sigma E$ means that E is true when its variables are interpreted according to σ.

- If $p(t_1, \ldots, t_n)$ is an atom, then

$$I \models_\sigma p(t_1, \ldots, t_n) \text{ iff } (\sigma(t_1), \ldots, \sigma(t_n)) \in p_I,$$

- if $A_1, \ldots, A_n$ is a query, then

$$I \models_\sigma A_1, \ldots, A_n \text{ iff } I \models_\sigma A_i \text{ for } i \in [1, n],$$

- if $\mathbf{A} \leftarrow \mathbf{B}$ is a resultant, then

$$I \models_\sigma \mathbf{A} \leftarrow \mathbf{B} \text{ iff } I \models_\sigma \mathbf{A} \text{ under the assumption of } I \models_\sigma \mathbf{B}.$$

In particular, if $H \leftarrow \mathbf{B}$ is a clause, then

$$I \models_\sigma H \leftarrow \mathbf{B} \text{ iff } I \models_\sigma H \text{ under the assumption of } I \models_\sigma \mathbf{B},$$

and for a unit clause $H \leftarrow$

$$I \models_\sigma H \leftarrow \text{ iff } I \models_\sigma H.$$

Finally, we say that an expression E *is true in the interpretation* I and write $I \models E$, when for all states σ we have $I \models_\sigma E$. Note that the empty query $\Box$ is true in every interpretation I. When E is not true in I, we write $I \not\models E$.

Exercise 29 Let E be a ground expression. Prove that for all interpretations I and states σ and τ, $I \models_\sigma E$ iff $I \models_\tau E$. Conclude that $I \models E$ iff for some σ, $I \models_\sigma E$. □

For further analysis it is useful to extend the class of considered syntactic constants by introducing for an expression E its *universal closure*, written as $\forall E$ and its *existential closure*, written as $\exists E$. We define their semantics by

- $I \models \forall E$ iff for all states σ, $I \models_\sigma E$,
- $I \models \exists E$ iff for some state σ, $I \models_\sigma E$.

Thus for any expression E we have $I \models \forall E$ iff $I \models E$.

Given a set S of expressions or their closures we say that an interpretation I is a *model* of S if all elements of S are true in I. In particular, an interpretation I is a *model for program* P if every clause from P is true in I.

Exercise 30 Consider the language of programs discussed in Example 4.2. Take the clause $x \cdot y < z + 1 \leftarrow x \cdot y < z$.

(i) Prove that the interpretation given in Example 4.2(i) is a model of this clause.

(ii) Prove that this clause is not true in the interpretation given in Example 4.2(ii). □

Given two sets of expressions or their closures S and T, we say that S *semantically implies* T or that T *is a semantic consequence of* S, if every model of S is also a model of T. We write then $S \models T$ and omit the $\{\ \}$ brackets if any of these sets has exactly one element. S and T are *semantically equivalent* if both $S \models T$ and $T \models S$ hold. In the sequel we assume tacitly several, easy to prove properties of semantic consequence and semantic equivalence. The specific ones used in the next section are listed in the following exercise.

Exercise 31 Let E, F be expressions, S, T, U sets of expressions and $\mathbf{A}, \mathbf{B}, \mathbf{C}$ queries. Prove that

(i) $E \models E\theta$, for all θ.

(ii) $E\theta \models \exists E$, for all θ.

(iii) If E and F are variants, then $E \models F$ and $F \models E$.

(iv) $S \cup \{E\} \models E$.

(v) $S \models T$ and $T \models U$ implies $S \models U$.

(vi) If $E \models F$, then $S \models E$ implies $S \models F$.

(vii) If $S \models \mathbf{A} \leftarrow \mathbf{B}$, then $S \models \mathbf{A}, \mathbf{C} \leftarrow \mathbf{B}, \mathbf{C}$ and $S \models \mathbf{C}, \mathbf{A} \leftarrow \mathbf{C}, \mathbf{B}$ for all $\mathbf{C}$.

(viii) If $S \models \mathbf{A} \leftarrow \mathbf{B}$ and $S \models \mathbf{B} \leftarrow \mathbf{C}$, then $S \models \mathbf{A} \leftarrow \mathbf{C}$. □

Given an expression E, we denote by $inst(E)$ the set of all instances of E. Similarly, for a set of expressions S, we denote by $inst(S)$ the set of all instances of elements from S. Analogously, we denote by $ground(E)$ the set of all ground instances of E and by $ground(S)$ the set of all ground instances of elements from S. We stress the fact that all these instances are obtained w.r.t. to the language $\mathcal{L}$.

4.3   Soundness of the SLD-resolution

Those familiar with the basics of first-order logic undoubtedly noticed that, as already stated in Section 3.1, the above definition of the semantics allows us to interpret the clause $H \leftarrow B_1, \ldots, B_n$ as the universally quantified implication

$$\forall x_1 \ldots \forall x_k (B_1 \wedge \ldots \wedge B_n \rightarrow H),$$

where $x_1, \ldots, x_k$ are the variables which occur in $H \leftarrow B_1, \ldots, B_n$.

However, in case of queries a mismatch between the interpretation suggested in Chapter 3 and here arises, since we now interpret the query $A_1, \ldots, A_n$ as

$$\forall x_1 \ldots \forall x_k (A_1 \wedge \ldots \wedge A_n),$$

where $x_1, \ldots, x_k$ are the variables which occur in $A_1, \ldots, A_n$, so the variables are quantified universally and *not* existentially. The point is that whenever a successful SLD-derivation of the query $A_1, \ldots, A_n$ exists, then the computed instance $(A_1, \ldots, A_n)\theta$ of it is semantically implied by the program. As a result the existential closure $\exists x_1 \ldots \exists x_k (A_1 \wedge \ldots \wedge A_n)$ of this query is also semantically implied by the program. This is the consequence of the soundness of SLD-derivation.

Let us make these claims precise. For the rest of this chapter, we fix an arbitrary program P. We have already mentioned in Chapter 3 that when reasoning about SLD-resolution it is useful to use resultants. In particular, the following lemma is now helpful. It justifies the informal statements concerning resultants, made in Section 3.4.

Lemma 4.3 (Resultant)

(i) Let $Q \xLongrightarrow[c]{\theta} Q_1$ be an SLD-derivation step and r the resultant associated with it. Then

$$c \models r.$$

(ii) Consider an SLD-derivation of $P \cup \{Q\}$ with the sequence $R_0, \ldots, R_n, \ldots$ of resultants associated with it. Then for all $i \geq 0$

$$P \models R_i.$$

Proof.
(i) Suppose that $Q := \mathbf{A}, B, \mathbf{C}$, where B is the selected atom of Q. Let $H \leftarrow \mathbf{B}$ be the input clause used. Then $Q_1 = (\mathbf{A}, \mathbf{B}, \mathbf{C})\theta$ and $r = (\mathbf{A}, B, \mathbf{C})\theta \leftarrow (\mathbf{A}, \mathbf{B}, \mathbf{C})\theta$.

Now $c \models H\theta \leftarrow \mathbf{B}\theta$, so $c \models B\theta \leftarrow \mathbf{B}\theta$, since θ is a unifier of B and H. Thus $c \models (\mathbf{A}, B, \mathbf{C})\theta \leftarrow (\mathbf{A}, \mathbf{B}, \mathbf{C})\theta$, i.e. $c \models r$.

(ii) Let

$$Q_0 \xLongrightarrow{\theta_1} Q_1 \cdots Q_n \xLongrightarrow{\theta_{n+1}} Q_{n+1} \cdots$$

with $Q_0 := Q$ be the considered SLD-derivation. We prove the claim by induction on i.

Base.

$i = 0$. Immediate.

$i = 1$. By (i) since R_1 is the resultant associated with $Q_0 \overset{\theta_1}{\Longrightarrow} Q_1$.

Induction step. Let r_i denote the resultant associated with $Q_i \overset{\theta_{i+1}}{\Longrightarrow} Q_{i+1}$. Thus

$$R_{i+1} = Q_0\theta_1\ldots\theta_i\theta_{i+1} \leftarrow Q_{i+1},$$

$$R_i\theta_{i+1} = Q_0\theta_1\ldots\theta_{i+1} \leftarrow Q_i\theta_{i+1},$$

$$r_i = Q_i\theta_{i+1} \leftarrow Q_{i+1}.$$

Note that R_{i+1} is a semantic consequence of $R_i\theta_{i+1}$ and r_i. So by the induction hypothesis and (i) $P \models R_{i+1}$. $\qquad\square$

As a consequence we obtain the following theorem, which justifies the statement made after Definition 3.6.

Theorem 4.4 (Soundness of SLD-resolution) Suppose that there exists a successful SLD-derivation of $P \cup \{Q\}$ with the c.a.s. θ. Then $P \models Q\theta$.

Proof. Let $\theta_1, \ldots, \theta_n$ be the mgus employed. Applying the Resultant Lemma 4.3 to the last resultant of the SLD-derivation in question we obtain $P \models Q\theta_1\ldots\theta_n \leftarrow \square$. But $\theta = (\theta_1\ldots\theta_n)\,|\,Var(Q)$, so we proved $P \models Q\theta$. $\qquad\square$

Corollary 4.5 (Soundness) Suppose that there exists a successful SLD-derivation of $P \cup \{Q\}$. Then $P \models \exists Q$. $\qquad\square$

The Soundness Theorem 4.4 motivates the following definition, which provides a declarative counterpart of the notion of the computed answer substitution.

Definition 4.6 Suppose that $P \models Q\theta$. Then $\theta\,|\,Var(Q)$ is called a *correct answer substitution* of Q and $Q\theta$ is called a *correct instance* of Q. $\qquad\square$

A natural question arises whether a converse of the above corollary or of the Soundness Theorem 4.4 can be proved, that is whether a certain form of *completeness* of SLD-resolution can be shown. To handle this question we introduce a special class of interpretations of logic programs, called term interpretations. The domain of these interpretations consists of all terms.

4.4   Term Interpretations

We begin by introducing some auxiliary concepts. By the *term universe* $TU_{\mathcal{L}}$ for the language of programs $\mathcal{L}$ we mean the set of all terms of $\mathcal{L}$. Since we assumed that the set of variables is infinite, $TU_{\mathcal{L}}$ is infinite, as well. By the *term base* $TB_{\mathcal{L}}$ for $\mathcal{L}$ we mean the set of all atoms of $\mathcal{L}$.

The *term algebra* for $\mathcal{L}$ is defined as follows:

- its domain is the term universe $TU_{\mathcal{L}}$,
- if f is an n-ary function symbol in $\mathcal{L}$, then it is assigned the mapping from $(TU_{\mathcal{L}})^n$ to $TU_{\mathcal{L}}$ which maps the sequence $t_1, \ldots, t_n$ of terms to the term $f(t_1, \ldots, t_n)$.

Now, a *term interpretation* for $\mathcal{L}$ is an interpretation I based on the term algebra for $\mathcal{L}$. Thus

- if p is an n-ary relation symbol in $\mathcal{L}$, then it is assigned a set p_I of n-tuples of terms.

Note that there is only one term algebra for $\mathcal{L}$ but in general many term interpretations for $\mathcal{L}$.

Finally, by a *term model* for a set S of expressions we mean a term interpretation which is a model of S.

Thus in each term interpretation for $\mathcal{L}$ the interpretation of the function symbols is fixed. Consequently, each term interpretation for $\mathcal{L}$ is uniquely determined by the interpretation of the relation symbols. In fact, there is a natural 1-1 correspondence between the term interpretations and the subsets of the term base $TB_{\mathcal{L}}$ made explicit by the mapping which assigns to the term interpretation I the set of atoms

$$\{p(t_1, \ldots, t_n) \mid p \text{ is an } n\text{-ary relation symbol and } (t_1, \ldots, t_n) \in p_I\}.$$

This allows us to identify term interpretations for $\mathcal{L}$ with (possibly empty) subsets of the term base $TB_{\mathcal{L}}$. This is what we shall do in the sequel.

Since the domain of term models consists of syntactic objects, it takes some time to develop appropriate intuitions when reasoning about them. In particular, it is important to realize that a state over the domain $TU_{\mathcal{L}}$ of term interpretations maps each variable to a term of $\mathcal{L}$. Given a state σ we denote its restriction to a set of variables X by $\sigma \,|\, X$. So for a state σ over $TU_{\mathcal{L}}$, when X is finite, $\sigma \,|\, X$ is a substitution.

The following lemma is useful. Parts (ii) and (iii) allow us to dispense with the notion of state when considering truth in term interpretations.

Lemma 4.7 (Term Interpretation) Let I be a term interpretation. Then

(i) for an atom A and a state σ

$$I \models_\sigma A \text{ iff } A(\sigma \,|\, Var(A)) \in I,$$

(ii) for an atom A

$$I \models A \text{ iff } inst(A) \subseteq I,$$

(iii) for a clause c

$$I \models c \text{ iff for all } A \leftarrow B_1, \ldots, B_n \text{ in } inst(c), \ \{B_1, \ldots, B_n\} \subseteq I \text{ implies } A \in I.$$

Proof.

(i) A straightforward proof by induction using Exercise 1(i) of Section 2.2 shows that for a term t and a finite set of variables X with $Var(t) \subseteq X$ we have $\sigma(t) = t(\sigma \mid X)$. That is, the value assigned to the term t by the state σ equals the result of applying the substitution $\sigma \mid X$ to t.

So for an atom $p(t_1, \ldots, t_n)$ we have

$$I \models_\sigma p(t_1, \ldots, t_n) \text{ iff } (t_1\theta, \ldots, t_n\theta) \in p_I \text{ iff } p(t_1, \ldots, t_n)\theta \in I,$$

where $\theta := \sigma \mid Var(p(t_1, \ldots, t_n))$.

(ii) By (i).

(iii) By (i) $I \models_\sigma A \leftarrow B_1, \ldots, B_n$ iff $\{B_1\theta, \ldots, B_n\theta\} \subseteq I$ implies $A\theta \in I$, where $\theta := \sigma \mid Var(A \leftarrow B_1, \ldots, B_n)$. This yields the claim. $\qquad\square$

Part (ii) shows that in general we cannot identify a term interpretation with the set of atoms true in it. But consider the following definition.

Definition 4.8 A term interpretation I is *closed under substitution* if $A \in I$ implies $inst(A) \subseteq I$. $\qquad\square$

Now, for term interpretations closed under substitutions the above identification is possible, that is for a term interpretation I closed under substitution we have

$$I = \{A \mid A \text{ is an atom and } I \models A\}.$$

Moreover, such interpretations satisfy an interesting property.

Note 4.9 (Substitution Closure) For a term interpretation I closed under substitution, $I \models \exists Q$ implies that for some substitution θ, $I \models Q\theta$.

Proof. Let $Q = A_1, \ldots, A_n$. For some state σ, $I \models_\sigma A_1, \ldots, A_n$. By the Term Interpretation Lemma 4.7(i) we obtain $A_i(\sigma \mid Var(Q)) \in I$ for $i \in [1, n]$, so by the Term Interpretation Lemma 4.7(ii) and the assumption about I, $I \models A_i(\sigma \mid Var(Q))$ for $i \in [1, n]$. Thus $I \models Q(\sigma \mid Var(Q))$. $\qquad\square$

Exercise 32 Find a term interpretation I and an atom A such that $I \models \exists A$ but for no substitution θ, $I \models A\theta$.

Hint. Take $I = \{p(x)\}$ and $A = p(x)$. $\qquad\square$

Given a program P we now construct a specific term model for P. We begin by introducing the following concept.

Definition 4.10 A finite tree whose nodes are atoms, is called an *implication tree* *w.r.t.* P if for each of its nodes A with the direct descendants $B_1, \ldots, B_n$, the clause $A \leftarrow B_1, \ldots, B_n$ is in $inst(P)$. In particular, for each leaf A the clause $A \leftarrow$ is in $inst(P)$. We say that an atom *has an implication tree w.r.t.* P if it is the root of an implication tree w.r.t. P. An implication tree is called *ground* iff all its nodes are ground. $\square$

In particular, when $A \leftarrow$ is in $inst(P)$ the tree with the single node A is an implication tree w.r.t. P. Note that an atom can be a root of several implication trees w.r.t. P. Ground implication trees will be used in Section 4.9.

Example 4.11 The atom *happy* has the following ground implication tree w.r.t. the program *SUMMER* of Example 3.1:

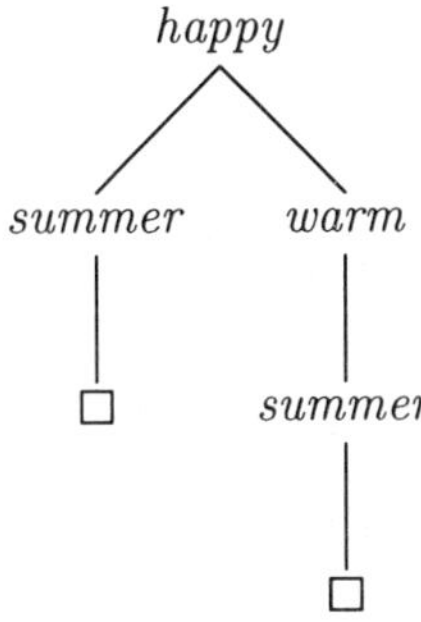

$\square$

For readers familiar with the basics of the proof theory the following intuitive explanation of implication trees can be useful. Given a program P, turn it into a proof system by writing each clause $A \leftarrow B_1, \ldots, B_n$ in $inst(P)$ as a proof rule:

$$\frac{B_1, \ldots, B_n}{A}$$

When $n = 0$ such a proof rule degenerates to an axiom. Then the implication trees w.r.t. P coincide with the proofs of atoms in the above proof system. So an atom has an implication tree w.r.t. P iff it is provable in this proof system.

An implication tree is a purely syntactic concept. Now we use them to construct a specific term model of a program P.

Lemma 4.12 ($\mathcal{C}(P)$) The term interpretation

$$\mathcal{C}(P) := \{A \mid A \text{ has an implication tree w.r.t. } P\}$$

is a model of P.

Proof. By the Term Interpretation Lemma 4.7(iii) it suffices to prove that for all $A \leftarrow B_1, \ldots, B_n$ in $inst(P)$, $\{B_1, \ldots, B_n\} \subseteq \mathcal{C}(P)$ implies $A \in \mathcal{C}(P)$. But this translates into an obvious property of the implication trees. $\square$

We shall use this result to establish completeness of the SLD-resolution.

Exercise 33 Prove that $\mathcal{C}(P)$ is closed under substitution. Conclude that for all atoms A, $\mathcal{C}(P) \models A$ iff $A \in \mathcal{C}(P)$. $\square$

4.5   Completeness of the SLD-resolution

The Soundness Theorem 4.4 relates provability with truth. The converse relation is provided by the completeness theorems. We establish here the strongest version which shows the existence of successful derivations independently of the selection rule.

Theorem 4.13 (Strong Completeness of SLD-resolution) Suppose that $P \models Q\theta$. Then for every selection rule $\mathcal{R}$ there exists a successful SLD-derivation of $P \cup \{Q\}$ via $\mathcal{R}$ with the c.a.s. η such that $Q\eta$ is more general than $Q\theta$.

The key step in the proof of this theorem we present here is the following purely proof-theoretical result which relates two concepts of provability — that by means of implication trees and that by means of SLD-resolution. We need an auxiliary concept first.

Definition 4.14 Given a program P and a query Q, we say that Q is n-*deep* if every atom in Q has an implication tree w.r.t. P and the total number of nodes in these implication trees is n. $\square$

Thus a query is 0-deep iff it is empty.

Lemma 4.15 (Implication Tree) Suppose that $Q\theta$ is n-deep for some $n \geq 0$. Then for every selection rule $\mathcal{R}$ there exists a successful SLD-derivation of $P \cup \{Q\}$ via $\mathcal{R}$ with the c.a.s. η such that $Q\eta$ is more general than $Q\theta$.

Proof. We construct by induction on $i \in [0, n]$ a prefix

$$Q_0 \overset{\theta_1}{\Longrightarrow} Q_1 \cdots \overset{\theta_i}{\Longrightarrow} Q_i$$

of an SLD-derivation of $P \cup \{Q\}$ via $\mathcal{R}$ and a sequence of substitutions $\gamma_0, \ldots, \gamma_i$, such that for the resultant $R_i := \mathbf{A}_i \leftarrow Q_i$ of level i

- $Q\theta = \mathbf{A}_i \gamma_i$,
- $Q_i \gamma_i$ is $(n - i)$-deep.

Then $Q_n\gamma_n$ is 0-deep, so $Q_n = \square$ and consequently

$$Q_0 \xstackrel{\theta_1}{\Longrightarrow} Q_1 \cdots \xstackrel{\theta_n}{\Longrightarrow} Q_n$$

is the desired SLD-derivation, since $\mathbf{A}_n$ is then more general than $Q\theta$ and $\mathbf{A}_n = Q\theta_1\ldots\theta_n$.

Base. $i = 0$. Define $Q_0 := Q$ and $\gamma_0 := \theta$.

Induction step. Let B be the atom of Q_i selected by $\mathcal{R}$. By the induction hypothesis $B\gamma_i$ has an implication tree with $r \geq 1$ nodes. Hence there exists a clause $c := H \leftarrow \mathbf{B}$ in P and a substitution τ such that $B\gamma_i = H\tau$ and

$$\mathbf{B}\tau \text{ is } (r-1)\text{-deep.} \tag{4.1}$$

Let π be a renaming such that $c\pi$ is variable disjoint with Q and with the substitutions and the input clauses used in the prefix constructed so far. Further, let α be the union of $\gamma_i \,|\, Var(R_i)$ and $(\pi^{-1}\tau) \,|\, Var(c\pi)$. By the Disjointness Lemma 3.11 α is well-defined. α acts on R_i as γ_i and on $c\pi$ as $\pi^{-1}\tau$. This implies that

$$B\alpha = B\gamma_i = H\tau = H\pi(\pi^{-1}\tau) = (H\pi)\alpha,$$

so B and $H\pi$ unify. Define θ_{i+1} to be an mgu of B and $H\pi$. Then there is γ_{i+1} such that

$$\alpha = \theta_{i+1}\gamma_{i+1}. \tag{4.2}$$

Q_i is of the form $\mathbf{A}, B, \mathbf{C}$. Let $Q_{i+1} := (\mathbf{A}, \mathbf{B}\pi, \mathbf{C})\theta_{i+1}$ be the next resolvent in the SLD-derivation being constructed. Then $\mathbf{A}_i\theta_{i+1} \leftarrow Q_{i+1}$ is the resultant of level $i + 1$. We have

$$Q\theta$$
$$=\quad \{\text{induction hypothesis}\}$$
$$\mathbf{A}_i\gamma_i$$
$$=\quad \{\text{definition of } \alpha\}$$
$$\mathbf{A}_i\alpha$$
$$=\quad \{(4.2)\}$$
$$\mathbf{A}_i\theta_{i+1}\gamma_{i+1},$$

and

$$Q_{i+1}\gamma_{i+1}$$
$$=\ (\mathbf{A}, \mathbf{B}\pi, \mathbf{C})\theta_{i+1}\gamma_{i+1}$$
$$=\quad \{(4.2)\}$$
$$(\mathbf{A}, \mathbf{B}\pi, \mathbf{C})\alpha$$
$$=\quad \{\text{definition of } \alpha\}$$
$$\mathbf{A}\gamma_i, \mathbf{B}\tau, \mathbf{C}\gamma_i.$$

So $Q_{i+1}\gamma_{i+1}$ is obtained from $Q_i\gamma_i$ by replacing $B\gamma_i$, that is $H\tau$, by $\mathbf{B}\tau$. By the induction hypothesis and (4.1) we conclude that $Q_{i+1}\gamma_{i+1}$ is $(n - (i + 1))$-deep. This completes the proof of the induction step. $\square$

The proof of the Strong Completeness Theorem 4.13 is now immediate.

Proof of Theorem 4.13. By the $\mathcal{C}(P)$ Lemma 4.12 and the Term Interpretation Lemma 4.7(ii) $P \models Q\theta$ implies that $Q\theta$ is n-deep for some $n \geq 0$. The claim now follows by the Implication Tree Lemma 4.15. $\square$

An interesting summary of the Strong Completeness Theorem 4.13 is given in Doets [Doe93]. Consider the following two-person game. Given is a program. A position in the game is a (possibly empty) query, say Q. The *selector* selects an atom in Q (if Q is non-empty), say A, upon which the *searcher* picks a clause applicable to A (if it exists), say c. An SLD-resolvent of the considered query and c, with the selected atom A, forms a new position in the game. The selector loses if the query is empty and the searcher loses if no clause is applicable to the selected atom. Now, the Strong Completeness Theorem states that, assuming that $P \models Q\theta$, in the game starting with the query Q the searcher has a winning strategy. Moreover, the searcher can additionally ensure that the produced sequence of queries, input clauses and mgus is a successful SLD-derivation of $P \cup \{Q\}$ that yields a c.a.s. η such that $Q\eta$ is more general than $Q\theta$.

Exercise 34 Suppose that $Q\theta$ is n-deep for some $n > 0$. Prove that for every atom A of Q there exists a query Q_1 and substitutions γ and θ_1 such that

- $Q \overset{\gamma}{\Longrightarrow} Q_1$ with A the selected atom of Q,

- $Q_1\theta_1$ is $(n - 1)$-deep. $\square$

Exercise 35 The above exercise suggests an alternative proof of the Strong Completeness Theorem 4.13 which uses a simpler induction. Complete this alternative proof. *Hint.* The details are rather delicate. Use the Composition Theorem 3.25 and Claim 1 used in its proof. $\square$

As a conclusion, we obtain the converse of the Soundness Corollary 4.5, which is often referred to as the "Completeness of SLD-resolution".

Corollary 4.16 (Completeness) Suppose that $P \models \exists Q$. Then there exists a successful SLD-derivation of $P \cup \{Q\}$.

Proof. $\mathcal{C}(P)$ is a model of P, so $\mathcal{C}(P) \models \exists Q$. By Exercise 33 and the Substitution Closure Note 4.9 for some substitution θ, $\mathcal{C}(P) \models Q\theta$. So, on account of the Term Interpretation Lemma 4.7(ii), in the terminology of the proof of Theorem 4.13 $Q\theta$ is n-deep for some $n \geq 0$. The result now follows by the Implication Tree Lemma 4.15. $\square$

Note that the Strong Completeness Theorem 4.13 does not allow us to conclude that the computed and correct answer substitutions coincide. In fact, they do not. Indeed, take $P := \{p(y) \leftarrow \}$ and $Q := p(x)$ and assume that the language $\mathcal{L}$ has a constant, say a. Then $\{y/a\}$ is a correct answer substitution, but not a c.a.s.

The Strong Completeness Theorem 4.13 is important. Together with the Soundness Theorem 4.4 it shows that a close correspondence exists between the declarative and procedural definition of logic programs independently of the chosen selection rule. However, this correspondence is not precise because, as we already have seen, the computed and correct answer substitutions do not need to coincide.

4.6   * Least Term Models

The term model $\mathcal{C}(P)$ turned out to be crucial for proving strong completeness of the SLD-resolution. Let us investigate now its properties. Recall that we identified each term interpretation with a set of atoms. A term model of a set of expressions S is called the *least term model* of S if it is included in every other term model of S. First, we have the following result.

Theorem 4.17 (Least Term Model) $\mathcal{C}(P)$ is the least term model of P.

Proof. Let I be a term model of P. Then I is also a model of $inst(P)$. We prove that $A \in \mathcal{C}(P)$ implies $I \models A$ by induction on the number i of nodes in the implication tree of A w.r.t. P. The claim then follows by the Term Interpretation Lemma 4.7(ii).

Base. $i = 1$. Then $A \leftarrow$ is in $inst(P)$, so $I \models A$.

Induction step. Suppose A is the root of an implication tree w.r.t. P with $i > 1$ nodes. Then for some $B_1, \ldots, B_n$ $(n > 1)$ the clause $A \leftarrow B_1, \ldots, B_n$ is in $inst(P)$ and every B_j $(j \in [1, n])$ has an implication tree w.r.t. P with $k_j < i$ nodes. By induction hypothesis $I \models B_j$ for $j \in [1, n]$. But $I \models A \leftarrow B_1, \ldots, B_n$, so $I \models A$. $\square$

Exercise 36 Prove that $P \models \exists Q$ implies that for some substitution θ, $P \models Q\theta$ without referring to the procedural interpretation. This provides an alternative proof of the Completeness Corollary 4.16.
Hint. Use the above theorem. $\square$

Another property of the term model $\mathcal{C}(P)$ shows that it is semantically equivalent to the declarative interpretation of the program.

Theorem 4.18 (Semantic Equivalence) For an atom A we have $P \models A$ iff $\mathcal{C}(P) \models A$.

Proof. First we prove the following claim.

Claim If an atom A is true in all term models of P, then $P \models A$.

Proof. Let I be a model of P. Then for $H \leftarrow B_1, \ldots, B_n$ in $inst(P)$,

$$I \models B_1, \ldots, I \models B_n \text{ implies } I \models H. \tag{4.3}$$

Indeed, I is a model of $inst(P)$, so for all states σ, $I \models_\sigma B_1, \ldots, B_n$ implies $I \models_\sigma H$.

Let now $I_T = \{A \mid A$ is an atom and $I \models A\}$ denote the term interpretation corresponding to I. By (4.3) and the Term Interpretation Lemma 4.7(iii) we conclude that I_T is a model of P, as well. Moreover, by the Term Interpretation Lemma 4.7(ii) the same atoms are true in I and I_T. This implies the result. $\square$

Fix now an atom A. By the $\mathcal{C}(P)$ Lemma 4.12 $\mathcal{C}(P)$ is a model of P, so $P \models A$ implies $\mathcal{C}(P) \models A$. The converse implication is an immediate consequence of the Term Interpretation Lemma 4.7(ii), the above claim and the Least Term Model Theorem 4.17. $\square$

To understand better the structure of the model $\mathcal{C}(P)$, following Falaschi *et al.* [FLMP93], we now introduce the following operator mapping term interpretations to term interpretations, that is sets of atoms to sets of atoms.

Definition 4.19 Given a program P we define the *immediate consequence operator* U_P by putting for a term interpretation I

$$U_P(I) = \{H \mid \exists B_1 \ldots \exists B_n \ (H \leftarrow B_1, \ldots, B_n \in inst(P), \ \{B_1, \ldots, B_n\} \subseteq I)\}.$$

$\square$

In particular, if $A \leftarrow$ is in P, then every instance of A is in $U_P(I)$ for every I. The following lemma due to Falaschi *et al.* [FLMP93] characterizes the term models of P in terms of the operator U_P and explains our interest in this operator.

Lemma 4.20 (U_P Characterization) A term interpretation I is a model of P iff $U_P(I) \subseteq I$.

Proof. We have

$\quad\quad\quad I$ is a model of P

$\quad$ iff $\quad$ {the Term Interpretation Lemma 4.7(iii)}

$\quad\quad\quad$ for every clause $H \leftarrow B_1, \ldots, B_n$ in $inst(P)$,

$\quad\quad\quad \{B_1, \ldots, B_n\} \subseteq I$ implies $H \in I$

$\quad$ iff $\quad$ {definition of the U_P operator}

$\quad\quad\quad U_P(I) \subseteq I$.

$\square$

Exercise 37 Find a counterexample to the following statement:

For a term interpretation I, I is a model of P iff $U'_P(I) \subseteq I$, where

$$U'_P(I) = \{H \mid \exists\, \mathbf{B}\ (H \leftarrow \mathbf{B} \in inst(P),\ I \models \mathbf{B})\}.$$

$\square$

When $T(I) \subseteq I$ holds, I is called a *pre-fixpoint* of T. Thus to study term models of a program P it suffices to study the pre-fixpoints of the operator U_P. This brings us to a study of operators and their pre-fixpoints in a general setting.

4.7   Operators and their Fixpoints

First, we need to fix the structure over which the operators are defined. We prefer to be as general as possible and consider operators over complete partial orderings. Let us recall here the definitions.

Consider now a partial ordering $(\mathcal{A}, \sqsubseteq)$ (for the definition of a partial ordering, see Section 2.6). Let $a \in \mathcal{A}$ and $X \subseteq \mathcal{A}$. Then a is called the *least* element of X if $a \in X$ and $a \sqsubseteq x$ for all $x \in X$. Further, a is called a *least upper bound* of X if $x \sqsubseteq a$ for all $x \in X$ and moreover a is the least element of $\mathcal{A}$ with this property. By antisymmetry, if a least upper bound of a set of elements exists, then it is unique.

A partial ordering $(\mathcal{A}, \sqsubseteq)$ is called *complete* (in short, a *cpo*) if $\mathcal{A}$ contains a least element and if for every increasing sequence

$$a_0 \sqsubseteq a_1 \sqsubseteq a_2 \ldots$$

of elements from $\mathcal{A}$, the set

$$\{a_0, a_1, a_2, \ldots\}$$

has a least upper bound.

In all subsequent uses of cpos, the set $\mathcal{A}$ will consist of a set of subsets of a specific domain, the least element will be the empty set, the partial ordering relation $\sqsubseteq$ will coincide with the subset relation $\subseteq$ and the least upper bound operator will coincide with the set theoretic union. So from now, in all applications, the least element of a cpo will be denoted by $\emptyset$, the partial ordering relation by $\subseteq$ and the least upper bound operator by $\bigcup$.

Consider now an arbitrary, but fixed cpo. We denote its elements by I, J (possibly with subscripts). Given a cpo and a set $X = \{I_n \mid n \geq 0\}$ of its elements, we denote $\bigcup X$ by $\bigcup_{n=0}^{\infty} I_n$. Note that when $I_0 \subseteq I_1 \subseteq \ldots$, the element $\bigcup_{n=0}^{\infty} I_n$ is guaranteed to exist.

Consider an operator T on a cpo. T is called *monotonic* if $I \subseteq J$ implies $T(I) \subseteq T(J)$, for all I, J. T is called *finitary*, if for every infinite sequence $I_0 \subseteq I_1 \subseteq \ldots$,

$$T(\bigcup_{n=0}^{\infty} I_n) \subseteq \bigcup_{n=0}^{\infty} T(I_n)$$

holds. If T is both monotonic and finitary, then it is called *continuous*. A more often used, equivalent definition of continuity is T is continuous if for every infinite sequence $I_0 \subseteq I_1 \subseteq \ldots$,

$$T(\bigcup_{n=0}^{\infty} I_n) = \bigcup_{n=0}^{\infty} T(I_n)$$

holds.

Exercise 38 Prove the equivalence of these two definitions. □

As already mentioned in the previous section, any I such that $T(I) \subseteq I$ is called a *pre-fixpoint of T*. If $T(I) = I$ then I is called a *fixpoint of T*.

We now define *powers* of an operator T. We put

$$\begin{aligned}
T \uparrow 0(I) &= I, \\
T \uparrow (n+1)(I) &= T(T \uparrow n(I)), \\
T \uparrow \omega(I) &= \bigcup_{n=0}^{\infty} T \uparrow n(I)
\end{aligned}$$

and abbreviate $T \uparrow \alpha(\emptyset)$ to $T \uparrow \alpha$. Informally, $T \uparrow n(I)$ is the result of the n-fold iteration of T starting at I. Thus $T \uparrow n$ is the result of the n-fold iteration of T starting at $\emptyset$. By the definition of a cpo, when the sequence $T \uparrow n(I)$ for $n \geq 0$ is increasing, $T \uparrow \omega(I)$ is guaranteed to exist.

Example 4.21 Extend the partial ordering $(N, \leq)$, where N is the set of natural numbers, by an element ω such that $\omega \geq n$ for $n \geq 0$. Note that the resulting ordering is a cpo. Consider an operator T on this ordering defined as follows:

$$T(n) := n+1 \text{ for } n \in N,$$

$$T(\omega) := \omega.$$

Note that T is monotonic, since for $m, n \in N$, $m \leq n$ implies $m+1 \leq n+1$ and $m \leq \omega$ implies $m+1 \leq \omega$.

Further, T is continuous, since for any sequence $n_0 \leq n_1 \ldots$ of natural numbers either $\bigcup_{i=0}^{\infty} n_i = n_j$ for some $j \geq 0$ and then $\bigcup_{i=0}^{\infty} T(n_i) = n_{j+1} = T(n_j) = T(\bigcup_{i=0}^{\infty} n_i)$, or $\bigcup_{i=0}^{\infty} n_i = \omega$ and then $\bigcup_{i=0}^{\infty} T(n_i) = \omega = T(\omega) = T(\bigcup_{i=0}^{\infty} n_i)$. □

The following well-known result will be of help.

Theorem 4.22 (Fixpoint) If T is continuous, then $T \uparrow \omega$ exists and is its least pre-fixpoint and its least fixpoint.

Proof. First we prove by induction on n that for $n \geq 0$, $T \uparrow n \subseteq T \uparrow (n+1)$. The base case is obvious and the induction step follows by the monotonicity of T.

This implies that $T \uparrow \omega$ exists. Moreover, $T \uparrow \omega$ is a fixpoint of T, because by the observation just made and the continuity of T we obtain

$$T(T \uparrow \omega) = T(\bigcup_{n=0}^{\infty} T \uparrow n) = \bigcup_{n=0}^{\infty} T(T \uparrow n),$$

so

$$T(T \uparrow \omega) = \bigcup_{n=1}^{\infty} T \uparrow n = \bigcup_{n=0}^{\infty} T \uparrow n,$$

as for any J we have $J = \emptyset \cup J$. So $T \uparrow \omega$ is also a pre-fixpoint of T.

To prove that $T \uparrow \omega$ is the least pre-fixpoint of T, we take a pre-fixpoint J of T and prove by induction on n that for $n \geq 0$, $T \uparrow n \subseteq J$. The base case is again obvious and for the induction step note that by the monotonicity $T \uparrow n \subseteq J$ implies $T \uparrow (n+1) \subseteq T(J)$, and hence $T \uparrow (n+1) \subseteq J$ by the fact that J is a pre-fixpoint. This implies that $T \uparrow \omega \subseteq J$. In particular $T \uparrow \omega$ is also the least fixpoint of T. $\square$

4.8   * Least Term Models, continued

Let us now return to the U_P operator. Note that the term interpretations of $\mathcal{L}$ with the usual set theoretic operations and the least element $\emptyset$ form a cpo, so when studying this operator we can apply the results of the previous section.

Lemma 4.23 (U_P Operator)

(i) U_P is finitary.
(ii) U_P is monotonic.

Proof.
(i) Consider an infinite sequence $I_0 \subseteq I_1 \subseteq \ldots$ of term interpretations and suppose that $A \in U_P(\bigcup_{n=0}^{\infty} I_n)$. Then for some atoms $B_1, \ldots, B_k$, the clause $A \leftarrow B_1, \ldots, B_k$ is in $inst(P)$ and $\{B_1, \ldots, B_k\} \subseteq \bigcup_{n=0}^{\infty} I_n$. So for some n we have $\{B_1, \ldots, B_k\} \subseteq I_n$. Hence $A \in U_P(I_n)$.

(ii) Immediate by definition. $\square$

We can now summarize various characterizations of the model $\mathcal{C}(P)$.

Theorem 4.24 (Characterization 1) The term interpretation $\mathcal{C}(P)$ satisfies the following properties.

(i) $\mathcal{C}(P)$ is the least term model of P.
(ii) $\mathcal{C}(P)$ is the least pre-fixpoint of U_P.
(iii) $\mathcal{C}(P)$ is the least fixpoint of U_P.
(iv) $\mathcal{C}(P) = U_P \uparrow \omega$.
(v) $\mathcal{C}(P) = \{A \mid A \text{ is an atom and } P \models A\}$.

Proof. (i) is the contents of the Least Term Model Theorem 4.17 and (ii)–(iv) are immediate consequences of the U_P Characterization Lemma 4.20, the U_P Operator Lemma 4.23 and the Fixpoint Theorem 4.22. In turn (v) is a consequence of the Semantic Equivalence Theorem 4.18 and Exercise 33. $\square$

Note that (v) provides a characterization of the semantic consequence relation $P \models A$ in terms of implication trees. Finally, the following theorem summarizes the relationship between the declarative interpretation based on term models and the procedural interpretation of logic programs.

We call here an SLD-derivation *trivially successful* if its computed instance is a variant of the original query.

Theorem 4.25 (Success 1) For an atom A the following are equivalent.

(i) $\mathcal{C}(P) \models A$.
(ii) $P \models A$.
(iii) Every SLD-tree for $P \cup \{A\}$ contains a trivially successful SLD-derivation.
(iv) There exists a trivially successful SLD-derivation of $P \cup \{A\}$.

Proof. It suffices to note the following implications:

(i) $\Rightarrow$ (ii) By the Semantic Equivalence Theorem 4.18.

(ii) $\Rightarrow$ (iii) This is the only part of the proof which requires an additional argument. Fix an SLD-tree $\mathcal{T}$ for $P \cup \{A\}$ via a selection rule $\mathcal{R}$. By Exercise 25 we can assume that $\mathcal{R}$ is variable independent.

By the Strong Completeness Theorem 4.13 there exists a successful SLD-derivation of $P \cup \{A\}$ via $\mathcal{R}$ with a c.a.s. η such that $A\eta$ is more general than A. But A is also more general than $A\eta$, so by the Variant Lemma 2.5 $A\eta$ is a variant of A.

Now by the Branch Theorem 3.38 a trivially successful SLD-derivation of $P \cup \{A\}$ via $\mathcal{R}$ is present as a branch in $\mathcal{T}$.

(iii) $\Rightarrow$ (iv) Immediate.

(iv) $\Rightarrow$ (i) By the Soundness Theorem 4.4 and the $\mathcal{C}(P)$ Lemma 4.12. $\square$

Exercise 39 Extend the above theorem to arbitrary queries. $\square$

Exercise 40
(i) Suppose that there exists a successful SLD-derivation of $P \cup \{A\}$ with a c.a.s. θ. Prove that for every selection rule $\mathcal{R}$ there exists a successful SLD-derivation of $P \cup \{A\theta\}$ via $\mathcal{R}$ with the empty c.a.s.

(ii) Fix a substitution θ and a program P. Suppose that the query A admits a successful SLD-derivation via the leftmost selection rule with the c.a.s. θ. Prove that then so does the query A, A.

Hint. Use the Closure Note 3.28. $\square$

4.9   Herbrand Interpretations

The declarative interpretation of a program tells us what semantically follows from the program. In order to prove that a query is true according to the declarative interpretation of a program one needs to show that this query is true in every model of the program. An obvious generalization of the Semantic Equivalence Theorem 4.18 to arbitrary queries allows us to reduce this problem to checking that the query is true in just one model — the least term model of the program. This is an important simplification. However, it is not completely clear how to compute this model for specific programs. Its characterization provided by the Characterization Theorem 4.24(iv) is apparently most useful. To this end for a given program P its operator U_P should be studied.

On the other hand, there exists an alternative approach to the problem of determining what semantically follows from a program that seems to be more convenient. It is based on the use of another class of interpretations, called Herbrand interpretations. They are obtained by choosing as the domain the set of all ground terms.

Assume now that the set of constants of $\mathcal{L}$ is not empty. By the *Herbrand universe* $HU_{\mathcal{L}}$ for $\mathcal{L}$ we mean the set of all ground terms of $\mathcal{L}$. By the above assumption $HU_{\mathcal{L}}$ is non-empty. By the *Herbrand base* $HB_{\mathcal{L}}$ for $\mathcal{L}$ we mean the set of all ground atoms of $\mathcal{L}$.

The *Herbrand algebra* for $\mathcal{L}$ is defined as follows:

- its domain is the Herbrand universe $HU_{\mathcal{L}}$,
- if f is an n-ary function symbol in $\mathcal{L}$, then it is assigned the mapping from $(HU_{\mathcal{L}})^n$ to $HU_{\mathcal{L}}$ which maps the sequence $t_1, \ldots, t_n$ of ground terms to the ground term $f(t_1, \ldots, t_n)$.

Now, a *Herbrand interpretation* for $\mathcal{L}$ is an interpretation I based on the Herbrand algebra for $\mathcal{L}$. Thus

- if p is an n-ary relation symbol in $\mathcal{L}$, then it is assigned a set p_I of n-tuples of ground terms.

So there exists exactly one Herbrand algebra for $\mathcal{L}$, but there are several Herbrand interpretations for $\mathcal{L}$.

By a *Herbrand model* for a set S of expressions we mean a Herbrand interpretation which is a model for S. A Herbrand model of a set of expressions S is called the *least Herbrand model* of S if it is included in every other Herbrand model of S.

Thus each Herbrand interpretation for $\mathcal{L}$ is uniquely determined by the interpretation of the relation symbols. As in the case of term interpretations, there is a natural 1-1 correspondence between the Herbrand interpretations and the subsets of the Herbrand base $HB_{\mathcal{L}}$ which is made explicit by the mapping which assigns to the Herbrand interpretation I the set of ground atoms

$$\{p(t_1, \ldots, t_n) \mid p \text{ is an } n\text{-ary relation symbol and } (t_1, \ldots, t_n) \in p_I\}.$$

This allows us to identify Herbrand interpretations for $\mathcal{L}$ with (possibly empty) subsets of the Herbrand base $HB_{\mathcal{L}}$. This is what we shall do in the sequel. It is important to realize that a set of ground atoms can now denote both a term interpretation and a Herbrand interpretation and that these two interpretations differ. In fact, each of them is based on another algebra.

We now investigate the properties of Herbrand interpretations by proceeding analogously to the case of term interpretations. First, note that for a state σ over $HU_{\mathcal{L}}$, when X is a finite set of variables, $\sigma|X$ is a ground substitution.

The following lemma is analogous to the Term Interpretation Lemma 4.7. It will allow us to determine that a Herbrand interpretation is a model of a program without using the notion of a state.

Lemma 4.26 (Herbrand Interpretation) Let I be a Herbrand interpretation. Then

(i) for an atom A and a state σ

$$I \models_\sigma A \text{ iff } A(\sigma\,|\, Var(A)) \in I,$$

(ii) for an atom A

$$I \models A \text{ iff } ground(A) \subseteq I,$$

(iii) for a clause c

$$I \models c \text{ iff for all } A \leftarrow B_1, \ldots, B_n \text{ in } ground(c),$$

$$\{B_1, \ldots, B_n\} \subseteq I \text{ implies } A \in I.$$

$\square$

Proof. Analogous to the proof of the Term Interpretation Lemma 4.7. $\square$

In particular, for a Herbrand interpretation I and a ground atom A, $I \models A$ iff $A \in I$. So every Herbrand interpretation can be identified with the set of ground atoms true in it. We shall often use this identification implicitly.

Example 4.27 Suppose that $\mathcal{L}$ consists of one constant, 0, one unary function symbol, s and one ternary relation symbol, sum. Then

$$I := \{sum(s^m(0), s^n(0), s^{m+n}(0)) \mid m \geq 0, n \geq 0\}$$

is a Herbrand interpretation for the program SUM of Example 3.7.

Actually, I is a Herbrand model of SUM. Indeed, it suffices to note that for $m \geq 0$, $sum(s^m(0), 0, s^m(0)) \in I$ and that if $sum(s^m(0), s^n(0), s^{m+n}(0)) \in I$, then $sum(s^m(0), s^{n+1}(0), s^{m+n+1}(0)) \in I$. The claim now follows by the Herbrand Interpretation Lemma 4.26(iii). $\square$

Exercise 41 Provide a proof of the above Lemma. $\square$

Exercise 42

(i) Prove that for a Herbrand interpretation I and an expression E

$$I \models E \text{ iff } I \models ground(E).$$

(ii) Prove that this above equivalence does not hold for term interpretations.   □

Exercise 43 Find a set of ground atoms I, a program P and an atom A such that

- when I is interpreted as a Herbrand interpretation, then $P \models A$,

- when I is interpreted as a term interpretation, then $P \not\models A$.   □

In Definition 4.10 we introduced ground implication trees w.r.t. a program P. Now we use them to construct a specific Herbrand model of a program. The following result is a counterpart of the $\mathcal{C}(P)$ Lemma 4.12.

Lemma 4.28 ($\mathcal{M}(P)$) The Herbrand interpretation

$$\mathcal{M}(P) := \{A \mid A \text{ has a ground implication tree w.r.t. } P\}$$

is a model of P.

Proof. By the Herbrand Interpretation Lemma 4.26(iii) it suffices to prove that for all $A \leftarrow B_1, \ldots, B_n$ in $ground(P)$, $\{B_1, \ldots, B_n\} \subseteq \mathcal{M}(P)$ implies $A \in \mathcal{M}(P)$. But this translates into an obvious property of the ground implication trees.   □

4.10   Least Herbrand Models

We now study the model $\mathcal{M}(P)$ in detail. The following result is a counterpart of the Least Term Model Theorem 4.17.

Theorem 4.29 (Least Herbrand Model) $\mathcal{M}(P)$ is the least Herbrand model of P.

Proof. Let I be a Herbrand model of P. Then I is also a model of $ground(P)$. We prove that $A \in \mathcal{M}(P)$ implies $I \models A$ by induction on the number of nodes in the ground implication tree A w.r.t. P. The claim then follows by the Herbrand Interpretation Lemma 4.26(ii).

Base. $i = 1$. Then $A \leftarrow$ is in $ground(P)$, so $I \models A$.

Induction step. Suppose A is the root of a ground implication tree w.r.t. P with $i > 1$ nodes. Then for some $B_1, \ldots, B_n$ $(n > 1)$ the clause $A \leftarrow B_1, \ldots, B_n$ is in $ground(P)$ and every B_j $(j \in [1, n])$ has a ground implication tree w.r.t. P with $k_j < i$ nodes. By induction hypothesis $I \models B_j$ for $j \in [1, n]$. But $I \models A \leftarrow B_1, \ldots, B_n$, so $I \models A$.   □

Exercise 44 Find another proof of the claim of Exercise 36 using the above theorem.

□

Another property of the Herbrand model $\mathcal{M}(P)$ shows that for ground atoms it is semantically equivalent to the declarative interpretation of the program.

Theorem 4.30 (Ground Equivalence) For a ground atom A we have $P \models A$ iff $\mathcal{M}(P) \models A$.

Proof. First we prove the following claim.

Claim If a ground atom A is true in all Herbrand models of P, then $P \models A$.

Proof. Let I be a model of P. By (4.3) for $H \leftarrow B_1, \ldots, B_n$ in $ground(P)$,

$$I \models B_1, \ldots, I \models B_n \text{ implies } I \models H. \tag{4.4}$$

Let now $I_H = \{A \mid A \text{ is a ground atom and } I \models A\}$ denote the Herbrand interpretation corresponding to I. By (4.4) and the Herbrand Interpretation Lemma 4.26(iii) I_H is a model of P, as well. Moreover, by the Herbrand Interpretation Lemma 4.26(ii), the same ground atoms are true in I and I_H. From this the claim follows.

□

Fix now a ground atom A. By the $\mathcal{M}(P)$ Lemma 4.28 $\mathcal{M}(P)$ is a model of P, so $P \models A$ implies $\mathcal{M}(P) \models A$. The converse implication follows by the Herbrand Interpretation Lemma 4.26(ii), the above claim and the Least Herbrand Model Theorem 4.29.

□

To study Herbrand models of programs, following Clark [Cla79], we now introduce an operator mapping Herbrand interpretations to Herbrand interpretations, that is sets of ground atoms to sets of ground atoms.

Definition 4.31 Given a program P we define the *immediate consequence operator T_P* by putting for a Herbrand interpretation I

$$T_P(I) = \{H \mid \exists\, \mathbf{B}\ (H \leftarrow \mathbf{B} \in ground(P),\ I \models \mathbf{B})\}.$$

□

In particular, if $A \leftarrow$ is in P, then every ground instance of A is in $T_P(I)$ for every I. The following observation of van Emden and Kowalski [vEK76] characterizes the Herbrand models of P by means of the operator T_P and explains the interest in this operator.

Lemma 4.32 (T_P Characterization) A Herbrand interpretation I is a model of P iff $T_P(I) \subseteq I$.

Proof. We have

$$I \text{ is a model of } P$$

iff {the Herbrand Interpretation Lemma 4.26(ii) }

  for every clause $H \leftarrow \mathbf{B}$ in $ground(P)$, $I \models \mathbf{B}$ implies $H \in I$

iff {definition of T_P operator}

  $T_P(I) \subseteq I$.

$\square$

Thus to study Herbrand models of a program P it suffices to study the pre-fixpoints of its immediate consequence operator T_P. First, we prove a result analogous to the U_P Operator Lemma 4.23.

Lemma 4.33 (T_P Operator)

(i) T_P is finitary.

(ii) T_P is monotonic.

Proof.
(i) Consider an infinite sequence $I_0 \subseteq I_1 \subseteq \ldots$ of Herbrand interpretations and suppose that $H \in T_P(\bigcup_{n=0}^{\infty} I_n)$. Then for some $\mathbf{B}$ the clause $H \leftarrow \mathbf{B}$ is in $ground(P)$ and $\bigcup_{n=0}^{\infty} I_n \models \mathbf{B}$. But the latter implies that for some I_n, namely the one containing all the atoms of $\mathbf{B}$, $I_n \models \mathbf{B}$. So $H \in T_P(I_n)$.

(ii) Immediate by definition. $\square$

Note that Herbrand interpretations of $\mathcal{L}$ with the usual set-theoretic operations form a cpo, so when studying the immediate consequence operator T_P we can now apply the results of Section 4.7. As a direct consequence of the above lemma we have the following analog of the Characterization 1 Theorem 4.24.

Theorem 4.34 (Characterization 2) The Herbrand interpretation $\mathcal{M}(P)$ satisfies the following properties:

(i) $\mathcal{M}(P)$ is the least Herbrand model of P.
(ii) $\mathcal{M}(P)$ is the least pre-fixpoint of T_P.
(iii) $\mathcal{M}(P)$ is the least fixpoint of T_P.
(iv) $\mathcal{M}(P) = T_P \uparrow \omega$.
(v) $\mathcal{M}(P) = \{A \mid A \text{ is a ground atom and } P \models A\}$.

Proof. (i) is the contents of the Least Herbrand Model Theorem 4.29 and (ii)–(iv) are immediate consequences of the T_P Characterization Lemma 4.32, the T_P Operator Lemma 4.33 and the Fixpoint Theorem 4.22. Finally, (v) is a consequence of the Ground Equivalence Theorem 4.30. $\square$

Example 4.35 Reconsider the program *SUMMER* from Example 3.1. We now show that

$$I := \{\texttt{summer}, \texttt{warm}, \texttt{happy}\}$$

is its least Herbrand model.

To this end note that

$$T_{SUMMER} \uparrow 0 = \emptyset,$$

$$T_{SUMMER} \uparrow 1 = \{\texttt{summer}\},$$

$$T_{SUMMER} \uparrow 2 = \{\texttt{summer}, \texttt{warm}\},$$

$$T_{SUMMER} \uparrow 3 = \{\texttt{summer}, \texttt{warm}, \texttt{happy}\},$$

$$T_{SUMMER} \uparrow 4 = \{\texttt{summer}, \texttt{warm}, \texttt{happy}\}.$$

Hence $T_{SUMMER} \uparrow 4 = T_{SUMMER} \uparrow \omega$, so by virtue of the Characterization Theorem 4.34(iv) I is indeed the least Herbrand model of *SUMMER*. $\square$

Exercise 45 Prove that the Herbrand interpretation of Example 4.27 is the least Herbrand model of *SUM*. $\square$

Note that clause (v) of the Characterization Theorem 2 4.34 provides a characterization of the semantic consequence relation $P \models A$ for a ground atom A in terms of ground implication trees. Another characterization of the model $\mathcal{M}(P)$ can be provided using the procedural interpretation of logic programs.

Definition 4.36 A *success set* of a program P is the set of all ground atoms A such that $P \cup \{A\}$ has a successful SLD-derivation. $\square$

The following theorem should be compared with the Success 1 Theorem 4.25. It summarizes the relationship between the declarative interpretation based on Herbrand models and procedural interpretation of logic programs.

Theorem 4.37 (Success 2) For a ground atom A the following are equivalent.

(i) $\mathcal{M}(P) \models A$.
(ii) $P \models A$.
(iii) Every SLD-tree for $P \cup \{A\}$ is successful.
(iv) A is in the success set of P.

Proof. It suffices to note the following implications.
(i) $\Rightarrow$ (ii) By the Ground Equivalence Theorem 4.30.
(ii) $\Rightarrow$ (iii) By the Strong Completeness Theorem 4.13.
(iii) $\Rightarrow$ (iv) Immediate.
(iv) $\Rightarrow$ (i) By the Soundness Theorem 4.4 and the $\mathcal{M}(P)$ Lemma 4.28. $\square$

Exercise 46 Extend this theorem to ground queries. $\square$

4.11   * Comparison of the Least Term and the Least Herbrand Models

We defined two models of a program — the least term model and the least Herbrand model. Each of them constitutes a natural interpretation of the meaning of the program. So let us clarify the relationship between them. First, as an immediate consequence of the Characterization 1 Theorem 4.24(v) and Characterization 2 Theorem 4.34(v) we obtain

$$\mathcal{M}(P) = \{A \mid A \text{ is a ground atom and } A \in \mathcal{C}(P)\}.$$

So the $\mathcal{M}(P)$ model can always be reconstructed from the $\mathcal{C}(P)$ model. The converse does not hold in general as the following argument from Falaschi *et al.* [FLMP93] shows. Consider the program $P_1 := \{p(x) \leftarrow \}$ and the program $P_2 := \{p(a) \leftarrow , p(b) \leftarrow \}$, both defined w.r.t. the language $\mathcal{L}$ which has only two constants a, b and no function symbols. Then $\mathcal{M}(P_1) = \mathcal{M}(P_2) = \{p(a), p(b)\}$. Moreover, $p(x) \in \mathcal{C}(P_1)$. However, $p(x)$ is false in the model I of P_2 with the domain $\{a, b, c\}$ and $p_I = \{a, b\}$. So by virtue of the Characterization 1 Theorem 4.24(v), $p(x) \notin \mathcal{C}(P_2)$. This shows that the $\mathcal{C}(P)$ model is not a function of the $\mathcal{M}(P)$ model.

However, in certain natural situations we can reconstruct the $\mathcal{C}(P)$ model from the $\mathcal{M}(P)$ model. More precisely, we have the following interesting result due to Maher [Mah88].

Theorem 4.38 (Reconstruction) Assume that the language $\mathcal{L}$ has infinitely many constants. Then $\mathcal{C}(P) = \{A \mid A \text{ is an atom and } \mathcal{M}(P) \models A\}$.

Proof. The inclusion $\mathcal{C}(P) \subseteq \{A \mid A \text{ is an atom and } \mathcal{M}(P) \models A\}$ always holds, since by the Characterization 1 Theorem 4.24(v)

$$\mathcal{C}(P) = \{A \mid A \text{ is an atom and } P \models A\}$$

and by the $\mathcal{M}(P)$ Lemma 4.28 $\mathcal{M}(P)$ is a model of P.

To prove the converse inclusion suppose $\mathcal{M}(P) \models A$. Let $x_1, \ldots, x_n$ be the variables of A and $c_1, \ldots, c_n$ distinct constants which do not appear in P or A. Let $\theta := \{x_1/c_1, \ldots, x_n/c_n\}$. Then $A\theta$ is ground and $\mathcal{M}(P) \models A\theta$, so $A\theta \in \mathcal{M}(P)$, that is $A\theta$ has a ground implication tree w.r.t. P. By replacing in this tree every occurrence of a constant c_i by x_i for $i \in [1, n]$ we conclude, by virtue of the choice of the constants $c_1, \ldots, c_n$, that A has an implication tree w.r.t. P, i.e. $A \in \mathcal{C}(P)$. $\square$

So, under the assumption of the above theorem,

$$\mathcal{M}(P_1) = \mathcal{M}(P_2) \text{ iff } \mathcal{C}(P_1) = \mathcal{C}(P_2),$$

that is both models identify the same pairs of programs.

Corollary 4.39 (Declarative Semantics) Assume that the language $\mathcal{L}$ has infinitely many constants. Then for a query Q the following are equivalent.

(i) $P \models Q$.
(ii) $\mathcal{M}(P) \models Q$.
(iii) $\mathcal{C}(P) \models Q$.

Proof. It suffices to note the following implications.
(i) $\Rightarrow$ (ii) By the $\mathcal{M}(P)$ Lemma 4.28.
(ii) $\Rightarrow$ (iii) By the Reconstruction Theorem 4.38, the Term Interpretation Lemma 4.7(i) and Exercise 33.
(iii) $\Rightarrow$ (i) By the Characterization 1 Theorem 4.24(v). $\qquad\qquad\square$

The assumption that the language $\mathcal{L}$ of programs has infinitely many constants sounds perhaps artificial. However, at a closer look it is quite natural. When considering in the next chapter pure Prolog programs we shall adhere to the syntax of Prolog. Now, any Prolog manual defines *infinitely* many constants. Of course, in practice only finitely many of them can be written or printed. But even in the case of one fixed program arbitrary queries can be posed and in these queries arbitrary constants can appear. So when studying the behaviour of a program, it is natural to assume a language in which all these constants are present.

This shows that under the assumption that the language $\mathcal{L}$ has infinitely many constants, the least term model and the least Herbrand model of a program are equivalent. So, by virtue of the above Corollary, the least Herbrand model of a program is equivalent to the declarative semantics of a program. (Hence the name of this corollary.) In the subsequent chapters we shall use this fact to study the declarative semantics of specific programs and to prove their correctness.

4.12   Concluding Remarks

In this chapter we studied the declarative interpretation of logic programs and related it to the procedural interpretation introduced in the previous chapter. The outcome were two theorems, the Soundness Theorem 4.4 and the Strong Completeness Theorem 4.13. While the Soundness Theorem is pretty natural and its proof is pretty routine, the Strong Completeness Theorem is quite subtle and in fact, it is easy to end up with an incorrect formulation of it.

In fact, the following version of the Strong Completeness of SLD-resolution is claimed in many places:

> Suppose that $P \models Q\theta$. Then for every selection rule $\mathcal{R}$ there exists a successful SLD-derivation of $P \cup \{Q\}$ via $\mathcal{R}$ with the c.a.s. η such that η is more general than θ.

Unfortunately, this version is incorrect as the following example due to H.-P. Ko and reported in Shepherdson [She94] shows.

Let $P := \{p(f(y,z)) \leftarrow \}$ and $Q := p(x)$, where x, y, z are distinct variables. Then any variant of the clause of P is of the form $p(f(u,v)) \leftarrow$, where u, v are distinct variables. By the Equivalence Lemma 2.23 any mgu of $p(x)$ and $p(f(u,v))$ is of the form $\{x/f(u,v)\}\eta$ where η is a renaming. So every c.a.s. of Q is of the form $\{x/f(u',v')\}$, where u', v' are distinct variables.

Now consider $\theta := \{x/f(a,a)\}$, where a is a constant. Clearly $P \models Q\theta$. However, as explained in Example 2.7(iii), $\{x/f(u',v')\}$ is not more general than θ.

Exercise 47

(i) Assume the definition of an SLD-derivation given in Exercise 19 of Chapter 3. Prove that in this case the above version of the Strong Completeness of SLD-resolution is incorrect, as well.

Hint. Take $P := \{p(f(y)) \leftarrow \}$, $Q := p(x)$ and $\theta := \{x/f(a)\}$, where x and y are distinct variables and a is a constant, and use Example 2.7(ii).

(ii) Show that when the definition of SLD-derivation adopted here is used, the counterexample of the hint of (i) is not a counterexample. $\square$

A small personal story concerning the above Exercise may be of interest to the reader. The above erroneous version of completeness of SLD-resolution was given in an early version of Apt [Apt90], where the definition of an SLD-derivation given in Exercise 19 is adopted. Fortunately, the counterexample given in (i), due to Ch. Lynch and W. Snyder, was sent to us just in time — at the moment of proofreading the galley proofs. We learned that it is not a correct counterexample in the case of the definition of SLD-derivation adopted here only five years later, while reading Shepherdson [She94].

The Strong Completeness Theorem 4.13 allows us to draw some conclusions about specific programs. To illustrate its use let us return to the *SUM* program from Example 3.7. Suppose that we checked by some means (for example using the Characterization 2 Theorem 4.34(iv) and the Declarative Semantics Corollary 4.39) that $SUM \models sum(x, s(s(0)), s(s(x)))$. Then we can draw conclusions about computed instances of various queries. For example, since $sum(x, s(s(0)), s(s(x))) = sum(x, y, z)\{y/s(s(0)), z/s(s(x))\}$, we conclude that there exists a successful SLD-derivation of the query $sum(x, y, z)$ with a c.a.s. η such that $sum(x, y, z)\eta$ is more general than $sum(x, s(s(0)), s(s(x)))$.

In the case of the *SUM* program the selection rules are hardly of relevance, but similar conclusions to the above ones, when applied to programs, the clauses of which have bodies with more than one atom (like the *PATH* program from Example 3.36), can additionally stipulate an arbitrary selection rule.

4.13 Bibliographic Remarks

Usually, following Lloyd [Llo84], the name "pre-interpretation" is used instead of algebra. Following the standard terminology of model theory and Doets [Doe94] we prefer to use the latter name.

The Soundness Theorem 4.4 and the Strong Completeness Theorem 4.13 are due to Clark [Cla79] (though the latter one was formulated in the incorrect form mentioned at the end of Section 4.12). The elegant proof presented here is due to Stärk [Stä90], who also defined the model $\mathcal{C}(P)$. Several other proofs of this result appeared in the literature. We only cite here the references in which the strongest version was proved: Doets [Doe93], Gallier [Gal86], Lloyd [Llo84], Sigal [Sig90] and Steiner and Komara [SK91]. The Completeness Corollary 4.16 is usually attributed to Hill [Hil74].

Term models in the context of logic programming were introduced in Clark [Cla79] and further investigated in Deransart and Ferrand [DF87] and Falaschi *et al.* [FLMP93]. The importance of Herbrand interpretations for the theory of logic programming was recognized in van Emden and Kowalski [vEK76] and Apt and van Emden [AvE82]. In the last reference the notion of a success set was introduced.

4.14 Summary

In this chapter we studied the semantics of logic programs. To this end we introduced

- algebras,
- interpretations

and proved soundness of the SLD-resolution. Then we introduced

- term interpretations

and used them to prove completeness of the SLD-resolution.
We also introduced

- Herbrand interpretations

and provided various characterizations of the least term models and the least Herbrand models.

4.15 References

[Apt90]   K. R. Apt. Logic programming. In J. van Leeuwen, editor, *Handbook of Theoretical Computer Science*, pages 493–574. Vol. B, Elsevier, Amsterdam, 1990.

[AvE82] K. R. Apt and M.H. van Emden. Contributions to the theory of logic programming. *Journal of the ACM*, 29(3):841–862, 1982.

[Cla79] K. L. Clark. Predicate logic as a computational formalism. Res. Report DOC 79/59, Imperial College, Department of Computing, London, 1979.

[DF87] P. Deransart and G. Ferrand. Programmation en logique avec negation: presentation formelle. Technical Report No. 87/3, Laboratoire d'Informatique, Département de Mathématiques et d'Informatique, Université d'Orléans, 1987.

[Doe93] H. C. Doets. Levationis laus. *Journal of Logic and Computation*, 3(5):487–516, 1993.

[Doe94] H.C. Doets. *From Logic to Logic Programming*. The MIT Press, Cambridge, MA, 1994.

[FLMP93] M. Falaschi, G. Levi, M. Martelli, and C. Palamidessi. A model-theoretic reconstruction of the operational semantics of logic programs. *Information and Computation*, 102(1):86–113, 1993.

[Gal86] J.H. Gallier. *Logic for Computer Science, Foundations of Automatic Theorem Proving*. Computer Science and Technology Series. Harper & Row, New York, 1986.

[Hil74] R. Hill. LUSH-resolution and its completeness. Technical Report DCL Memo 78, Department of Artificial Intelligence, University of Edinburgh, 1974.

[Llo84] J. W. Lloyd. *Foundations of Logic Programming*. Springer-Verlag, Berlin, 1984.

[Mah88] M. J. Maher. Equivalences of logic programs. In J. Minker, editor, *Foundations of Deductive Databases and Logic Programming*, pages 627–658. Morgan Kaufmann, Los Altos, CA, 1988.

[She94] J. C. Shepherdson. The role of standardising apart in logic programming. *Theoretical Computer Science*, 129:143–166, 1994.

[Sig90] R. Sigal. SLD-resolution completeness without lifting, without switching. In A. Bossi, editor, *5° Convegno sulla Programmazione Logica GULP '90*, pages 295–308. Universitá di Padova, Padova, 1990.

[SK91] J. Steiner and J. Komara. An algebraic approach to the computation of logic programs. In J. Zlatuška, editor, *LOP '91:-!. (Logic Programming Winter School and Seminar)*, pages 187–198. Masaryk University, Brno, 1991.

[Stä90] R. Stärk. A direct proof for the completeness of SLD-resolution. In Börger, H. Kleine Büning, and M.M. Richter, editors, *Computer Science Logic 89*, Lecture Notes in Computer Science 440, pages 382–383. Springer-Verlag, Berlin, 1990.

[vEK76] M. H. van Emden and R. A. Kowalski. The semantics of predicate logic as a programming language. *Journal of the ACM*, 23(4):733–742, 1976.

Chapter 5

Programming in Pure Prolog

We learned in Chapter 3 that logic programs can be used for computing. This means that logic programming can be used as a *programming language*. However, to make it a viable tool for programming the problems of efficiency and of ease of programming have to be adequately addressed. Prolog is a programming language based on logic programming and in which these two objectives were met in an adequate way. The aim of this chapter is to provide an introduction to programming in a subset of Prolog, which corresponds with logic programming. We call this subset "pure Prolog".

Every logic program, when viewed as a sequence instead of as a set of clauses, is a pure Prolog program, but not conversely, because we extend the syntax by a couple of useful Prolog features. Computing in pure Prolog is obtained by imposing certain restrictions on the computation process of logic programming in order to make it more efficient. All the programs presented here can be run using any well-known Prolog system.

To provide a better insight into the programming needs, we occasionally explain some features of Prolog which are not present in pure Prolog.

In the next section we explain various aspects of pure Prolog, including its syntax, the way computing takes place and an interaction with a Prolog system. In the remainder of the chapter we present several pure Prolog programs. This part is divided according to the domains over which computing takes place. So, in Section 5.2 we give an example of a program computing over the empty domain and in Section 5.3 we discuss programming over finite domains.

The simplest infinite domain is that of the numerals. In Section 5.4 we present a number of pure Prolog programs computing over this domain. Then, in Section 5.5 we introduce a fundamental data structure of Prolog — that of lists and provide several classic programs that use them. In the subsequent section an example of a program is given which illustrates Prolog's use of terms to represent complex objects. Then in Section 5.7 we introduce another important data structure — that of binary trees and present various programs computing over them. We conclude the chapter by trying to assess in Section 5.8 the relevant aspects of programming in pure Prolog. We also summarize there the shortcomings of this subset of Prolog.

5.1   Introduction

5.1.1   Syntax

When presenting pure Prolog programs we adhere to the usual syntactic conventions of Prolog. So each query and clause ends with the period "." and in the unit clauses " $\leftarrow$ " is omitted. Unit clauses are called *facts* and non-unit clauses are called *rules*. Of course, queries and clauses can be broken over several lines. To maintain the spirit of logic programming, when presenting the programs, instead of Prolog's ":-" we use here the logic programming " $\leftarrow$ ".

By a *definition* of a relation symbol p in a given program P we mean the set of all clauses of P which use p in their heads. In Prolog terminology *relation symbol* is synonymous with *predicate*.

Strings starting with a lower-case letter are reserved for the names of function or relation symbols. For example f stands for a constant, function or relation symbol. Additionally, we use here integers as constants. In turn, each string starting with a capital letter or "_" (underscore) is identified with a variable. For example Xs is a variable. Comment lines start by the "%" symbol.

There are, however two important differences between the syntax of logic programming and of Prolog which need to be mentioned here.

Ambivalent Syntax
In first-order logic and, consequently, in logic programming, it is assumed that function and relation symbols of different arity form mutually disjoint classes of symbols. While this assumption is rarely stated explicitly, it is a folklore postulate in mathematical logic which can be easily tested by exposing a logician to Prolog syntax and wait for his protests. Namely, in contrast to first-order logic, in Prolog the *same* name can be used for function or relation symbols of different arity. Moreover, the same name with the same arity can be used for function and relation symbols. This facility is called *ambivalent syntax*.

A function or a relation symbol f of arity n is then referred to as f/n. So in a Prolog program we can use both a relation symbol p/2 and function symbols p/1 and p/2 and build syntactically legal facts like p(p(a,b), [c,p(a)]).

In the presence of ambivalent syntax the distinction between function symbols and relation symbols and, consequently, between terms and atoms, disappears but in the context of queries and clauses it is clear which symbol refers to which syntactic category. The ambivalent syntax facility allows us to use the same name for naturally related function or relation symbols.

In the presence of the ambivalent syntax we need to modify the Martelli–Montanari algorithm given in Section 2.6 by allowing in action (2) the possibility that the function symbols are equal. The appropriate modification is the following one:

$$(2') \ f(s_1, ..., s_n) = g(t_1, ..., t_m) \text{ where } f \neq g \text{ or } n \neq m \quad \textit{halt with failure.}$$

Throughout this chapter we refer to nullary function symbols as constants, and to function symbols of positive arity as function symbols.

Anonymous Variables

Prolog allows so-called *anonymous variables*, written as "_" (underscore). These variables have a special interpretation, because each occurrence of "_" in a query or in a clause is interpreted as a *different* variable. Thus by definition each anonymous variable occurs in a query or a clause only once.

At this stage it is too early to discuss the advantages of the use of anonymous variables. We shall return to their use within the context of specific programs. Anonymous variables form a simple and elegant device which sometimes increases the readability of programs in a remarkable way.

Modern versions of Prolog, like SICStus Prolog [CW93], encourage the use of anonymous variables by issuing a warning if a non-anonymous variable that occurs only once in a clause is encountered.

We incorporate both of these syntactic facilities into pure Prolog.

5.1.2   Computing

We now explain the computation process used in Prolog. First of all, the leftmost selection rule is used. To simplify the subsequent discussion we now introduce the following terminology. By an *LD-resolvent* we mean an SLD-resolvent w.r.t. the leftmost selection rule and by an *LD-tree* an SLD-tree w.r.t. the leftmost selection rule. The notions of LD-resolution and LD-derivation have the expected meaning.

Next, the clauses are tried in the order in which they appear in the program text. So the program is viewed as a *sequence* and not as a set of clauses. In addition, for the efficiency reasons, the occur-check is omitted from the unification algorithm. We adopt these choices in pure Prolog.

The Strong Completeness of SLD-resolution (Theorem 4.13) tells us that (up to renaming) all computed answers to a given query can be found in any SLD-tree. However, without imposing any further restrictions on the SLD-resolution, the computation process of logic programming, the resulting programs can become hopelessly inefficient even if we restrict our attention to the leftmost selection rule. In other words, the way the answers to the query are searched for becomes crucial from the efficiency point of view.

If we traverse an LD-tree by means of breadth-first search, that is level by level, it is guaranteed that an answer will be found, if there is any, but this search process can take exponential time in the depth of the tree and also requires exponential space in the depth of the tree to store all the visited nodes. If we traverse this tree by means of a depth-first search (to be explained more precisely in a moment), that is informally, by pursuing the search first down each branch, often the answer can be found in linear time in the depth of the tree but a divergence may result in the presence of an infinite branch.

In Prolog the latter alternative, that is the depth-first search, is taken. Let us explain now this search process in more detail.

Depth-first Search

By an *ordered tree* we mean here a tree in which the direct descendants of every node are totally ordered.

The *depth-first search* is a search through a finitely branching ordered tree, the main characteristic of which is that for each node all of its descendants are visited before its siblings lying to its right. In this search no edge of the tree is traversed more than once.

Depth-first search can be described as follows. Consider a finitely branching ordered tree all the leaves of which are marked by a *success* or a *fail* marker. The search starts at the root of the tree and proceeds by descending to its first descendant. This process continues as long as a node has some descendants (so it is not a leaf).

If a leaf marked *success* is encountered, then this fact is reported. If a leaf marked *fail* is encountered, then *backtracking* takes place, that is the search proceeds by moving back to the parent node of the leaf whereupon the next descendant of this parent node is selected. This process continues until control is back at the root node and all of its descendants have been visited. If the depth-first search enters an infinite path before visiting a node marked *success*, then a divergence results.

In the case of Prolog the depth-first search takes place on an LD-tree for the query and program under consideration. If a leaf marked *success* (that is the node with the empty query) is encountered, then the associated c.a.s. is printed and the search is suspended. The request for more solutions ("`;`") results in a resumption of the search from the last node marked *success* until a new noded marked *success* is visited. If the tree has no (more) nodes marked *success*, then failure is reported, by printing the answer "no".

For the LD-tree given in Figure 3.1 the depth-first search is depicted in Figure 5.1.

The above description of the depth-first search is still somewhat informal, so we provide an alternative description of it which takes into account that in an LD-tree the nodes lying to the right of an infinite branch will not be visited. To this end we define the subtree of the LD-tree which consists of the nodes that will be generated during the depth-first search. As the order of the program clauses is now taken into account this tree will be ordered.

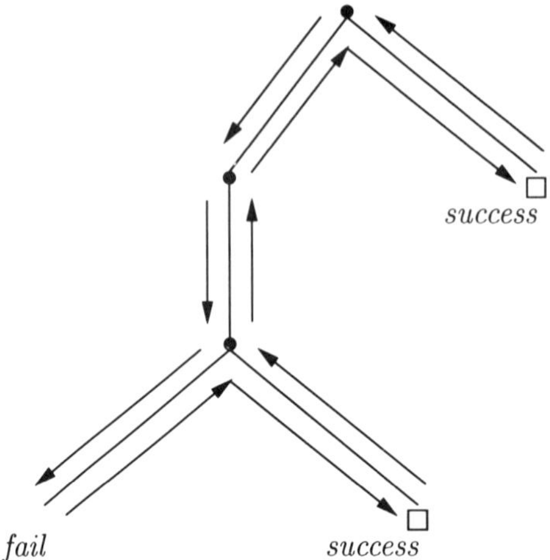

Figure 5.1 Backtracking over the LD-tree of Figure 3.1

Definition 5.1 For a given program we build a finitely branching ordered tree of queries, possibly marked with the markers *success* and *fail*, by starting with the initial query and repeatedly applying to it an operator *expand(T, Q)* where T is the current tree and Q is the leftmost unmarked query.

expand(T, Q) is defined as follows.

- **success**: Q is the empty query;
  mark Q with *success*,
- **fail**: Q has no LD-resolvents;
  mark Q with *fail*,
- **expand**: Q has LD-resolvents;
  let k be the number of clauses of the program that are applicable to the selected atom. Add to T as direct descendants of Q k LD-resolvents of Q, each with a different program clause. Choose these resolvents in such a way that the paths of the tree remain initial fragments of LD-derivations. Order them according to the order the applicable clauses appear in the program.

The limit of this process is an ordered tree of (possibly marked) queries. We call this tree a *Prolog tree*.   □

Example 5.2

(i) Consider the following program P_1:

```
p ← q.
p.
q ← r.
q ← s.
```

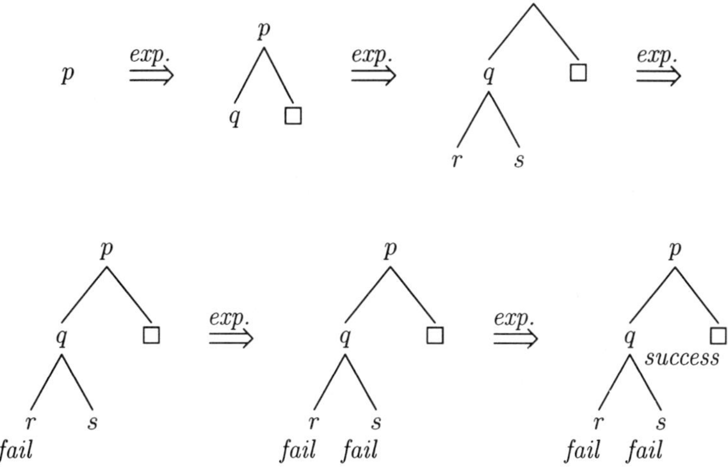

Figure 5.2   Step-by-step construction of the Prolog tree for the program P_1 and the query p

In Figure 5.2 we show a step-by-step construction of the Prolog tree for the query p. Note that this tree is finite and the empty query is eventually marked with *success*. In other words this tree is successful.

(ii) Consider now the following program P_2:

```
p ← q.
p.
q ← r.
q ← s.
s ← s.
```

The last clause forms the only difference with the previous program. In Figure 5.3 we depict a step-by-step construction of the Prolog tree for the query p. Note that this tree is infinite and the empty query is never visited. In this case the Prolog tree is infinite and unsuccessful.   □

The step-by-step construction of the Prolog tree generates a sequence of consecutively selected nodes; in Figure 5.2 these are the following five queries: p, q, r, s and □. These nodes correspond to the nodes successively visited during the depth-first search over the corresponding LD-tree with the only difference that the backtracking to the parent node has become "invisible". Finally, note that the unmarked leaves of a Prolog tree are never visited during the depth-first search. Consequently, their descendants are not even generated during the depth-first search.

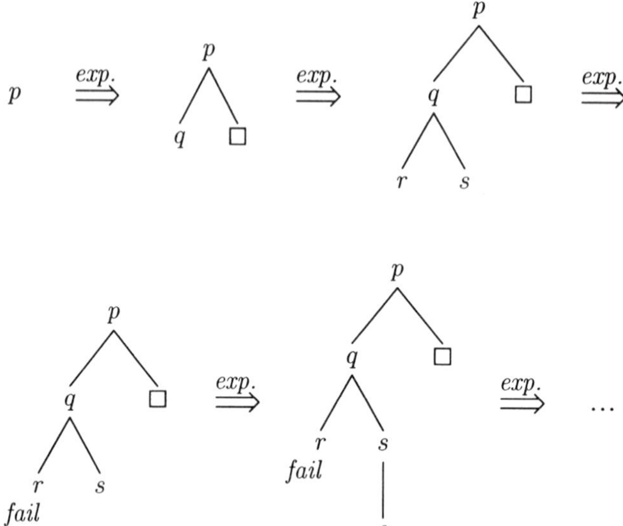

Figure 5.3   Step-by-step construction of the Prolog tree for the program P_2 and the query **p**

To summarize, the basic search mechanism for answers to a query in pure Prolog is a depth-first search in an LD-tree. The construction of a Prolog tree is an abstraction of this process but it approximates it in a way sufficient for our purposes.

Note that the LD-trees can be obtained by a simple modification of the above expansion process by disregarding the order of the descendants and applying the *expand* operator to *all* unmarked queries each time. This summarizes in a succinct way the difference between the LD-trees and Prolog trees.

Exercise 48 Characterize the situations in which the Prolog tree and the corresponding LD-tree coincide if the markers and the order of the descendants are disregarded.

□

So pure Prolog differs from logic programming in a number of aspects. Consequently, after explaining how to program in the resulting programming language we shall discuss the consequences of the above choices in the subsequent chapters.

Outcomes of Prolog Computations
When considering pure Prolog programs it is important to understand what are the possible outcomes of Prolog computations. For the sake of this discussion assume that in LD-trees:

- the descendants of each node are ordered in a way conforming to the clause ordering,

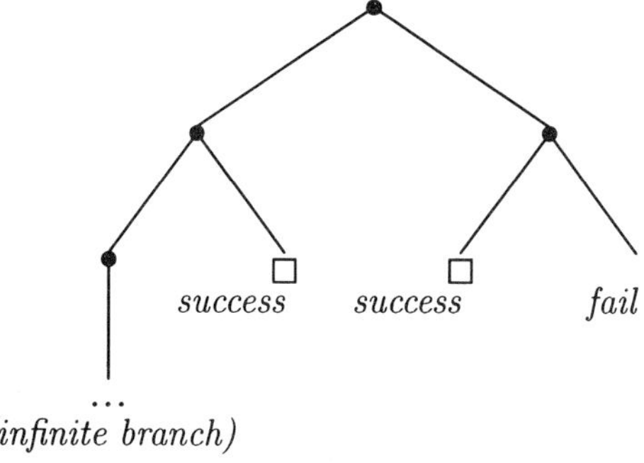

Figure 5.4 A query diverges

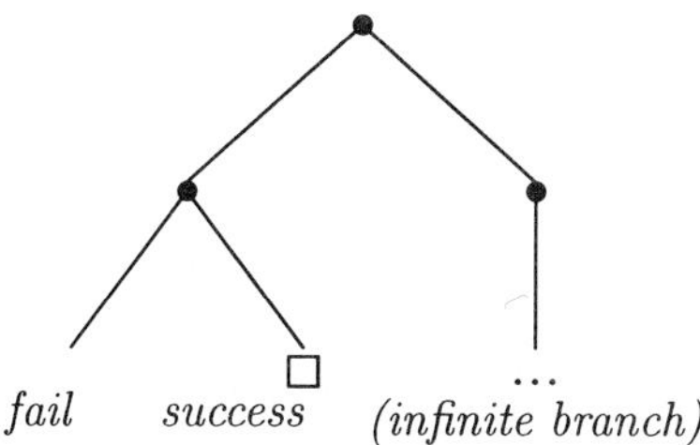

Figure 5.5 A query potentially diverges

- the input clauses are obtained in a fixed way (for example, as already suggested in Section 3.2, by adding a subscript "$_i$" at the level i to all clause variables),
- the mgus are chosen in a fixed way.

Then for every query Q and a program P exactly one LD-tree for $P \cup \{Q\}$ exists. Given a query Q and a program P, we introduce the following terminology.

- Q *universally terminates* if the LD-tree for $P \cup \{Q\}$ is finite.
  For example the query p(X,c) for the program *PATH* of Example 3.36 universally terminates as Figure 3.1 shows.
- Q *diverges* if in the LD-tree for $P \cup \{Q\}$ an infinite branch exists to the left of any success node. In particular, Q diverges if the LD-tree is not successful and infinite. This situation is represented in Figure 5.4.
- Q *potentially diverges* if in the LD-tree for $P \cup \{Q\}$ a success node exists such that

  - all branches to its left are finite,

  - an infinite branch exists to its right.

  This situation is represented in Figure 5.5.
- Q *produces infinitely many answers* if the LD-tree for $P \cup \{Q\}$ has infinitely many success nodes and all infinite branches lie to the right of them; Figure 5.6 represents this situation.

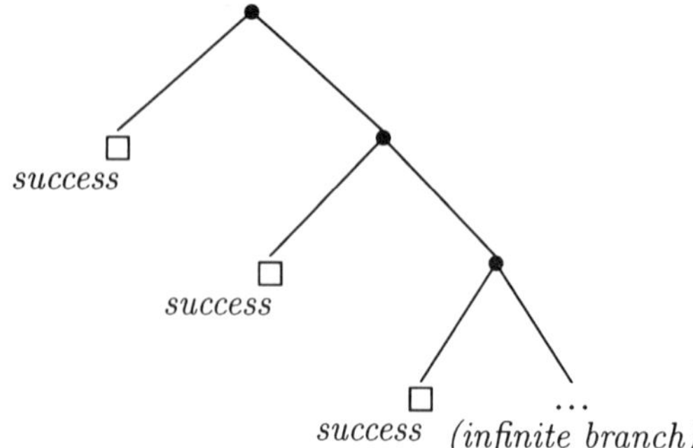

Figure 5.6 A query produces infinitely many answers

- *Q fails* if the LD-tree for $P \cup \{Q\}$ is finitely failed.

Note that if Q produces infinitely many answers, then it potentially diverges, but not conversely. Each of these possible outcomes will be illustrated later in the chapter.

5.1.3   Pragmatics of Programming

The details of the procedural interpretation of logic programming — unification, standardization apart and generation of new resolvents — are quite subtle. Adding to it the above mentioned modifications — leftmost selection rule, ordering of the clauses, depth-first search and omission of the occur-check — results in a pretty involved computation mechanism which is certainly difficult to grasp.

Fortunately, the declarative interpretation of logic programs comes to our rescue. Using it we can simply view logic programs and pure Prolog programs as formulas in a fragment of first-order logic. Thinking in terms of the declarative interpretation instead of in terms of the procedural interpretation turns out to be of great help. Declarative interpretation allows us to concentrate on *what* is to be computed, in contrast to the procedural interpretation which explains *how* to compute.

Now, program specification is precisely a description of what the program is to compute. In many cases to solve a computational problem in Prolog it just suffices to formalize its specification in the clausal form. Of course such a formalization often becomes a very inefficient program. But after some experience it is possible to identify the causes of inefficiency and to learn to program in such a way that more efficient solutions are offered.

5.1.4 Interaction with a Prolog System

Here is the shortest possible description of how a Prolog system can be used. For a more complete description the reader is referred to a language manual. The interaction starts by typing cprolog for C-Prolog or sicstus for SICStus Prolog. There are some small differences in interaction with these two systems which we shall disregard. The system replies by the prompt "| ?-". Now the program can be read in by typing [file-name] followed by the period ".". Assuming that the program is syntactically correct, the system replies with the answer "yes" followed by the prompt "| ?-". Now a query to the program can be submitted, by typing it with the period "." at its end. The system replies are of two forms. If the query succeeds, the corresponding computed answer substitution is printed in an equational form; "**yes**" is used to denote the empty substitution.

At this point typing the return key terminates the computation, whereas typing ";" followed by the return key is interpreted as the request to produce the next computed answer substitution. If the query or the request to produce the next answer (finitely) fails, "no" is printed. Below, we use queries both to find *one* answer (the first one found by the depth-first search procedure) and to find *all* answers. Finally, typing halt. finishes the interaction with the system.

Here is an example of an interaction with C-Prolog:

```
cprolog
C-Prolog version 1.5
| ?- [test].               % read in the file called test;
test consulted 5112 bytes 0.15 sec.

yes                        % the file read in;
| ?- app([a,b], [c,d], Zs). % compute an answer to the query
                           % app([a,b], [c,d], Zs);
Zs = [a,b,c,d]             % an answer is produced;

yes                        % an answer to typing the return key;
| ?- sum(0, s(0), Z).      % compute an answer to the query
                           % sum(0, s(0), Z);
Z = s(0) ;                 % ``;'' is a request for more solutions;

no                         % no more solutions;
| ?- halt.                 % leave the system.

[ Prolog execution halted ]
```

Below, when listing the interactions with the Prolog system, the queries are written with the prompt string "| ?-" preceding them and the period "." succeeding them.

5.2   The Empty Domain

We found it convenient to organize the exposition in terms of domains over which computing takes place. The simplest possible domain is the empty domain. Not much can be computed over it. Still, for pure academic interest, legal Prolog programs which compute over this domain can be written. An example is the program considered in Chapter 3, now written conforming to the above syntax conventions:

```
summer.
warm  ←  summer.
warm  ←  sunny.
happy  ←  summer, warm.
```

Program: SUMMER

We can query this program to obtain answers to simple questions. In absence of variables all computed answer substitutions are empty. For example, we have

```
| ?- happy.


yes
| ?- sunny.


no
```

Exercise 49 Draw the Prolog trees for these two queries.   □

Prolog provides three built-in nullary relation symbols — true/0, fail/0 and repeat/0. true/0 is defined internally by the single clause:

```
true.
```

so the query true always succeeds. fail/0 has the empty definition, so the query fail always fails. Finally, repeat/0 is internally defined by the following clauses:

```
repeat.
repeat  ←  repeat.
```

The qualification "built-in" means that these relations cannot be redefined, so clauses, the heads of which refer to the built-in relations, are ignored. In more modern versions of Prolog, like SICStus Prolog, a warning is issued in case such an attempt at redefining a built-in relation is encountered.

Exercise 50
(i) Draw the LD-tree and the Prolog tree for the query repeat, fail.

(ii) The command write('a') of Prolog prints the string a on the screen and the command nl produces a new line. What is the effect of the query repeat, write('a'), nl, fail? Does this query diverge or potentially diverge?   □

5.3   Finite Domains

Slightly less trivial domains are the finite ones. With each element in the domain there corresponds a constant in the language; no other function symbols are available.

Even such limited domains can be useful. Consider for example a simple database providing an information which countries are neighbours. To save toner let us consider Central America (see Figure 5.7).

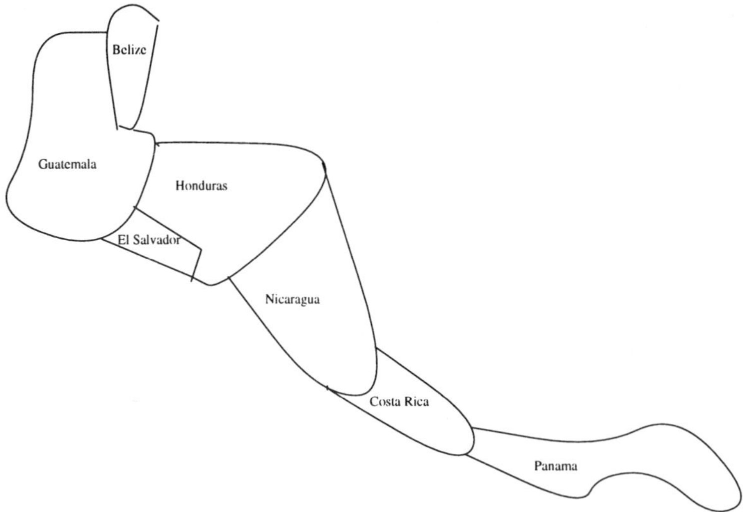

Figure 5.7 Map of Central America

```
% neighbour(X, Y)  ←  X is a neighbour of Y.
neighbour(belize, guatemala).
neighbour(guatemala, belize).
neighbour(guatemala, el_salvador).
neighbour(guatemala, honduras).
neighbour(el_salvador, guatemala).
neighbour(el_salvador, honduras).
neighbour(honduras, guatemala).
neighbour(honduras, el_salvador).
neighbour(honduras, nicaragua).
neighbour(nicaragua, honduras).
neighbour(nicaragua, costa_rica).
neighbour(costa_rica, nicaragua).
neighbour(costa_rica, panama).
neighbour(panama, costa_rica).
```

Program: CENTRAL_AMERICA

Here and elsewhere we precede the definition of each relation symbol by a comment line explaining its intended meaning.

We can now ask various simple questions, like

"are Honduras and El Salvador neighbours?"

```
| ?- neighbour(honduras, el_salvador).
```

yes

"which countries are neighbours of Nicaragua?"

```
| ?-  neighbour(nicaragua, X).
```

```
X = honduras ;
```

```
X = costa_rica ;
```

no

"which countries have both Honduras and Costa Rica as a neighbour?"

```
| ?- neighbour(X, honduras), neighbour(X, costa_rica).
```

```
X = nicaragua ;
```

no

The query `neighbour(X, Y)` lists all pairs of countries in the database (we omit the listing) and, not unexpectedly, we have

```
| ?- neighbour(X, X).
```

no

Exercise 51 Formulate a query that computes all the triplets of countries which are neighbours of each other. □

Exercise 52
(i) Define a relation `diff` such that `diff(X, Y)` iff X and Y are different countries. How many clauses are needed to define `diff`?

(ii) Formulate a query that computes all the pairs of countries that have Guatemala as a neighbour. □

Exercise 53 Consider the following question:

"are there triplets of countries which are neighbours of each other?"

and the following formalization of it as a query:

```
neighbour(X, Y), neighbour(Y, Z), neighbour(X, Z).
```

Why is it not needed to state in the query that X, Y and Z are different countries? □

Some more complicated queries require addition of rules to the considered program. Consider for example the question

"which countries can one reach from Guatemala by crossing one other country?"

It is answered by first formulating the rule

```
one_crossing(X, Y)  ←  neighbour(X, Z), neighbour(Z, Y), diff(X, Y).
```

where `diff` is the relation defined in Exercise 52, and adding it to the program `CENTRAL_AMERICA`. Now we obtain

```
| ?- one_crossing(guatemala, Y).

Y = honduras ;

Y = el_salvador ;

Y = nicaragua ;

no
```

This rule allowed us to "mask" the local variable Z. A variable of a clause is called *local* if it occurs only in its body. One should not confuse anonymous variables with local ones. For example, replacing in the above clause Z by "_" would change its meaning, as each occurrence of "_" denotes a different variable.

Next, consider the question

"which countries have Honduras or Costa Rica as a neighbour?"

In pure Prolog, clause bodies are simply sequences of atoms, so we need to define a new relation by means of two rules:

```
neighbour_h_or_c(X)  ←  neighbour(X, honduras).
neighbour_h_or_c(X)  ←  neighbour(X, costa_rica).
```

and add them to the above program. Now we get

```
| ?- neighbour_h_or_c(X).

X = guatemala ;

X = el_salvador ;
```

```
X = nicaragua ;

X = nicaragua ;

X = panama ;

no
```

The answer `nicaragua` is listed twice due to the fact that it is a neighbour of both countries. The above representation of the `neighbour` relation is very simple minded and consequently various natural questions, like "which country has the largest number of neighbours?" or "which countries does one need to cross when going from country X to country Y?" cannot be easily answered. A more appropriate representation is where for each country an explicit list of its neighbours is made. We shall return to this issue after we have introduced the concept of lists.

Exercise 54 Assume the unary relations `female` and `male` and the binary relations `mother` and `father`. Write a pure Prolog program that defines the binary relations `son`, `daughter`, `parent`, `grandmother`, `grandfather` and `grandparent`. Set up a small database of some family and run some example queries that involve the new relations.

□

5.4 Numerals

Natural numbers can be represented in many ways. Perhaps the most simple representation is by means of a constant 0 (zero), and a unary function symbol s (successor). We call the resulting ground terms *numerals*. Formally, numerals are defined inductively as follows:

- 0 is a numeral,
- if x is a numeral, then $s(x)$, the successor of x, is a numeral.

Numeral
This definition directly translates into the following program:

```
% num(X)  ←  X is a numeral.
num(0).
num(s(X))  ←  num(X).
```

Program: NUMERAL

It is easy to see that

- for a numeral $s^n(0)$, where $n \geq 0$, the query $num(s^n(0))$ successfully terminates,

- for a *ground* term t which is not a numeral, the query num(t) finitely fails.

The above program is *recursive*, which means that its relation, num, is defined in terms of itself. In general, recursion introduces a possibility of non-termination. For example, consider the program NUMERAL1 obtained by reordering the clauses of the program NUMERAL and take the query num(Y) with a variable Y. As Y unifies with s(X), we see that, using the first clause of NUMERAL1, num(X) is a resolvent of num(Y). By repeating this procedure we obtain an infinite computation which starts with num(Y). Thus the query num(Y) diverges w.r.t. NUMERAL1.

In contrast, the query num(Y), when used with the original program NUMERAL, yields a c.a.s. {Y/0}. Upon backtracking the c.a.s.s {Y/s(0)}, {Y/s(s(0))}, ... are successively produced. So, in the terminology of Section 5.1, the query num(Y) produces infinitely many answers and *a fortiori* potentially diverges.

Exercise 55 Draw the LD-tree and the Prolog tree for the query num(Y) w.r.t. to the programs NUMERAL and NUMERAL1. $\square$

So we see that termination depends on the clause ordering, which considerably complicates an understanding of the programs. Therefore it is preferable to write the programs in such a way that the desired queries terminate for *all* clause orderings, that is that these queries universally terminate.

Another aspect of the clause ordering is efficiency. Consider the query $num(s^n(0))$ with n > 0. With the program NUMERAL1 the first clause will be successfully used for n times, then it will "fail" upon which the second clause will be successfully used. So in total n+2 unification attempts will be made. With the clause ordering used in the program NUMERAL this number equals 2n+1, so is $\geq$ n+2.

Of course, the above query is not a "typical" one but one can at least draw the conclusion that usually in a term there are more occurrences of the function symbol s than of 0. Consequently, the first clause of NUMERAL succeeds less often than the second one.

This seems to suggest that the program NUMERAL1 is more efficient than NUMERAL. However, this discussion assumes that the clauses forming the definition of a relation are tried sequentially in the order they appear in the program. In most implementations of Prolog this is not the case. Namely an indexing mechanism is used (see e.g. Aït-Kaci [Ait91, pages 65–72]), according to which initially the first argument of the selected atom with a relation p is compared with the first argument of the head of each of the clauses defining p and all incompatible clauses are discarded. Then the gain obtained from the clause ordering in NUMERAL1 is lost.

Addition

The program NUMERAL can only be used to test whether a term is a numeral. Let us see now how to compute with numerals. Addition is an operation defined on numerals by the following two axioms of Peano arithmetic (see e.g. Shoenfield [Sho67, page 22]):

- $x + 0 = x$,
- $x + s(y) = s(x + y)$.

They translate into the following program already mentioned in Chapter 3:

```
% sum(X, Y, Z) ← X, Y, Z are numerals such that Z is the sum of X and Y.
sum(X, 0, X).
sum(X, s(Y), s(Z)) ← sum(X, Y, Z).
```

Program: SUM

where, intuitively, Z holds the result of adding X and Y.

To see better the connection between the second axiom and the second clause note that this axiom could be rewritten as

- $x + s(y) = s(z)$, where $z = x + y$.

This program can be used in a number of ways. First, we can compute the sum of two numbers, albeit in a cumbersome, unary notation:

```
| ?- sum(s(s(0)), s(s(s(0))), Z).
```

```
Z = s(s(s(s(s(0)))))
```

However, we can also obtain answers to more complicated questions. For example, the query below produces all pairs of numerals X, Y such that $X + Y = s^3(0)$:

```
| ?- sum(X, Y, s(s(s(0)))).
```

```
X = s(s(s(0)))
Y = 0 ;

X = s(s(0))
Y = s(0) ;

X = s(0)
Y = s(s(0)) ;

X = 0
Y = s(s(s(0))) ;

no
```

In turn, the query $\mathrm{sum}(s(X), s(Y), s(s(s(s(s(0))))))$ yields all pairs X, Y such that $s(X) + s(Y) = s^5(0)$, etc. In addition, recall that the answers to a query need not be ground. Indeed, we have

```
| ?- sum(X, s(0), Z).
```

```
Z = s(X) ;
```

no

Finally, some queries, like the query sum(X, Y, Z) already discussed in Chapter 3, produce infinitely many answers. Other programs below can be used in similar, diverse ways.

Exercise 56 Draw the the LD-tree and the Prolog tree for the query sum(X, Y, Z).

□

Notice that we did not enforce anywhere that the arguments of the sum relation should be terms which instantiate to numerals. Indeed, we obtain the following expected answer

```
| ?- sum(a,0,X).
```

```
X = a
```

... but also an unexpected one:

```
| ?- sum([a,b,c],s(0),X).
```

```
X = s([a,b,c])
```

To safeguard oneself against such unexpected (ab)uses of SUM we need to insert the test num(X) in the first clause, i.e. to change it to

$$sum(X, 0, X) \leftarrow num(X).$$

Omitting this test puts the burden on the user; including it puts the burden on the system — each time the first clause of SUM is used, the inserted test is carried out. Note that with the sum so modified the above considered query sum(X, s(0), Z) produces infinitely many answers, since num(X) produces infinitely many answers. These answers are $\{X/0, Z/s(0)\}$, $\{X/s(0), Z/s(s(0))\}$, etc.

Multiplication

In Peano arithmetic, multiplication is defined by the following two axioms (see Shoenfield [Sho67, page 22]):

- $x \cdot 0 = 0$,
- $x \cdot s(y) = (x \cdot y) + x$.

They translate into the following program:

```
% mult(X, Y, Z) ← X, Y, Z are numerals such that Z is the product of X
                   and Y.
mult(_, 0, 0).
mult(X, s(Y), Z) ← mult(X, Y, W), sum(W, X, Z).
```

augmented by the SUM program.

Program: MULT

In this program the local variable W is used to hold the intermediate result of multiplying X and Y. Note the use of an anonymous variable in the first clause.

Again, the second clause can be better understood if the second axiom for multiplication is rewritten as

- $x \cdot s(y) = w + x$, where $w = x \cdot y$.

Exercise 57 Write a program that computes the sum of three numerals.   □

Exercise 58 Write a program computing the exponent X^Y of two numerals.   □

Less than

Finally, the relation $<$ (*less than*) on numerals can be defined by the following two axioms:

- $0 < s(x)$,
- if $x < y$, then $s(x) < s(y)$.

They translate into following program:

```
% less(X, Y) ← X, Y are numerals such that X < Y.
less(0, s(_)).
less(s(X), s(Y)) ← less(X, Y).
```

Program: LESS

It is worthwhile to note here that the above two axioms differ from the formalization of the $<$ relation in Peano arithmetic, where among others the linear ordering axiom is used:

- $x < y \lor x = y \lor y < x$.

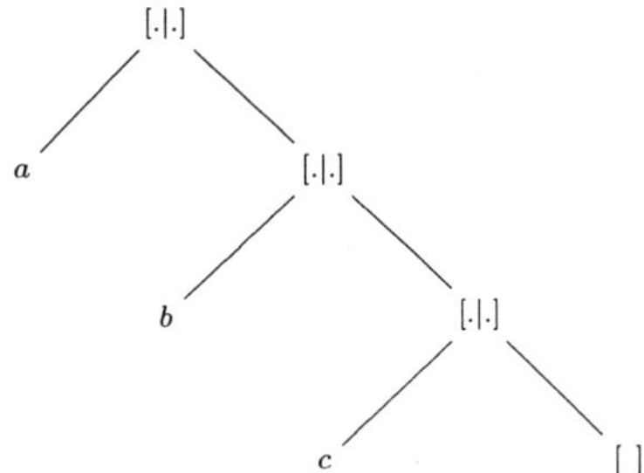

Figure 5.8 A list

5.5 Lists

To represent sequences in Prolog we can use any constant, say 0 and any binary function symbol, say f. Then the sequence a, b, c can be represented by the term $f(a, f(b, f(c, 0)))$. This representation trivially supports an addition of an element at the front of a sequence — if e is an element and s represents a sequence, then the result of this addition is represented by $f(e, s)$. However, other operations on sequences, like the deletion of an element or insertion at the end have to be programmed. A data structure which supports just one operation on sequences — an insertion of an element at the front — is usually called a *list*.

Lists form such a fundamental data structure in Prolog that special, built-in notational facilities for them are available. In particular, the pair consisting of a constant [] and a binary function symbol [.|..] is used to define them. Formally, lists are defined inductively as follows:

- [] is a list,
- if xs is a list, then [x | xs] is a list; x is called its *head* and xs is called its *tail*.

[] is called the *empty list*.

For example, [s(0)|[]] and [0|[X|[]]] are lists, whereas [0|s(0)] is not, because s(0) is not a list. In addition, the tree depicted in Figure 5.8 represents the list [a|[b|[c|[]]]].

As already stated, lists can also be defined using *any* pair consisting of a constant and a binary function symbol. (Often the pair *nil* and *cons* is used.) However, the use of the above pair makes it easier to recognize when lists are used in programs. This notation is not very readable, and even short lists become then difficult to parse. So the following shorthands are introduced inductively for $n \geq 1$:

- $[s_0|[s_1, ..., s_n|t]]$ abbreviates to $[s_0, s_1, ..., s_n|t]$,
- $[s_0, s_1, ..., s_n|[\ ]]$ abbreviates to $[s_0, s_1, ..., s_n]$.

Thus for example, [a|[b|c]] abbreviates to [a,b|c], and [a|[b,c|[]]] abbreviates to [a,b,c].

The following interaction with a Prolog system shows that these simplifications are also carried out internally. Here =/2 is Prolog's built-in written using the infix notation (that is, between the arguments) and defined internally by a single clause:

```
% X = Y  ←  X and Y are unifiable.
X = X.
```

```
| ?- X = [a | [b | c]].
```

```
X = [a,b|c]
```

```
| ?- [a,b|c]  = [a | [b | c]].
```

```
yes
| ?- X = [a | [b, c | []]].
```

```
X = [a,b,c]
```

```
| ?- [a,b,c] = [a | [b, c | []]].
```

```
yes
```

To enhance the readability of the programs that use lists we incorporate the above notation and abbreviations into pure Prolog.

The above abbreviations easily confuse a beginner. To test your understanding of this notation please solve the following exercise.

Exercise 59 Which of the following terms are lists:

```
[a,b], [a|b], [a|[b|c]], [a,[b,c]], [a,[b|c]], [a|[b,c]]?
```

$\square$

Further, to enhance the readability, we also use in programs the names ending with "s" to denote variables which are meant to be instantiated to lists. Note that the elements of a list need not to be ground.

We now present a pot-pourri of programs that use lists.

List

The definition of lists directly translates into the following simple program which recognizes whether a term is a list:

```
% list(Xs)  ←  Xs is a list.
list([]).
list([_ | Ts])  ←  list(Ts).
```

Program: LIST

As with the program NUMERAL we note the following:

- for a list t the query `list(t)` successfully terminates,
- for a *ground* term t which is not a list, the query `list(t)` finitely fails,
- for a variable X, the query `list(X)` produces infinitely many answers.

Exercise 60 Draw the LD-tree and the Prolog tree for the query `list(X)`. □

Length

The length of a list is defined inductively:

- the length of the empty list [] is 0,
- if n is the length of the list xs, then n+1 is the length of the list [x|xs].

This yields the following program:

```
% len(Xs, X)  ←  X is the length of the list Xs.
len([], 0).
len([_ | Ts], s(N))  ←  len(Ts, N).
```

Program: LENGTH

which can be used to compute the length of a list in terms of numerals:

```
| ?- len([a,b,a,d],N).

N = s(s(s(s(0))))
```

Less expectedly, this program can also be used to generate a list of different variables of a given length. For example, we have:

```
| ?-  len(Xs, s(s(s(s(0)))) ).

Xs = [_A,_B,_C,_D]
```

(_A,_B,_C,_D are variables generated by the Prolog system). We shall see at the end of this section an example of a program where such lists will be of use.

Member

Note that an element x is a member of a list l iff

- x is the head of l or
- x is a member of the tail of l.

This leads to the following program which tests whether an element is present in the list:

```
% member(Element, List)  ←  Element is an element of the list List.
member(X, [X | _]).
member(X, [_ | Xs])  ←  member(X, Xs).
```

Program: MEMBER

This program can be used in a number of ways. First, we can check whether an element is a member of a list:

```
| ?-  member(august, [june, july, august, september]).
```

yes

Next, we can generate all members of a list (this is a classic example from the original *C-Prolog User's Manual*):

```
| ?-  member(X, [tom, dick, harry]).
```

X = tom ;

X = dick ;

X = harry ;

no

In addition, as already mentioned in Chapter 1, we can easily find all elements which appear in two lists:

```
| ?- member_both(X, [1,2,3], [2,3,4,5]).
```

X = 2 ;

X = 3 ;

no

Again, as in the case of SUM, some ill-typed queries may yield a puzzling answer:

```
| ?- member(0,[0 | s(0)]).
```

yes

Recall that [0 | s(0)] is not a list. A "no" answer to such a query can be enforced by replacing the first clause by

```
member(X, [X | Xs])  ←  list(Xs).
```

Subset

The MEMBER program is used in the following program SUBSET which tests whether a list is a subset of another one:

```
% subset(Xs, Ys)  ←  each element of the list Xs is a member of the list Ys.
subset([], _).
subset([X | Xs], Ys)  ←  member(X, Ys), subset(Xs, Ys).
```

augmented by the MEMBER program.

Program: SUBSET

Note that multiple occurrences of an element are allowed here. So we have for example

```
| ?- subset([a, a], [a]).

yes
```

Append

More complex lists can be formed by concatenation. The inductive definition is as follows:

- the concatenation of the empty list [] and the list ys yields the list ys,
- if the concatenation of the lists xs and ys equals zs, the concatenation of the lists [x | xs] and ys equals [x | zs].

This translates into the perhaps most often cited Prolog program:

```
% app(Xs, Ys, Zs)  ←  Zs is the result of concatenating the lists Xs and Ys.
app([], Ys, Ys).
app([X | Xs], Ys, [X | Zs])  ←  app(Xs, Ys, Zs).
```

Program: APPEND

Note that the computation of concatenation of two lists takes linear time in the length of the first list. Indeed, for a list of length n, $n + 1$ calls of the app relation are generated. APPEND can be used not only to concatenate the lists:

```
| ?- app([a,b], [a,c], Zs).

Zs = [a,b,a,c]
```

but also to split a list in all possible ways:

```
| ?- app(Xs, Ys, [a,b,a,c]).

Xs = []
Ys = [a,b,a,c] ;

Xs = [a]
Ys = [b,a,c] ;

Xs = [a,b]
Ys = [a,c] ;

Xs = [a,b,a]
Ys = [c] ;

Xs = [a,b,a,c]
Ys = [] ;

no
```

Combining these two ways of using APPEND we can delete an occurrence of an
element from the list:

```
| ?- app(X1s, [a | X2s], [a,b,a,c]), app(X1s, X2s, Zs).

X1s = []
X2s = [b,a,c]
Zs = [b,a,c] ;

X1s = [a,b]
X2s = [c]
Zs = [a,b,c] ;

no
```

Here the result is computed in Zs and X1s and X2s are auxiliary variables. In
addition, we can generate all results of deleting an occurrence of an element from
a list:

```
| ?- app(X1s, [X | X2s], [a,b,a,c]), app(X1s, X2s, Zs).

X = a
X1s = []
X2s = [b,a,c]
Zs = [b,a,c] ;
```

```
X = b
X1s = [a]
X2s = [a,c]
Zs = [a,a,c] ;

X = a
X1s = [a,b]
X2s = [c]
Zs = [a,b,c] ;

X = c
X1s = [a,b,a]
X2s = []
Zs = [a,b,a] ;

no
```

To eliminate the printing of the auxiliary variables X1s and X2s we could define a new relation by the rule

```
select(X, Xs, Zs) ← app(X1s, [X | X2s], Xs), app(X1s, X2s, Zs).
```

and use it in the queries.

Exercise 61 Write a program for concatenating three lists. □

Select
Alternatively, we can define the deletion of an element from a list inductively. The following program performs this task:

```
% select(X, Xs, Zs) ← Zs is the result of deleting one occurrence of X
                       from the list Xs.
select(X, [X | Xs], Xs).
select(X, [Y | Xs], [Y | Zs]) ← select(X, Xs, Zs).
```

Program: SELECT

Now we have

```
| ?- select(a, [a,b,a,c], Zs).

Zs = [b,a,c] ;

Zs = [a,b,c] ;

no
```

and also

```
| ?- select(X, [a,b,a,c], Zs).

X = a
Zs = [b,a,c] ;

X = b
Zs = [a,a,c] ;

X = a
Zs = [a,b,c] ;

X = c
Zs = [a,b,a] ;

no
```

Permutation

Deleting an occurrence of an element from a list is helpful when generating all permutations of a list. The program below uses the following inductive definition of a permutation:

- the empty list [] is the only permutation of itself,
- [x|ys] is a permutation of a list xs if ys is a permutation of the result zs of deleting one occurrence of x from the list xs.

Using the first method of deleting one occurrence of an element from a list we are brought to the following program:

```
% perm(Xs, Ys)  ←  Ys is a permutation of the list Xs.
perm([], []).
perm(Xs, [X | Ys])  ←
    app(X1s, [X | X2s], Xs),
    app(X1s, X2s, Zs),
    perm(Zs, Ys).
```

augmented by the **APPEND** program.

Program: PERMUTATION

```
| ?- perm([here,we,are], Ys).

Ys = [here,we,are] ;

Ys = [here,are,we] ;
```

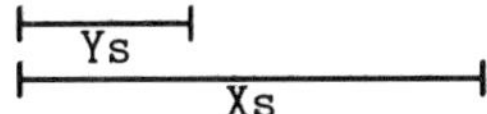

Figure 5.9 Prefix of a list

```
Ys = [we,here,are] ;

Ys = [we,are,here] ;

Ys = [are,here,we] ;

Ys = [are,we,here] ;

no
```

Permutation1

An alternative version uses the **SELECT** program to remove an element from the list:

```
% perm(Xs, Ys)  ←  Ys is a permutation of the list Xs.
perm([], []).
perm(Xs, [X | Ys]) ←
    select(X, Xs, Zs),
    perm(Zs, Ys).
```

augmented by the **SELECT** program.

Program: PERMUTATION1

Prefix and Suffix

The **APPEND** program can also be elegantly used to formalize various sublist operations. An initial segment of a list is called a *prefix* and its final segment is called a *suffix*. Using the **APPEND** program both relations can be defined in a straightforward way:

```
% prefix(Xs, Ys)  ←  Xs is a prefix of the list Ys.
prefix(Xs, Ys) ←  app(Xs, _, Ys).
```

augmented by the **APPEND** program.

Program: PREFIX

Figure 5.9 illustrates this situation in a diagram.

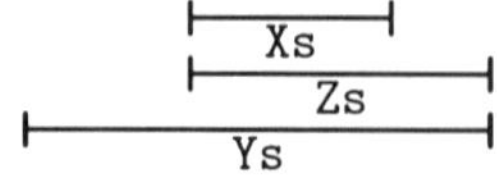

Figure 5.10 Suffix of a list

Figure 5.11 Sublist of a list

```
% suffix(Xs, Ys)  ←  Xs is a suffix of the list Ys.
suffix(Xs, Ys)  ←  app(_, Xs, Ys).
```

augmented by the APPEND program.

Program: SUFFIX

Again, Figure 5.10 illustrates this situation in a diagram.

Exercise 62 Define the `prefix` and `suffix` relations directly, without the use of the APPEND program.   □

Sublist

Using the `prefix` and `suffix` relations we can easily check whether one list is a (consecutive) sublist of another one. The program below formalizes the following definition of a sublist:

- the list `as` is a sublist of the list `bs` if `as` is a prefix of a suffix of `bs`.

```
% sublist(Xs, Ys)  ←  Xs is a sublist of the list Ys.
sublist(Xs, Ys)  ←  app(_, Zs, Ys), app(Xs, _, Zs).
```

augmented by the APPEND program.

Program: SUBLIST

In this clause `Zs` is a suffix of `Ys` and `Xs` is a prefix of `Zs`. The diagram in Figure 5.11 illustrates this relation.

This program can be used in an expected way, for example,

```
| ?- sublist([2,6], [5,2,3,2,6,4]).
```

yes

and also in a less expected way,

```
| ?- sublist([1,X,2], [4,Y,3,2]).


X = 3
Y = 1 ;


no
```

Here as an effect of the call of **SUBLIST** both lists become instantiated so that the first one becomes a sublist of the second one. At the end of this section we shall see a program where this type of instantiation is used in a powerful way to solve a combinatorial problem.

Exercise 63 Write another version of the **SUBLIST** program which formalizes the following definition:

the list **as** is a sublist of the list **bs** if **as** is a suffix of a prefix of **bs**. □

Naive Reverse

To reverse a list, the following program is often used:

```
% reverse(Xs, Ys)  ←   Ys is the result of reversing the list Xs.
reverse([], []).
reverse([X | Xs], Ys)  ←  reverse(Xs, Zs), app(Zs, [X], Ys).
```

augmented by the **APPEND** program.

Program: NAIVE_REVERSE

This program is very inefficient and is often used as a benchmark program. It leads to a number of computation steps, which is quadratic in the length of the list. Indeed, translating the clauses into recurrence relations over the length of the lists we obtain for the first clause:

$$r(x + 1) = r(x) + a(x),$$
$$a(x) = x + 1,$$

and for the second one:

$$r(0) = 1.$$

This yields $r(x) = x \cdot (x + 1)/2 + 1$.

Reverse with Accumulator

A more efficient program is the following one:

```
% reverse(Xs, Ys)  ←   Ys is the reverse of the list Xs.
reverse(X1s, X2s)  ←  reverse(X1s, [], X2s).

% reverse(Xs, Ys, Zs)  ←  Zs is the result of concatenating
                          the reverse of the list Xs and the list Ys.
reverse([], Xs, Xs).
reverse([X | X1s], X2s, Ys)  ←  reverse(X1s, [X | X2s], Ys).
```

Program: REVERSE

Here, the middle argument of `reverse/3` is used as an *accumulator*. This makes the number of computation steps linear in the length of the list. To understand better the way this program works consider its use for the query `reverse([a,b,c],Ys)`. It leads to the following successful derivation:

$$\text{reverse}([a, b, c], Ys) \xRightarrow[1]{\theta_1} \text{reverse}([a, b, c], [\ ], Ys) \xRightarrow[3]{\theta_2} \text{reverse}([b, c], [a], Ys) \xRightarrow[3]{\theta_3}$$
$$\text{reverse}([c], [b, a], Ys) \xRightarrow[3]{\theta_4} \text{reverse}([\ ], [c, b, a], Ys) \xRightarrow[2]{\theta_5} \square,$$

where θ_5 instantiates `Ys` to `[c,b,a]`.

NAIVE_REVERSE and REVERSE can be used in a number of ways. For example, the query `reverse(xs, [X | Ls])` produces the last element of the list `xs`:

```
| ?-  reverse([a,b,a,d], [X|Ls]).


Ls = [a,b,a]
X = d
```

Exercise 64 Write a program which computes the last element of a list directly, without the use of other programs. □

So far we have used the anonymous variables only in program clauses. They can also be used in queries. They are not printed in the answer, so we obtain

```
| ?- reverse([a,b,a,d], [X|_]).


X = d
```

Recall, that each occurrence of "_" is interpreted as a *different* variable, so we have (compare it with the query `neighbour(X, X)` used on page 116)

```
| ?- neighbour(_,_).

yes
```

One has to be careful and not to confuse the use of "_" with existential quantification. For example, note that we cannot eliminate the printing of the values of `X1s` and `X2s` in the query

```
| ?- app(X1s, [X | X2s], [a,b,a,c]), app(X1s, X2s, Zs).
```

by replacing them by "_", i.e. treating them as anonymous variables, as each of them occurs more than once in the query.

Palindrome

Another use of the **REVERSE** program is present in the following program which tests whether a list is a palindrome.

```
% palindrome(Xs)  ←  the list Xs is equal to its reverse.
palindrome(Xs)  ←  reverse(Xs, Xs).
```

augmented by the **REVERSE** program.

Program: PALINDROME

For example:

```
| ?-  palindrome(
        [t,o,o,n, n,e,v,a,d,a, n,a, c,a,n,a,d,a, v,e,n,n,o,o,t]
     ).
```

yes

It is instructive to see for which programs introduced in this section it is possible to run successfully ill-typed queries, i.e. queries which do not have lists as arguments in the places one would expect a list from the specification. These are **SUBSET**, **APPEND**, **SELECT** and **SUBLIST**. For other programs the ill-typed queries never succeed, essentially because the unit clauses can succeed only with properly typed arguments.

A Sequence

The following delightful program (see Coelho and Cotta [CC88, page 193]) shows how the use of anonymous variables can dramatically improve the program readability. Consider the following problem: arrange three 1s, three 2s, ..., three 9s in sequence so that for all $i \in [1,9]$ there are exactly i numbers between successive occurrences of i.

The desired program is an almost verbatim formalization of the problem in Prolog.

```
% sequence(Xs)  ←  Xs is a list of 27 elements.
sequence([_,_,_,_,_,_,_,_,_,_,_,_,_,_,_,_,_,_,_,_,_,_,_,_,_,_,_]).

% question(Ss)  ←  Ss is a list of 27 elements forming the desired sequence.
question(Ss)  ←
    sequence(Ss),
    sublist([1,_,1,_,1], Ss),
    sublist([2,_,_,2,_,_,2], Ss),
    sublist([3,_,_,_,3,_,_,_,3], Ss),
    sublist([4,_,_,_,_,4,_,_,_,_,4], Ss),
    sublist([5,_,_,_,_,_,5,_,_,_,_,_,5], Ss),
```

```
sublist([6,_,_,_,_,_,_,6,_,_,_,_,_,_,6], Ss),
sublist([7,_,_,_,_,_,_,_,7,_,_,_,_,_,_,_,7], Ss),
sublist([8,_,_,_,_,_,_,_,_,8,_,_,_,_,_,_,_,_,8], Ss),
sublist([9,_,_,_,_,_,_,_,_,_,9,_,_,_,_,_,_,_,_,_,9], Ss).
```

augmented by the SUBLIST program.

Program: SEQUENCE

The following interaction with Prolog shows that there are exactly six solutions
to this problem.

```
| ?- question(Ss).
```

```
Ss = [1,9,1,2,1,8,2,4,6,2,7,9,4,5,8,6,3,4,7,5,3,9,6,8,3,5,7] ;
```

```
Ss = [1,8,1,9,1,5,2,6,7,2,8,5,2,9,6,4,7,5,3,8,4,6,3,9,7,4,3] ;
```

```
Ss = [1,9,1,6,1,8,2,5,7,2,6,9,2,5,8,4,7,6,3,5,4,9,3,8,7,4,3] ;
```

```
Ss = [3,4,7,8,3,9,4,5,3,6,7,4,8,5,2,9,6,2,7,5,2,8,1,6,1,9,1] ;
```

```
Ss = [3,4,7,9,3,6,4,8,3,5,7,4,6,9,2,5,8,2,7,6,2,5,1,9,1,8,1] ;
```

```
Ss = [7,5,3,8,6,9,3,5,7,4,3,6,8,5,4,9,7,2,6,4,2,8,1,2,1,9,1] ;
```

```
no
```

5.6   Complex Domains

By a complex domain we mean here a domain built from some constants by means
of function symbols. Of course, both numerals and lists are examples of such
domains. In this section our interest lies in domains built by means of other,
application dependent, function symbols. Such domains correspond to compound
data types in imperative and functional languages.

A Map Colouring Program

As an example consider the problem of colouring a map in such a way that no
two neighbours have the same colour. Below we call such a colouring *correct*. A
solution to the problem can be greatly simplified by the use of an appropriate data
representation. The map is represented below as a list of regions and colours as a
list of available colours. This is hardly surprising.

The main insight lies in the representation of regions. In the program below each
region is determined by its name, colour and the colours of its neighbours, so it is

represented as a term `region(name, colour, neighbours)`, where `neighbours` is a list of colours of the neighbouring regions.

The program below is a pretty close translation of the following definition of a correct colouring:

- A map is correctly coloured iff each of its regions is correctly coloured.
- A region `region(name,colour,neighbours)` is correctly coloured, iff `colour` and the elements of `neighbours` are members of the list of the available colours and `colour` is not a member of the list `neighbours`.

```
% colour_map(Map, Colours)  ←  Map is correctly coloured using Colours.
colour_map([], _).
colour_map([Region | Regions], Colours) ←
    colour_region(Region, Colours),
    colour_map(Regions, Colours).

% colour_region(Region, Colours)  ←  Region and its neighbours are
                                      correctly coloured using Colours.
colour_region(region(_, Colour, Neighbors), Colours) ←
    select(Colour, Colours, Colours1),
    subset(Neighbors, Colours1).
```

augmented by the `SELECT` program.

augmented by the `SUBSET` program.

Program: `MAP_COLOUR`

Thus to use this program one first needs to represent the map in an appropriate way. Here is the appropriate representation for the map of Central America expressed as a single atom with the relation symbol `map`:

```
map([
     region(belize, Belize, [Guatemala]),
     region(guatemala, Guatemala, [Belize, El_Salvador, Honduras]),
     region(el_salvador, El_Salvador, [Guatemala, Honduras]),
     region(honduras, Honduras, [Guatemala, El_Salvador, Nicaragua]),
     region(nicaragua, Nicaragua, [Honduras, Costa_rica]),
     region(costa_rica, Costa_rica, [Nicaragua, Panama]),
     region(panama, Panama, [Costa_rica])
    ]).
```

Program: `MAP_OF_CENTRAL_AMERICA`

Now, to link this representation with the `MAP_COLOUR` program we just need to use the following query which properly "initializes" the variable `Map` and where for simplicity we already fixed the choice of available colours:

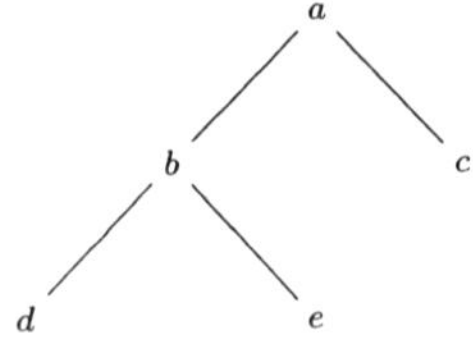

Figure 5.12 A binary tree

```
| ?- map(Map), colour_map(Map, [green, blue, red]).

Map = [region(belize,green,[blue]),
       region(guatemala,blue,[green,green,red]),
       region(el_salvador,green,[blue,red]),
       region(honduras,red,[blue,green,green]),
       region(nicaragua,green,[red,blue]),
       region(costa_rica,blue,[green,green]),
       region(panama,green,[blue])
      ]
```

5.7 Binary Trees

Binary trees form another fundamental data structure. Prolog does not provide
any built-in notational facilities for them, so we adopt the following inductive
definition:

- void is a (n empty) binary tree,
- if left and right are trees, then tree(x, left, right) is a binary tree; x
  is called its *root*, left its *left subtree* and right its *right subtree*.

Empty binary trees serve to "fill" the nodes in which no data is stored. To
visualize the trees it is advantageous to ignore their presence in the binary tree.
Thus the binary tree tree(c, void, void) corresponds to the tree with just one
node — the root c, and the binary tree

```
tree(a, tree(b, tree(d, void, void), tree(e, void, void)),
        tree(c, void, void))
```

can be visualized as the tree depicted in Figure 5.12. So the leaves are represented
by the terms of the form tree(s, void, void).

From now on we abbreviate binary tree to a *tree* and hope that no confusion
arises between a term that is a (binary) tree and the tree such a term visualizes.

The above definition translates into the following program which tests whether
a term is a tree.

```
% bin_tree(T)  ←  T is a tree.
bin_tree(void).
bin_tree(tree(_, Left, Right))  ←
    bin_tree(Left),
    bin_tree(Right).
```

Program: TREE

As with the programs `NUMERAL` and `LIST` we note the following:

- for a tree t the query `bin_tree(t)` successfully terminates,
- for a *ground* term t which is not a tree the query `bin_tree(t)` finitely fails,
- for a variable `X`, the query `bin_tree(X)` produces infinitely many answers.

Trees can be used to store data and to maintain various operations on this data.

Tree Member

Note that an element x is present in a tree T iff

- x is the root of T or
- x is in the left subtree of T or
- x is in the right subtree of T.

This directly translates into the following program:

```
% tree_member(E, Tree)  ←  E is an element of the tree Tree.
tree_member(X, tree(X, _, _)).
tree_member(X, tree(_, Left, _))  ←  tree_member(X, Left).
tree_member(X, tree(_, _, Right))  ←  tree_member(X, Right).
```

Program: TREE_MEMBER

This program can be used both to test whether an element x is present in a given tree t — by using the query `tree_member(x, t)`, and to list all elements present in a given tree t — by using the query `tree_member(X, t)`.

In-order Traversal

To traverse a tree three methods are most common: a *pre-order* — (in every subtree) first the root is visited, then the nodes of left subtree and then the nodes of right subtree; an *in-order* — first the nodes of the left subtree are visited, then the root and then the nodes of the right subtree; and a *post-order* — first the nodes of the left subtree are visited, then the nodes of the right subtree and then the root. Each of them translates directly into a Prolog program. For example the in-order traversal translates to

```
% in-order(Tree, List)  ←  List is a list obtained by the in-order
                                traversal of the tree Tree.
in-order(void, []).
in-order(tree(X, Left, Right), Xs)  ←
    in-order(Left, Ls),
    in-order(Right, Rs),
    app(Ls, [X | Rs], Xs).
```

augmented by the APPEND program.

Program: IN_ORDER

Exercise 65 Write the programs computing the pre-order and post-order traversals of
a tree.   □

Frontier

The *frontier* of a tree is a list formed by its leaves. Recall that the leaves of a tree
are represented by the terms of the form tree(a, void, void). To compute a
frontier of a tree we need to distinguish three types of trees:

- the empty tree, that is the term void,
- a leaf, that is a term of the form tree(a, void, void),
- a non-empty, non-leaf tree (in short a *nel-tree*), that is a term tree(x, l,
  r), such that either l or r does not equal void.

We now have:

- for the empty tree its frontier is the empty list,
- for a leaf tree(a, void, void) its frontier is the list [a],
- for a nel-tree its frontier is obtained by appending to the frontier of the left
  subtree the frontier of the right subtree.

This leads to the following program in which the auxiliary relation nel_tree is
used to enforce that a tree is a nel-tree:

```
% nel_tree(t)  ←  t is a nel-tree.
nel_tree(tree(_, tree(_,_,_), _)).
nel_tree(tree(_, _, tree(_,_,_))).

% front(Tree, List)  ←  List is a frontier of the tree Tree.
front(void, []).
front(tree(X, void, void), [X]).
front(tree(X, L, R), Xs)  ←
    nel_tree(tree(X, L, R)),
    front(L, Ls),
    front(R, Rs),
    app(Ls, Rs, Xs).
```

augmented by the APPEND program.

Program: FRONTIER

Note that the test `nel_tree(t)` can also succeed for terms which are not trees, but in the above program it is applied to trees only. In addition, observe that the apparently simpler program

```
% front(Tree, List)  ←  List is a frontier of the tree Tree.
front(void, []).
front(tree(X, void, void), [X]).
front(tree(_, L, R), Xs)  ←
    front(L, Ls),
    front(R, Rs),
    app(Ls, Rs, Xs).
```

augmented by the `APPEND` program is incorrect. Indeed, the query `front(tree(X, void, void), Xs)` yields two different answers: $\{Xs/[X]\}$ by means of the second clause and $\{Xs/[]\}$ by means of the third clause.

5.8   Concluding Remarks

The aim of this chapter was to provide an introduction to programming in a subset of Prolog, called pure Prolog. We organized the exposition in terms of different domains. Each domain was obtained by fixing the syntax of the underlying language. In particular, we note the following interesting progression between the language choices and resulting domains:

Language	Domain
1 constant, 1 unary function	numerals
1 constant, 1 binary function	lists
1 constant, 1 ternary function	trees

Prolog is an original programming language and several algorithms can be coded in it in a remarkably elegant way. From the programming point of view, the main interest in logic programming and pure Prolog is in its capability to support *declarative programming*.

Recall from Chapter 1 that declarative programming was described as follows. *Specifications* written in an appropriate format can be used as a *program*. The desired conclusions follow *semantically* from the program. To compute these conclusions some *computation mechanism* is available.

Clearly, logic programming comes close to this description of declarative programming. The soundness and completeness results relate the declarative and procedural interpretations and consequently the concepts of correct answer substitutions and computed answer substitutions. However, these substitutions do not need to coincide, so a mismatch may arise.

Moreover, when moving from logic programming to pure Prolog new difficulties arise due to the use of the depth-first search strategy combined with the ordering of the clauses, the fixed selection rule and the omission of the occur-check in the unification. Consequently, pure Prolog does not completely support declarative programming and additional arguments are needed to justify that these modifications do not affect the correctness of specific programs. This motivates the next three chapters which will be devoted to the study of various aspects of correctness of pure Prolog programs.

It is also important to be aware that pure Prolog and *a fortiori* Prolog suffers from a number of deficiencies. To make the presentation balanced we tried to make the reader aware of these weaknesses. Let us summarize them here.

5.8.1   Redundant Answers

In certain cases it is difficult to see whether redundancies will occur when generating all answers to a query. Take for instance the program SUBLIST. The list [1, 2] has four different sublists. However, the query sublist(Xs, [1, 2]) generates in total six answers:

```
| ?- sublist(Xs, [1, 2]).

Xs = [] ;

Xs = [1] ;

Xs = [1,2] ;

Xs = [] ;

Xs = [2] ;

Xs = [] ;

no
```

5.8.2 Lack of Types

Types are used in programming languages to structure the data manipulated by the program and to ensure its correct use. As we have seen Prolog allows us to define various types, like lists or binary trees. However, Prolog does not support types, in the sense that it does not check whether the queries use the program in the intended way. The type information is not part of the program but rather constitutes a part of the commentary on its use.

Because of this absence of types in Prolog it is easy to abuse Prolog programs by using them with unintended inputs. The obtained answers are then not easy to predict. Consequently the "type" errors are easy to make but are difficult to find. Suppose for example that we wish to use the query `sum(A, s(0), X)` with the `SUM` program, but we typed instead `sum(a, s(0), X)`. Then we obtain

```
| ?- sum(a, s(0), X).
```

```
X = s(a)
```

which does not make much sense, because `a` is not a numeral. However, this error is difficult to catch, especially if this query is part of a larger computation.

5.8.3 Termination

In many programs it is not easy to see which queries are guaranteed to terminate. Take for instance the `SUBSET` program. The query `subset(Xs, s)` for a list `s` produces infinitely many answers. For example, we have

```
| ?- subset(Xs, [1, 2, 3]).
```

```
Xs = [] ;
```

```
Xs = [1] ;
```

```
Xs = [1,1] ;
```

```
Xs = [1,1,1] ;
```

```
Xs = [1,1,1,1] ;
```

etc.

Consequently, the query `subset(Xs, [1, 2, 3]), len(Xs, s(s(0)))`, where the `len` relation is defined by the `LENGTH` program, does not generate all subsets of `[1, 2, 3]`, but diverges after producing the answer `Xs = [1,1]`.

5.9 Bibliographic Remarks

The notion of a Prolog tree is from Apt and Teusink [AT95]. Almost all programs listed here were taken from other sources. In particular, we heavily drew on two books on Prolog — Bratko [Bra86] and Sterling and Shapiro [SS86]. The book of Coelho and Cotta [CC88] contains a large collection of interesting Prolog programs. The book of Clocksin and Mellish [CM84] explains various subtle points of the language and the book of O'Keefe [O'K90] discusses in depth the efficiency and pragmatics of programming in Prolog.

We shall return to Prolog in Chapters 9 and 11.

5.10 Summary

In this chapter we introduced a subset of Prolog, called pure Prolog. We defined its syntax and computation mechanism and discussed several programs written in this subset. These programs were arranged according to the domains over which they compute, that is

- the empty domain,
- finite domains,
- numerals,
- lists,
- complex domains,
- binary trees.

5.11 References

[Ait91] H. Aït-Kaci. *Warren's Abstract Machine.* MIT Press, Cambridge, MA, 1991.

[AT95] K.R. Apt and F. Teusink. Comparing negation in logic programming and in Prolog. In K.R. Apt and F. Turini, editors, *Meta-logics and Logic Programming*, pages 111–133. The MIT Press, Cambridge, MA, 1995.

[Bra86] I. Bratko. *PROLOG Programming for Artificial Intelligence.* International Computer Science Series. Addison-Wesley, Reading, MA, 1986.

[CC88] H. Coelho and J. C. Cotta. *Prolog by Example.* Springer-Verlag, Berlin, 1988.

[CM84] W.F. Clocksin and C.S. Mellish. *Programming in Prolog.* Springer-Verlag, Berlin, second edition, 1984.

[CW93] M. Carlsson and J. Widén. *SICStus Prolog User's Manual.* SICS, P.O. Box 1263, S-164 28 Kista, Sweden, January 1993.

[O'K90] R.A. O'Keefe. *The Craft of Prolog.* MIT Press, Cambridge, MA, 1990.

[Sho67]   J. R. Shoenfield. *Mathematical Logic.* Addison-Wesley, Reading, MA, 1967.

[SS86]   L. Sterling and E. Shapiro. *The Art of Prolog.* MIT Press, Cambridge, MA, 1986.

Chapter 6

Termination

With this chapter we begin our study of the verification of pure Prolog programs. We start by observing that the use of the leftmost selection rule combined with the depth-first search in the resulting search trees makes pure Prolog and logic programming different. As a consequence the completeness results linking the procedural and declarative interpretation of logic programs cannot be directly applied to reason about the termination of pure Prolog programs. Indeed, even when the completeness result guarantees an existence of a solution to a query, a Prolog system will miss a solution if all success nodes lie to the right of an infinite path in the search tree, that is if, in the terminology of Section 5.1, the query diverges. So termination is the key issue.

The aim of this chapter is to provide a method for proving the termination of logic and pure Prolog programs. By termination we mean here finiteness of *all* possible SLD-derivations of the initial query w.r.t. the leftmost selection rule. This notion of termination is called universal termination in Section 5.1. It does not depend on the ordering of the program clauses.

The main tool used is the multiset ordering discussed in the next section. In Section 6.2 we fix the language in which the programs and queries are supposed to be defined and study universal termination w.r.t. all selection rules. This sets a useful basis for a study of universal termination w.r.t. the leftmost selection rule.

Then, in Section 6.3 we show how this form of termination can be established for a number of pure Prolog programs and in Section 6.4 characterize the class of pure Prolog programs that terminate in the sense studied in Section 6.2.

In Section 6.5 we move on to the study of universal termination w.r.t. the leftmost selection rule. In Section 6.6 we illustrate the usefulness of the proposed method by applying it successfully to programs studied in Chapter 5 and to which the method of Section 6.2 does not apply. Then, in Section 6.7 we characterize the class of pure Prolog programs that terminate w.r.t. the leftmost selection rule in the sense studied in Section 6.5. Finally, in Section 6.8 we discuss the limitations of the proposed methods and suggest their improvement.

6.1   Multiset Ordering

In what follows we shall use a specific well-founded ordering, called the multiset ordering. A *multiset,* sometimes called *bag,* is an unordered sequence. We denote a multiset consisting of elements $a_1, \ldots, a_n$ by $bag\,(a_1, \ldots, a_n)$.

The *multiset ordering* is an ordering on finite multisets of natural numbers. It is defined as the transitive closure of the relation in which X is smaller than Y if X can be obtained from Y by replacing an element a of Y by a finite (possibly empty) multiset of natural numbers each of which is smaller than a. (For the definition of the transitive closure of a relation see Section 2.6.)

In symbols, first we define the relation $\prec$ by

$$X \prec Y \text{ iff } X = Y - \{a\} \cup Z \text{ for some } a \in Y \text{ and } Z \text{ such that } b < a \text{ for } b \in Z,$$

where X, Y and Z are finite multisets of natural numbers and then define the multiset ordering $\prec_m$ as the transitive closure of the relation $\prec$. We denote a by $old(X, Y)$ and Z by $new(X, Y)$.

Example 6.1 Consider two multisets, $bag(3, 3, 6, 7)$ and $bag(2, 2, 2, 3, 7, 5)$. Then $bag(2, 2, 2, 3, 7, 5) \prec_m bag(3, 3, 6, 7)$, because by replacing one occurrence of 3 by three occurrences of 2 we obtain $bag(2, 2, 2, 3, 7, 5) \prec bag(3, 3, 7, 5)$ and by replacing 6 by 5 we have $bag(3, 3, 7, 5) \prec bag(3, 3, 6, 7)$. $\qquad\qquad \square$

To reason about the multiset ordering we use the following classical result of König [Kön27].

Lemma 6.2 (König) An infinite, finitely branching tree has an infinite path.

Proof. Consider an infinite, but finitely branching tree T. We construct by induction an infinite branch

$$\xi := n_0,\ n_1,\ n_2 \ldots$$

in T such that for $i \geq 0$, n_i is the root of an infinite subtree of T.

Base. $i = 0$. As n_0 we take the root of T.

Induction step. By induction hypothesis, n_i is the root of an infinite subtree of T. Since T is finitely branching, there are only finitely many children of n_i. At least one of these children is a root of an infinite subtree of T, so we take n_{i+1} to be such a child of n_i. This completes the inductive definition of ξ. $\qquad \square$

We also need the following simple observation.

Note 6.3 (Well-foundedness) An ordering is well-founded iff its transitive closure is well-founded. $\qquad \square$

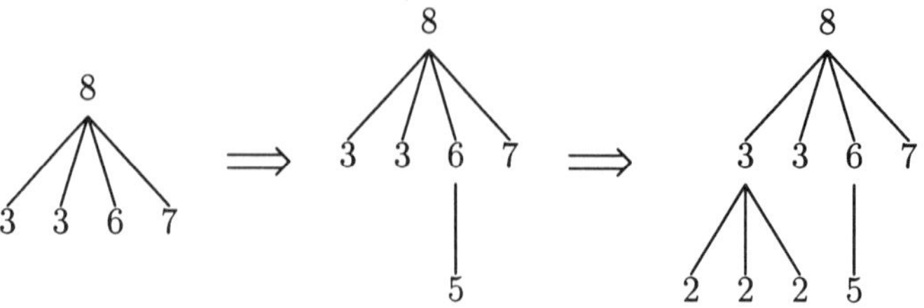

Figure 6.1 From multisets to trees

Exercise 66 Prove the above Note.   □

Theorem 6.4 (Multiset) The multiset ordering is well-founded.

Proof. By the Well-foundedness Note 6.3 it suffices to prove that the ordering $\prec$ is well-founded. Consider a sequence $\xi := m_0,\ m_1,\ m_2,\ \ldots$ of finite multisets of natural numbers such that $m_{i+1} \prec m_i$ for $i \geq 0$. We construct by induction a finitely branching tree T whose nodes are natural numbers, such that at the stage i all the elements of m_i are leaves of the tree so far constructed and in such a way that

$$\text{each element of } T \text{ is larger than its children.} \tag{6.1}$$

As the root of T we choose a natural number n larger than all the elements of m_0.

Base. $i = 0$. Extend T by adding all the elements of m_0 as the children of n in T.

Induction step. Extend T by adding all the elements of $new(m_{i+1}, m_i)$ as the children of $old(m_{i+1}, m_i)$ in T. In case $new(m_{i+1}, m_i)$ is empty, no action is performed.

In the case of the multisets studied in Example 6.1 this construction is summarized in Figure 6.1, where 8 is chosen as the root of the tree.

Suppose now by contradiction that ξ is infinite. Then infinitely often the set $new(m_{i+1}, m_i)$ is non-empty, since otherwise from some moment on the cardinality of m_i would strictly decrease. Thus infinitely often new elements were added to T, i.e. T is infinite. By König's Lemma 6.2 T has an infinite branch which contradicts (6.1).   □

This theorem has a charming interpretation in the form of a ball game (see Smullyan [Smu79]). Consider balls labelled with natural numbers. Suppose that we have a box filled with a finite number of such balls. We are allowed to repeatedly replace a ball by a finite number of balls, all with smaller numbers. For example, a ball with number 100 can be replaced by $10^{10^{10}}$ balls with number 99. Then eventually the box will be empty.

6.2   Terminating Programs

6.2.1   Syntactic Issues

When studying logic and pure Prolog programs we should first fix a first-order language w.r.t. which they are analyzed. Usually, one associates with the program the language determined by it — its function and relation symbols are the ones occurring in the program (see, e.g., Lloyd [Llo87] and Apt [Apt90]).

Another choice was made by Kunen [Kun89] who assumed a universal first-order language $\mathcal{L}$ with infinitely many function and relation symbols in each arity, in which all programs and queries are written. One can think of this language as the language defined by a Prolog manual, so this choice better reflects the reality of programming, In practise, of course only finitely many function and relation symbols will be supported by an implementation.

In this chapter we follow the latter alternative. At first sight a choice of such a universal language seems to be unusual, because only finitely many function and relation symbols occur in every program and a query. However, for each query this set of symbols is different and it is artificial to impose a syntactic restriction on the queries which may be used for a given program. It is useful to add that the specific results obtained in this chapter do not depend on this choice of the language.

All considered interpretations are interpretations for this universal language $\mathcal{L}$. In addition, all notions referring to the syntax, like $ground(P)$ are defined with respect to $\mathcal{L}$.

Finally, recall that in Chapter 5 we used ambivalent syntax. To be able to deal formally with all pure Prolog programs we allow ambivalent syntax in $\mathcal{L}$ as well. Thus, $\mathcal{L}$ is not a first-order language, but rather an extension of a first-order language in which ambivalent syntax is used. This generalization does not lead to any complications and allows us to use here all the formal results established in Chapters 2–4.

6.2.2   Recurrent Programs

We begin our study of termination by analyzing termination in a very strong sense, namely w.r.t. all selection rules. This notion of termination is more applicable to logic programs than to Prolog programs. However, it is easier to handle and it will provide us with a useful basis from which a transition to the case of pure Prolog programs will be quite natural.

In this section we study the terminating programs in the following sense.

Definition 6.5 A program is called *terminating* if all its SLD-derivations starting with a ground query are finite. $\qquad\qquad$ □

Hence, terminating programs have the property that the SLD-trees of ground queries are finite and any search procedure in such trees will always terminate independently from the adopted selection rule. When studying Prolog programs, one is actually interested in proving the termination of a given program not only for all ground queries but also for a class of non-ground queries constituting the intended queries. The method of proving termination considered here will allow us to identify such a class of non-ground queries for each program. As we shall see below, many Prolog programs, including SUM, LIST and APPEND are terminating.

To prove that a program is terminating the following concepts due to Bezem [Bez93] and Cavedon [Cav89] play a crucial role.

Definition 6.6

- A *level mapping* for a program P is a function $| \ | : HB_P \rightarrow N$ of ground atoms to natural numbers. For $A \in HB_P$, $|A|$ is the *level of A*.
- A clause of P is called *recurrent with respect to a level mapping* $| \ |$, if for every ground instance $A \leftarrow \mathbf{A}, B, \mathbf{B}$ of it

$$|A| > |B|.$$

- A program P is called *recurrent with respect to a level mapping* $| \ |$, if all its clauses are. P is called *recurrent* if it is recurrent with respect to some level mapping. $\qquad\square$

First, following Bezem [Bez93], let us "lift" the concept of level mapping to non-ground atoms.

Definition 6.7

- An atom A is called *bounded with respect to a level mapping* $| \ |$, if for some $k \geq 0$ for every ground instance A' of A we have $|A'| \leq k$. For A bounded w.r.t. $| \ |$, we define $|A|$, the *level of A* w.r.t. $| \ |$, as the maximum $| \ |$ takes on $ground(A)$.
- A query is called *bounded with respect to a level mapping* $| \ |$, if all its atoms are. For $Q := A_1, \ldots, A_n$ bounded w.r.t. $| \ |$, we define $|Q|$, the *level of Q* w.r.t. $| \ |$, as the multiset $bag\,(|A_1|, \ldots, |A_n|)$. If $|A_i| \leq k$ for $i \in [1, n]$, we say that Q is *bounded by k*. $\qquad\square$

Strictly speaking, for an atomic query A, the notation $|A|$ has now a double meaning, depending whether we view A as an atom or as a query. In the sequel it will be always clear which of these two interpretations is used.

6.2.3 Relating Recurrent and Terminating Programs

We now prove that every recurrent program is terminating. To this end the concept of boundedness is helpful, as the following lemma shows. Recall that $\prec_m$ stands for the multiset ordering defined in Section 6.1.

Lemma 6.8 (Boundedness 1) Let P be a program that is recurrent w.r.t. a level mapping $|\ |$. Let Q_1 be a query that is bounded w.r.t. $|\ |$ and let Q_2 be an SLD-resolvent of Q_1 and a clause from P. Then

- Q_2 is bounded w.r.t. $|\ |$,
- $|Q_2| \prec_m |Q_1|$.

Proof. An SLD-resolvent of a query and a clause is obtained by means of the following three operations:

- instantiation of the query,
- instantiation of the clause,
- replacement of an atom, say H, of a query by the body of a clause whose head is H.

Thus the lemma is an immediate consequence of the following claims in which we refer to the given level mapping.

Claim 1 An instance Q' of a bounded query Q is bounded and $|Q'| \preceq_m |Q|$.

Proof. It suffices to note that an instance A' of a bounded atom A is bounded and $|A'| \leq |A|$. $\qquad\square$

Claim 2 An instance of a recurrent clause is recurrent.

Proof. Obvious. $\qquad\square$

Claim 3 For every recurrent clause $H \leftarrow \mathbf{B}$ and sequences of atoms $\mathbf{A}$ and $\mathbf{C}$, if $\mathbf{A}, H, \mathbf{C}$ is bounded, then $\mathbf{A}, \mathbf{B}, \mathbf{C}$ is bounded and $|\mathbf{A}, \mathbf{B}, \mathbf{C}| \prec_m |\mathbf{A}, H, \mathbf{C}|$.

Proof. First we prove the claim when both $\mathbf{A}$ and $\mathbf{C}$ are empty. Consider an atom C occurring in a ground instance of $\mathbf{B}$. Then it occurs in the body of a ground instance of $H \leftarrow \mathbf{B}$, say $H\theta \leftarrow \mathbf{B}\theta$. By Claim 2 $|C| < |H\theta|$, so $|C| < |H|$. This proves that $\mathbf{B}$ is bounded and $|\mathbf{B}| \prec_m |H|$.

The general case now follows from the definition of the multiset ordering. $\quad\square$
$\qquad\qquad\qquad\qquad\qquad\qquad\qquad\qquad\qquad\qquad\qquad\qquad\qquad\qquad\qquad\quad\square$

The following conclusions are now immediate.

Corollary 6.9 (Finiteness 1) Let P be an recurrent program and Q a bounded query. Then all SLD-derivations of $P \cup \{Q\}$ are finite.

Proof. By the Boundedness 1 Lemma 6.8 and the Multiset Theorem 6.4. $\qquad\square$

Corollary 6.10 (Termination 1) Every recurrent program is terminating.

Proof. Every ground query is bounded.   □

These corollaries can be easily applied to various pure Prolog programs. The level mapping can be usually defined as a simple function of the terms of the ground atom. The following natural concept will be useful.

Define by induction a function $|\ |$, called *listsize*, which assigns natural numbers to ground terms:

$$\begin{aligned}
|[x|xs]| &= |xs| + 1, \\
|f(x_1, \ldots, x_n)| &= 0 \text{ if } f \neq [.\,|\,.].
\end{aligned}$$

In particular, $|[\,]| = 0$. Note that for a list xs, $|xs|$ equals its length.

For queries with one atom it is often easy to establish boundedness by proving a stronger property.

Definition 6.11 Let $|\ |$ be a level mapping. An atom A is called *rigid* w.r.t. $|\ |$ if $|\ |$ is constant on the set $ground(A)$ of ground instances of A.   □

Obviously, rigid atoms are bounded. Let us see now how the above results can be applied to prove termination.

Example 6.12 Consider the program LIST:

```
% list(Xs)  ←  Xs is a list.
list([]).
list([_ | Ts])  ←  list(Ts).
```

Define

$$|\texttt{list(t)}| = |\texttt{t}|.$$

It is straightforward to see that LIST is recurrent w.r.t. $|\ |$ and that for a list t, the atom list(t) is rigid w.r.t. $|\ |$. By the Termination 1 Corollary 6.10 we conclude that LIST is terminating and by the Finiteness 1 Corollary 6.9 for a list t, all SLD-derivations of LIST $\cup$ {list(t)} are finite.   □

6.3   Applications

The notion of termination introduced in Definition 6.5 is very strong. We now show that quite a few simple programs are terminating in this sense.

Member
To start with, consider the program MEMBER:

```
% member(Element, List)  ←  Element is an element of the list List.
member(X, [X | _]).
member(X, [_ | Xs])  ←  member(X, Xs).
```

Using the level mapping

$$|\mathtt{member}(\mathrm{x}, \mathrm{y})| = |\mathrm{y}|$$

we conclude by the Termination 1 Corollary 6.10 that MEMBER is terminating and by the Finiteness 1 Corollary 6.9 that for a list t, all SLD-derivations of MEMBER $\cup$ {member(s, t)} are finite.

Subset

So far we have dealt with the termination of programs which have a very simple structure — their clause bodies had at most one atom. For such programs and atomic queries termination for all selection rules coincides with termination for one selection rule. The program SUBSET:

```
% subset(Xs, Ys) ←  each element of the list Xs is a member of the list Ys.
subset([], _).
subset([X | Xs], Ys) ← member(X, Ys), subset(Xs, Ys).
```

augmented by the MEMBER program.

has a slightly more complicated structure. We now prove that SUBSET is recurrent. To this end we use the following level mapping:

$$\begin{aligned} |\mathtt{member}(\mathrm{x}, \mathrm{xs})| &= |\mathrm{xs}|, \\ |\mathtt{subset}(\mathrm{xs}, \mathrm{ys})| &= |\mathrm{xs}| + |\mathrm{ys}|. \end{aligned}$$

By the Termination 1 Corollary 6.10 SUBSET is terminating and consequently by the Finiteness 1 Corollary 6.9 if xs and ys are lists, all SLD-derivations of SUBSET $\cup$ {subset(xs, ys)} are finite. Consequently, for the query subset(xs,ys) we may reorder the atoms in the body of the second clause without affecting the termination.

In general, various choices for the level mapping exist and for each choice different conclusions can be drawn. The following three simple examples illustrate this point.

Append

In general, different level mappings may yield different classes of bounded queries. An example is the program APPEND:

```
% app(Xs, Ys, Zs) ←  Zs is the result of concatenating the lists Xs and Ys.
app([], Ys, Ys).
app([X | Xs], Ys, [X | Zs]) ← app(Xs, Ys, Zs).
```

It is easy to check that APPEND is recurrent w.r.t. the level mapping

$$|\mathtt{app}(\mathrm{xs}, \mathrm{ys}, \mathrm{zs})| = |\mathrm{xs}|$$

and also with respect to the level mapping

$$|\mathtt{app}(\mathrm{xs}, \mathrm{ys}, \mathrm{zs})| = |\mathrm{zs}|.$$

In each case we obtain different class of bounded queries. The level mapping

$$|\mathrm{app}(\mathrm{xs}, \mathrm{ys}, \mathrm{zs})| = \min(|\mathrm{xs}|, |\mathrm{zs}|)$$

combines the advantages of both of them. APPEND is easily seen to be recurrent w.r.t. this level mapping and if xs is a list or zs is a list, app(xs, ys, zs) is bounded (though not rigid). By the Termination 1 Corollary 6.10 APPEND is terminating and by the Finiteness 1 Corollary 6.9 if xs is a list or zs is a list, all SLD-derivations of APPEND ∪ {app(xs, ys, zs)} are finite.

Select
Next, analyze the program SELECT:

```
% select(X, Xs, Zs)  ←  Zs is the result of deleting one occurrence of X
                         from the list Xs.
select(X, [X | Xs], Xs).
select(X, [Y | Xs], [Y | Zs])  ←  select(X, Xs, Zs).
```

As in the case of the APPEND program, it is more advantageous to use the level mapping

$$|\mathrm{select}(\mathrm{x}, \mathrm{ys}, \mathrm{zs})| = \min(|\mathrm{ys}|, |\mathrm{zs}|).$$

Then SELECT is recurrent w.r.t | | and if ys is a list or zs is a list, all SLD-derivations of SELECT ∪ {select(x, ys, zs)} are finite.

Sum
Now consider the program SUM:

```
% sum(X, Y, Z)  ←  X, Y, Z are numerals such that Z is the sum of X and Y.
sum(X, 0, X).
sum(X, s(Y), s(Z))  ←  sum(X, Y, Z).
```

Again, it is more advantageous to use here the level mapping

$$|\mathrm{sum}(\mathrm{x}, \mathrm{y}, \mathrm{z})| = \min(\mathrm{size}(\mathrm{y}), \mathrm{size}(\mathrm{z})),$$

where for a term t, size(t) denotes the number of symbols in t.

Then SUM is recurrent w.r.t. | | and for a ground y or z, sum(x, y, z) is bounded w.r.t. | |. By the Termination 1 Corollary 6.10 SUM is terminating and by the Finiteness 1 Corollary 6.9 for a ground y or z, all SLD-derivations of SUM ∪ {sum(x, y, z)} are finite.

Palindrome
In some circumstances the level mappings needed to prove termination are a bit
artificial since a strict decrease of the level mapping is required from the clause
head to the atoms of the clause body. We shall return to this problem in Section
6.8. An example is the case of the program PALINDROME:

```
% palindrome(Xs)  ←  the list Xs is equal to its reverse.
palindrome(Xs)  ←  reverse(Xs, Xs).

% reverse(Xs, Ys)  ←   Ys is the reverse of the list Xs.
reverse(X1s, X2s)  ←  reverse(X1s, [], X2s).

% reverse(Xs, Ys, Zs)  ←  Zs is the result of concatenating
                          the reverse of the list Xs and the list Ys.
reverse([], Xs, Xs).
reverse([X | X1s], X2s, Ys)  ←  reverse(X1s, [X | X2s], Ys).
```

We leave it to the reader to check that PALINDROME is indeed recurrent w.r.t.
the following level mapping $|\ |$:

$$
\begin{aligned}
|\texttt{palindrome}(\mathtt{xs})| &= 2 \cdot |\mathtt{xs}| + 2, \\
|\texttt{reverse}(\mathtt{xs}, \mathtt{ys})| &= 2 \cdot |\mathtt{xs}| + 1, \\
|\texttt{reverse}(\mathtt{xs}, \mathtt{ys}, \mathtt{zs})| &= 2 \cdot |\mathtt{xs}| + |\mathtt{ys}|.
\end{aligned}
$$

Consequently, again by the Finiteness 1 Corollary 6.9 for a ground xs all SLD-
derivations of PALINDROME $\cup$ {palindrome(xs)} are finite.

Exercise 67 Prove that the programs NUMERAL, LESS and LENGTH are terminating. $\square$

6.4   * Characterizing Terminating Programs

In this section we prove the converse of the Termination 1 Corollary 6.10. This
provides us with an exact characterization of terminating programs.

In what follows with a query Q we associate a tree of SLD-derivations of $P \cup \{Q\}$.
In this tree, for every query its children consist of all its SLD-resolvents "modulo
renaming" w.r.t. all program clauses and all atoms. More precisely, we introduce
the following definition.

Definition 6.13 An *S-tree for* $P \cup \{Q\}$ is a tree such that

- its branches are SLD-derivations of $P \cup \{Q\}$,
- every node Q has exactly one descendant for every atom A of Q and every
  clause c from P which is applicable to A. This descendant is a resolvent of
  Q and c w.r.t. A. $\square$

Informally, an S-tree for $P \cup \{Q\}$ groups all SLD-derivations of $P \cup \{Q\}$ provided
choices (C) and (D) defined in Section 3.5 are discarded.

Lemma 6.14 (S-tree 1) An S-tree for $P \cup \{Q\}$ is finite iff all SLD-derivations of $P \cup \{Q\}$ are finite.

Proof. By definition the S-trees are finitely branching. The claim now follows by König's Lemma 6.2. $\qquad\square$

This lemma allows us to concentrate on S-trees when studying termination.

Exercise 68 Let P be a program and Q a query.

(i) Prove that an S-tree for $P \cup \{Q\}$ is finite iff all S-trees for $P \cup \{Q\}$ are finite.

(ii) Prove that if an S-tree for $P \cup \{Q\}$ is finite, then all S-trees for $P \cup \{Q\}$ have the same height. $\qquad\square$

For a program P and a query Q, we denote by $nodes_P(Q)$ the number of nodes in an S-tree for $P \cup \{Q\}$. The above exercise shows that this notation is well-defined. The following properties of S-trees will be needed.

Lemma 6.15 (S-tree 2) Let P be a program and Q a query such that an S-tree for $P \cup \{Q\}$ is finite. Then

(i) for all substitutions θ, $nodes_P(Q\theta) \leq nodes_P(Q)$,
(ii) for all atoms A of Q, $nodes_P(A) \leq nodes_P(Q)$,
(iii) for all non-root nodes H in the S-tree for $P \cup \{Q\}$, $nodes_P(H) < nodes_P(Q)$.

Proof.
(i) Immediate by the Lifting Theorem 3.22.

(ii), (iii) Immediate by the definition. $\qquad\square$

We can now prove the desired result.

Theorem 6.16 (Recurrence) Let P be a terminating program. Then for some level mapping $|\ |$

(i) P is recurrent w.r.t. $|\ |$,
(ii) for every query Q, Q is bounded w.r.t. $|\ |$ iff all SLD-derivations of $P \cup \{Q\}$ are finite.

Proof. Define the level mapping by putting for $A \in HB_{\mathcal{L}}$

$$|A| = nodes_P(A).$$

Since P is terminating, by the S-tree 1 Lemma 6.14 this level mapping is well defined. First we prove one implication of (ii).

(ii1) Consider a query Q such that all SLD-derivations of $P \cup \{Q\}$ are finite. We prove that Q is bounded by $nodes_P(Q)$ w.r.t. $|\ |$.

To this end take an atom A occurring in a ground instance of Q. By the S-tree 2 Lemma 6.15 (i) and (ii) we have $nodes_P(A) \leq nodes_P(Q)$, so by the definition of the level mapping

$$|A| \leq nodes_P(Q) \tag{6.2}$$

which proves the claim.

(i) We now prove that P is recurrent w.r.t. $|\ |$. Take a clause $A \leftarrow B_1, \ldots, B_n$ in P and its ground instance $A\theta \leftarrow B_1\theta, \ldots, B_n\theta$. We need to show that

$$|A\theta| > |B_i\theta| \text{ for } i \in [1, n].$$

We have $A\theta\theta = A\theta$, so θ is a unifier of $A\theta$ and A. Let μ be an mgu of $A\theta$ and A. Then $\theta = \mu\delta$ for some δ, so $B_1\mu, \ldots, B_n\mu$ is an SLD-resolvent of $A\theta$ and $A \leftarrow B_1, \ldots, B_n$.

Fix $i \in [1, n]$. By the S-tree 2 Lemma 6.15 (iii) we have

$$nodes_P(A\theta) > nodes_P(B_1\mu, \ldots, B_n\mu).$$

But by (6.2) $nodes_P(B_1\mu, \ldots, B_n\mu) \geq nodes_P(B_i\theta)$, so $|A\theta| > |B_i\theta|$ by the definition of the level mapping.

(ii2) Consider a query Q which is bounded w.r.t. $|\ |$. Then by (i) and the Finiteness 1 Corollary 6.9 all SLD-derivations of $P \cup \{Q\}$ are finite. $\square$

Corollary 6.17 (Equivalence 1) A program is terminating iff it is recurrent.

Proof. By the Termination 1 Corollary 6.10 and the Recurrence Theorem 6.16. $\square$

6.5   Left Terminating Programs

6.5.1   Motivation

Because of the Equivalence 1 Corollary 6.17, recurrent programs and bounded queries are too restrictive concepts to deal with Prolog programs, as a larger class of programs and queries is terminating when adopting a specific selection rule, e.g. the leftmost selection rule.

When studying the termination of Prolog programs we need to study LD-derivations. Recall from Section 5.1 that by an *LD-derivation* we mean an SLD-derivation via the leftmost selection rule.

Example 6.18
(i) First we exhibit a terminating program P such that for a query Q of interest all LD-derivations of $P \cup \{Q\}$ are finite, whereas some SLD-derivation of $P \cup \{Q\}$ is infinite.

Consider the following program APPEND3, which is a solution to Exercise 61 of Section 5.5.

```
% app3(Xs, Ys, Zs, Us)  ←  Us is the result of concatenating the lists
                               Xs, Ys and Zs.
app3(Xs, Ys, Zs, Us)  ←  app(Xs, Ys, Vs), app(Vs, Zs, Us).
```

augmented by the `APPEND` program.

Program: APPEND3

It is easy to prove that `APPEND3` is recurrent by using the following level mapping $| \ |$:

$$|\text{app}(xs, ys, zs)| = \min(|xs|, |zs|),$$
$$|\text{app3}(xs, ys, zs, us)| = |xs| + |us| + 1.$$

Thus by the Termination 1 Corollary 6.10 `APPEND3` is terminating. Now, a typical use of the program involves a query of the form `app3(xs, ys, zs, Us)`, where `xs, ys, zs` are lists and `Us` is a variable. We shall show at the end of this section that all LD-derivations of `app3(xs, ys, zs, Us)` are finite.

On the other hand it is easy to see that an infinite SLD-derivation exists when the rightmost selection rule is used. As a consequence of the Finiteness 1 Corollary 6.9 the query `app3(xs, ys, zs, Us)` is not bounded, although according to the terminology of Section 5.1 it universally terminates, that is it can be evaluated by a finite Prolog computation.

(ii) Next, we consider a program which is not terminating but is such that all LD-derivations starting with a ground query are finite. An example of such a program is `NAIVE REVERSE`:

```
% reverse(Xs, Ys)  ←  Ys is a reverse of the list Xs.
reverse([], []).
reverse([X | Xs], Ys)  ←
    reverse(Xs, Zs),
    app(Zs, [X], Ys).
```

augmented by the `APPEND` program.

It is easy to check that the ground query `reverse(xs, ys)`, for a list `xs` with at least two elements and an arbitrary list `ys` has an infinite SLD-derivation, obtained by using the selection rule which selects the leftmost atom at the first two steps and the second leftmost atom afterwards. Thus `REVERSE` is not terminating. However, one can show that all LD-derivations starting with a query `reverse(s,y)` for s ground (or s list) are finite. □

To cope with these difficulties we first modify the definition of a terminating program in such a way that it takes into account the leftmost selection rule.

Definition 6.19 A program is called *left terminating* if all its LD-derivations starting with a ground query are finite. □

The notion of left termination is clearly more appropriate for the study of Prolog programs than that of a terminating program.

6.5.2   Acceptable Programs

To prove that a program is left terminating, and to characterize the queries that terminate w.r.t. such a program, we introduce the following concepts from Apt and Pedreschi [AP93].

Definition 6.20 Let P be a program, $|\,|$ a level mapping for P and I an interpretation of P.

- A clause of P is called *acceptable with respect to $|\,|$ and I*, if I is its model and for every ground instance $A \leftarrow \mathbf{A}, B, \mathbf{B}$ of it such that $I \models \mathbf{A}$

  $$|A| > |B|.$$

  In other words, for every ground instance $A \leftarrow B_1, \ldots, B_n$ of the clause

  $$|A| > |B_i| \text{ for } i \in [1, \bar{n}],$$

  where

  $$\bar{n} = \min(\{n\} \cup \{i \in [1, n] \mid I \not\models B_i\}).$$

- A program P is called *acceptable with respect to $|\,|$ and I*, if all its clauses are. P is called *acceptable* if it is acceptable with respect to some level mapping and an interpretation of P. □

The use of the premise $I \models \mathbf{A}$ forms the *only* difference between the concepts of recurrence and acceptability. Intuitively, this premise expresses the fact that when in the evaluation of the query $\mathbf{A}, B, \mathbf{B}$ using the leftmost selection rule the atom B is reached, the atoms $\mathbf{A}$ are already resolved. Consequently, by the soundness of the SLD-resolution (Theorem 4.4), these atoms are all true in I.

Alternatively, we may define $\bar{n}$ by

$$\bar{n} \;=\; \begin{cases} n & \text{if } I \models B_1, \ldots, B_n, \\ i & \text{if } I \models B_1, \ldots, B_{i-1} \text{ and } I \not\models B_1, \ldots, B_i. \end{cases}$$

Thus, given a level mapping $|\,|$ for P and an interpretation I of P, in the definition of acceptability w.r.t. $|\,|$ and I, for every ground instance $A \leftarrow B_1, \ldots, B_n$ if a clause in P we only require that the level of A is higher than the level of B_is in a certain prefix of $B_1, \ldots, B_n$. Which B_is are taken into account is determined by the model I. If $I \models B_1, \ldots, B_n$ then all of them are considered and otherwise only those whose index is $\leq \bar{n}$, where $\bar{n}$ is the least index i for which $I \not\models B_i$.

The following observation shows that the notion of acceptability generalizes that of recurrence.

Note 6.21 (Generalization 1) A program is P recurrent w.r.t. $|\,|$ iff it is acceptable w.r.t. $|\,|$ and $HB_{\mathcal{L}}$. □

6.5.3   Relating Acceptable and Left Terminating Programs

We now proceed in an analogous way to Section 6.2 and prove that every acceptable program is left terminating. To this end we use again the notion of boundedness. The concept of a bounded query employed here differs from that introduced in Definition 6.7 in that it takes into account the interpretation I. This results in a more complicated definition.

Given a set A, denote now the set of all subsets of A by $\mathcal{P}(A)$. In what follows, assume that the maximum function $max : \mathcal{P}(N) \to N \cup \{\omega\}$, from the set of all subsets of natural numbers to the set of natural numbers augmented by ω, is defined as

$$max\ S \ = \ \begin{cases} 0 & \text{if } S = \emptyset, \\ n & \text{if } S \text{ is finite and non-empty, and } n \text{ is the maximum of } S, \\ \omega & \text{if } S \text{ is infinite.} \end{cases}$$

Then, assuming that $n < \omega$ for all natural numbers n, $max\ S < \omega$ iff the set S is finite.

Definition 6.22 Let P be a program, $||$ a level mapping for P, I an interpretation of P and k a natural number.

- A query Q is called *bounded by k* w.r.t. $||$ and I if for every ground instance $\mathbf{A}, B, \mathbf{B}$ of it such that $I \models \mathbf{A}$

  $$|B| \leq k.$$

  A query Q is called *bounded* w.r.t. $||$ and I if it is bounded by some k w.r.t. $||$ and I.
- With each query Q with n atoms we associate n sets of natural numbers defined as follows, for $i \in [1, n]$:

  $$|Q|_i^I := \{|A_i| \mid A_1, \ldots, A_n \text{ is a ground instance of } Q \text{ and } I \models A_1, \ldots, A_{i-1}\}.$$

- With a query Q with n atoms, bounded w.r.t. $||$ and I, we associate the following multiset $|Q|_I$ of natural numbers:

  $$|Q|_I := \ bag\,(max\ |Q|_1^I, \ldots, max\ |Q|_n^I).$$

$\square$

Note that $|Q|_i^I$ is constructed as follows. First one takes the set of those ground instances of Q the first $i - 1$ atoms of which are true in I. Then $|Q|_i^I$ is the set of the i-th atoms of these instances. The following exercise clarifies the introduced notions.

Exercise 69

(i) Prove that a query Q is bounded by k w.r.t. $|\ |$ and I if $k \geq h$ for $h \in |Q|_I$.

(ii) Prove that a query Q is bounded w.r.t. $|\ |$ and I iff $|Q|_i^I$ is finite, for $i \in [1, n]$. (This shows that, for a bounded query Q, $|Q|_I$ is indeed a multiset of natural numbers.)

(iii) Prove that a query Q is bounded w.r.t. $|\ |$ and $HB_{\mathcal{L}}$ iff it is bounded w.r.t. $|\ |$ in the sense of Definition 6.7. $\square$

Note that the first atom of a bounded query is bounded and that a query with only one atom is bounded iff this atom is bounded.

We now prove a lemma analogous to the Boundedness 1 Lemma 6.8.

Lemma 6.23 (Boundedness 2) Let P be a program that is acceptable w.r.t. a level mapping $|\ |$ and an interpretation I. Let Q_1 be a query that is bounded w.r.t. $|\ |$ and I, and let Q_2 be an LD-resolvent of Q_1 and of a clause from P. Then

(i) Q_2 is bounded w.r.t. $|\ |$ and I,
(ii) $|Q_2|_I \prec_m |Q_1|_I$.

Proof. An LD-resolvent of a query and a clause is obtained by means of the following three operations:

- instantiation of the query,
- instantiation of the clause,
- replacement of the first atom, say H, of a query by the body of a clause whose head is H.

Thus the lemma is an immediate consequence of the following claims in which we refer to the given level mapping and interpretation I.

Claim 1 An instance Q' of a bounded query Q is bounded and $|Q'|_I \preceq_m |Q|_I$.

Proof. It suffices to note that $|Q'|_i^I \subseteq |Q|_i^I$ for $i \in [1, n]$, where n is the number of atoms in Q (and Q'). $\square$

Claim 2 An instance of an acceptable clause is acceptable.

Proof. Obvious. $\square$

Claim 3 For every acceptable clause $A \leftarrow \mathbf{B}$ and sequence of atoms $\mathbf{C}$, if $A, \mathbf{C}$ is bounded, then $\mathbf{B}, \mathbf{C}$ is bounded and $|\mathbf{B}, \mathbf{C}|_I \prec_m |A, \mathbf{C}|_I$.

Proof. Let $\mathbf{B} = B_1, \ldots, B_n$ and $\mathbf{C} = C_1, \ldots, C_m$, for $n, m \geq 0$. We first prove the following facts.

Fact 1 For $i \in [1, n]$, $|B_1, \ldots, B_n, C_1, \ldots, C_m|_i^I$ is finite, and

$$max|B_1, \ldots, B_n, C_1, \ldots, C_m|_i^I < max|A, C_1, \ldots, C_m|_1^I.$$

Proof. We have

$$max|B_1, \ldots, B_n, C_1, \ldots, C_m|_i^I$$

$= \quad \{\text{Definition 6.22}\}$

$$max\{|B_i'| \mid B_1', \ldots, B_n' \text{ is a ground instance of } \mathbf{B}$$
$$\text{and } I \models B_1', \ldots, B_{i-1}'\}$$

$= \quad \{\text{for some } A', \ A' \leftarrow B_1', \ldots, B_n' \text{ is a ground instance of } A \leftarrow \mathbf{B}\}$

$$max\{|B_i'| \mid A' \leftarrow B_1', \ldots, B_n' \text{ is a ground instance of } A \leftarrow \mathbf{B}$$
$$\text{and } I \models B_1', \ldots, B_{i-1}'\}$$

$< \quad \{\text{Definition 6.20 and the fact that for finite } R, S,$

$$\forall x \in S \; \exists y \in R : x < y \text{ implies } max \; S < max \; R\}$$

$$max\{|A'| \mid A' \text{ is a ground instance of } A\}$$

$= \quad \{\text{Definition 6.22}\}$

$$max|A, C_1, \ldots, C_m|_1^I.$$

$\square$

Fact 2 For $j \in [1, m]$, $|B_1, \ldots, B_n, C_1, \ldots, C_m|_{j+n}^I$ is finite, and

$$max|B_1, \ldots, B_n, C_1, \ldots, C_m|_{j+n}^I \leq max|A, C_1, \ldots, C_m|_{j+1}^I.$$

Proof. We have

$$max|B_1, \ldots, B_n, C_1, \ldots, C_m|_{j+n}^I$$

$= \quad \{\text{Definition 6.22}\}$

$$max\{|C_j'| \mid B_1', \ldots, B_n', C_1', \ldots, C_m' \text{ is a ground instance of } \mathbf{B}, \mathbf{C}$$
$$\text{and } I \models B_1', \ldots, B_n', C_1', \ldots, C_{j-1}'\}$$

$\leq \quad \{\text{for some } A', \ A' \leftarrow B_1', \ldots, B_n' \text{ is a ground instance of } A \leftarrow \mathbf{B},$

$$I \text{ is a model of } P \text{ and } S \subseteq R \text{ implies } max \; S \leq max \; R\}$$

$$max\{|C_j'| \mid A', C_1', \ldots, C_m' \text{ is a ground instance of } A, \mathbf{C}$$
$$\text{and } I \models A', C_1', \ldots \wedge C_{j-1}'\}$$

$= \quad \{\text{Definition 6.22}\}$

$$max|A, C_1, \ldots, C_m|_{j+1}^I.$$

$\square$

As a consequence of Facts 1 and 2 $\mathbf{B}, \mathbf{C}$ is bounded and

$$bag(max|\mathbf{B}, \mathbf{C}|_1^I, \ldots, max|\mathbf{B}, \mathbf{C}|_{n+m}^I) \prec_m bag(max|A, \mathbf{C}|_1^I, \ldots, max|A, \mathbf{C}|_{m+1}^I)$$

which establishes the claim.

$\square$
$\square$

This brings us to the conclusions analogous to those of Subsection 6.2.3.

Corollary 6.24 (Finiteness 2) Let P be an acceptable program and Q a bounded query. Then all LD-derivations of $P \cup \{Q\}$ are finite.

Proof. By the Boundedness 2 Lemma 6.23 and the Multiset Theorem 6.4. $\quad\square$

Corollary 6.25 (Termination 2) Every acceptable program is left terminating.

Proof. Every ground query is bounded. $\quad\square$

Let us see now how these results can be used to establish left termination of specific programs.

Example 6.26 We use here the function defined in Subsection 6.2.2, *listsize* $| \ |$, which assigns natural numbers to ground terms. Reconsider the APPEND3 program of Example 6.18. Define

$$
\begin{aligned}
|\mathrm{app}(\mathrm{xs}, \mathrm{ys}, \mathrm{zs})| &= |\mathrm{xs}|, \\
|\mathrm{app3}(\mathrm{xs}, \mathrm{ys}, \mathrm{zs}, \mathrm{us})| &= |\mathrm{xs}| + |\mathrm{ys}| + 1.
\end{aligned}
$$

and take the Herbrand interpretation

$$
\begin{aligned}
I \;:=\; &\{\mathrm{app}(\mathrm{xs}, \mathrm{ys}, \mathrm{zs}) \mid |\mathrm{xs}| + |\mathrm{ys}| = |\mathrm{zs}|\} \\
&\cup \; ground(\mathrm{app3}(\mathrm{Xs}, \mathrm{Ys}, \mathrm{Zs}, \mathrm{Us})).
\end{aligned}
$$

It is easy to see that I is a model of APPEND3. Indeed, we have $|[]|+|\mathrm{ys}| = |\mathrm{ys}|$ and if $|\mathrm{xs}|+|\mathrm{ys}| = |\mathrm{zs}|$, then $|[\mathrm{x}|\mathrm{xs}]|+|\mathrm{ys}| = 1+|\mathrm{xs}|+|\mathrm{ys}| = 1+|\mathrm{zs}| = |[\mathrm{x}|\mathrm{zs}]|$, so I is a model of APPEND. Further, the clause defining the app3 relation is obviously true in I.

We already noted in Section 6.3 that APPEND is recurrent w.r.t. $| \ |$. To see that the clause defining the app3 relation is acceptable w.r.t. $| \ |$ and I it suffices to note that $|\mathrm{xs}|+|\mathrm{ys}|+1 > |\mathrm{xs}|$ and that $|\mathrm{xs}|+|\mathrm{ys}| = |\mathrm{vs}|$ implies $|\mathrm{xs}|+|\mathrm{ys}|+1 > |\mathrm{vs}|$.

We conclude by the Termination 2 Corollary 6.25 that APPEND3 is left terminating. In addition, for all lists xs, ys, zs and an arbitrary term u, the query $\mathrm{app3}(\mathrm{xs},\mathrm{ys},\mathrm{zs},\mathrm{u})$ is bounded w.r.t. $| \ |$ and I, so by the Finiteness 2 Corollary 6.24 all LD-derivations of APPEND3 $\cup \{\mathrm{app3}(\mathrm{xs}, \mathrm{ys}, \mathrm{zs}, \mathrm{u})\}$ are finite. $\quad\square$

6.6 Applications

We now show the usefulness of the results established in the previous section by means of two further examples. In the following, we present the proof of acceptability (w.r.t. a level mapping $| \ |$ and an interpretation I) of a given clause

$c := A_0 \leftarrow A_1, \ldots, A_n$ by means of the following *proof outline*:

$$
\begin{array}{lll}
\{f_0\} & & \\
A_0 & \leftarrow & \{t_0\} \\
A_1, & & \{t_1\} \\
\quad \{f_1\} & & \\
\quad \vdots & & \\
A_{n-1}, & & \{t_{n-1}\} \\
\quad \{f_{n-1}\} & & \\
A_n. & & \{t_n\} \\
\quad \{f_n\} & &
\end{array}
$$

Here, t_i and f_i, for $i \in [0, n]$ are integer expressions and statements respectively, such that all ground instances of the following properties are satisfied:

- $t_i = |A_i|$, for $i \in [0, n]$,
- f_i holds iff $I \models A_i$, for $i \in [0, n]$,
- $f_1 \wedge \ldots \wedge f_n \Rightarrow f_0$,
- For $i \in [1, n]$: $f_1 \wedge \ldots \wedge f_{i-1} \Rightarrow t_0 > t_i$.

We omit in the proof outlines $\{f_i\}$ if $f_i = \mathbf{true}$. In addition, if we only wish to prove that an interpretation I is a model of a clause, we omit in the proof outlines $\{t_i\}$.

It is immediate that a proof outline satisfying the above properties corresponds to the proofs that I is a model of the clause c and that c is acceptable w.r.t. $|\ |$ and I.

Permutation

Consider the program PERMUTATION:

```
% perm(Xs, Ys)  ←  Ys is a permutation of the list Xs.
perm([], []).
perm(Xs, [X | Ys])  ←
    app(X1s, [X | X2s], Xs),
    app(X1s, X2s, Zs),
    perm(Zs, Ys).
```

augmented by the APPEND program.

Observe the following:

- PERMUTATION is not recurrent. Indeed, take xs, x, ys ground and consider an SLD-derivation of PERMUTATION $\cup$ {perm(xs, [x | ys])} constructed as follows. In the second query select the middle atom app(x1s, x2s, zs) and subsequently apply repeatedly the recursive clause of APPEND. In this way we obtain an infinite SLD-derivation. Thus PERMUTATION is not terminating and so by the Termination 1 Corollary 6.10 it is not recurrent.

- We already noticed in Example 6.26 that the Herbrand interpretation

$$I_{APP} = \{\mathrm{app}(\mathrm{xs},\mathrm{ys},\mathrm{zs}) \mid |\mathrm{xs}| + |\mathrm{ys}| = |\mathrm{zs}|\}$$

  is a model of the program APPEND.
- The program PERMUTATION is acceptable w.r.t. the level mapping $|\;|$ and the interpretation I_{PERM} defined by

$$|\mathrm{perm}(\mathrm{xs},\mathrm{ys})| = |\mathrm{xs}| + 1,$$
$$|\mathrm{app}(\mathrm{xs},\mathrm{ys},\mathrm{zs})| = \min(|\mathrm{xs}|,|\mathrm{zs}|),$$

$$I_{PERM} = ground(\mathrm{perm}(\mathrm{Xs},\mathrm{Ys})) \cup I_{APP}.$$

We already noticed in Subsection 6.2 that APPEND is recurrent w.r.t. $|\;|$. The proof outline for the non-recursive clause of the perm relation is obvious. For the recursive clause take the following proof outline:

$$
\begin{aligned}
\mathrm{perm}(\mathrm{xs},[\mathrm{x}|\mathrm{ys}]) \;\;\leftarrow\;\; & &\{|\mathrm{xs}|+1\}\\
& \mathrm{app}(\mathrm{x1s},[\mathrm{x}|\mathrm{x2s}],\mathrm{xs}), &\{\min(|\mathrm{x1s}|,|\mathrm{xs}|)\}\\
& \quad\{|\mathrm{x1s}|+1+|\mathrm{x2s}|=|\mathrm{xs}|\}\\
& \mathrm{app}(\mathrm{x1s},\mathrm{x2s},\mathrm{zs}), &\{\min(|\mathrm{x1s}|,|\mathrm{zs}|)\}\\
& \quad\{|\mathrm{x1s}|+|\mathrm{x2s}|=|\mathrm{zs}|\}\\
& \mathrm{perm}(\mathrm{zs},\mathrm{ys}). &\{|\mathrm{zs}|+1\}
\end{aligned}
$$

Using the Termination 2 Corollary 6.25 we conclude that PERMUTATION is left terminating. Moreover, we obtain that, for a list s and a term t, the atom perm(s,t) is rigid and hence bounded. Consequently, by the Finiteness 2 Corollary 6.24, all LD-derivations of PERMUTATION $\cup\{\mathrm{perm}(\mathrm{s},\mathrm{t})\}$ are finite.

Sequence
The choice of the level mapping and of the model can affect the class of queries whose termination can be established. To see this consider the program SEQUENCE:

```
% sequence(Xs)  ←  Xs is a list of 27 elements.
sequence([_,_,_,_,_,_,_,_,_,_,_,_,_,_,_,_,_,_,_,_,_,_,_,_,_,_,_]).

% question(Ss)  ←  Ss is a list of 27 elements forming the desired sequence.
question(Ss)  ←
    sequence(Ss),
    sublist([1,_,1,_,1], Ss),
    sublist([2,_,_,2,_,_,2], Ss),
    sublist([3,_,_,_,3,_,_,_,3], Ss),
    sublist([4,_,_,_,_,4,_,_,_,_,4], Ss),
    sublist([5,_,_,_,_,_,5,_,_,_,_,_,5], Ss),
    sublist([6,_,_,_,_,_,_,6,_,_,_,_,_,_,6], Ss),
    sublist([7,_,_,_,_,_,_,_,7,_,_,_,_,_,_,_,7], Ss),
```

```
sublist([8,_,_,_,_,_,_,_,_,8,_,_,_,_,_,_,_,_,_,8], Ss),
sublist([9,_,_,_,_,_,_,_,_,_,9,_,_,_,_,_,_,_,_,_,9], Ss).
```

```
% sublist(Xs, Ys)  ←  Xs is a sublist of the list Ys.
sublist(Xs, Ys)  ←  app(_, Zs, Ys), app(Xs, _, Zs).
```

augmented by the APPEND program.

It is straightforward to verify that SEQUENCE is recurrent (so by the Generalization 1 Note 6.21 acceptable when the model $HB_\mathcal{L}$ is used) w.r.t. the level mapping $|\ |$ defined by

$$
\begin{aligned}
|\texttt{question(xs)}| &= |\texttt{xs}| + 23, \\
|\texttt{sequence(xs)}| &= 0, \\
|\texttt{sublist(xs,ys)}| &= |\texttt{xs}| + |\texttt{ys}| + 1, \\
|\texttt{app(xs,ys,zs)}| &= \min(|\texttt{xs}|, |\texttt{zs}|).
\end{aligned}
$$

Consequently, by the Finiteness 1 Corollary 6.9, for all ground terms s, all SLD-derivations (thus *a fortiori* all LD-derivations) of SEQUENCE $\cup$ {question(s)} are finite. However, with this choice of the level mapping we face the problem that the atom question(Ss) is not bounded. Consequently, we cannot use the Finiteness 2 Corollary 6.24 to prove termination of this query w.r.t. the leftmost selection rule. The situation is analogous to that of the program APPEND3 of Example 6.18(i).

To prove this stronger termination property we change the above level mapping by putting

$$
|\texttt{question(xs)}| = 50,
$$

and choose any model I of SEQUENCE such that for a ground s

$$
I \models \texttt{sequence(s)} \text{ iff s is a list of 27 elements.}
$$

Then SEQUENCE is acceptable w.r.t. $|\ |$ and I. Moreover, the query question(Ss) is now bounded w.r.t. $|\ |$ and, consequently, by the Finiteness 2 Corollary 6.24, all LD-derivations of SEQUENCE $\cup$ {question(Ss)} are finite.

Exercise 70 Provide a proof outline showing that with the above choice of the level mapping and the interpretation SEQUENCE is acceptable. □

Exercise 71 The level mapping used in the proof of acceptability of SEQUENCE implies that for all lists s,t all LD-derivations of sublist(s,t) are finite. Show that the requirement that s is a list is not needed to draw this conclusion. □

6.7   * Characterizing Left Terminating Programs

We now characterize the class of left terminating programs by proving the converse of the Termination 2 Corollary 6.25. To this end we proceed analogously as in the case of terminating programs and analyze the size of finite LD-trees.

Exercise 72 Let P be a program and Q a query.

   (i) Prove that an LD-tree for $P \cup \{Q\}$ is finite iff all LD-trees for $P \cup \{Q\}$ are finite.

   (ii) Prove that if an LD-tree for $P \cup \{Q\}$ is finite, then all LD-trees for $P \cup \{Q\}$ have the same height.   □

We need the following analog of the S-tree 2 Lemma 6.15, where for a program P and a query Q we now denote by $lnodes_P(Q)$ the number of nodes in an LD-tree for $P \cup \{Q\}$. Exercise 72 shows that this notation is well-defined.

Lemma 6.27 (LD-tree) Let P be a program and Q a query such that an LD-tree for $P \cup \{Q\}$ is finite. Then

   (i) for all substitutions θ, $lnodes_P(Q\theta) \leq lnodes_P(Q)$,
   (ii) for all prefixes Q' of Q, $lnodes_P(Q') \leq lnodes_P(Q)$,
   (iii) for all non-root nodes Q' in the LD-tree for $P \cup \{Q\}$, $lnodes_P(Q') < lnodes_P(Q)$.

Proof.
(i) Immediate by the Lifting Theorem 3.22.

(ii) Consider a prefix $Q' := A_1, \ldots, A_k$ of $Q := A_1, \ldots, A_n$ $(n \geq k)$. By an appropriate renaming of variables, we can assume on the account of the Variant Corollary 3.19 that all input clauses used in an LD-tree for $P \cup \{Q'\}$ have no variables in common with Q. We can now transform the LD-tree for $P \cup \{Q'\}$ into an initial subtree of an LD-tree for $P \cup \{Q\}$ by replacing in it a node $\mathbf{B}$ by $\mathbf{B}, A_{k+1}\theta, \ldots, A_n\theta$, where θ is the composition of the mgus used on the path from the root Q' to the node $\mathbf{B}$. This implies the claim.

(iii) Immediate by the definition.   □

We can now demonstrate the desired result which is a counterpart of the Recurrence Theorem 6.16.

Theorem 6.28 (Acceptability) Let P be a left terminating program. Then for some level mapping $|\ |$ and an interpretation I of P

   (i) P is acceptable w.r.t. $|\ |$ and I,
   (ii) for every query Q, Q is bounded w.r.t. $|\ |$ and I iff all LD-derivations of $P \cup \{Q\}$ are finite.

Proof. Define the level mapping by putting for $A \in HB_{\mathcal{L}}$

$$|A| = lnodes_P(A).$$

Since P is left terminating, this level mapping is well defined. Next, choose

$$I := \{A \in HB_{\mathcal{L}} \mid \text{there is a successful LD-derivation of } P \cup \{A\}\}.$$

By the Success Theorem 2 4.37 we have $I = \mathcal{M}(P)$, so I is a model of P.

First we prove one implication of (ii).

(ii1) Consider a query Q such that all LD-derivations of $P \cup \{Q\}$ are finite. We prove that Q is bounded by $lnodes_P(Q)$ w.r.t. $|\,|$ and I.

To this end take $\ell \in |Q|_I$. For some ground instance $A_1, \ldots, A_n$ of Q and $i \in [1, \bar{n}]$, where

$$\bar{n} = \min(\{n\} \cup \{i \in [1, n] \mid I \not\models A_i\}),$$

we have $\ell = |A_i|$. We now calculate

$$
\begin{array}{rl}
& lnodes_P(Q) \\
\geq & \{\text{LD-tree Lemma 6.27 (i)}\} \\
& lnodes_P(A_1, \ldots, A_n) \\
\geq & \{\text{LD-tree Lemma 6.27 (ii)}\} \\
& lnodes_P(A_1, \ldots, A_{\bar{n}}) \\
\geq & \{\text{LD-tree Lemma 6.27 (iii), noting that for } j \in [1, \bar{n} - 1] \\
& \quad \text{there is a successful LD-derivation of } P \cup \{A_1, \ldots, A_j\}\} \\
& lnodes_P(A_i, \ldots, A_{\bar{n}}) \\
\geq & \{\text{LD-tree Lemma 6.27 (ii)}\} \\
& lnodes_P(A_i) \\
= & \{\text{definition of } |\,|\} \\
& |A_i| \\
= & \ell.
\end{array}
$$

(i) We now prove that P is acceptable w.r.t. $|\,|$ and I. Take a clause $A \leftarrow B_1, \ldots, B_n$ in P and its ground instance $A\theta \leftarrow B_1\theta, \ldots, B_n\theta$. We need to show that

$$|A\theta| > |B_i\theta| \text{ for } i \in [1, \bar{n}],$$

where

$$\bar{n} := \min(\{n\} \cup \{i \in [1, n] \mid I \not\models B_i\theta\}).$$

We have $A\theta\theta = A\theta$, so $A\theta$ and A unify. Let μ be an mgu of $A\theta$ and A. Then $\theta = \mu\delta$ for some δ. By the definition of LD-resolution, $B_1\mu, \ldots, B_n\mu$ is an LD-resolvent of $A\theta$.

Then for $i \in [1, \bar{n}]$

$$
\begin{array}{rl}
& |A\theta| \\
= & \{\text{definition of } |\,|\} \\
& lnodes_P(A\theta) \\
> & \{\text{LD-tree Lemma 6.27 (iii), } B_1\mu, \ldots, B_n\mu \text{ is a resolvent of } A\theta\}
\end{array}
$$

$$lnodes_P\,(B_1\mu,\ldots,B_n\mu)$$
$$\geq\quad \{\text{part (ii1), with } Q := B_1\mu,\ldots,B_n\mu \text{ and } A_i := B_i\theta\}$$
$$|B_i\theta|.$$

(ii2) Consider a query Q which is bounded w.r.t. $|\ |$ and I. Then by (i) and the Finiteness 2 Corollary 6.24 all LD-derivations of $P \cup \{Q\}$ are finite. $\qquad\square$

Corollary 6.29 (Equivalence 2) A program is left terminating iff it is acceptable.

Proof. By the Termination 2 Corollary 6.25 and the Acceptability Theorem 6.28. $\qquad\square$

6.8   * An Improvement

6.8.1   Motivation

The notions of recurrence and of acceptability stipulate that level mappings decrease from clause heads to clause bodies. This is used for two different purposes:

(i) in (mutually) recursive calls, to ensure termination of (mutually) recursive procedures, and

(ii) in non- (mutually) recursive calls, to ensure that non- (mutually) recursive procedures are called with terminating queries.

Although a decreasing of the level mappings is apparently essential for the first purpose, this is not the case for the second purpose, since a weaker condition can be adopted to ensure that non-recursive procedures are properly called.

In this section we elaborate on this idea, by presenting alternative definitions of recurrence and of acceptability, that we qualify with the prefix *semi*. These notions are actually proved equivalent to the original ones, but they give rise to more flexible proof methods.

Following the intuition that recursive and non-recursive procedures should be handled separately in proving termination, we introduce a natural ordering over the relation names occurring in a program P, with the intention that for relations p and q, $p \sqsupseteq q$ holds if p can "call" q. The next definition makes this concept precise by defining first when two relation symbols occurring in a program are mutually recursive.

We use here the notion of a transitive reflexive closure of a relation defined in Section 2.6.

Definition 6.30 Let P be a program and p, q be relation symbols occurring in it.

- We say that p *refers to* q *in* P if there is a clause in P that uses p in its head and q in its body.

- We say that p *depends on* q *in* P and write $p \sqsupseteq q$, if (p, q) is in the transitive, reflexive closure of the relation *refers to*.
- We say that p and q are *mutually recursive* and write $p \simeq q$, if $p \sqsupseteq q$ and $q \sqsupseteq p$. In particular, p and p are mutually recursive. $\square$

We also write $p \sqsupset q$ when $p \sqsupseteq q$ and $q \not\sqsupseteq p$. According to the above definition, $p \simeq q := p \sqsupseteq q$ and $q \sqsupseteq p$ means that p and q are mutually recursive and $p \sqsupset q := p \sqsupseteq q$ and $q \not\sqsupseteq p$ means that p calls q as a subprogram.

Exercise 73 Prove that for every program the ordering $\sqsupset$ over its relation symbols is well-founded. $\square$

6.8.2 Semi-recurrent programs

The following definition of *semi-recurrence* exploits the introduced orderings over the relation symbols. The level mapping is required to decrease from an atom A in the head of a clause to an atom B in the body of that clause only if the relations of A and B are mutually recursive. Additionally, the level mapping is required not to increase from A to B if the relations of A and B are not mutually recursive.

We denote here by $rel(A)$ the relation symbol occurring in atom A.

Definition 6.31

- A clause is called *semi-recurrent with respect to a level mapping* $|\ |$, if for every ground instance $A \leftarrow \mathbf{A}, B, \mathbf{B}$ of it

  (i) $|A| > |B|$ if $rel(A) \simeq rel(B)$,

  (ii) $|A| \geq |B|$ if $rel(A) \sqsupset rel(B)$.

- A program P is called *semi-recurrent with respect to a level mapping* $|\ |$, if all its clauses are. P is called *semi-recurrent* if it is semi-recurrent with respect to some level mapping. $\square$

The following observation is immediate.

Note 6.32 (Semi-recurrence) If a program is recurrent w.r.t. $|\ |$, then it is semi-recurrent w.r.t. $|\ |$. $\square$

The converse of the Semi-recurrence Note 6.32 also holds, in a sense made precise by the following result.

Lemma 6.33 (Reduction 1) If a program is semi-recurrent w.r.t. $|\ |$, then it is recurrent w.r.t. a level mapping $||\ ||$. Moreover, for each atom A, if A is bounded w.r.t. $|\ |$, then A is bounded w.r.t. $||\ ||$.

Proof. In order to define the level mapping $\| \ \|$, we first introduce a mapping $| \ |$ from the relation symbols of P to natural numbers such that, for two relation symbols p, q occurring in P,

$$p \simeq q \quad \text{implies} \quad |p| = |q|, \tag{6.3}$$
$$p \sqsupset q \quad \text{implies} \quad |p| > |q|. \tag{6.4}$$

A mapping $| \ |$ satisfying these two properties obviously exists.

Next, we define a level mapping $\| \ \|$ for P by putting for $A \in HB_{\mathcal{L}}$:

$$\|A\| = |A| + |rel(A)|.$$

We now prove that P is recurrent w.r.t. $\| \ \|$. Let $A \leftarrow \mathbf{A}, B, \mathbf{B}$ be a ground instance of a clause from P. Two cases arise.

Case 1 $rel(A) \simeq rel(B)$.
Then $\|A\| > \|B\|$ on account of Definition 6.31(i) and (6.3).

Case 2 $rel(A) \sqsupset rel(B)$.
Then $\|A\| > \|B\|$ on account of Definition 6.31(ii) and (6.4).

So in both cases $\|A\| > \|B\|$, which establishes the first claim. The second claim follows directly from the definition of $\| \ \|$. $\square$

The following is an immediate conclusion of the Semi-recurrence Note 6.32 and the Reduction 1 Lemma 6.33.

Corollary 6.34 (Equivalence 3) A program is recurrent iff it is semi-recurrent. $\square$

6.8.3   Semi-acceptable programs

An analogous modification of the notion of acceptability yields a more flexible approach to the proofs of left termination.

Definition 6.35 Let P be a program, $| \ |$ a level mapping for P and I a (not necessarily Herbrand) interpretation of P.

- A clause of P is called *semi-acceptable with respect to $| \ |$ and I*, if I is its model and for every ground instance $A \leftarrow \mathbf{A}, B, \mathbf{B}$ of it such that $I \models \mathbf{A}$

  (i) $|A| > |B|$ if $rel(A) \simeq rel(B)$,

  (ii) $|A| \geq |B|$ if $rel(A) \sqsupset rel(B)$.

- A program P is called *semi-acceptable with respect to $\| \ \|$ and I*, if all its clauses are. P is called *semi-acceptable* if it is semi-acceptable with respect to some level mapping and an interpretation of P. $\square$

The use of the premise $I \models \mathbf{A}$ forms the *only* difference between the concepts of semi-recurrence and semi-acceptability.

The following observations are immediate. The first one is a counterpart of the Generalization 1 Note 6.21.

Note 6.36 (Generalization 2) A program P is semi-recurrent w.r.t. $|\ |$ iff it is semi-acceptable w.r.t. $|\ |$ and $HB_{\mathcal{L}}$. $\square$

Lemma 6.37 (Semi-acceptability) If a program P is acceptable w.r.t. $|\ |$ and I, then it is semi-acceptable w.r.t. $|\ |$ and I. $\square$

In addition, the following analog of the Reduction 1 Lemma 6.33 holds.

Lemma 6.38 (Reduction 2) If a program is semi-acceptable w.r.t. $|\ |$ and I, then it is acceptable w.r.t. a level mapping $||\ ||$ and the same interpretation I. Moreover, for each atom A, if A is bounded w.r.t. $|\ |$, then A is bounded w.r.t. $||\ ||$. $\square$

Exercise 74 Prove the Reduction 2 Lemma 6.38. $\square$

We conclude by noting the following direct consequence of the Semi-acceptability Lemma 6.37 and the Reduction 2 Lemma 6.38.

Corollary 6.39 (Equivalence 4)   A program is acceptable iff it is semi-acceptable. $\square$

6.8.4   Examples

To see that the notions of semi-recurrence and semi-acceptability indeed lead to more natural level mappings reconsider two programs studied before.

Palindrome
When proving in Section 6.3 that `PALINDROME` is recurrent we had to repeatedly use "+1" to ensure the decrease of the level mapping. Now a simpler level mapping $|\ |$ suffices:

$$
\begin{aligned}
|\mathtt{palindrome(xs)}| &= 2 \cdot |\mathtt{xs}|, \\
|\mathtt{reverse(xs,ys)}| &= 2 \cdot |\mathtt{xs}|, \\
|\mathtt{reverse(xs,ys,zs)}| &= 2 \cdot |\mathtt{xs}| + |\mathtt{ys}|.
\end{aligned}
$$

It is straightforward to check that `PALINDROME` is semi-recurrent w.r.t. the level mapping $|\ |$.

Sequence

It is easy to see that SEQUENCE is semi-acceptable w.r.t. the level mapping $| \ |$ defined by

$$
\begin{aligned}
|\texttt{question(xs)}| &= 48, \\
|\texttt{sequence(xs)}| &= 0, \\
|\texttt{sublist(xs, ys)}| &= |\texttt{xs}| + |\texttt{ys}|, \\
|\texttt{app(xs, ys, zs)}| &= \min(|\texttt{xs}|, |\texttt{zs}|).
\end{aligned}
$$

and (as before) any model I of SEQUENCE such that for a ground s

$$I \models \texttt{sequence(s)} \text{ iff s is a list of 27 elements.}$$

Again, in the above level mapping it was possible to disregard the accumulated use of "+1s". In addition, it is somewhat more natural to use 48 instead of 50 as in Section 6.6, because for a ground list s of 27 elements we have

$$|\texttt{sublist}([9, \_, \_, \_, \_, \_, \_, \_, \_, \_, 9, \_, \_, \_, \_, \_, \_, \_, \_, \_, \_, 9], \ \texttt{s})| = 48.$$

Exercise 75 Show that the program PERMUTATION is left terminating by exhibiting a more natural level mapping than the one given in Section 6.6 and using the notion of semi-acceptability. □

6.9 Concluding Remarks

Now that we have presented a method allowing us to deal with the termination of logic and pure Prolog programs let us assess its merits and limitations. As pointed out at the beginning of this chapter, termination is one of the basic problems one has to deal with when studying the correctness of logic and pure Prolog programs. The method proposed here provides us with some insights into the nature of the problem and offers some heuristics which can be helpful when dealing with specific programs.

First, note that by the Success 2 Theorem 4.37, the least Herbrand model uniquely determines ground queries which succeed and terminate w.r.t. the leftmost selection rule. By the Lifting Corollary 3.23 all generalizations of these ground queries also succeed but only in the case of logic programming. In pure Prolog such a generalization can fail to terminate. So first we should think in terms of ground queries and then "lift" each of them, but "carefully", so that left termination w.r.t. the leftmost selection rule is preserved.

Further, observe that the proposed method to prove left termination requires in general only a limited declarative knowledge about the considered program in the form of a model in which only certain properties of the program are valid. Often this model is easy to guess and usually it can be defined in terms of simple relations involving such elementary concepts as the *listsize* function or the size of a ground term. In fact, this method seems to capture the employed informal reasoning.

The formal results justify this approach (Finiteness 1 Corollary 6.9 and Finiteness 2 Corollary 6.24) and also show its limitations (Equivalence 1 Corollary 6.17 and Equivalence 2 Corollary 6.29).

In the terminology of Section 5.1 we dealt here only with universal termination. This allows us to prove termination independently of the clause ordering. Still, there are natural queries which terminate only in a weaker sense. As an example consider the program

```
% even(X)  ←  X is an even numeral.
even(0).
even(s(s(X)))  ←  even(X).
```

augmented by the LESS program.

Then the pure Prolog query `even(X)`, `less(X, `$s^{10}(0)$`)` generates the first five even numerals and then diverges. In the terminology of Section 5.1 this query potentially diverges.

The method proposed in this chapter cannot be used to reason about this query. Even though some methods dealing with potential divergence (sometimes called *existential termination*) were proposed in the literature, we are not aware of any intuitive and simple method which could use an informal reasoning.

6.10   Bibliographic Remarks

This chapter follows the exposition of Apt and Pedreschi [AP94], where refinements of the presented methods that deal with modular termination proofs are also discussed. These modifications were applied there to a number of non-trivial examples including the MAP_COLOR program. Dershowitz [Der87] discussed in detail various uses of the multiset ordering in the area of term rewriting systems.

The results of Sections 6.3 and 6.4 are from Bezem [Bez93]. The function *listsize* defined in Section 6.2.2 was first considered in Ullman and van Gelder [UvG88].

The termination of logic programs has been a subject of intense research in recent years. Without aiming at completeness let us mention here the following related work.

Vasak and Potter [VP86] identified two forms of termination for logic programs — the existential and universal one — and characterized the class of universal terminating queries for a given program with selected selection rules. However, this characterization cannot be easily used to prove termination.

Baudinet [Bau88] presented a method for proving existential termination of the Prolog program in which with each program a system of equations is associated whose least fixpoint is the meaning of the program. By analyzing this least fixpoint various termination properties can be proved.

Bal Wang and Shyamasundar [BS94] provided a method of proving universal termination based on a concept of the so-called U-graph in which the relevant connections through unification between the atoms of the query and of the program are recorded. This method calls for the use of pre- and post-conditions that are associated with the nodes of the U-graph.

Bossi *et al.* [BCF91] refined this method by exploiting level mappings applied to non-ground atoms. These level mappings are constructed from level mappings defined on non-ground terms. The key concept is that of *rigidity* that allows us to identify the terms whose level mapping is invariant under instantiation.

Rao *et al.* [RKS92] proposed yet another approach to proving universal termination according to which logic programs are translated into term rewriting systems and subsequently the (sometimes automated) methods of proving termination of these systems are used.

Ullman and Van Gelder [UvG88] considered the problem of automatic verification of termination of a Prolog program and a query. In their approach, first some sufficient set of inequalities between the sizes of the arguments of the relation symbols is generated and then it is verified if they indeed hold. This approach was improved in Plümer [Plü90b], [Plü90a], who allowed a more general form of the inequalities and the way sizes of the arguments are measured. As pointed out in Apt and Pedreschi [AP93], left termination of some natural programs remains beyond the scope of this approach while it can be handled in a simple way using the notion of acceptability.

In addition, Apt and Pedreschi [AP93] noted that some fragments of the proof of acceptability can be automated as in many cases the task of checking the guesses for both the level mapping | | and the model I can be reduced to checking the validity of universal formulas in an extension of the so-called Presburger arithmetic by the *min* and *max* operators. In Shostak [Sho77] an exponential decision algorithm for this theory was presented. Pieramico [Pie91] implemented this procedure for checking left termination w.r.t. a level mapping and a Herbrand interpretation which are expressible in the above language and verified mechanically left termination of some pure Prolog programs.

De Schreye *et al.* [SVB92] studied the problem of automatic generation of level mappings and Herbrand interpretations w.r.t. which the program is left terminating.

Finally, De Schreye and Decorte [SD94] surveyed various methods of proving the termination of logic and Prolog programs and list several other relevant references.

6.11   Summary

In this chapter we provided a method for proving termination of logic and pure Prolog programs. To this end we introduced

- the multiset ordering

and combined it with the use of the

- level mappings,
- recurrent programs,
- bounded queries,

to deal with logic programs. Then we modified this approach to deal with the termination of pure Prolog programs by introducing the notion of

- acceptable programs.

6.12 References

[AP93] K. R. Apt and D. Pedreschi. Reasoning about termination of pure Prolog programs. *Information and Computation*, 106(1):109–157, 1993.

[AP94] K. R. Apt and D. Pedreschi. Modular termination proofs for logic and pure Prolog programs. In G. Levi, editor, *Advances in Logic Programming Theory*, pages 183–229. Oxford University Press, Oxford, 1994.

[Apt90] K. R. Apt. Logic programming. In J. van Leeuwen, editor, *Handbook of Theoretical Computer Science*, pages 493–574. Vol. B, Elsevier, Amsterdam, 1990.

[Bau88] M. Baudinet. Proving termination properties of Prolog programs. In *Proceedings of the 3rd Annual Symposium on Logic in Computer Science (LICS)*, pages 336–347. IEEE Computer Society, Edinburgh, 1988.

[BCF91] A. Bossi, N. Cocco, and M. Fabris. Termination of logic programs by exploiting term properties. In S. Abramsky and T.S.E. Maibaum, editors, *Proceedings CCPSD-TAPSOFT '91*, Lecture Notes in Computer Science 494, pages 153–180. Springer-Verlag, Berlin, 1991.

[Bez93] M. A. Bezem. Strong termination of logic programs. *Journal of Logic Programming*, 15(1 & 2):79–98, 1993.

[BS94] Bal Wang and R.K. Shyamasundar. A methodology for proving termination of logic programs. *Journal of Logic Programming*, 21(1):1–30, 1994.

[Cav89] L. Cavedon. Continuity, consistency, and completeness properties for logic programs. In G. Levi and M. Martelli, editors, *Proceedings of the Sixth International Conference on Logic Programming*, pages 571–584. The MIT Press, Cambridge, MA, 1989.

[Der87] N. Dershowitz. Termination of rewriting. *Journal of Symbolic Computation*, 8:69–116, 1987.

[Kön27] D. König. Über eine Schlußweise aus dem Endlichen ins Unendliche. *Acta Litt. Ac. Sci.*, 3:121–130, 1927.

[Kun89] K. Kunen. Signed data dependencies in logic programs. *Journal of Logic Programming*, 7:231–246, 1989.

[Llo87] J. W. Lloyd. *Foundations of Logic Programming.* Springer-Verlag, Berlin, second edition, 1987.

[Pie91] C. Pieramico. Metodi formali di ragionamento sulla terminazione di programmi Prolog. Technical report, Dipartimento di Informatica, Universitá di Pisa, 1991. Tesi di Laurea. In Italian.

[Plü90a] L. Plümer. *Termination Proofs for Logic Programs.* Lecture Notes in Artificial Intelligence 446, Springer-Verlag, Berlin, 1990.

[Plü90b] L. Plümer. Termination proofs for logic programs based on predicate inequalities. In D. H. D. Warren and P. Szeredi, editors, *Proceedings of the Seventh International Conference on Logic Programming*, pages 634–648. The MIT Press, Cambridge, MA, 1990.

[RKS92] K. Rao, D. Kapur, and R.K. Shyamasundar. A transformational methodology for proving termination of logic programs. In *Proceedings of the Fifth Conference on Computer Science Logic*, Lecture Notes in Computer Science 626, pages 213–226. Springer-Verlag, Berlin, 1992.

[SD94] D. De Schreye and S. Decorte. Termination of logic programs: the never-ending story. *Journal of Logic Programming*, 19-20:199–260, 1994.

[Sho77] R. E. Shostak. On the SUP-INF method for proving Presburger formulas. *Journal of the ACM*, 24(4):529–543, 1977.

[Smu79] R. Smullyan. Trees and ball games. *Annals of the New York Academy of Sciences*, 321:86–90, 1979.

[SVB92] D. De Schreye, K. Verschaetse, and M. Bruynooghe. A framework for analyzing the termination of definite logic programs with respect to call patterns. In ICOT Staff, editors, *Proceedings of the International Conference on Fifth Generation Computer Systems 1992*, pages 481–488. Institute for New Generation Computer Technology, 1992.

[UvG88] J. D. Ullman and A. van Gelder. Efficient tests for top-down termination of logical rules. *Journal of the ACM*, 35(2):345–373, 1988.

[VP86] T. Vasak and J. Potter. Characterization of terminating logic programs. In *Proceedings of the 1986 IEEE Symposium on Logic Programming*, pages 140–147, IEEE Computer Society, Salt Lake City, Utah, 1986.

Chapter 7

The Occur-check Problem

In Section 5.1 we explained the computation mechanism of pure Prolog programs. One of its striking features was that, conforming to most Prolog implementations, the occur-check was omitted from the unification algorithm. This omission may result in an incorrect use of unification and the resulting complications are usually termed as the *occur-check problem*. As an illustration of the difficulties consider the following interrupted listing:

```
| ?- X = f(X).
```

```
X = f(f(f(f(f(f(f(f(f(f(f(f(f(f(f(f(f(f(f(f(f(f(f(f(f(f(f(f(f(f(f(f(f(f(f(
```

Recall from Section 5.5 that =/2 is Prolog's built-in defined internally by a single clause:

```
%  X = Y  ←  X and Y are unifiable.
   X = X.
```

Note that for two terms, s, t, the query $s = t$ succeeds iff for a variable x such that $x \notin Var(s, t)$ the set of equations $\{x = s, x = t\}$ is unifiable. But $\{x/s\}$ is an mgu of $\{x = s\}$, so by the Iteration Lemma 2.24 $\{x = s, x = t\}$ is unifiable iff $\{s = t\}$ is unifiable, that is iff s and t unify. This justifies the comment line in the above program.

The above interrupted listing shows that even very simple queries can lead to divergence due to the omission of the occur-check. The aim of this chapter is to propose and justify various easy to check conditions that ensure that the occur-check problem does not arise and to explain how to deal with the occur-check problem when it does arise.

Our analysis is based on various syntactic properties which are introduced for programs that use so-called modes. We begin by defining formally in the next section the class of the occur-check programs and queries. An important tool in our considerations is the so-called NSTO Lemma, studied in detail in Section 7.2.

It provides sufficient conditions for proving occur-check freedom for sets of term equations.

In Section 7.3 we introduce modes. Modes indicate which argument positions of a relation symbol should be viewed as an input and which as an output. So, informally, modes indicate how a relation symbol is to be turned into a function symbol. Then we define for programs and queries the property of being well-moded. In Section 7.4 we apply this property to prove occur-check freedom.

However, the property of being well-moded is rather restrictive. In particular, it requires that atomic queries are ground in their input positions. Therefore, in Section 7.5, we introduce another property of programs and queries, called nice modedness which, as shown in Section 7.6, allows us to prove occur-check freedom for another class of programs and queries.

The above results show that by means of simple syntactic checks it is possible to establish occur-check freedom. However, the occur-check problem is in general undecidable, so the above results cannot provide a complete solution to the occur-check problem.

To address this issue in general, we propose program transformations which allow us to insert so-called occur-checks in the program and the query. To relate the behaviour of the original and of the transformed program, in Section 7.7 we introduce the notion of an unfolding. Unfolding is a general technique allowing us to increase program efficiency. Then, in Section 7.8, we show how every program and a query can be transformed into a new program and a new query in which only one single relation needs to be dealt with by the unification algorithm with the occur-check. Unfolding allows us to relate this new program to the original one.

7.1   Occur-check Free Programs

To define formally the occur-check problem we need to return to the Martelli–Montanari algorithm presented in Section 2.6. As already stated in Sections 2.3 and 2.6 the test "x does not occur in t" in action (5) of the algorithm is called the *occur-check*. In Section 5.1 we already mentioned that in most Prolog implementations it is omitted for efficiency reasons.

Consider now the consequences of omitting the occur-check from the Martelli–Montanari algorithm, that is of omitting the occur-check in action (5) and deleting action (6) from the algorithm. In principle we are still then left with two options depending on whether we also wish to perform the substitution $\{x/t\}$ on t itself. (Of course, if x does not occur in t, these alternatives are irrelevant.) If we do, then divergence can result, because x occurs in t implies that x occurs in $t\{x/t\}$. If we do not, then an incorrect result can be produced, as in the case of the single equation $x = f(x)$ which determines the substitution $\{x/f(x)\}$. The above interrupted listing suggests that in SICStus Prolog the first option is actually taken.

None of the above mentioned options is desirable. It is natural then to seek conditions which guarantee that, in the absence of the occur-check, in all Prolog computations of a given query and a program, unification is correctly performed. The idea is to ensure that during these computations action (6) of the Martelli–Montanari algorithm can never be performed. If this is the case, then it is indeed immaterial which of the two modifications of this algorithm just discussed is used, as both of them then behave in the same way as the original algorithm.

In the sequel we drop the qualification "term" when talking about term equations and for two atoms $A := p(s_1, \ldots, s_n)$ and $H := p(t_1, \ldots, t_n)$ with the same relation symbol we denote the set of equations $\{s_1 = t_1, \ldots, s_n = t_n\}$ by $A = H$.

The above discussion leads us to the following notions.

Definition 7.1 A set of equations E is called *not subject to occur-check* (NSTO in short) if in no execution of the Martelli–Montanari algorithm started with E action (6) can be performed. $\qquad\square$

Definition 7.2 Let P be a program.

- Let ξ be an LD-derivation for P and A an atom selected in ξ. Suppose that H is a variant of the head of a clause of P such that A and H have the same relation symbol. Then we say that the set of equations $A = H$ *is available in ξ*.
- Suppose that all sets of equations available in the LD-derivations of $P \cup \{Q\}$ are NSTO. Then we say that $P \cup \{Q\}$ is *occur-check free*. $\qquad\square$

Thus the notion of occur-check freedom does not depend on the ordering of the program clauses. Note that the above definition assumes a specific unification algorithm but allows us to derive precise results. Moreover, the nondeterminism built into the Martelli–Montanari algorithm allows us to model executions of various other unification algorithms, including Robinson's algorithm (see Exercise 7 in Chapter 2). In contrast, no specific unification algorithm in the definition of the LD-derivation is assumed.

By the Unification 2 Theorem 2.16 if the available set of equations is unifiable, then it is NSTO, as well. Thus the property of being occur-check free rests exclusively upon those available sets which are not unifiable. In the definition of the occur-check freedom *all* LD-derivations of $P \cup \{Q\}$ are considered, so all sets of equations that can be available in a possibly backtracking Prolog execution of a query Q w.r.t. the program P are taken into account.

7.2   NSTO Lemma

To prove that a program is occur-check free we need to have some means to establish that a set of equations is NSTO. In this section we provide a criterion that will be sufficient for our purposes. We need some preparatory definitions first.

Definition 7.3

- We call a family of terms *linear* if every variable occurs at most once in it.
- We call a set of equations *left linear* if the family of terms formed by their left-hand sides is linear. □

Thus a family of terms is linear iff no variable has two distinct occurrences in any term and no two terms have a variable in common.

Definition 7.4 Let E be a set of equations. We denote by $\to_E$ the following relation defined on the elements of E:
$e_1 \to_E e_2$ iff the left-hand side of e_1 and the right-hand side of e_2 have a variable in common. □

So for example $x = f(y) \to_E a = x$ for any E containing these two equations. Note that if a variable occurs both in the left-hand and right-hand side of an equation e of E, then $e \to_E e$.

We can now prove the desired result from Deransart *et al.* [DFT91].

Lemma 7.5 (NSTO) Suppose that the equations in E can be reoriented in such a way that the resulting set F is left linear and the relation $\to_F$ is acyclic. Then E is NSTO.

Proof. Call a set of equations *good* if it satisfies the assumptions of the lemma. We prove two claims.

Claim 1 Goodness is preserved by the actions of the Martelli–Montanari algorithm.

Proof. We consider each action separately. We write "$E \dot\cup \{e\}$" as a shorthand for "$E \cup \{e\}$, where $e \notin E$".

Action (1). Suppose that $E \dot\cup \{f(s_1, \ldots, s_n) = f(t_1, \ldots, t_n)\}$ is left linear. Then so is $F := E \cup \{s_1 = t_1, \ldots, s_n = t_n\}$.

Consider now a path $e_1 \to_F e_2 \to_F \ldots \to_F e_m$ in the relation $\to_F$. Then by replacing in it every equation of the form $s_i = t_i$ by $f(s_1, \ldots, s_n) = f(t_1, \ldots, t_n)$ we obtain a path in the relation $\to_{E \cup \{f(s_1,\ldots,s_n)=f(t_1,\ldots,t_n)\}}$. Thus if the relation $\to_{E \cup \{f(s_1,\ldots,s_n)=f(t_1,\ldots,t_n)\}}$ is acyclic, then so is $\to_F$.

Action (3). Note that $x = x \to_E x = x$ for any set of equations E containing $x = x$. Thus if E is good, then $x = x \notin E$ and, consequently, action (3) cannot be applied to E.

Action (4). By definition $E \dot\cup \{x = t\}$ is good iff $E \cup \{t = x\}$ is good, so action (4) preserves goodness.

Action (5). Assume that x does not occur in t. Then $x = t \to_{E\{x/t\} \cup \{x=t\}} e\{x/t\}$, where $e \in E$, cannot hold, since x does not occur in $e\{x/t\}$. So $x = t$ has no successor in the relation $\to_{E\{x/t\} \cup \{x=t\}}$.

For a set of equations E denote now by $lhs(E)$ (respectively $rhs(E)$) the set of variables that occur in the left-hand side (respectively right-hand side) of an equation from E and introduce an analogous notation for an equation e. We consider two situations.

(i) Suppose that $E\dot{\cup}\{x = t\}$ is left linear and that the relation $\to_{E\cup\{x=t\}}$ is acyclic. Then $x \notin lhs(E)$, so $E\{x/t\} \cup \{x = t\}$ is left linear, as well.

We now prove that the relation $\to_{E\{x/t\}\cup\{x=t\}}$ is acyclic. To this end suppose that $e_1\{x/t\} \to_{E\{x/t\}\cup\{x=t\}} e_2\{x/t\}$, where $e_1, e_2 \in E$. So for a variable y, both $y \in lhs(e_1\{x/t\})$ and $y \in rhs(e_2\{x/t\})$ hold. But $x \notin lhs(e_1)$, so $y \in lhs(e_1)$. Two cases arise.

Case 1 $y \in rhs(e_2)$.
Then $e_1 \to_{E\cup\{x=t\}} e_2$.

Case 2 $y \notin rhs(e_2)$.
Then $x \in rhs(e_2)$ and $y \in Var(t)$. Thus we have $e_1 \to_{E\cup\{x=t\}} x = t \to_{E\cup\{x=t\}} e_2$.

We conclude that if a cycle exists in the relation $\to_{E\{x/t\}\cup\{x=t\}}$, then a cycle also exists in the relation $\to_{E\cup\{x=t\}}$. Thus $\to_{E\{x/t\}\cup\{x=t\}}$ is acyclic.

(ii) Suppose now that $E\dot{\cup}\{t = x\}$ is left linear and that the relation $\to_{E\cup\{t=x\}}$ is acyclic. Then x occurs at most once in a left-hand side of an equation of E and $Var(t) \cap lhs(E) = \emptyset$. Thus $E\{x/t\} \cup \{x = t\}$ (note the reorientation of $t = x$) is left linear, since x does not occur in t.

We now prove that the relation $\to_{E\{x/t\}\cup\{x=t\}}$ is acyclic. Suppose as before that $e_1\{x/t\} \to_{E\{x/t\}\cup\{x=t\}} e_2\{x/t\}$, where $e_1, e_2 \in E$. So for a variable y, both $y \in lhs(e_1\{x/t\})$, and $y \in rhs(e_2\{x/t\})$. Four cases arise.

Case 1 $y \in lhs(e_1)$ and $y \in rhs(e_2)$.
Then $e_1 \to_{E\cup\{t=x\}} e_2$.

Case 2 $y \in lhs(e_1)$ and $y \notin rhs(e_2)$.
Then $x \in rhs(e_2)$ and $y \in Var(t)$. But $Var(t) \cap lhs(E) = \emptyset$, so actually this case cannot take place.

Case 3 $y \notin lhs(e_1)$ and $y \in rhs(e_2)$.
Then $x \in lhs(e_1)$ and $y \in Var(t)$. Thus we have $e_1 \to_{E\cup\{t=x\}} t = x \to_{E\cup\{t=x\}} e_2$.

Case 4 $y \notin lhs(e_1)$ and $y \notin rhs(e_2)$.
Then $x \in lhs(e_1)$ and $x \in rhs(e_2)$, so $e_1 \to_{E\cup\{t=x\}} e_2$.

We conclude that if a cycle exists in the relation $\to_{E\{x/t\}\cup\{x=t\}}$, then also a cycle exists in the relation $\to_{E\cup\{t=x\}}$. Thus $\to_{E\{x/t\}\cup\{x=t\}}$ is acyclic. $\square$

Claim 2 If a set of equations is good, then action (6) cannot be applied to it.

Proof. Consider an equation of the form $x = t$, where x occurs in t. Then for any set of equations E both $x = t \to_{E\cup\{x=t\}} x = t$ and $t = x \to_{E\cup\{t=x\}} t = x$.

This shows that if action (6) can be applied to a set of equations E, then for any set of equations F resulting from a reorientation of the equations of E the relation $\rightarrow_F$ is cyclic, and consequently E is not good. $\quad\square$

The desired conclusion now follows immediately from Claims 1 and 2. $\quad\square$

Example 7.6 As an illustration of the use of the above result consider the set of equations

$$E := \{z = f(v), f(v) = z, x = f(y), u = a, g(u, z, z) = y\}.$$

Then E is NSTO because the following reorientation of it satisfies the assumptions of the NSTO Lemma 7.5:

$$\{z = f(v), x = f(y), u = a, y = g(u, z, z)\}.$$

Note that the resulting set of equations has one element less than the original set.
$\quad\square$

Exercise 76 Prove the following properties of sets of equations.

(i) $E \cup \{f(s_1, \ldots, s_n) = f(t_1, \ldots, t_n)\}$ is NSTO iff $E \cup \{s_1 = t_1, \ldots, s_n = t_n\}$ is NSTO.

(ii) $E \cup \{x = x\}$ is NSTO iff E is NSTO.

(iii) $E \cup \{s = t\}$ is NSTO iff $E \cup \{t = s\}$ is NSTO. $\quad\square$

Exercise 77 Call an equation *semi-ground* if one side of it is ground and call a set of equations *semi-ground* if all its elements are semi-ground. Prove that for E_1 semi-ground, $E_1 \cup E_2$ is NSTO iff E_2 is NSTO. $\quad\square$

Note that these exercises allow us to strengthen the NSTO Lemma 7.5 by applying it to a larger class of sets of equations.

7.3   Well-moded Queries and Programs

For further analysis we introduce modes. Modes indicate how the arguments of a relation should be used.

Definition 7.7 Consider an n-ary relation symbol p. By a *mode* for p we mean a function m_p from $\{1, \ldots, n\}$ to the set $\{+, -\}$. If $m_p(i) = $ "+", we call i an *input position* of p and if $m_p(i) = $ "−", we call i an *output position* of p (both w.r.t. m_p). By a *moding* we mean a collection of modes, each for a different relation symbol. $\quad\square$

We write m_p in a more suggestive form $p(m_p(1), \ldots, m_p(n))$. For example, `member(-,+)` denotes a binary relation `member` with the first position moded as output and the second position moded as input.

The definition of moding assumes one mode per relation in a program. Multiple modes may be obtained by simply renaming the relations. In the remainder of this chapter we adopt the following.

Assumption *Every considered relation* has a fixed mode associated with it.

This assumption will allow us to talk about the input and output positions of an atom. Intuitively, the modes indicate how the arguments of a relation should be used: the given, known arguments should be put in the input positions and the terms (usually variables) in which the values should be computed should be put in the output positions. However, this distinction between the input and output positions is not so clear when all the positions in an atom of a query are filled in by compound terms.

We now introduce a restriction which constrains the "flow of data" through the query and through the clauses of the programs. To simplify the notation, when writing an atom as $p(\mathbf{u}, \mathbf{v})$, we now assume that $\mathbf{u}$ is a sequence of terms filling in the input positions of p and that $\mathbf{v}$ is a sequence of terms filling in the output positions of p.

Definition 7.8

(i) A query $p_1(\mathbf{s_1}, \mathbf{t_1}), \ldots, p_n(\mathbf{s_n}, \mathbf{t_n})$ is called *well-moded* if for $i \in [1, n]$

$$Var(\mathbf{s_i}) \subseteq \bigcup_{j=1}^{i-1} Var(\mathbf{t_j}).$$

(ii) A clause

$$p_0(\mathbf{t_0}, \mathbf{s_{n+1}}) \leftarrow p_1(\mathbf{s_1}, \mathbf{t_1}), \ldots, p_n(\mathbf{s_n}, \mathbf{t_n})$$

is called *well-moded* if for $i \in [1, n+1]$

$$Var(\mathbf{s_i}) \subseteq \bigcup_{j=0}^{i-1} Var(\mathbf{t_j}).$$

(iii) A program is called *well-moded* if every clause of it is. $\square$

Thus, a query is well-moded if

- every variable occurring in an input position of an atom ($i \in [1, n]$) occurs in an output position of an earlier ($j \in [1, i-1]$) atom.

And a clause is well-moded if

- ($i \in [1, n]$) every variable occurring in an input position of a body atom occurs either in an input position of the head ($j = 0$) or in an output position of an earlier ($j \in [1, i - 1]$) body atom,
- ($i = n + 1$) every variable occurring in an output position of the head occurs in an input position of the head ($j = 0$) or in an output position of a body atom ($j \in [1, n]$).

Note that a unit clause $p(\mathbf{s}, \mathbf{t})$ is well-moded iff $Var(\mathbf{t}) \subseteq Var(\mathbf{s})$, whereas a query with only one atom is well-moded iff this atom is ground in its input positions.

Intuitively, in a Prolog computation of a well-moded query $A_1, \ldots, A_n$ and well-moded program P, "data" passes from the input positions of A_1 to the output positions of A_1, then to the input positions of A_2, etc., until it reaches the output positions of A_n.

And within each well-moded clause $H \leftarrow B_1, \ldots, B_n$ of P a Prolog computation begins by passing "data" to the input positions of the H, from which it is passed to the input positions of B_1, etc., until it reaches the output positions of B_n from which it is finally passed to the output positions of H.

A test whether a query or clause is well-moded can be efficiently performed by noting that a query Q is well-moded iff every first from the left occurrence of a variable in Q is within an output position. And a clause $p(\mathbf{s}, \mathbf{t}) \leftarrow \mathbf{B}$ is well-moded iff every first from the left occurrence of a variable in the sequence $\mathbf{s}, \mathbf{B}, \mathbf{t}$ is within an input position of $p(\mathbf{s}, \mathbf{t})$ or within an output position in $\mathbf{B}$. (We assume in this description that in every atom the input positions occur first.)

The following lemma shows the "persistence" of the notion of well-modedness.

Lemma 7.9 (Well-modedness) An SLD-resolvent of a well-moded query and a well-moded clause is well-moded.

Proof. An SLD-resolvent of a query and a clause is obtained by means of the following three operations:

- instantiation of a query,
- instantiation of a clause,
- replacement of an atom, say H, of a query by the body of a clause whose head is H.

So we only need to prove the following two claims.

Claim 1 An instance of a well-moded query (respectively clause) is well-moded.

Proof. It suffices to note that for any sequences of terms $\mathbf{s}, \mathbf{t}_1, \ldots, \mathbf{t}_n$ and a substitution θ, $Var(\mathbf{s}) \subseteq \bigcup_{j=1}^{n} Var(\mathbf{t}_j)$ implies $Var(\mathbf{s}\theta) \subseteq \bigcup_{j=1}^{n} Var(\mathbf{t}_j\theta)$. $\square$

Claim 2 Suppose that $\mathbf{A}, H, \mathbf{C}$ is a well-moded query and $H \leftarrow \mathbf{B}$ is a well-moded clause. Then $\mathbf{A}, \mathbf{B}, \mathbf{C}$ is a well-moded query.

Proof.   Let
$$\mathbf{A} := p_1(\mathbf{s}_1, \mathbf{t}_1), \ldots, p_k(\mathbf{s}_k, \mathbf{t}_k),$$
$$H := p(\mathbf{s}, \mathbf{t}),$$
$$\mathbf{B} := p_{k+1}(\mathbf{s}_{k+1}, \mathbf{t}_{k+1}), \ldots, p_{k+l}(\mathbf{s}_{k+l}, \mathbf{t}_{k+l}),$$
$$\mathbf{C} := p_{k+l+1}(\mathbf{s}_{k+l+1}, \mathbf{t}_{k+l+1}), \ldots, p_{k+l+m}(\mathbf{s}_{k+l+m}, \mathbf{t}_{k+l+m}).$$

Fix now $i \in [1, k + l + m]$. We need to prove $Var(\mathbf{s}_i) \subseteq \bigcup_{j=1}^{i-1} Var(\mathbf{t}_j)$. Three cases arise.

Case 1 $i \in [1, k]$.
Note that $\mathbf{A}$ is well-moded, since $\mathbf{A}, H, \mathbf{C}$ is well-moded. Hence the claim follows.

Case 2 $i \in [k + 1, k + l]$.
$H \leftarrow \mathbf{B}$ is well-moded, so $Var(\mathbf{s}_i) \subseteq Var(\mathbf{s}) \cup \bigcup_{j=k+1}^{i-1} Var(\mathbf{t}_j)$. Moreover, $\mathbf{A}, H, \mathbf{C}$ is well-moded, so $Var(\mathbf{s}) \subseteq \bigcup_{j=1}^{k} Var(\mathbf{t}_j)$. This implies the claim.

Case 3 $i \in [k + l + 1, k + l + m]$.
$\mathbf{A}, H, \mathbf{C}$ is well-moded, so $Var(\mathbf{s}_i) \subseteq \bigcup_{j=1}^{k} Var(\mathbf{t}_j) \cup Var(\mathbf{t}) \cup \bigcup_{j=k+l+1}^{i-1} Var(\mathbf{t}_j)$ and $Var(\mathbf{s}) \subseteq \bigcup_{j=1}^{k} Var(\mathbf{t}_j)$. Moreover, $H \leftarrow \mathbf{B}$ is well-moded, so $Var(\mathbf{t}) \subseteq Var(\mathbf{s}) \cup \bigcup_{j=k+1}^{k+l} Var(\mathbf{t}_j)$. This implies the claim. $\qquad\square$

$\qquad\square$

Corollary 7.10 (Well-modedness) Let P and Q be well-moded. Then all queries in all SLD-derivations of $P \cup \{Q\}$ are well-moded. $\qquad\square$

This allows us to draw the following conclusion which is not needed for the study of the occur-check problem but is of independent interest.

Corollary 7.11 (Computed Answer) Let P and Q be well-moded. Then for every computed answer substitution θ for $P \cup \{Q\}$, $Q\theta$ is ground.

Proof. Let $\mathbf{x}$ stand for the sequence of all variables that appear in Q. Let p be a new relation of arity equal to the length of $\mathbf{x}$ and with all positions moded as input. Then $Q, p(\mathbf{x})$ is a well-moded query, because every variable occurring in a well-moded query has an occurrence within an output position.

Suppose now that θ is a computed answer substitution for $P \cup \{Q\}$. Then $p(\mathbf{x})\theta$ is a query in an SLD-derivation of $P \cup \{Q, p(\mathbf{x})\}$. By the Well-modedness Corollary 7.10 $p(\mathbf{x})\theta$ is well-moded, that is ground. This implies the claim. $\qquad\square$

Exercise 78 Let P be well-moded and θ a c.a.s. of $P \cup \{p(\mathbf{s}, \mathbf{t})\}$. Prove that then $Var(\mathbf{t}\theta) \subseteq Var(\mathbf{s}\theta)$.
Hint. Let r be a new relation of arity equal to the length of $\mathbf{s}$ and with all positions moded as output and q be a new relation of arity equal to the length of $\mathbf{t}$ and with all positions moded as input. Consider the query $r(\mathbf{s}), p(\mathbf{s}, \mathbf{t}), q(\mathbf{t})$. $\qquad\square$

Exercise 79 Let P and $A, \mathbf{B}$ be well-moded. Suppose that $\mathbf{B}\theta$ is a descendant of $A, \mathbf{B}$ in an LD-derivation of $P \cup \{A, \mathbf{B}\}$, where θ is the composition of the mgus used in resolving A. Prove that $A\theta$ is ground. $\qquad\square$

By the Soundness Theorem 4.4 every computed answer substitution is a correct answer substitution. However, we noticed in Section 4.5 that the converse in general does not hold. It is interesting to note that under the assumption of well-modedness these two notions do coincide. Namely, we have the following result.

Theorem 7.12 (Well-modedness) Let P and Q be well-moded. Then every correct answer substitution is a computed answer substitution.

Proof. Let θ be a correct answer substitution for $P \cup \{Q\}$. By the Strong Completeness Theorem 4.13 there exists a computed answer substitution η for $P \cup \{Q\}$ such that $Q\eta$ is more general than $Q\theta$. But by the Computed Answer Corollary 7.11 $Q\eta$ is ground. Thus $Q\theta$ is ground and $Q\theta$ and $Q\eta$ coincide. Hence θ and η coincide. $\qquad\qquad\square$

7.3.1   Examples

Let us consider now some examples. They show how and to what extent the notion of well-modedness can be applied to specific programs. When dealing with the programs below we apply the Computed Answer Corollary 7.11. Note that this corollary refers to an arbitrary selection rule.

Append
First, consider the program **APPEND**:

```
app([], Ys, Ys).
app([X | Xs], Ys, [X | Zs]) ← app(Xs, Ys, Zs).
```

with the mode app(+,+,-). It is easy to check that **APPEND** is then well-moded. Indeed, the following inclusions obviously hold:

$$Var(\texttt{Ys}) \subseteq Var([\ ],\texttt{Ys}),$$

$$Var(\texttt{Xs},\texttt{Ys}) \subseteq Var([\texttt{X}|\texttt{Xs}],\texttt{Ys}),$$

$$Var([\texttt{X}|\texttt{Zs}]) \subseteq Var([\texttt{X}|\texttt{Xs}],\texttt{Ys}) \cup Var(\texttt{Zs}).$$

We conclude that for ground $\texttt{s},\texttt{t}$ all computed answer substitutions θ for **APPEND** $\cup$ $\{\texttt{app(s, t, u)}\}$ are such that $u\theta$ is ground.

Exercise 80 Check that **APPEND** is well-moded with the following modes:

(i) app(-,-,+),

(ii) app(+,-,+),

(iii) app(-,+,+).

Is APPEND well-moded with the mode app(+,+,+)?   □

This example and the exercise indicate various natural uses of the APPEND program. They show that in general it is not clear how to mode the relation app in such a way as to conform to the intuition concerning the use of modes.

Moreover, not all uses of APPEND can be properly taken into account by means of modes. First of all, APPEND can be used to concatenate non-ground lists. In this case the considered query is not well-moded. Further, there is no way to mode the relation app so that the program APPEND and the query app([X,2], [Y,U], [3,Z,0,Z]) are well-moded. Note that this query succeeds with the c.a.s. $\{X/3, Z/2, Y/0, U/2\}$ and app([X,2], [Y,U], [3,Z,0,Z]) $\{X/3, Z/2, Y/0, U/2\}$ is ground. However, this fact cannot be established on the basis of the Computed Answer Corollary 7.11.

Permutation

To make certain programs well-moded a relation has to be moded in two different ways. For example, take the program PERMUTATION:

```
% perm(Xs, Ys)  ←  Ys is a permutation of the list Xs.
perm([], []).
perm(Xs, [X | Ys])  ←
    app(X1s, [X | X2s], Xs),
    app(X1s, X2s, Zs),
    perm(Zs, Ys).
```

augmented by the APPEND program.

Conforming to the customary use of this program, we wish to use the moding perm(+,-) for the perm relation.

Exercise 81 Prove that there is no way to extend the moding perm(+,-) by assigning a single mode to the relation app, so that PERMUTATION becomes well-moded.   □

To extend the moding perm(+,-) so that the PERMUTATION program becomes well-moded, we thus need to use different modings for the relation app. It is easy to check that with the mode app(-,-,+) for the first call to APPEND and app(+,+,-) for the second call to APPEND, PERMUTATION is well-moded.

As stated at the beginning of this section, such multiple modes can be formally handled by renaming of the relations used. Intuitively, each call of the app relation refers to a different copy of the APPEND program. Formally, it suffices to rename the second call to APPEND to app1(X1s, X2s, Zs) and add to the program a renamed version of APPEND which defines the relation app1.

On account of the fact that PERMUTATION is well-moded, we conclude that for s ground all the computed answer substitutions θ for PERMUTATION $\cup$ {perm(s, t)} are such that $t\theta$ is ground.

Note also that in the case of the PERMUTATION program some of its uses cannot be properly taken into account by means of modes either. Indeed, this program can be also used to compute permutations of a non-ground list. In this case the relevant query is not well-moded.

Sequence

Finally, we exhibit an example of a natural program such that a customary use of it is not well-moded for any moding. Namely, consider the SEQUENCE program:

```
% sequence(Xs)  ←  Xs is a list of 27 elements.
sequence([_,_,_,_,_,_,_,_,_,_,_,_,_,_,_,_,_,_,_,_,_,_,_,_,_,_,_]).

% question(Ss)  ←  Ss is a list of 27 elements forming the desired sequence.
question(Ss)  ←
    sequence(Ss),
    sublist([1,_,1,_,1], Ss),
    sublist([2,_,_,2,_,_,2], Ss),
    sublist([3,_,_,_,3,_,_,_,3], Ss),
    sublist([4,_,_,_,_,4,_,_,_,_,4], Ss),
    sublist([5,_,_,_,_,_,5,_,_,_,_,_,5], Ss),
    sublist([6,_,_,_,_,_,_,6,_,_,_,_,_,_,6], Ss),
    sublist([7,_,_,_,_,_,_,_,7,_,_,_,_,_,_,_,7], Ss),
    sublist([8,_,_,_,_,_,_,_,_,8,_,_,_,_,_,_,_,_,8], Ss),
    sublist([9,_,_,_,_,_,_,_,_,_,9,_,_,_,_,_,_,_,_,_,9], Ss).

% sublist(Xs, Ys)  ←  Xs is a sublist of the list Ys.
sublist(Xs, Ys)  ←  app(_, Zs, Ys), app(Xs, _, Zs).
```

augmented by the APPEND program.

We call here a list of 27 elements "a desired sequence" if it satisfies the description given on page 135, so "it is a sequence containing three 1s, three 2s, ..., three 9s such that for all $i \in [1, 9]$ there are exactly i numbers between successive occurrences of i". Take now the query question(Ss). To get it well-moded we have to use the mode question(-). This implies that to obtain the clause defining the question relation well-moded, we have to use the mode sequence(-). But then we cannot satisfy the requirement of well-modedness for the unit clause defining the sequence relation.

We conclude that the Computed Answer Corollary 7.11 cannot be applied to SEQUENCE $\cup$ {sequence(Ss)}.

Exercise 82 Consider other programs discussed in Chapter 5. Find natural modings in which these programs are used and check which programs are then well-moded. $\square$

7.4 Occur-check Freedom via Well-modedness

After this incursion into the world of modes let us return to our original problem — that of establishing that a program is occur-check free. In this section we show

how the notion of well-modedness can be of help. To this end we introduce the following concepts.

Definition 7.13

- An atom is called *input* (respectively *output*) *linear* if the family of terms occurring in its input (respectively output) positions is linear.
- An atom is called *input–output disjoint* if the family of terms occurring in its input positions has no variable in common with the family of terms occurring in its output positions. □

We can now link the NSTO Lemma 7.5 to the notion of mode.

Lemma 7.14 (NSTO via Modes) Consider two atoms A and H with the same relation symbol. Suppose that

- they have no variable in common,
- one of them is input–output disjoint,
- one of them is input linear and the other is output linear.

Then $A = H$ is NSTO.

Proof. Suppose first that A is input–output disjoint and input linear and H is output linear. Let $i_1^A, \ldots, i_m^A$ (respectively $i_1^H, \ldots, i_m^H$) be the terms filling in the input positions of A (respectively H) and $o_1^A, \ldots, o_n^A$ (respectively $o_1^H, \ldots, o_n^H$) the terms filling in the output positions of A (respectively H).

The set of equations under consideration is

$$E := \{i_1^A = i_1^H, \ldots, i_m^A = i_m^H, o_1^A = o_1^H, \ldots, o_n^A = o_n^H\}.$$

Reorient it as follows:

$$F := \{i_1^A = i_1^H, \ldots, i_m^A = i_m^H, o_1^H = o_1^A, \ldots, o_n^H = o_n^A\}.$$

By assumption A and H have no variable in common. This implies that

- F is left linear (because additionally A is input linear and H is output linear),
- the equations $i_j^A = i_j^H$ have no successor in the $\rightarrow_F$ relation and the equations $o_j^H = o_j^A$ have no predecessor (because additionally A is input–output disjoint).

Thus by the NSTO Lemma 7.5 $A = H$ is NSTO. The proofs for the remaining three cases are analogous and omitted. □

Exercise 83 Complete the proof of the NSTO via modes Lemma 7.14. □

We now apply this result to the study of pure Prolog programs. To this end we need to consider LD-derivations. The following notion is due to Dembiński and Małuszyński [DM85].

Definition 7.15 We call an LD-derivation *data driven* if all atoms selected in it are ground in their input positions. $\square$

We now prove a result allowing us to conclude that $P \cup \{Q\}$ is occur-check free.

Theorem 7.16 (Occur-check 1) Suppose that

- the head of every clause of P is output linear,
- all LD-derivations of $P \cup \{Q\}$ are data driven.

Then $P \cup \{Q\}$ is occur-check free.

Proof. Consider an LD-derivation of $P \cup \{Q\}$. Let A be an atom selected in it and suppose that H is a variant of the head of a clause of P such that A and H have the same relation symbol. By assumption A is ground in its input positions, so it is input–output disjoint and input linear. By assumption H is output linear and A and H have no variable in common. So by the NSTO via Modes Lemma 7.14 $A = H$ is NSTO. $\square$

Exercise 84 Suppose that the head of every clause of P is linear. Prove that then $P \cup \{Q\}$ is occur-check free for every query Q. $\square$

The above exercise is applicable to some pure Prolog programs, for example to **LESS** and **LENGTH**. However, most natural programs do not satisfy its assumption, so it is of limited use. Hence we should rather try to exploit the Occur-check 1 Theorem 7.16 in a different way. To apply this theorem to specific programs we need to have a means to establish its second assumption. But the definition of a well-moded program is designed in such a way that the following result holds.

Lemma 7.17 (Data Drivenness) Let P and Q be well-moded. Then all LD-derivations of $P \cup \{Q\}$ are data driven.

Proof. Note that the first atom of a well-moded query is ground in its input positions, so the conclusion follows by the Well-modedness Corollary 7.10. $\square$

This brings us to the following conclusion which involves the concept of well-modedness.

Corollary 7.18 (Occur-check 1) Let P and Q be well-moded. Suppose that

- the head of every clause of P is output linear.

Then $P \cup \{Q\}$ is occur-check free.

Proof. By the Occur-check 1 Theorem 7.16 and the Data Drivenness Lemma 7.17. $\square$

7.4.1   Examples

This Corollary can be easily applied to various pure Prolog programs. We limit ourselves here to the programs considered in Section 7.3.1. We use here the conclusions there established, namely that these programs are well-moded in the discussed modings.

Append

First, consider the program APPEND with the mode app(+,+,-). It is easy to see that in this mode the head of every clause is output linear. We conclude that for s and t ground, APPEND ∪ {app(s, t, u)} is occur-check free.

Append, again

In addition, in the mode app(-,-,+) the head of every clause of APPEND is output linear. Again, we conclude that for u ground, APPEND ∪ {app(s, t, u)} is occur-check free.

Exercise 85 Draw the appropriate conclusions concerning the occur-check freedom for APPEND used in the following modes: app(+,-,+), app(-,+,+).   □

Permutation

Finally, consider the program PERMUTATION with the previously considered moding, that is perm(+,-), app(-,-,+) for the first call to APPEND and app(+,+,-) for the second call to APPEND.

Again, the heads of all clauses are output linear. We obtain that for s ground, PERMUTATION ∪ {perm(s, t)} is occur-check free.

To apply the Occur-check 1 Corollary 7.18 to specific programs it is natural to start by moding the relations used in the query so that this query becomes well-moded. The important clue comes from the fact that the input positions of the first atom of a well-moded query are filled in by ground terms. Then one should try to mode other relations used in the program, so that the remaining conditions of this Corollary are satisfied.

Exercise 86 Consider the program PALINDROME:

```
% palindrome(Xs)  ←   the list Xs is equal to its reverse.
palindrome(Xs)  ←  reverse(Xs, Xs).

% reverse(Xs, Ys)  ←   Ys is the reverse of the list Xs.
reverse(X1s, X2s)  ←  reverse(X1s, [], X2s).

% reverse(Xs, Ys, Zs)  ←  Zs is the result of concatenating
                          the reverse of the list Xs and the list Ys.
reverse([], Xs, Xs).
reverse([X | X1s], X2s, Ys)  ←  reverse(X1s, [X | X2s], Ys).
```

Prove that for s ground, PALINDROME ∪ { palindrome(s)} is occur-check free.   □

7.5 Nicely Moded Programs

The above conclusions are of a restrictive kind, because in each case we had to assume that the input positions of one atom queries are ground. Moreover, for some natural programs the above results are not applicable. For example, the Occur-check 1 Corollary 7.18 cannot be used to establish that SEQUENCE $\cup$ {question(Ss)} is occur-check free. Indeed, we have already noted in Section 7.3.1, that there is no way to mode this program and query so that both of them are well-moded.

To deal with these difficulties we now consider different syntactic restrictions.

Definition 7.19

- A query $p_1(\mathbf{s_1}, \mathbf{t_1}), \ldots, p_n(\mathbf{s_n}, \mathbf{t_n})$ is called *nicely moded* if $\mathbf{t_1}, \ldots, \mathbf{t_n}$ is a linear family of terms and for $i \in [1, n]$

$$Var(\mathbf{s_i}) \cap (\bigcup_{j=i}^{n} Var(\mathbf{t_j})) = \emptyset. \tag{7.1}$$

- A clause

$$p_0(\mathbf{s_0}, \mathbf{t_0}) \leftarrow p_1(\mathbf{s_1}, \mathbf{t_1}), \ldots, p_n(\mathbf{s_n}, \mathbf{t_n})$$

is called *nicely moded* if $p_1(\mathbf{s_1}, \mathbf{t_1}), \ldots, p_n(\mathbf{s_n}, \mathbf{t_n})$ is nicely moded and

$$Var(\mathbf{s_0}) \cap (\bigcup_{j=1}^{n} Var(\mathbf{t_j})) = \emptyset. \tag{7.2}$$

  In particular, every unit clause is nicely moded.
- A program is called *nicely moded* if every clause of it is. $\qquad\square$

Thus, assuming that in every atom the input positions occur first, a query is nicely moded if

- every variable occurring in an output position of an atom does not occur earlier in the query.

And a clause is nicely moded if

- every variable occurring in an output position of a body atom occurs neither earlier in the body nor in an input position of the head.

Note that a one atom query is nicely moded iff it is output linear and input–output disjoint.

Intuitively, the concept of being nicely moded prevents a "speculative binding" of the variables which occur in output positions — these variables are required to be "fresh", that is to say not used before the Prolog computation reaches the output positions in which they occur.

The following lemma shows the "persistence" of the notion of being nicely moded when the leftmost selection rule is used.

Lemma 7.20 (Nice Modedness) An LD-resolvent of a nicely moded query and a nicely moded clause is nicely moded.

Proof. The proof is quite long and tedious and is omitted. The interested reader is referred to Apt and Pellegrini [AP94, pages 719–724].   □

This lemma leads to the following conclusion.

Corollary 7.21 (Nice Modedness) Let P and Q be nicely moded. Then all queries in all LD-derivations of $P \cup \{Q\}$ are nicely moded.

Proof. A variant of a nicely moded clause is nicely moded. The conclusion now follows by the Nice Modedness Lemma 7.20.   □

Exercise 87 Show that the above corollary does not hold for SLD-derivations.   □

7.5.1   Examples

The main use of the notion of nicely modedness lies in ensuring that the output positions of the atoms selected in the LD-derivations do not share variables, both between themselves and with the input positions. To get familiar with the definition let us now consider the programs analyzed in Section 7.3.1.

Append
Note that APPEND is nicely moded in the mode app(+,+,-). Indeed, the first clause is a unit clause and hence nicely moded. For the second clause it suffices to note that its body app(Xs, Ys, Zs) is output linear and input–output disjoint and hence nicely moded as a query. Moreover, $Var([X|Xs], Ys) \cap Var(Zs) = \emptyset$ so condition (7.2) is satisfied.

Append, again
It is equally straightforward to check that in the mode app(-,-,+) APPEND is nicely moded, as well.

Exercise 88 Check whether APPEND is nicely moded in the modes app(+,-,+) and app(-,+,+).   □

Permutation
Consider now PERMUTATION with the previously considered moding, so perm(+,-) and app(-,-,+) for the first call to APPEND and app(+,+,-) for the second call to APPEND. We just checked that in each of these two modes APPEND is nicely moded, so it suffices to consider the clauses defining the relation perm. The first clause is a unit clause and hence nicely moded. For the second clause notice that the query

```
app(X1s, [X | X2s], Xs), app(X1s, X2s, Zs), perm(Zs, Ys)
```

is nicely moded because

- $\texttt{X1s}, [\texttt{X}|\texttt{X2s}], \texttt{Zs}, \texttt{Ys}$ is a linear family of terms,
- $Var(\texttt{Xs}) \cap (Var(\texttt{X1s}, [\texttt{X}|\texttt{X2s}]) \cup Var(\texttt{Zs}) \cup Var(\texttt{Ys})) = \emptyset$,
  $Var(\texttt{X1s}, \texttt{X2s}) \cap (Var(\texttt{Zs}) \cup Var(\texttt{Ys})) = \emptyset$, and
  $Var(\texttt{Zs}) \cap Var(\texttt{Ys}) = \emptyset$,

and that condition (7.2) holds since

$$Var(\texttt{Xs}) \cap (Var(\texttt{X1s}, [\texttt{X}|\texttt{X2s}]) \cup Var(\texttt{Zs}) \cup Var(\texttt{Ys})) = \emptyset.$$

Sequence

Finally, consider the **SEQUENCE** program with the following moding: $\texttt{app(-,-,+)}$, $\texttt{sublist(-,+)}$, $\texttt{sequence(+)}$, $\texttt{question(+)}$.

We already checked that **APPEND** is nicely moded in the mode $\texttt{app(-,-,+)}$. Proving nice modedness of the remaining clauses is straightforward thanks to the use of anonymous variables. We conclude that **SEQUENCE** is nicely moded.

7.6   Occur-check Freedom via Nice Modedness

Let us now return to the problem of proving occur-check freedom. In this section we show how the notion of nice modedness can be of use. The presentation is analogous to that of Section 7.4. So first we introduce the following concept.

Definition 7.22 We call an LD-derivation *output driven* if all atoms selected in it are output linear and input–output disjoint.   □

This brings us to the following alternative way of proving occur-check freedom.

Theorem 7.23 (Occur-check 2) Suppose that

- the head of every clause of P is input linear,
- all LD-derivations of $P \cup \{Q\}$ are output driven.

Then $P \cup \{Q\}$ is occur-check free.

Proof. Let A and H be as in the proof of the Occur-check 1 Theorem 7.16. The NSTO via Modes Lemma 7.14 applies and yields that $A = H$ is NSTO.   □

To apply this result to specific programs it suffices to link it with the concept of nice modedness. The following lemma is analogous to the Data Drivenness Lemma 7.17 and clarifies our interest in nicely moded programs.

Lemma 7.24 (Output Drivenness) Let P and Q be nicely moded. Then all LD-derivations of $P \cup \{Q\}$ are output driven.

Proof. Note that the first atom of a nicely moded query is output linear and input–output disjoint, so the conclusion follows by the Nice Modedness Lemma 7.20. □

Corollary 7.25 (Occur-check 2) Let P and Q be nicely moded. Suppose that

- the head of every clause of P is input linear.

Then $P \cup \{Q\}$ is occur-check free.

Proof. By the Occur-check 2 Theorem 7.23 and the the Output Drivenness Lemma 7.24. □

7.6.1   Examples

Let us see now how this corollary can be applied to the previously studied programs. We use here the conclusions established in Subsection 7.5.1, namely that these programs are nicely moded in the modings discussed there and in each case apply the Occur-check 2 Corollary 7.25.

Append
Consider APPEND with the mode `app(+,+,-)`. Clearly, the head of every clause is input linear. We conclude that when the query `app(s, t, u)` is nicely moded, so when u is linear and $Var(\mathbf{s},\mathbf{t}) \cap Var(\mathbf{u}) = \emptyset$, APPEND $\cup$ {`app(s, t, u)`} is occur-check free.

Append, again
In the mode `app(-,-,+)` the head of every clause of APPEND is input linear, as well. We obtain that when s,t is a linear family of terms and $Var(\mathbf{s},\mathbf{t}) \cap Var(\mathbf{u}) = \emptyset$, APPEND $\cup$ {`app(s, t, u)`} is occur-check free.

Permutation
It is straightforward to check that the heads of all clauses of PERMUTATION are input linear. We conclude that when t is linear and $Var(\mathbf{s}) \cap Var(\mathbf{t}) = \emptyset$, PERMUTATION $\cup$ {`perm(s, t)`} is occur-check free.

Sequence
Finally, consider the program SEQUENCE. The heads of its clauses are obviously input linear in the moding discussed before. We now obtain that for every term s, SEQUENCE $\cup$ {`question(s)`} is occur-check free.

Palindrome
So far it seems that the Occur-check 2 Corollary 7.25 allows us to draw more useful conclusions than the Occur-check 1 Corollary 7.18. However, reconsider the program PALINDROME discussed in Exercise 86.

Exercise 89 Show that no moding exists in which `PALINDROME` is nicely moded with the heads of all clauses being input linear.   □

This exercise implies that the Occur-check 2 Corollary 7.25 cannot be applied to this program.

A natural question arises of how to apply the above corollary to specific programs. We have already noticed in Section 7.4 that in the case of well-moded queries the input positions of the first atom are filled in by ground terms. This helps to find the appropriate modings so that the Occur-check 1 Corollary 7.18 could be applied.

However, no analogous property holds for for the nicely moded queries. As a result it is not clear how to mode the relations so that the Occur-check 2 Corollary 7.25 could be applied. For example, we have already noticed in Section 7.3 that it is not clear how to mode the relation `app` when considering the query `app([X,2], [Y,U], [3,Z,0,Z])`. Note that to conclude that `APPEND` $\cup$ {`app([X,2], [Y,U], [3,Z,0,Z])`} is occur-check free it suffices to use the mode `app(-,-,+)` and apply a conclusion established above.

As observed in Chadha and Plaisted [CP94], to apply the Occur-check 2 Corollary 7.25 it is probably more natural to investigate first all the modings for which the program is nicely moded and the heads of all clauses are input linear. Then one should check for which modings the given query is nicely moded. To this end in Chadha and Plaisted [CP94] two efficient algorithms are proposed for generating modings with the minimal number of input positions, for which the program is nicely moded.

Exercise 90 Prove that in the case of `APPEND` out of eight modes only for five of them are the conditions of the Occur-check 2 Corollary 7.25 satisfied. Show that out of these five modes only the mode `app(-,-,+)` can be used to deal with the occur-check freedom for the query `app([X,2], [Y,U], [3,Z,0,Z])`.   □

Exercise 91 Consider the `MEMBER` program:

```
% member(Element, List)  ←  Element is an element of the list List.
member(X, [X | _]).
member(X, [_ | Xs])  ←  member(X, Xs).
```

Prove that when $X \notin Var(\mathbf{t})$, `MEMBER` $\cup$ {`member(X, t)`} is occur-check free.   □

Exercise 92

(i) Suppose that all LD-derivations of $P \cup \{Q\}$ are both data and output driven. Prove that then $P \cup \{Q\}$ is occur-check free.

(ii) Let P and Q be well-moded and nicely moded. Prove that then $P \cup \{Q\}$ is occur-check free.   □

7.7   * Unfolding

Unfolding is a program transformation technique that allows us to improve the program efficiency through so-called partial evaluation. It was originally considered in Komorowski [Kom82] and formally studied by Tamaki and Sato [TS84] and others. In the next section we shall use this notion in the context of the problem of inserting the occur-checks. Here we define this notion and mention its relevant properties.

First, we generalize the notion of a resolvent to the case of two clauses. Recall from Definition 3.5 that a clause is applicable to an atom if a variant of its head unifies with the atom.

Definition 7.26 Let $c := H_1 \leftarrow \mathbf{A}, B, \mathbf{C}$ and d be clauses such that d is applicable to B. Let $H_2 \leftarrow \mathbf{B}$ be a variant of d with no common variables with c and let θ be an mgu of B and H_2. Then we call

$$(H_1 \leftarrow \mathbf{A}, \mathbf{B}, \mathbf{C})\theta$$

a resolvent of c and d via B. □

Definition 7.27 Let c be a clause of P with an atom A occurring in its body. Suppose that $d_1, \ldots, d_n$ are all the clauses of P which are applicable to A and let, for $i \in [1, n]$, c_i be the resolvent of c and d_i via A. Then we define

$$unfold(P, A, c) := (P - \{c\}) \cup \{c_1, \ldots, c_n\}.$$

We say that $unfold(P, A, c)$ is the result of *unfolding A in c in P* and call it an *unfolding of P*.   In particular, if no clause of P is applicable to A, then $unfold(P, A, c) := P - \{c\}$. □

As an example consider the program SUFFIX:

```
% suffix(Xs, Ys)  ←  Xs is a suffix of the list Ys.
suffix(Xs, Ys)  ←  app(_, Xs, Ys).
```

augmented by the APPEND program.

We leave to the reader to check that

```
suffix(Ys, Ys).
suffix(Xs, [_ | Ys])  ←  app(_, Xs, Ys).
```

augmented by the APPEND program.

is the result of unfolding the **app**-atom in the above clause.

Exercise 93

(i) Compute the result of unfolding the `member`-atom in the second clause of the SUBSET program:

```
% subset(Xs, Ys)  ←  each element of the list Xs is a member of the list Ys.
subset([], _).
subset([X | Xs], Ys)  ←  member(X, Ys), subset(Xs, Ys).
```

augmented by the MEMBER program.

(ii) Compute the result of unfolding of all the `sublist`-atoms in the program SEQUENCE discussed in the previous sections.   □

A program and its unfolding are closely related as the following theorem by Kawamura and Kanamori [KK88] shows.

Theorem 7.28 (Unfolding 1) Let P be a program, P_1 an unfolding of P and Q a query. Then θ is a c.a.s. for $P \cup \{Q\}$ iff θ is a c.a.s. for $P_1 \cup \{Q\}$.

Proof. Omitted.   □

Note that this theorem states nothing about termination. In fact, the following simple example shows that in general termination with respect to a program and its unfolding can differ.

Example 7.29 Consider the following program P:

```
r  ←  p, q.
p  ←  p.
```

By unfolding q in the first clause of P we actually delete this clause and obtain the following program P_1:

```
p  ←  p.
```

Now the only LD-derivation of $P \cup \{r\}$ is infinite, whereas the only LD-derivation of $P_1 \cup \{r\}$ is failed, so finite.   □

It is useful, however, to point out that unfolding of a program maintains universal termination of a query in the sense defined in Section 5.1. Namely, the following result was established by Bossi and Cocco [BC94]. It also justifies the intuition that unfolding improves efficiency.

Theorem 7.30 (Unfolding 2) Let P be a program, P_1 an unfolding of P and Q a query. Suppose that all LD-derivations of $P \cup \{Q\}$ are finite. Then all LD-derivations of $P_1 \cup \{Q\}$ are finite. Moreover, the height of all LD-trees for $P_1 \cup \{Q\}$ is then smaller than or equal to the height of all LD-trees for $P \cup \{Q\}$.

Proof. Omitted. The reader is referred to Exercise 72 of Section 6.7 for the justification of the reference to "the height of all LD-trees".   □

Exercise 94 Prove that an unfolding of a well-moded program is well-moded.   □

7.8   * Insertion of the Occur-checks

So far we explained how to prove the occur-check freedom for certain programs and queries. But, as already noted at the beginning of this chapter, it is very easy to run into difficulties due to the occur-check problem. In fact, for almost every program of Chapter 5 we can find a query which causes the occur-check problem. Consider for example the MEMBER program. Take then the query member(Y, [f(Y)]). Then one of the available sets of equations is { Y = X, f(Y) = X, [] = Xs } which *is* subject to occur-check. This set of equations is generated during a program execution and we obtain the already familiar interrupted listing:

```
| ?- member(Y, [f(Y)]).


Y = f(f(f(f(f(f(f(f(f(f(f(f(f(f(f(f(f(f(f(f(f(f(f(f(f(f(f(f(f(f(f(f(f(f(f(f(f(
```

In general, it is undecidable whether the occur-check can take place in a program execution (see Deransart and Małuszyński [DM85] and Apt and Pellegrini [AP94]), so the Occur-check 1 Corollary 7.18 and the Occur-check 2 Corollary 7.25 cannot offer a complete solution to the occur-check problem. The aim of this section is to explain how this problem can be taken care of by inserting the occur-checks. By this we mean insertion at the selected places in the program and the query of calls to the unification algorithm with the occur-check. The following strengthening of the Occur-check 2 Corollary 7.25 is essential.

Lemma 7.31 (Occur-check) Let P and Q be nicely moded. All sets of equations which are available in the LD-derivations of $P \cup \{Q\}$ and are obtained using a clause whose head is input linear are NSTO.

Proof. By the Nice Modedness Corollary 7.21 all queries in all LD-derivations of $P \cup \{Q\}$ are nicely moded. But the first atom of a nicely moded query is output linear and input–output disjoint. So when the head of the input clause used is input linear, by the NSTO via Modes Lemma 7.14 the corresponding set of equations is NSTO.   □

To use this result we transform a program and a query into a nicely moded program and a nicely moded query using the relation "$=_{oc}$" which is defined by the single clause

$$X =_{oc} X.$$

moded completely input. In the transformed program only this relation symbol is dealt with by the unification algorithm with the occur-check. The subscript $_{oc}$ was added to distinguish it from the Prolog built-in "=" which, according to our assumption, performs unification without the occur-check. Note that the clause X $=_{oc}$ X is not input linear, so the Occur-check 2 Corollary 7.25 cannot be applied in its presence.

The following result summarizes the effect of the yet to be defined program and query transformations.

Theorem 7.32 (Occur-check Insertion) For every program P and query Q there exists a program P' and a query Q' such that

- P' and Q' are nicely moded,
- the head of every clause of P' different from X $=_{oc}$ X is input linear,
- P is the result of unfolding some calls of "$=_{oc}$" in P',
- Q is the result of resolving some calls of "$=_{oc}$" in Q',
- all sets of equations available in the LD-derivations of $P' \cup \{Q'\}$, but not associated with the calls of "$=_{oc}$", are NSTO.

Proof. The idea is to replace the variables which "contradict nice modedness" by "fresh" variables. Consider a clause $H \leftarrow \mathbf{B}$. Assume for simplicity that in every atom input positions occur first. We say that a given occurrence of a variable x in $\mathbf{B}$ *contradicts nice modedness* of $H \leftarrow \mathbf{B}$ if x occurs in an output position of an atom in $\mathbf{B}$ and x occurs earlier in $\mathbf{B}$ or in an input position of H.

Consider now an occurrence of x in $\mathbf{B}$ which contradicts nice modedness. Let A be the atom in $\mathbf{B}$ in which this occurrence of x takes place and let z be a fresh variable. Replace this occurrence of x in A by z and denote the resulting atom A'. Replace A in $\mathbf{B}$ by $A', z =_{oc} x$.

Scan now $\mathbf{B}$ and perform this replacement repeatedly for all occurrences of variables which contradict the nice modedness of the original clause $H \leftarrow \mathbf{B}$. Call the resulting sequence of atoms $\mathbf{B}'$. It is easy to see that $H \leftarrow \mathbf{B}'$ is nicely moded. Note that by unfolding the inserted calls of "$=_{oc}$" in $H \leftarrow \mathbf{B}'$, we obtain the original clause $H \leftarrow \mathbf{B}$.

The same transformation applied to an arbitrary query transforms it into a nicely moded query. Finally, a similar transformation ensures that the head H of $H \leftarrow \mathbf{B}$ is input linear. It suffices to repeatedly replace every occurrence of a variable x which contradicts linearity of H by a fresh variable z and replace $\mathbf{B}$ by $z =_{oc} x, \mathbf{B}$. Clearly, the head of the resulting clause $H \leftarrow \mathbf{B}'$ is input linear and this transformation does not destroy the nice modedness of the clause. Again, the original clause $H \leftarrow \mathbf{B}$ can be obtained by unfolding the inserted calls of "$=_{oc}$".

The claim now follows by the Occur-check Lemma 7.31. $\qquad\square$

The Unfolding 1 Theorem 7.28 and Unfolding 2 Theorem 7.30 show that the behaviour of an unfolded program is closely related to the original program. So it is justified to summarize the above result by saying that every program and query is equivalent to a nicely moded program and nicely moded query such that the heads of all clauses, except X $=_{oc}$ X, are input linear. In the Prolog execution of the latter program and query *only* the inserted calls of "$=_{oc}$" need to be dealt with by means of a unification algorithm with the occur-check. These inserted calls of "$=_{oc}$" can be viewed as the overhead needed to implement correctly the original program without the occur check.

Alternatively, the part of the transformation which ensures that the head of each clause is input linear could be dropped and the Occur-check Lemma 7.31 could be applied.

Let us see now how this transformation can be applied to specific programs and queries.

Member

Consider the MEMBER program and the above discussed query member(Y, [f(Y)]) in the moding member(-,+). MEMBER is then nicely moded, so no transformation of the program is needed. The transformation of the query results in member(Z, [f(Y)]), $Z=_{oc}$ Y.

Palindrome

Exercise 86 shows that when s is a ground term, PALINDROME $\cup$ {palindrome(s)} is occur-check free. On the other hand, it is easy to see that when s is a non-ground term, then the occur-check freedom can be established neither by the Occur-check 1 Corollary 7.18 nor by the Occur-check 2 Corollary 7.25. (For the latter see Exercise 89.) In fact, the query palindrome([X, f(X)]) yields the already familiar interrupted listing.

Take now the following moding for PALINDROME: palindrome(+), reverse(+,+), reverse(+,-,+). Then for an arbitrary term s the query palindrome(s) is nicely moded. In addition, all clauses of PALINDROME are then input linear. However, the clause reverse([X | X1s], X2s, Ys) $\leftarrow$ reverse(X1s, [X | X2s], Ys) is not nicely moded. Indeed, the last occurrence of X contradicts the nice modedness of this clause. Using the above program transformation we obtain the clause

reverse([X | X1s], X2s, Ys) $\leftarrow$ reverse(X1s, [Z | X2s], Ys), Z $=_{oc}$ X.

Denote by PALINDROME1 the program obtained from PALINDROME by replacing the clause reverse([X | X1s], X2s, Ys) $\leftarrow$ reverse(X1s, [X | X2s], Ys) by its transformed version and by adding the clause X $=_{oc}$ X. By the Occur-check Insertion Theorem 7.32 we conclude that all sets of equations available in the LD-derivations of PALINDROME1 $\cup$ {palindrome(s)}, but not associated with the calls of "$=_{oc}$", are NSTO.

7.9   Concluding Remarks

The original motivation of the implementers of Prolog for omiting the occur-check from the unification algorithm was to ensure that the unification of a variable and a term can be done in constant time. This special case of unification often takes place — for example, when the output positions of the selected atoms are filled in by different variables.

It should be mentioned here that some modern Prolog systems, for example ECL^{i}PS^e [Agg95], allow us to set a flag to perform unification with the occur-check. This does not obviate the work discussed here, because not all Prolog systems have this facility and moreover the omission of the occur-check is desired from the efficiency point of view.

The occur-check freedom is an example of a run-time property, that is a property which refers to the program execution. In general, such properties are undecidable and the occur-check freedom is no exception (see Section 7.8). In this chapter we proposed simple methods allowing us to deal with the occur-check problem. These methods are based on a syntactic analysis and can be easily implemented. It was shown in Apt and Pellegrini [AP94] that these methods and their modifications deal satisfactorily with most common Prolog programs.

Because of the above undecidability results it is easy to find examples of programs and queries to which these methods cannot be applied. In such situations one can use the program transformation proposed in the previous section. Note that such a transformation can be efficiently implemented using two passes through the query and the program, one to ensure nice modedness and the other to ensure the input linearity of the heads of the program clauses. Its usefulness is crucially dependent on the generation of the modes which reflect the use of the program relations.

Finally, a digression about the actions of the Martelli–Montanari algorithm. We showed that whenever the conditions of the Occur-check 1 Corollary 7.18 or of the Occur-check 2 Corollary 7.25 are satisfied for P and Q, action (6) cannot be performed in any LD-derivation of $P \cup \{Q\}$. In fact, as the proofs of the NSTO Lemma 7.5 and of the NSTO via Modes Lemma 7.14 show, in these situations action (3) cannot be performed either, so it can be deleted from the algorithm. The gain is, however, negligible.

7.10 Bibliographic Remarks

This chapter is based on Apt and Pellegrini [AP94], where refinements of the presented methods are also discussed that allow us to deal with more complex Prolog programs. The notion of an NSTO set of equations is from Deransart *et al.* [DFT91]. Exercise 76 is from Deransart and Małuszyński [DM93].

Modes were first considered in Mellish [Mel81] and more extensively studied in Reddy [Red84]. The concept of a well-moded program is essentially from Dembiński and Małuszyński [DM85], where a more complicated definition is given and the Data Drivenness Lemma 7.17 is stated without proof. We used here an elegant formulation from Rosenblueth [Ros91], which is equivalent to that of Drabent [Dra87], where well-moded programs are called simple. The Well-modedness Lemma 7.9 is from Apt and Luitjes [AL95]. In Apt and Pellegrini [AP94] a weaker version was proved that dealt only with the LD-resolvents. In Rao [Rao93] the notion of well-modedness is generalized so that the Computed

Answer Corollary 7.11 becomes applicable to more programs and different selection rules.

Exercise 84 is stated in Clark [Cla79, page 15]. P. Deransart (private communication) pointed out to us that the Occur-check 2 Corollary 7.25 is also a consequence of the results established in Deransart *et al.* [DFT91] and based on the use of the attribute grammars. Exercises 89 and 90 are due to Chadha and Plaisted [CP94].

The subject of transformations of logic programs, which we barely touch in this book, is extensively studied in Deville [Dev90] and Pettorossi and Proietti [PP94]. Example 7.29 is due to Bossi and Cocco [BC94].

Two other approaches to the subject of proving occur-check freedom were proposed in the literature. One is based on the abstract interpretations and another uses the attribute grammars. The first approach originated with Plaisted [Pla84], where the occur-check problem was originally formulated and was further developed in Søndergaard [Son86]. The second approach was originated by Deransart and Małuszyński [DM85] and was further developed in Deransart *et al.* [DFT91]. More recently, it was applied in Dumant [Dum92] to deal with the problem of inserting occur-checks for arbitrary resolution strategies.

7.11   Summary

In this chapter we dealt with the occur-check problem. For this purpose we introduced the following notions:

- occur-check free programs and queries,
- modes,
- input (respectively output) linearity,
- well-moded queries and programs,
- nicely moded queries and programs

and showed how to use them to prove occur-check freedom by means of syntactic means. We also dealt with the problem of the insertion of the occur-checks. To this end we defined

- unfolding,
- insertion of the occur-checks by means of program and query transformations.

7.12   References

[Agg95]   A. Aggoun *et al. ECL^{i}PS^e 3.5 User Manual.* ECRC, Munich, Germany, February 1995.

[AL95]   K. R. Apt and I. Luitjes. Verification of logic programs with delay declarations. In V.S. Alagar and M. Nivat, editors, *Proceedings of the Fourth International*

Conference on Algebraic Methodology and Software Technology, (AMAST'95), Lecture Notes in Computer Science 936, pages 66–90, Springer-Verlag, Berlin, 1995. Invited Lecture.

[AP94] K. R. Apt and A. Pellegrini. On the occur-check free Prolog programs. *ACM Toplas*, 16(3):687–726, 1994.

[BC94] A. Bossi and N. Cocco. Preserving universal termination through unfold/fold. In G. Levi and M. Rodriguez-Artalejo, editors, *Proceeding of the Fourth International Conference on Algebraic and Logic Programming (ALP 94)*, Lecture Notes in Computer Science 850, pages 269–286, Springer-Verlag, Berlin, 1994.

[Cla79] K. L. Clark. Predicate logic as a computational formalism. Res. Report DOC 79/59, Imperial College, Department of Computing, London, 1979.

[CP94] R. Chadha and D. A. Plaisted. Correctness of unification without occur check in Prolog. *Journal of Logic Programming*, 18(2):99–122, 1994.

[Dev90] Y. Deville. *Logic Programming. Systematic Program Development*. International Series in Logic Programming. Addison-Wesley, Reading, MA, 1990.

[DFT91] P. Deransart, G. Ferrand, and M. Téguia. NSTO programs (not subject to occur-check). In V. Saraswat and K. Ueda, editors, *Proceedings of the International Logic Symposium*, pages 533–547. The MIT Press, Cambridge, MA, 1991.

[DM85] P. Deransart and J. Małuszyński. Relating logic programs and attribute grammars. *Journal of Logic Programming*, 2:119–156, 1985.

[Dra87] W. Drabent. Do logic programs resemble programs in conventional languages? In *International Symposium on Logic Programming*, pages 389–396. IEEE Computer Society, San Francisco, CA, August 1987.

[DM85] P. Dembiński and J. Małuszyński. AND-parallelism with intelligent backtracking for annotated logic programs. In *Proceedings of the International Symposium on Logic Programming*, pages 29–38. IEEE Computer Society, Boston, MA, 1985.

[DM93] P. Deransart and J. Małuszyński. *A Grammatical View of Logic Programming*. The MIT Press, Cambridge, MA, 1993.

[Dum92] B. Dumant. Checking soundness of resolution schemes. In K. R. Apt, editor, *Proceedings of the Joint International Conference and Symposium on Logic Programming*, pages 37–51. MIT Press, Cambridge, MA, 1992.

[KK88] T. Kawamura and T. Kanamori. Preservation of stronger equivalence in unfold/fold logic programming transformation. In ICOT Staff, editors, *Proceedings of the International Conference on Fifth Generation Computer Systems*, pages 413–422. Institute for New Generation Computer Technology, Tokyo, 1988.

[Kom82]   H. J. Komorowski. Partial evaluation as a means for inferencing data structures in an applicative language: a theory and implementation in case of Prolog. In *Proceedings of the Ninth ACM Symposium on Principles of Programming Languages*, pages 255–267. The Association for Computing Machinery, New York, 1982.

[Mel81]   C. S. Mellish. The Automatic Generation of Mode Declarations for Prolog Programs. DAI Research Paper 163, Department of Artificial Intelligence, University of Edinburgh, August 1981.

[Pla84]   D.A. Plaisted. The occur-check problem in Prolog. *New Generation Computing*, 2:309–322, 1984.

[PP94]   A. Pettorossi and M. Proietti. Transformation of logic programs: foundations and techniques. *Journal of Logic Programming*, 19-20:261–320, 1994.

[Rao93]   K. Rao. *Termination characteristics of logic programs*. Ph.D. Thesis, University of Bombay, 1993.

[Red84]   U. S. Reddy. Transformation of logic programs into functional programs. In *International Symposium on Logic Programming*, pages 187–198, Silver Spring, MD, February 1984. Atlantic City, IEEE Computer Society.

[Ros91]   D.A. Rosenblueth. Using program transformation to obtain methods for eliminating backtracking in fixed-mode logic programs. Technical Report 7, Universidad Nacional Autonoma de Mexico, Instituto de Investigaciones en Matematicas Aplicadas y en Sistemas, 1991.

[Son86]   H. Søndergaard. An application of abstract interpretation of logic programs: occur check reduction. In *Proceedings of ESOP'86*, pages 327–338, Saarbrücken, 1986.

[TS84]   H. Tamaki and T. Sato. Unfold/fold transformations of logic programs. In Sten-Åke Tärnlund, editor, *Proceedings of the Second International Conference on Logic Programming*, pages 127–138, Uppsala, 1984.

Chapter 8

Partial Correctness

In Chapter 1 we mentioned several program properties which should be taken into account when proving that a program is correct. One of them is partial correctness the study of which forms the subject of this chapter.

As logic and pure Prolog programs can yield several answers, partial correctness can be interpreted in two ways. In the next section we identify these two possible interpretations. The first of them aims at determining the form of computed instances of a query. In Section 8.2 we introduce assertions and define for programs and queries the property of being well-asserted. Then, in Section 8.3 we show how these notions can be applied to determine the form of computed instances for specific programs and queries.

The second interpretation of the notion of partial correctness aims at computing the set of all computed instances of a query. In Section 8.4 we provide a method allowing us to compute such sets using the least Herbrand model of a program. Then, in Section 8.5 we show how this method can be applied for specific programs.

Finally, in Section 8.6, we deal with a program property that is specific to the logic programming paradigm, namely absence of failures, that is the existence of successful derivations. The first interpretation of the notion of correctness cannot be used to establish the existence of such derivations but the second interpretation can. We also show that absence of failures can be established in a more direct way, using the least Herbrand model of a program.

8.1 Introduction

In Chapter 1 we defined partial correctness as the property that the program delivers correct results for relevant queries. However, logic and pure Prolog programs can yield several answers and consequently partial correctness can be interpreted in two ways.

Take as an example the already familiar APPEND program. It is natural that for the query app([1,2], [3,4], Zs) we would like to prove that upon successful termination the variable Zs is instantiated to [1,2,3,4], that is that $\{Zs/[1,2,3,4]\}$ is the computed answer substitution.

On the other hand, for the query app(Xs, Ys, [1,2,3,4]) we would like to prove that *all* possible splittings of the list [1,2,3,4] can be produced. This means that we would like to prove that each of the following substitutions:

$$\{Xs/[\ ], Ys/[1,2,3,4]\},$$
$$\{Xs/[1], Ys/[2,3,4]\},$$
$$\{Xs/[1,2], Ys/[3,4]\},$$
$$\{Xs/[1,2,3], Ys/[4]\},$$
$$\{Xs/[1,2,3,4], Ys/[\ ]\}$$

is a possible computed answer substitution to the query app(Xs, Ys, [1,2,3,4]).

Moreover, we should also prove that *no* other answer can be produced. This boils down to the claim that the above set of substitutions coincides with the set of all computed answer substitutions to app(Xs, Ys, [1,2,3,4]).

A similar strengthening is possible in the case of the first query. We could prove that the query app([1,2], [3,4], Zs) admits *precisely* one c.a.s., namely $\{Zs/[1,2,3,4]\}$. Note that the previous formulation only guarantees that the query app([1,2], [3,4], Zs) admits at *most* one c.a.s., namely $\{Zs/[1,2,3,4]\}$.

Both formulations of the partial correctness can be conveniently formalized using the notion of a computed instance. Recall from Section 3.2 (Definition 3.6) that given a program P and a query Q, the query Q' is called a computed instance of Q if for some c.a.s. θ of Q we have $Q' = Q\theta$.

In what follows, the program P, w.r.t. which the computed instances are considered, is always clear from the context, so we omit a reference to it.

We are now ready to define formally both notions of partial correctness.

Definition 8.1 Consider a program P and a query Q and a set of queries $\mathcal{Q}$.

- We write $\{Q\}\ P\ \mathcal{Q}$ to denote the fact that all computed instances of Q are elements of $\mathcal{Q}$.
- We denote by $sp(Q, P)$ the set of all computed instances of Q. $\qquad\square$

Here "*sp*" is an abbreviation for "strongest postcondition", a notion originally introduced in the context of imperative programs. The first notion of partial correctness aims at establishing formulas of the form $\{Q\}\ P\ \mathcal{Q}$ while the second one aims at computing the sets of the form $sp(Q, P)$. Note that $\{Q\}\ P\ \mathcal{Q}$ iff $sp(Q, P) \subseteq \mathcal{Q}$, so the first notion of correctness deals with the inclusions between two sets of queries, while the second notion deals with the equality between two sets of queries.

Note that both notions of correctness refer to successful SLD-derivations and not to successful LD-derivations. This is not a problem because, by virtue of the Independence Theorem 3.33, the notion of a computed instance does not depend on the selection rule.

In the subsequent sections we introduce methods that allow us to establish the above two properties. In particular, using these methods we can prove the above mentioned properties of the APPEND program, so

$$\{\mathrm{app}([1,2],[3,4],\mathrm{Zs})\}\ \text{APPEND}\ \{\mathrm{app}([1,2],[3,4],[1,2,3,4])\}$$

and

$$sp(\mathrm{app}(\mathrm{Xs},\mathrm{Ys},[1,2,3,4]),\text{APPEND}) =$$

```
{app([],[1,2,3,4],[1,2,3,4]),
 app([1],[2,3,4],[1,2,3,4]),
 app([1,2],[3,4],[1,2,3,4]),
 app([1,2,3],[4],[1,2,3,4]),
 app([1,2,3,4],[],[1,2,3,4])
}.
```

8.2   Well-asserted Queries and Programs

We begin by providing a method that allows us to prove properties of the first kind, that is statements of the form $\{Q\}\ P\ Q$. We call an atom a *p-atom* if its relation symbol is p. Recall from Section 6.8 that we denoted the relation symbol occurring in atom A by $rel(A)$. So an atom A is a $rel(A)$-atom.

The following very general definition of the notions of assertion and specification is sufficient for our purposes.

Definition 8.2 Consider a relation symbol p.

- An *assertion for p* is a set of p-atoms closed under substitution.
- An *assertion* is an assertion for a relation symbol p.
- We say that an assertion $\mathcal{A}$ *holds for an atom* A if $A \in \mathcal{A}$.
- A *specification for p* is a pair pre_p, $post_p$ of assertions for p. We call pre_p (respectively $post_p$) a *pre-assertion* (respectively a *post-assertion*) associated with p.
- A *specification* is a collection of specifications for different relation symbols.

$\square$

Example 8.3 Consider the following specification for the relation member:

$$pre_{\mathrm{member}} = \{\mathrm{member}(s,t) \mid t \text{ is a list}\},$$

$$post_{\mathrm{member}} = \{\mathrm{member}(s,t) \mid s \text{ is an element of the list } t\}.$$

Then pre_{member} holds for member(s,t) iff t is a list and $post_{\mathrm{member}}$ holds for member(s,t) iff s is an element of the list t. In contrast, the set

$$\{\mathrm{member}(s,t) \mid s \text{ is a variable and } t \text{ is a list}\},$$

is not an assertion since it is not closed under substitution. $\square$

In the remainder of this section we adopt the following.

Assumption *Every considered relation* has a fixed specification associated with it.

This assumption will allow us to talk about pre- and post-assertions of a relation symbol. The assumption is somewhat limiting if we wish to associate different specifications with different occurrences of a relation in a program. This can be achieved by simply renaming the relations.

The idea behind the use of the specifications is the following. We associate with each relation a specification with the intention that the post-assertions hold for the computed instances of each atomic query. So, for example, in the case of the APPEND program the intention is that the post-assertion associated with the relation app holds for the atom app([1,2], [3,4], [1,2,3,4]). More generally, this post-assertion should contain all the computed instances of the app-atoms of the form app(s,t,u) where s,t are lists.

As not every choice of specifications meets the above intention, we impose appropriate restrictions on them. These restrictions ensure that a stronger property holds, namely that the pre-assertions hold for all atoms selected in the LD-derivations and that the post-assertions hold for the computed instances of all selected atoms.

The appropriate conditions generalize the notion of a well-moded query and well-moded program introduced in Section 7.3. First, we need the following notation.

Definition 8.4 Given atoms $A_1, \ldots, A_n, A_{n+1}$ and assertions $\mathcal{A}_1, \ldots, \mathcal{A}_n, \mathcal{A}_{n+1}$, where $n \geq 0$, we write

$$\models A_1 \in \mathcal{A}_1, \ldots, A_n \in \mathcal{A}_n \;\Rightarrow\; A_{n+1} \in \mathcal{A}_{n+1}$$

to denote the fact that for all substitutions θ, if $A_1\theta \in \mathcal{A}_1, \ldots, A_n\theta \in \mathcal{A}_n$, then $A_{n+1}\theta \in \mathcal{A}_{n+1}$. $\qquad\square$

Exercise 95 Call a statement of the form $A \in \mathcal{A}$, where A is an atom and $\mathcal{A}$ an assertion, an *assertion claim*. Let $\phi, \phi_1, \phi_2, \phi_3$ and ψ be sequences of assertion claims. Suppose that $\models \phi_2 \Rightarrow A \in \mathcal{A}$ and $\models \phi_1, A \in \mathcal{A}, \phi_3 \Rightarrow B \in \mathcal{B}$. Prove then that

$$\models \phi_1, \phi_2, \phi_3 \;\Rightarrow\; B \in \mathcal{B}.$$

$\qquad\square$

We now abbreviate $A \in pre_{rel(A)}$ to $pre(A)$ and analogously for *post*. So given an atom $p(\mathbf{s})$ and a pre-assertion pre_p, we write $pre(p(\mathbf{s}))$ when $p(\mathbf{s}) \in pre_p$.

Definition 8.5

- A query $A_1, \ldots, A_n$ is called *well-asserted* if for $j \in [1, n]$

$$\models post(A_1), \ldots, post(A_{j-1}) \;\Rightarrow\; pre(A_j).$$

- A clause $H \leftarrow B_1, \ldots, B_n$ is called *well-asserted* if

    for $j \in [1, n+1]$

    $$\models pre(H), post(B_1), \ldots, post(B_{j-1}) \ \Rightarrow \ pre(B_j),$$

    where $pre(B_{n+1}) := post(H)$.

- A program is called *well-asserted* if every clause of it is.   □

Thus, a query is well-asserted if

- the pre-assertion of every atom is implied in the sense of Definition 8.4 by the conjunction of the post-assertions of the previous atoms.

And a clause is well-asserted if

- ($j \in [1, n]$) the pre-assertion of every body atom is implied by the conjunction of the pre-assertion of the head and the post-assertions of the previous body atoms,
- ($j = n+1$) the post-assertion of the head is implied by the conjunction of the pre-assertion of the head and the post-assertions of the body atoms.

In particular, an atomic query A is well-asserted if $\models pre(A)$, and a unit clause $A \leftarrow$ is well-asserted if $\models pre(A) \Rightarrow post(A)$.

The following lemma, analogous to the Well-modedness Lemma 7.9, shows the "persistence" of the notion of well-assertedness.

Lemma 8.6 (Well-assertedness) An SLD-resolvent of a well-asserted query and a well-asserted clause is well-asserted.

Proof. We reason as in the proof of the Well-modedness Lemma 7.9. It suffices to prove the following two claims.

Claim 1 An instance of a well-asserted query (respectively clause) is well-asserted.

Proof. Immediate by the assumption that the assertions are closed under substitution.

□

Claim 2 Suppose that $\mathbf{A}, H, \mathbf{C}$ is a well-asserted query and $H \leftarrow \mathbf{B}$ is a well-asserted clause. Then $\mathbf{A}, \mathbf{B}, \mathbf{C}$ is a well-asserted query.

Proof. Let
$$\mathbf{A} := A_1, \ldots, A_k,$$
$$\mathbf{B} := A_{k+1}, \ldots, A_{k+l},$$
$$\mathbf{C} := A_{k+l+1}, \ldots A_{k+l+m}.$$

Fix now $i \in [1, k + l + m]$. We need to prove

$$\models post(A_1), \ldots, post(A_{i-1}) \;\Rightarrow\; pre(A_i).$$

Three cases arise.

Case 1 $i \in [1, k]$.
Note that $\mathbf{A}$ is well-asserted, since $\mathbf{A}, H, \mathbf{C}$ is well-asserted. Hence the claim follows.

Case 2 $i \in [k + 1, k + l]$.
$H \leftarrow \mathbf{B}$ is well-asserted, so

$$\models pre(H), post(A_{k+1}), \ldots, post(A_{i-1}) \;\Rightarrow\; pre(A_i).$$

Moreover, $\mathbf{A}, H, \mathbf{C}$ is well-asserted, so

$$\models post(A_1), \ldots, post(A_k) \;\Rightarrow\; pre(H).$$

This implies the claim by virtue of Exercise 95.

Case 3 $i \in [k + l + 1, k + l + m]$.
$\mathbf{A}, H, \mathbf{C}$ is well-asserted, so

$$\models post(A_1), \ldots, post(A_k), post(H), post(A_{k+l+1}), \ldots, post(A_{i-1}) \;\Rightarrow\; pre(A_i)$$

and

$$\models post(A_1), \ldots, post(A_k) \;\Rightarrow\; pre(H).$$

Moreover, $H \leftarrow \mathbf{B}$ is well-asserted, so

$$\models pre(H), post(A_{k+1}), \ldots, post(A_{k+l}) \;\Rightarrow\; post(H).$$

Applying Exercise 95 twice we obtain the claim. $\qquad\square$
$\hfill\square$

We can now draw the following conclusions. The first one is analogous to the Well-modedness Corollary 7.10.

Corollary 8.7 (Well-assertedness) Let P and Q be well-asserted. Then all queries in all SLD-derivations of $P \cup \{Q\}$ are well-asserted. $\qquad\square$

The next one deals with LD-derivations and is analogous to the Data Drivenness Lemma 7.17.

Corollary 8.8 (Pre-assertion) Let P and Q be well-asserted, and let ξ be an LD-derivation of $P \cup \{Q\}$. Then $\models pre(A)$ for every atom A selected in ξ.

Proof. Note that for a well-asserted query $A_1, \ldots, A_n$ we have $\models pre(A_1)$, so the claim follows from the Well-assertedness Corollary 8.7. $\square$

The final conclusion is analogous to the Computed Answer Corollary 7.11.

Corollary 8.9 (Post-assertion) Let P and Q be well-asserted. Then for every computed instance $A_1, \ldots, A_n$ of Q we have $\models post(A_j)$ for $j \in [1, n]$.

Proof. Let $Q = p_1(\mathbf{s}_1), \ldots, p_k(\mathbf{s}_k)$ and let p be a new relation of arity equal to the sum of the arities of $p_1, \ldots, p_k$.

We now define a pre-assertion for p as follows:

$$p(\mathbf{s}_1, \ldots, \mathbf{s}_k) \in pre_p \text{ iff } p_1(\mathbf{s}_1) \in post_{p_1}, \ldots, p_k(\mathbf{s}_k) \in post_{p_k}.$$

Note that pre_p is closed under substitution, since each $post_{p_i}$ is, so it is indeed an assertion. Define the post-assertion for p arbitrarily.

Then $Q, p(\mathbf{s}_1, \ldots, \mathbf{s}_k)$ is a well-asserted query because by the definition of pre_p

$$\models post(p_1(\mathbf{s}_1)), \ldots, post(p_k(\mathbf{s}_k)) \ \Rightarrow \ pre(p(\mathbf{s}_1, \ldots, \mathbf{s}_k)).$$

Suppose now that θ is a c.a.s. of Q. Then $p(\mathbf{s}_1, \ldots, \mathbf{s}_k)\theta$ is a query in an SLD-derivation of $P \cup \{Q, p(\mathbf{s}_1, \ldots, \mathbf{s}_k)\}$. By the Well-assertedness Corollary 8.7 we have $\models pre(p(\mathbf{s}_1, \ldots, \mathbf{s}_k)\theta)$ and by the definition of pre_p

$$\models pre(p(\mathbf{s}_1, \ldots, \mathbf{s}_k)\theta) \ \Rightarrow \ post(p_1(\mathbf{s}_1)\theta), \ldots, post(p_k(\mathbf{s}_k)\theta),$$

so the conclusion follows. $\square$

Exercise 96 Prove that an unfolding of a well-asserted program is well-asserted. $\square$

8.3   Applications

We now explain how the results of the previous section allow us to establish properties of the form $\{Q\} \ P \ Q$. For simplicity, in the examples below we restrict our attention to atomic queries. We shall use the following immediate conclusion of the Post-assertion Corollary 8.9. Recall from Section 4.2 that for an atom A we denote by $inst(A)$ the set of all instances of A.

Corollary 8.10 (Partial Correctness) Let P and A be well-asserted, where A is a p-atom. Then $\{A\} \ P \ inst(A) \cap post_p$. $\square$

To see the usefulness of this corollary let us apply it to specific programs.

Append

First, consider the program APPEND:

```
app([], Ys, Ys).
app([X | Xs], Ys, [X | Zs]) ← app(Xs, Ys, Zs).
```

Let

$$pre_{\mathbf{app}} = \{\mathtt{app}(s, t, u) \mid s, t \text{ are lists}\},$$

$$post_{\mathbf{app}} = \{\mathtt{app}(s, t, u) \mid s, t, u \text{ are lists and } s * t = u\},$$

where "$*$" denotes the list concatenation, that is

$$[s_1, \ldots, s_m] * [t_1, \ldots, t_n] := [s_1, \ldots, s_m, t_1, \ldots, t_n],$$

where $m, n \geq 0$. Let us check that APPEND is then well-asserted. To this end we need to prove the following statements:

$$\models pre(\mathtt{app}([\ ], \mathtt{Ys}, \mathtt{Ys})) \Rightarrow post(\mathtt{app}([\ ], \mathtt{Ys}, \mathtt{Ys})),$$

$$\models pre(\mathtt{app}([\mathtt{X}|\mathtt{Xs}], \mathtt{Ys}, [\mathtt{X}|\mathtt{Zs}])) \Rightarrow pre(\mathtt{app}(\mathtt{Xs}, \mathtt{Ys}, \mathtt{Zs})),$$

$$\models pre(\mathtt{app}([\mathtt{X}|\mathtt{Xs}], \mathtt{Ys}, [\mathtt{X}|\mathtt{Zs}])), post(\mathtt{app}(\mathtt{Xs}, \mathtt{Ys}, \mathtt{Zs})) \Rightarrow \\ post(\mathtt{app}([\mathtt{X}|\mathtt{Xs}], \mathtt{Ys}, [\mathtt{X}|\mathtt{Zs}])).$$

All of them are completely straightforward and we limit ourselves to checking the last one. So suppose that for some substitution θ both $\mathtt{app}([\mathtt{X}|\mathtt{Xs}], \mathtt{Ys}, [\mathtt{X}|\mathtt{Zs}])\theta \in pre_{\mathbf{app}}$ and $\mathtt{app}(\mathtt{Xs}, \mathtt{Ys}, \mathtt{Zs})\theta \in post_{\mathbf{app}}$. This means that $[\mathtt{X}|\mathtt{Xs}]\theta$, $\mathtt{Ys}\theta$, $\mathtt{Xs}\theta$, and $\mathtt{Zs}\theta$ are lists and $\mathtt{Xs}\theta * \mathtt{Ys}\theta = \mathtt{Zs}\theta$. From this we conclude that $[\mathtt{X}|\mathtt{Zs}]\theta$ is also a list and $[\mathtt{X}|\mathtt{Xs}]\theta * \mathtt{Ys}\theta = [\mathtt{X}|\mathtt{Zs}]\theta$.

Now let $\mathtt{s}, \mathtt{t}$ be ground lists and consider the query $\mathtt{app}(\mathtt{s}, \mathtt{t}, \mathtt{Zs})$. Note that this query is well-asserted and

$$inst(\mathtt{app}(s, t, \mathtt{Zs})) \cap post_{\mathbf{app}} = \{\mathtt{app}(s, t, s * t)\},$$

so by the Partial Correctness Corollary 8.10 we conclude

$$\{\mathtt{app}(s, t, \mathtt{Zs})\} \text{ APPEND } \{\mathtt{app}(s, t, s * t)\}.$$

Exercise 97 Prove that the program MEMBER:

```
member(X, [X | _]).
member(X, [_ | Xs]) ← member(X, Xs).
```

is well-asserted w.r.t. the specification given in Example 8.3.   □

Append, again

Consider now the query app(Xs, Ys, u), where u is a ground list. Note that this query is not well-asserted w.r.t. the considered specification of app. So to deal with its partial correctness we need to use a different specification for the app relation.

Now let

$$pre_{\mathbf{app}} = \{\mathrm{app}(s, t, u) \mid u \text{ is a list}\},$$

$$post_{\mathbf{app}} = \{\mathrm{app}(s, t, u) \mid s, t, u \text{ are lists and } s * t = u\}.$$

Exercise 98 Prove that APPEND is well-asserted w.r.t. this specification. □

Note that now the query app(Xs, Ys, u) is well-asserted. By the Partial Correctness Corollary 8.10 we conclude that

$$\{\mathrm{app}(\mathtt{Xs}, \mathtt{Ys}, \mathtt{u})\} \text{ APPEND } inst(\mathrm{app}(\mathtt{Xs}, \mathtt{Ys}, \mathtt{u})) \cap post_{app}.$$

But it is easy to see that

$$inst(\mathrm{app}(\mathtt{Xs}, \mathtt{Ys}, \mathtt{u})) \cap post_{app} = \{\mathrm{app}(s, t, u) \mid s * t = u\},$$

so we conclude that every successful SLD-derivation of APPEND $\cup$ $\{\mathrm{app}(\mathtt{Xs}, \mathtt{Ys}, \mathtt{u})\}$ yields a computed instance app(s,t,u) such that s*t = u.

Notice that for each of the uses of APPEND we considered only ground lists. The reasons for this restriction will be discussed in Section 8.7.

Exercise 99 To avoid separate consideration of the two uses of APPEND discussed above we can introduce the following specification which is a set-theoretical union of the previous two ones:

$$pre_{\mathbf{app}} = \{\mathrm{app}(s, t, u) \mid s, t \text{ are lists or } u \text{ is a list}\},$$

$$post_{\mathbf{app}} = \{\mathrm{app}(s, t, u) \mid s, t, u \text{ are lists and } s * t = u\}.$$

Prove that APPEND is well-asserted w.r.t. this specification. □

Sequence

As a somewhat less trivial example consider now the SEQUENCE program:

```
% sequence(Xs)  ←  Xs is a list of 27 elements.
sequence([_,_,_,_,_,_,_,_,_,_,_,_,_,_,_,_,_,_,_,_,_,_,_,_,_,_,_]).

% question(Ss)  ←  Ss is a list of 27 elements forming the desired sequence.
question(Ss)  ←
    sequence(Ss),
    sublist([1,_,1,_,1], Ss),
    sublist([2,_,_,2,_,_,2], Ss),
    sublist([3,_,_,_,3,_,_,_,3], Ss),
```

```
sublist([4,_,_,_,_,4,_,_,_,_,4], Ss),
sublist([5,_,_,_,_,_,5,_,_,_,_,_,5], Ss),
sublist([6,_,_,_,_,_,_,6,_,_,_,_,_,_,6], Ss),
sublist([7,_,_,_,_,_,_,_,7,_,_,_,_,_,_,_,7], Ss),
sublist([8,_,_,_,_,_,_,_,_,8,_,_,_,_,_,_,_,_,8], Ss),
sublist([9,_,_,_,_,_,_,_,_,_,9,_,_,_,_,_,_,_,_,_,9], Ss).
```

```
% sublist(Xs, Ys) ← Xs is a sublist of the list Ys.
sublist(Xs, Ys) ← app(_, Zs, Ys), app(Xs, _, Zs).
```

augmented by the APPEND program.

Here, as in Section 7.3 we call a list of 27 elements a "desired sequence" if it is a
sequence containing three 1s, three 2s, ..., three 9s such that for all $i \in [1, 9]$ there
are exactly i numbers between successive occurrences of i.

Take now the following specifications:

$$pre_{\mathsf{sequence}} = \{\mathsf{sequence}(\mathsf{s}) \mid \mathsf{s} \text{ is a term}\},$$

$$post_{\mathsf{sequence}} = \{\mathsf{sequence}(\mathsf{s}) \mid \mathsf{s} \text{ is a list of 27 elements}\},$$

$$pre_{\mathsf{question}} = \{\mathsf{question}(\mathsf{s}) \mid \mathsf{s} \text{ is a term}\},$$

$$post_{\mathsf{question}} = \{\mathsf{question}(\mathsf{s}) \mid \mathsf{s} \text{ is a desired sequence}\},$$

$$pre_{\mathsf{sublist}} = \{\mathsf{sublist}(\mathsf{s}, \mathsf{t}) \mid \mathsf{s}, \mathsf{t} \text{ are lists}\},$$

$$post_{\mathsf{sublist}} = \{\mathsf{sublist}(\mathsf{s}, \mathsf{t}) \mid \text{ the list } \mathsf{s} \text{ is a sublist of the list } \mathsf{t}\},$$

and assume for the app relation the specification given in Exercise 99.

We now prove that SEQUENCE is well-asserted w.r.t. the above specification. The
clause defining the sequence relation is well-asserted because every instance of a
term of the form $[\_, \_, \_, \_, \_, \_, \_, \_, \_, \_, \_, \_, \_, \_, \_, \_, \_, \_, \_, \_, \_, \_, \_, \_, \_, \_, \_]$ is a list of 27
elements.

Let us now prove that the clause defining the sublist relation is well-asserted.
To this end we need to prove the following statements:

$$\models pre(\mathsf{sublist}(\mathsf{Xs}, \mathsf{Ys})) \Rightarrow pre(\mathsf{app}(\mathsf{Us}, \mathsf{Zs}, \mathsf{Ys})),$$

$$\models pre(\mathsf{sublist}(\mathsf{Xs}, \mathsf{Ys})), post(\mathsf{app}(\mathsf{Us}, \mathsf{Zs}, \mathsf{Ys})) \Rightarrow pre(\mathsf{app}(\mathsf{Xs}, \mathsf{Vs}, \mathsf{Zs})),$$

$$\models pre(\mathsf{sublist}(\mathsf{Xs}, \mathsf{Ys})), post(\mathsf{app}(\mathsf{Us}, \mathsf{Zs}, \mathsf{Ys})), post(\mathsf{app}(\mathsf{Xs}, \mathsf{Vs}, \mathsf{Zs})) \Rightarrow$$
$$post(\mathsf{sublist}(\mathsf{Xs}, \mathsf{Ys})).$$

As an illustration let us check the last claim. Suppose that for some substitution θ $\mathtt{sublist(Xs,Ys)}\theta \in pre_{\mathtt{sublist}}$, $\mathtt{app(Us,Zs,Ys)}\theta \in post_{\mathtt{app}}$ and $\mathtt{app(Xs,Vs,Zs)}\theta \in post_{\mathtt{app}}$. This means that $\mathtt{Xs}\theta, \mathtt{Ys}\theta, \mathtt{Us}\theta, \mathtt{Zs}\theta, \mathtt{Vs}\theta$ are lists such that $\mathtt{Us}\theta * \mathtt{Zs}\theta = \mathtt{Ys}\theta$ and $\mathtt{Xs}\theta * \mathtt{Vs}\theta = \mathtt{Zs}\theta$. So $\mathtt{Us}\theta * (\mathtt{Xs}\theta * \mathtt{Vs}\theta) = \mathtt{Ys}\theta$. Hence $\mathtt{Xs}\theta$ is a sublist of $\mathtt{Ys}\theta$, that is $\mathtt{sublist(Xs,Ys)}\theta \in post_{\mathtt{sublist}}$.

Finally, we prove that the clause defining the **question** relation is well-asserted. The only statement, the proof of which requires some justification, is the following one:

$$
\begin{aligned}
\models \ &pre(\mathtt{question(Ss)}), \\
&post(\mathtt{sequence(Ss)}), \\
&post(\mathtt{sublist([1,\_,1,\_,1], Ss)}), \\
&post(\mathtt{sublist([2,\_,\_,2,\_,\_,2], Ss)}), \\
&post(\mathtt{sublist([3,\_,\_,\_,3,\_,\_,\_,3], Ss)}), \\
&post(\mathtt{sublist([4,\_,\_,\_,\_,4,\_,\_,\_,\_,4], Ss)}), \\
&post(\mathtt{sublist([5,\_,\_,\_,\_,\_,5,\_,\_,\_,\_,\_,5], Ss)}), \\
&post(\mathtt{sublist([6,\_,\_,\_,\_,\_,\_,6,\_,\_,\_,\_,\_,\_,6], Ss)}), \\
&post(\mathtt{sublist([7,\_,\_,\_,\_,\_,\_,\_,7,\_,\_,\_,\_,\_,\_,\_,7], Ss)}), \\
&post(\mathtt{sublist([8,\_,\_,\_,\_,\_,\_,\_,\_,8,\_,\_,\_,\_,\_,\_,\_,\_,8], Ss)}), \\
&post(\mathtt{sublist([9,\_,\_,\_,\_,\_,\_,\_,\_,\_,9,\_,\_,\_,\_,\_,\_,\_,\_,\_,9], Ss)}) \Rightarrow \\
&post(\mathtt{question(Ss)}).
\end{aligned}
$$

So assume that for some substitution θ the term $\mathtt{Ss}\theta$ is such that

- it is a list of 27 elements,
- for all $i \in [1,9]$ a list of the form $[i,\ldots,i,\ldots,i]$, where there are exactly i numbers between successive occurrences of i, is a sublist of $\mathtt{Ss}\theta$.

This implies that $\mathtt{Ss}\theta$ is a desired sequence, that is $\mathtt{question(Ss}\theta) \in post_{\mathtt{question}}$.

We conclude that **SEQUENCE** is well-asserted. Note that the query $\mathtt{question(Ss)}$ is well-asserted as well. By the Partial Correctness Corollary 8.10 we conclude that

$$\{\mathtt{question(Ss)}\}\ \textbf{SEQUENCE}\ inst(\mathtt{question(Ss)}) \cap post_{\mathtt{question}},$$

which implies that every successful SLD-derivation of **SEQUENCE** $\cup$ $\{\mathtt{question(Ss)}\}$ yields a computed instance $\mathtt{question(s)}$ such that $\mathtt{s}$ is a desired sequence.

Palindrome

Finally, consider the program **PALINDROME**:

```
% palindrome(Xs)  ←  the list Xs is equal to its reverse.
palindrome(Xs)  ←  reverse(Xs, Xs).

% reverse(Xs, Ys)  ←  Ys is the reverse of the list Xs.
reverse(X1s, X2s)  ←  reverse(X1s, [], X2s).

% reverse(Xs, Ys, Zs)  ←  Zs is the result of concatenating
                          the reverse of the list Xs and the list Ys.
reverse([], Xs, Xs).
reverse([X | X1s], X2s, Ys)  ←  reverse(X1s, [X | X2s], Ys).
```

Given a list s, let `rev(s)` denote its reverse. We now use the following specifications:

$$pre_{\texttt{palindrome}} = \{\texttt{palindrome(s)} \mid \texttt{s is a list}\},$$

$$post_{\texttt{palindrome}} = \{\texttt{palindrome(s)} \mid \texttt{s is a list such that s = rev(s)}\},$$

$$pre_{\texttt{reverse/2}} = \{\texttt{reverse(s,t)} \mid \texttt{s is a list}\},$$

$$post_{\texttt{reverse/2}} = \{\texttt{reverse(s,t)} \mid \texttt{s,t are lists and t = rev(s)}\},$$

$$pre_{\texttt{reverse/3}} = \{\texttt{reverse(s,t,u)} \mid \texttt{s,t are lists}\},$$

$$post_{\texttt{reverse/3}} = \{\texttt{reverse(s,t,u)} \mid \texttt{s,t,u are lists and } \texttt{rev(s)} * \texttt{t} = \texttt{u}\}.$$

In the proof that **PALINDROME** is well-asserted w.r.t. the above specification, we limit ourselves to checking that the last clause is well-asserted. We need to prove the following two statements:

$$\models pre(\texttt{reverse([X|X1s], X2s, Ys)}) \Rightarrow pre(\texttt{reverse(X1s, [X|X2s], Ys)}),$$

$$\models pre(\texttt{reverse([X|X1s], X2s, Ys)}), post(\texttt{reverse(X1s, [X|X2s], Ys)}) \Rightarrow$$
$$post(\texttt{reverse([X|X1s], X2s, Ys)}).$$

The proof of the first statement boils down to the obvious implication: if `[x|x1s]` and x2s are lists then x1s and `[x|x2s]` are lists.

To prove the second statement it suffices to observe that for any term x and lists `x1s, x2s`

$$\texttt{rev([x|x1s])} * \texttt{x2s} = \texttt{rev(x1s)} * \texttt{[x|x2s]}. \tag{8.1}$$

Take now a ground list s. Then the query `palindrome(s)` is well-asserted. By the Partial Correctness Corollary 8.10 we conclude that

$$\{\texttt{palindrome(s)}\} \text{ PALINDROME } inst(\texttt{palindrome(s)}) \cap post_{\texttt{palindrome}}.$$

Consequently if an SLD-derivation of **PALINDROME** $\cup$ `{palindrome(s)}` is successful, then the set $inst(\texttt{palindrome(s)}) \cap post_{\texttt{palindrome}}$ is non-empty. In this case it consists of just one element: `palindrome(s)`, where `s = rev(s)`.

8.4   Computing Strongest Postconditions

We now turn our attention to a method that allows us to compute the strongest postcondition of a query, that is sets of the form $sp(Q, P)$ where Q is a query and P a program.

Recall from Section 4.3 (Definition 4.6) that given a program P and a query Q, the query Q' is called a correct instance of Q if Q' is an instance of Q such that $P \models Q'$.

Our approach is based on the following simple result the proof of which uses the basic properties of the SLD-resolution.

Theorem 8.11 (Intersection) Assume that the Herbrand universe of the underlying language $\mathcal{L}$ is infinite. Consider a program P and a query Q. Suppose that the set $\mathcal{Q}$ of ground correct instances of Q is finite. Then $sp(Q, P) = \mathcal{Q}$.

Proof. First note that

$$\text{every correct instance } Q' \text{ of } Q \text{ is ground.} \tag{8.2}$$

Indeed, otherwise, by the fact that the Herbrand universe is infinite, the set $\mathcal{Q}$ would be infinite.

Consider now $Q_1 \in \mathcal{Q}$. By the Strong Completeness Theorem 4.13, there exists a computed instance Q_2 of Q such that Q_2 is more general than Q_1. By the Soundness Theorem 4.4, Q_2 is a correct instance of Q, so by (8.2) Q_2 is ground. Consequently $Q_2 = Q_1$, that is Q_1 is a computed instance of Q.

Conversely, take a computed instance Q_1 of Q. By the Soundness Theorem 4.4 Q_1 is a correct instance of Q. By (8.2) Q_1 is ground, so $Q_1 \in \mathcal{Q}$. $\qquad\square$

The assumption that the Herbrand universe is infinite is a very natural one since it can be rephrased as "the underlying language $\mathcal{L}$ has infinitely many constants or at least one constant and one (non-nullary) function symbol".

In the sequel we shall use the following consequence of this theorem which explains the relevance of the least Herbrand model $\mathcal{M}(P)$ in our approach.

Corollary 8.12 (Intersection 1) Assume that the Herbrand universe of $\mathcal{L}$ is infinite. Consider a program P and an atom A. Suppose that the set $ground(A) \cap \mathcal{M}(P)$ is finite. Then $sp(A, P) = ground(A) \cap \mathcal{M}(P)$.

Proof. It suffices to notice the following string of equivalences:

$$
\begin{aligned}
&\quad A\theta \text{ is a ground correct instance of } A\\
\text{iff} \quad & P \models A\theta \text{ and } A\theta \text{ is ground}\\
\text{iff} \quad & \{\text{Success 2 Theorem 4.37}\}\\
&\quad \mathcal{M}(P) \models A\theta \text{ and } A\theta \text{ is ground}\\
\text{iff} \quad & A\theta \in ground(A) \cap \mathcal{M}(P),
\end{aligned}
$$

and use the Intersection Theorem 8.11. $\qquad\square$

Exercise 100 Show that the assumption that the Herbrand universe of $\mathcal{L}$ is infinite is in the above Corollary necessary.
Hint. Take the language $\mathcal{L}$ with only one constant, a, the program {p(X)., p(a).} and the query p(X).
$\square$

Exercise 101 Show that for well-moded programs and queries the assumption that the Herbrand universe of $\mathcal{L}$ is infinite is not needed in the above Corollary.
Hint. Use the Computed Answer Corollary 7.11 and the Well-modedness Theorem 7.12.
$\square$

To be able to use the Intersection 1 Corollary 8.12 we need to construct for a given program its least Herbrand model $\mathcal{M}(P)$. One possibility is to use the Characterization 2 Theorem 4.34(iv) according to which $\mathcal{M}(P) = T_P \uparrow \omega$.

However, the least Herbrand model also admits another characterization: by virtue of the Success 2 Theorem 4.37 it coincides with the set of ground atoms A such that $P \cup \{A\}$ has a successful LD-derivation. Often this set coincides with the "specification" of a program limited to its ground atomic queries.

In the case of left terminating programs there exists a simple test allowing us to verify whether a given set of atoms is the least Herbrand model of a program.

Theorem 8.13 (Unique Fixed Point 1) Let P be a left terminating program. Then $\mathcal{M}(P)$ is a unique fixpoint of T_P.

Proof. First note that by the Characterization 2 Theorem 4.34(iii) for every program P, $\mathcal{M}(P)$ is the least fixpoint of T_P.

Take now a left terminating program P. By the Acceptability Theorem 6.28 P is acceptable w.r.t. some level mapping $|\ |$ and a model of P. By definition P is acceptable w.r.t. $|\ |$ and $\mathcal{M}(P)$.

Suppose now that I is a fixpoint of T_P. Then $\mathcal{M}(P) \subseteq I$. We now prove that for every $A \in I - \mathcal{M}(P)$ there exists $B \in I - \mathcal{M}(P)$ such that $|A| > |B|$, which implies that $I = \mathcal{M}(P)$.

So fix some $A \in I - \mathcal{M}(P)$. By the choice of I there exists $\mathbf{B}$ such that $I \models \mathbf{B}$ and $A \leftarrow \mathbf{B} \in ground(P)$. Then $\mathcal{M}(P) \not\models \mathbf{B}$ since $\mathcal{M}(P) \not\models A$. Let B be the first atom in $\mathbf{B}$ such that $\mathcal{M}(P) \not\models B$. Then $B \in I - \mathcal{M}(P)$ and by the definition of acceptability $|A| > |B|$.
$\square$

To see the usefulness and the limitations of the above results let us construct by way of example the least Herbrand model of the **APPEND** program.

In Section 5.5 we defined some shorthands concerning lists. We now call a construct of the form $[s_1, ..., s_n | t]$, where $n \geq 1$, a *partial list*. Then a non-empty list is a partial list since $[s_0, s_1, ..., s_n]$ equals $[s_0, s_1, ..., s_n | []]$.

In Section 8.3 we defined concatenation of two lists. We now extend this definition to pairs consisting of a list s and a term t. If $s = [\ ]$, then

$$s * t := t$$

and if $s = [s_1, ..., s_n]$, where $n \geq 1$, then

$$s * t := [s_1, ..., s_n | t].$$

We now prove that

$$\mathcal{M}(\text{APPEND}) = \{\text{app}(s, t, s * t) \mid s \text{ is a ground list}, t \text{ is a ground term}\}.$$

As we showed in Section 6.2 that APPEND is terminating (so *a fortiori* left terminating) we can use the Unique Fixed Point Theorem 1 8.13. So let us check that

$$I := \{\text{app}(s, t, s * t) \mid s \text{ is a ground list}, t \text{ is a ground term}\}$$

is a fixed point of T_{APPEND}.

For the proof of the inclusion $T_{\text{APPEND}}(I) \subseteq I$ first observe that `[]`$*$`t=t`, so by the definition of I, $ground(\text{app}([\ ], \text{Ys}, \text{Ys})) \subseteq I$.

Take now a ground instance $\text{app}([v|s], t, [v|u]) \leftarrow \text{app}(s, t, u)$ of the clause

```
app([X | Xs], Ys, [X | Zs])  ←  app(Xs, Ys, Zs)
```

such that $\text{app}(s, t, u) \in I$. Then s is a list and $u = s*t$. On account of the notation introduced in Section 5.5, $[s_0|[s_1, ..., s_n|t]]$ abbreviates to $[s_0, s_1, ..., s_n|t]$, so $[v|s] * t = [v|s * t]$. Hence $\text{app}([v|s], t, [v|s * t]) \in I$, that is $\text{app}([v|s], t, [v|u]) \in I$.

For the proof of the inclusion $I \subseteq T_{\text{APPEND}}(I)$ take a ground list s and a ground term t. If $s = [\ ]$, then $s * t = t$, so $\text{app}(s,t,s*t)$ is a ground instance of the atom $\text{app}(\text{[]}, \text{Ys}, \text{Ys})$ and consequently is an element of $T_{\text{APPEND}}(I)$.

If s is a non-empty list, say $s = [v|s']$, then by definition $\text{app}(s', t, s' * t) \in I$, so $\text{app}([v|s'], t, [v|s' * t]) \in T_{\text{APPEND}}(I)$. But, as already noted, $[v|s' * t] = [v|s'] * t$, so we proved that $\text{app}(s, t, s * t) \in T_{\text{APPEND}}(I)$.

We can now proceed and use the Intersection 1 Corollary 8.12 to compute the strongest postcondition of various atomic queries for APPEND. However, this example shows that even for simple programs it is quite clumsy to construct their least Herbrand model. The problem has to do with the lack of types in Prolog. This forces us to consider some "ill-typed" atoms like $\text{app}(s,t,s*t)$ where t is not a list.

As a remedy we now modify the above approach by limiting our attention to a "well-typed" fragment of the least Herbrand model. To this end we use the notion of a well-asserted program.

Definition 8.14 Consider a well-asserted program P. Let

$$pre := \bigcup_{p \text{ is in } P} ground(pre_p),$$

$$post := \bigcup_{p \text{ is in } P} ground(post_p),$$

$$\mathcal{M}_{(pre,post)}(P) := \mathcal{M}(P) \cap pre,$$

$$pre(P) := \{H \leftarrow \mathbf{B} \in ground(P) \mid H \in pre\}.$$

$\square$

Exercise 102 Check that for an atom A

$$pre \models A \text{ iff } \models pre(A),$$

$$post \models A \text{ iff } \models post(A).$$

$\square$

Intuitively, $\mathcal{M}_{(pre,post)}(P)$ is the "well-typed" fragment of the least Herbrand model of the well-asserted program P. This interpretation depends on the specifications used. Note that the $\mathcal{M}_{(pre,post)}$ semantics does not depend on *post*, but the following observation shows that for well-asserted programs $\mathcal{M}_{(pre,post)}(P)$ can be equivalently defined as $\mathcal{M}(P) \cap pre \cap post$.

Note 8.15 (Pre-post) For a well-asserted program P, we have $\mathcal{M}_{(pre,post)}(P) \subseteq post$.

Proof. Consider a ground atom $A \in \mathcal{M}(P) \cap pre$. Then the atomic query A is well-typed. Since $A \in \mathcal{M}(P)$, by the Success 2 Theorem 4.37 there exists a successful LD-derivation of $P \cup \{A\}$. By the Post-assertion Corollary 8.9 $A \in post$.
$\square$

Exercise 103 Give an example showing that $\mathcal{M}_{(pre,post)}(P)$ is not a model of P. $\square$

Now, using the previously obtained characterization of $\mathcal{M}(\mathbf{APPEND})$ we obtain for the specification of $\mathbf{APPEND}$ considered in Exercise 99

$$\mathcal{M}_{(pre,post)}(\mathbf{APPEND}) = \{\mathtt{app(s,t,u)} \mid \mathtt{s,t,u} \text{ are ground lists and } \mathtt{s*t=u}\},$$

which is closer to the intended description of $\mathbf{APPEND}$ than $\mathcal{M}(\mathbf{APPEND})$ is. This example shows how to construct the set $\mathcal{M}_{(pre,post)}(P)$ using the least Herbrand model $\mathcal{M}(P)$. But, as we have already noted, the construction of $\mathcal{M}(P)$ can be quite cumbersome, so we would prefer to define $\mathcal{M}_{(pre,post)}(P)$ directly, without constructing $\mathcal{M}(P)$ first. To this end we use the program $pre(P)$. The fact that this program is possibly infinite causes no complications in our considerations.

Theorem 8.16 ($\mathcal{M}_{(pre,post)}(P)$) For a well-asserted program P

$$\mathcal{M}_{(pre,post)}(P) = \mathcal{M}(pre(P)).$$

Proof. By the Characterization 2 Theorem 4.34(iv) $\mathcal{M}_{(pre,post)}(P) = T_P \uparrow \omega \cap pre$ and $\mathcal{M}(pre(P)) = T_{pre(P)} \uparrow \omega$.

Thus to show the claim it suffices to prove by induction that for $n \geq 0$

$$T_{pre(P)} \uparrow n = T_P \uparrow n \cap pre.$$

Base. $n = 0$. Immediate.

Induction step. $n > 0$. Assume that $T_{pre(P)} \uparrow (n-1) = T_P \uparrow (n-1) \cap pre$ and consider the two inclusions separately. For the inclusion $\subseteq$ we calculate:

$$
\begin{aligned}
& T_{pre(P)} \uparrow n \\
= \quad & \{T_{pre(P)}(I) = T_P(I) \cap pre \text{ for every Herbrand interpretation } I\} \\
& T_P(T_{pre(P)} \uparrow (n-1)) \cap pre \\
= \quad & \{\text{induction hypothesis}\} \\
& T_P(T_P \uparrow (n-1) \cap pre) \cap pre \\
\subseteq \quad & \{T_P \text{ is monotonic}\} \\
& T_P \uparrow n \cap pre.
\end{aligned}
$$

To prove the other inclusion take $H \in T_P \uparrow n \cap pre$. Then there exists $H \leftarrow B_1 \ldots B_m \in ground(P)$ such that

$$\{B_1 \ldots B_m\} \subseteq T_P \uparrow (n-1). \tag{8.3}$$

We now prove by induction on m that also the inclusion

$$\{B_1 \ldots B_m\} \subseteq pre \tag{8.4}$$

holds.

Base. $m = 0$. The claim holds vacuously.

Induction step. $m > 0$. Assume that $\{B_1 \ldots B_{m-1}\} \subseteq pre$. This together with (8.3) implies $\{B_1 \ldots B_{m-1}\} \subseteq \mathcal{M}_{(pre,post)}(P)$ and, hence, by the Pre-post Note 8.15 $\{B_1 \ldots B_{m-1}\} \subseteq post$ holds. Since by assumption $H \in pre$, it follows by the definition of well-assertedness and Exercise 102 that $B_m \in pre$. This proves (8.4).

Now by the induction hypothesis, (8.3) and (8.4) imply $\{B_1 \ldots B_m\} \subseteq T_{pre(P)} \uparrow (n-1)$ and consequently $H \in T_{pre(P)} \uparrow n$ which concludes the main induction proof. $\qquad\square$

So $\mathcal{M}_{(pre,post)}(P)$ is the least Herbrand model of the program $pre(P)$. We can now prove the modifications of the previous two results that dealt with $\mathcal{M}(P)$, now reformulated for the case of the Herbrand interpretation $\mathcal{M}_{(pre,post)}(P)$.

Corollary 8.17 (Intersection 2) Assume that the Herbrand universe of $\mathcal{L}$ is infinite. Consider a well-asserted program P and a well-asserted atomic query A. Suppose that the set $ground(A) \cap \mathcal{M}_{(pre,post)}(P)$ is finite. Then $sp(A, P) = ground(A) \cap \mathcal{M}_{(pre,post)}(P)$.

Proof. For a well-asserted atomic query A we have $\models pre(A)$, so $ground(A) \subseteq pre$. Hence

$$ground(A) \cap \mathcal{M}_{(pre,post)}(P) = ground(A) \cap \mathcal{M}(P), \tag{8.5}$$

so the claim follows from the Intersection 1 Corollary 8.12. $\square$

Exercise 104 Prove that for a well-asserted program P and a well-asserted query Q

$$\mathcal{M}(P) \models Q \text{ iff } \mathcal{M}_{(pre,post)}(P) \models Q.$$

Hint. Proceed by induction on the number of atoms in Q and use the Pre-post Note 8.15. $\square$

Theorem 8.18 (Unique Fixed Point 2) Let P be a left well-asserted terminating program. Then $\mathcal{M}_{(pre,post)}(P)$ is a unique fixpoint of $T_{pre(P)}$.

Proof. By Exercise 17 of Section 3.5 the (possibly infinite) program $ground(P)$ is left terminating, so *a fortiori* $pre(P)$. The result now follows by the $\mathcal{M}_{(pre,post)}(P)$ Theorem 8.16 combined with the Unique Fixed Point 1 Theorem 8.13 applied to the program $ground(P)$. $\square$

Exercise 105 Provide an alternative proof of the implication "if P is left terminating then $ground(P)$ is left terminating" using the Equivalence 2 Corollary 6.29.
Hint. Note that the implication "P be acceptable implies that P is left terminating" holds for infinite programs, as well. $\square$

8.5   Applications

We now show how the last two results can be used to draw stronger conclusions about the example programs considered in Section 8.3. Throughout this section we assume that the Herbrand universe of $\mathcal{L}$ is infinite so that we can apply the Intersection 2 Corollary 8.17.

Append
Assume the specification of `APPEND` considered in Exercise 99. We have already noted in the previous section then that

$$\mathcal{M}_{(pre,post)}(\texttt{APPEND}) = \{\texttt{app(s,t,u)} \mid \texttt{s,t,u} \text{ are ground lists and } \texttt{s*t=u}\}.$$

Exercise 106 Provide a direct proof of this fact by checking that the set

$$\{\texttt{app}(s,t,u) \mid \texttt{s,t,u} \text{ are ground lists and } \texttt{s*t=u}\}$$

is a fixed point of $T_{pre(\texttt{APPEND})}$. $\square$

Now let s,t be ground lists and consider the well-asserted query app(s, t, Zs). Note that the set $ground(app(s,t,Zs)) \cap \mathcal{M}_{(pre,post)}(APPEND)$ consists of just one element: app(s,t,s*t). Thus by the Intersection 2 Corollary 8.17 we conclude that

$$sp(app(s,t,Zs), APPEND) = \{app(s,t,s*t)\}.$$

Consider now the well-asserted query app(Xs, Ys, u), where u is a ground list. Note that

$$ground(app(Xs,Ys,u)) \cap \mathcal{M}_{(pre,post)}(APPEND) =$$

$$\{app(s,t,u) \mid s,t \text{ are ground lists, } s*t = u\}.$$

But each list can be split only in finitely many ways, so the set

$$ground(app(Xs,Ys,u)) \cap \mathcal{M}_{(pre,post)}(APPEND)$$

is finite. Thus, again by the Intersection 2 Corollary 8.17,

$$sp(app(Xs,Ys,u), APPEND) = \{app(s,t,u) \mid s,t \text{ are ground lists, } s*t = u\}.$$

Sequence
Next, consider the SEQUENCE program with its specification used in Section 8.3.

Exercise 107 Check then that

$$
\begin{aligned}
\mathcal{M}_{(pre,post)}(SEQUENCE) \;=\;& \mathcal{M}_{(pre,post)}(APPEND) \\
\cup\;& \{sublist(s,t) \mid s,t \text{ are ground lists, } s \text{ is a sublist of } t\} \\
\cup\;& \{sequence(s) \mid s \text{ is a ground list of length } 27\} \\
\cup\;& \{question(s) \mid s \text{ is a desired list}\}
\end{aligned}
$$

by applying the Unique Fixed Point 2 Theorem 8.18. □

By virtue of the above exercise

$$ground(question(Ss)) \cap \mathcal{M}_{(pre,post)}(SEQUENCE) =$$

$$\{question(s) \mid s \text{ is a desired list}\}.$$

But the number of desired lists is obviously finite. (In fact, the listing of the execution of this program given in Section 5.5 shows that there are six of them.) Consequently, by the Intersection 2 Corollary 8.17

$$sp(question(Ss), SEQUENCE) = \{question(s) \mid s \text{ is a desired list}\}.$$

Palindrome

Finally, we treat again the program PALINDROME. Assume its specification used in Section 8.3. Recall from Section 8.3 that for a list s we denoted by `rev(s)` its reverse.

Exercise 108 Check then that

$$\mathcal{M}_{(pre,post)}(\text{PALINDROME}) \;=\; \{\text{palindrome(s)} \mid \text{s is a ground list, rev(s) = s}\}$$
$$\cup \;\; \{\text{reverse(s,t)} \mid \text{s,t are ground lists, rev(s) = t}\}$$
$$\cup \;\; \{\text{reverse(s,t,u)} \mid \text{s,t,u are ground lists, rev(s)*t = u}\}$$

using (8.1) and applying the Unique Fixed Point 2 Theorem 8.18. □

Thus for a ground list s

- when `rev(s) = s`,

$$sp(\text{palindrome(s)}, \text{PALINDROME}) = \{\text{palindrome(s)}\};$$

- when `rev(s) ≠ s`,

$$sp(\text{palindrome(s)}, \text{PALINDROME}) = \emptyset.$$

Exercise 109 Prove that for the REVERSE program (which is a part of the PALINDROME program) we have for a ground list s

$$sp(\text{reverse(s,Ys)}, \text{REVERSE}) = \{\text{reverse(s,rev(s))}\}.$$

□

Exercise 110 Prove that for the MEMBER program (see Exercise 97) we have for a ground list s

$$sp(\text{member(X,s)}, \text{MEMBER}) = \{\text{member(a,s)} \mid \text{a is an element of s}\}.$$

□

8.6   Absence of Failures

In our considerations concerning program correctness so far we have ignored one program property which is specific to logic and pure Prolog programs, namely the *absence of failures*, that is an existence of successful LD-derivations. This issue does not arise in the study of program verification for other programming paradigms because there is no concept of failure present there.

Note that the method discussed in Sections 8.2 and 8.3 does not allow us to conclude that in the case of the APPEND program, for ground lists s,t the query app(s,t,Zs) actually successfully terminates, that is that there exists a successful

LD-derivation of $\mathtt{APPEND} \cup \{\mathtt{app(s,t,Zs)}\}$. All that we proved there was that $\mathtt{app(s,t,s*t)}$ is the only possible computed instance of this query.

On the other hand, the method considered in Sections 8.4 and 8.5 does allow us to draw such a conclusion, because we were able to prove there that the set $sp(\mathtt{app(s,t,Zs)}, \mathtt{APPEND})$ is non-empty.

In other words, the use of the strongest postconditions allows us to establish the absence of failures. However, to prove this property a somewhat simpler method is sufficient. Namely, we have the following simple consequence of the results established in Chapter 4.

Corollary 8.19 (Absence of Failures) Assume that the language $\mathcal{L}$ has infinitely many constants. Consider a program P and an atom A. Suppose that the set $ground(A) \cap \mathcal{M}(P)$ is non-empty. Then there exists a successful LD-derivation of $P \cup \{A\}$.

Proof. By the Herbrand Interpretation Lemma 4.26(i) the set $ground(A) \cap \mathcal{M}(P)$ is non-empty iff for some substitution θ such that $A\theta$ is ground, $\mathcal{M}(P) \models A\theta$. Now by the Success 2 Theorem 4.37 we obtain $P \models A\theta$ and by the Strong Completeness Theorem 4.13 we can draw the desired conclusion. $\square$

As in Section 8.4 for a well-asserted program P and a well-asserted atomic query A we can, by virtue of (8.5), refine this result so that the "well-typed" fragment $\mathcal{M}_{(pre,post)}(P)$ of the least Herbrand model of P is used.

As a simple application of this result note that for lists s', t' there exists a successful LD-derivation of $\mathtt{APPEND} \cup \{\mathtt{app(s',t',Zs)}\}$ because the set

$$ground(\mathtt{app(s',t',Zs)}) \cap \{\mathtt{app(s,t,u)} \mid \mathtt{s,t,u}\ \text{are ground lists and}\ \mathtt{s*t=u}\}$$

is non-empty.

Note that this result cannot be established using the Intersection 1 Corollary 8.12 because for non-ground lists s', t' the above set is infinite.

Exercise 111 Take a list s such that $\mathtt{s = rev(s)}$. Prove that there exists a successful LD-derivation of $\mathtt{PALINDROME} \cup \{\mathtt{palindrome(s)}\}$. $\square$

8.7   Concluding Remarks

With this chapter we conclude the study of correctness of pure Prolog programs. In general, given a program P and a "relevant" query Q we would like to establish the following properties:

- all the LD-derivations of $P \cup \{Q\}$ terminate,
- $P \cup \{Q\}$ is occur-check free,
- all successful LD-derivations of $P \cup \{Q\}$ yield the desired results,

- there exists a successful LD-derivation of $P \cup \{Q\}$.

In the last three chapters we proposed proof methods that allow us to establish these properties. In the course of this study we noticed that at least two meaningful notions of termination exist. In addition, because logic and pure Prolog programs can yield several answers, we found that it is natural to consider two notions of partial correctness: one which identifies the shape of computed instances and another which aims at computing all computed instances to a given query. Finally, we identified the absence of failures as a program property specific to the logic programming paradigm.

None of the proposed proof methods allows us to deal with all programs and all queries. However, in each case we were able to show that the proposed methods are sufficiently powerful to deal with most programs of interest.

In the previous two chapters we explained the limitations of the approaches to termination and to the occur-check freedom. Let us briefly assess now the limitations of the methods proposed in this chapter.

First, notice that in Sections 8.2 and 8.4 we limited our attention to the study of queries with *ground* lists. For example, nothing was proved for the case of the query app(s,t, Zs), where s,t are arbitrary lists. Using the approach of Section 8.2 we can establish the following conclusion to the Partial Correctness Corollary 8.10:

$$\{\text{app}(s, t, Zs)\} \ \text{APPEND} \ inst(\text{app}(s, t, Zs)) \cap post_{\text{app}}.$$

We noted that in the case when s,t are ground lists, the set $inst(\text{app}(s, t, Zs)) \cap post_{\text{app}}$ consists of just one element. Now it admits a more complex description. Namely, we have

$$inst(\text{app}(s, t, Zs)) \cap post_{\text{app}} = \{\text{app}(s\theta, t\theta, Zs\theta) \mid s\theta * t\theta = Zs\theta\}.$$

So for example, for s:= [X], t:=[Y] and the constants a,b, we have

$$\text{app}([a], [b], [a, b]) \in inst(\text{app}([X], [Y], Zs)) \cap post_{\text{app}}.$$

Turning our attention to the the approach studied in Section 8.4 we note that it does not allow us to draw any conclusions in the case when some correct instances are not ground. Indeed, this approach is based on the Intersection Theorem 8.11 the assumptions of which imply (8.2). In particular, nothing can be deduced about the query app([X], [Y], Zs) which does admit a non-ground correct instance app([X], [Y], [X,Y]).

However, as already noticed in Section 8.6, we can prove the existence of a successful LD-derivation of $\text{APPEND} \cup \{\text{app}([X], [Y], Zs)\}$.

In Apt *et al.* [AGP96] a generalization of the method given in Section 8.4 is proposed that for certain programs allows us to compute the strongest postconditions of arbitrary queries. In particular, one can conclude that for arbitrary lists s,t we have

$$sp(\text{app}(s, t, Zs), \text{APPEND}) = Variant(\{\text{app}(s, t, s * t)\}),$$

where for a set of atoms I, $Variant(I) := \{A\theta \mid A \in I, \theta \text{ is a renaming}\}$. This implies that `app([a], [b], [a,b])` is not a computed instance of `app([X], [Y], Zs)`.

To establish various results of this section we occasionally used certain assumptions about the underlying language $\mathcal{L}$. If, as in Chapter 6, we assume that $\mathcal{L}$ is a universal language in which all queries and programs are written, then all of these assumptions are satisfied. In Section 6.1 we argued that the use of such a universal language better reflects the reality of programming.

8.8   Bibliographic Remarks

The partial correctness of logic programs has been studied for a long time. For early references see, e.g. Clark and Tärnlund [CT77], Clark [Cla79] and Hogger [Hog84]. In Deransart [Der93] various approaches are discussed and compared. Among them the most powerful one is the inductive assertion method of Drabent and Małuszyński [DM88] that allows us to prove various program properties that can be expressed only using non-monotonic assertions, that is assertions not closed under substitution.

In all these approaches, specifications are associated with the relations occurring in the program. In Colussi and Marchiori [CM91] an alternative proof method is introduced in which assertions are attached to the program points. This allows them to study global run-time properties, such as the variable disjointness of two atoms during the program execution.

The method used here and based on the notion of a well-asserted query and program and discussed in Section 8.2, coincides with the partial correctness method of Bossi and Cocco [BC89], though in our presentation we abstracted from the concrete syntax introduced in this paper. In Apt and Marchiori [AM94] it is shown that this method is a special case of the method of Drabent and Małuszyński [DM88].

The approach to partial correctness that aims at computing the strongest postcondition of a query and based on the use of the Intersection Theorem 8.11 and the Intersection 1 Corollary 8.12 is from Apt [Apt95]. The Unique Fixed Point 1 Theorem 8.13 is from Apt and Pedreschi [AP93].

The refinement of this approach to well-asserted programs and queries, based on the use of the $\mathcal{M}_{(pre,post)}(P)$ interpretation and the $\mathcal{M}_{(pre,post)}(P)$ Theorem 8.16, Intersection 2 Corollary 8.17 and the Unique Fixed Point 2 Theorem 8.18, is from Apt *et al.* [AGP96].

The Pre-post Note 8.15 is from Ruggieri [Rug94] and Exercise 104 is from Apt *et al.* [AGP96].

8.9 Summary

In this chapter we discussed various aspects concerning the partial correctness of logic and pure Prolog programs. To determine the form of computed instances of a query we introduced the notions of

- well-asserted queries and programs.

To compute the set of all computed instances of a query we introduced the notion of a

- strongest postcondition of a query

and showed how to compute such sets using the least Herbrand model of a program.
  We also indicated that usually this model is rather clumsy to construct and proposed to use instead, for well-asserted programs and well-asserted queries, the "well-typed" fragment of this model. Finally, we explained how to establish the absence of failures, that is the existence of successful LD-derivations.

8.10 References

[AGP96] K.R. Apt, M. Gabbrielli, and D. Pedreschi. A closer look at declarative interpretations. *Journal of Logic Programming*, 28(2): 147–180, 1996.

[AM94] K. R. Apt and E. Marchiori. Reasoning about Prolog programs: from modes through types to assertions. *Formal Aspects of Computing*, 6(6A):743–765, 1994.

[AP93] K. R. Apt and D. Pedreschi. Reasoning about termination of pure Prolog programs. *Information and Computation*, 106(1):109–157, 1993.

[Apt95] K. R. Apt. Program verification and Prolog. In E. Börger, editor, *Specification and Validation Methods for Programming Languages and Systems*, pages 55–95. Oxford University Press, Oxford, 1995.

[BC89] A. Bossi and N. Cocco. Verifying correctness of logic programs. In J. Diaz and F. Orejas, editors, *Proceedings of TAPSOFT '89*, Lecture Notes in Computer Science 352, pages 96–110. Springer-Verlag, Berlin, 1989.

[Cla79] K. L. Clark. Predicate logic as a computational formalism. Res. Report DOC 79/59, Imperial College, Department of Computing, London, 1979.

[CM91] L. Colussi and E. Marchiori. Proving correctness of logic programs using axiomatic semantics. In K. Furukawa, editor, *Proceedings of the 1991 International Conference on Logic Programming*, pages 629–644. MIT Press, Cambridge, MA, 1991.

[CT77]   K. Clark and S-Å. Tärnlund. A first order theory of data and programs. In B. Gilchrist, editor, *Information Processing '77*, pages 939–944. North-Holland, Toronto, 1977.

[Der93]   P. Deransart. Proof methods of declarative properties of definite programs. *Theoretical Computer Science*, 118:99–166, 1993.

[DM88]   W. Drabent and J. Małuszyński. Inductive assertion method for logic programs. *Theoretical Computer Science*, 59(1):133–155, 1988.

[Hog84]   C.J. Hogger. *Introduction to Logic Programming*. Academic Press, London, 1984.

[Rug94]   S. Ruggieri. Metodi formali per lo sviluppo di programmi logici. Technical report, Dipartimento di Informatica, Università di Pisa, 1994. Tesi di Laurea. In Italian.

Chapter 9

Programming in Pure Prolog with Arithmetic

Every realistic programming language needs to provide some facilities to deal with arithmetic. In Chapter 5 we formalized natural numbers by means of zero and the successor function. This representation allows us to write programs that deal with natural numbers. However, programming based on this formalization is very laborious and hardly useful for computation.

The aim of this chapter is to discuss Prolog facilities for dealing with numbers or more generally with arithmetic. For simplicity we limit our attention in this book to integers.

We begin our presentation by discussing arithmetic operations in the next section. We also explain there Prolog's facilities for dealing with the binding power and for allowing the use of arbitrary function symbols in the so-called infix and bracketless prefix notation.

Next, we discuss in Section 9.2 arithmetic comparison relations.

Then we resume the style of presentation adopted in Chapter 5, so we introduce programs according to the domains over which they compute.

More specifically, in Section 9.3 we provide an example of a program computing over a complex domain (in the sense of Section 5.6) that involves integers. Then, in Section 9.4, we present programs that compute over an often used domain — lists of integers.

In Section 9.5 we introduce an important programming technique called "difference lists", that allows us to concatenate the lists in constant time and illustrate its use on a number of examples.

Next, in Section 9.6, we consider programs that compute over binary search trees, a subclass of the binary trees studied in Chapter 5 which remain properly "balanced".

In Section 9.7, we explain Prolog's way of evaluating arithmetic expressions — by means of an arithmetic evaluator "is" and introduce some programs that use this construct. Finally, in Section 9.8, we summarize the relevant aspects Prolog's arithmetic facilities and assess their shortcomings.

9.1   Operators

Prolog provides integers as a built-in data structure, with various operations on them. In the case of SICStus Prolog these operations include the following binary operations:

- addition, written as +,
- subtraction, written as -,
- multiplication, written as *,
- integer division, written as //,
- remainder of the integer division, written as mod,

and the following unary operations:

- negation of a natural number, written as -,
- absolute value, written as abs.

We call the above operations *arithmetic operators*.

According to the usual notational convention of logic programming and Prolog, the relation and function symbols are written in a *prefix form*, that is in front of the arguments. In contrast, in accordance with the usage in arithmetic, the binary arithmetic operators are written in the *infix form*, that is between the arguments, while the unary arithmetic operators are written in the prefix form. On the other hand, negation of a natural number can be written in the *bracketless prefix form*, that is without brackets surrounding its argument.

Recall that the integer division is defined as the integer part of the usual division outcome and given two integers x and y such that $y \neq 0$, x mod y is defined as x - y*(x//y).

The use of the infix and bracketless prefix form for arithmetic operators leads to well-known ambiguities. For example, 4+3*5 could be interpreted either as (4+3)*5 or 4+(3*5) and -3+4 could be interpreted either as (-3)+4 or -(3+4). Further, 12//4//3 could be interpreted either as (12//4)//3 or 12//(4//3), etc.

Such ambiguities are resolved in Prolog in a way that also allows for the presence of other function symbols written in the infix or bracketless prefix form. To this end Prolog provides a means to declare an *arbitrary* function symbol as an infix binary symbol or as a bracketless prefix unary symbol, with a fixed *priority* that determines its binding power and a certain *mnemonics* that implies some (or no) form of associativity. Function symbols that are declared in such a way are called *operators*.

The priority and mnemonics information allows us to associate with each term written using the infix or bracketless prefix notation, a unique term written in the customary prefix notation, that serves as the *interpretation* of the original one.

In SICStus Prolog priority is a natural number between 1 and 1200 inclusive. Informally, the higher the priority the lower the binding power.

There are seven mnemonics. We list them together with (if any) the associativity information each of them implies. For the binary function symbols these are

- **xfx** (no associativity),
- **xfy** (right associativity),
- **yfx** (left associativity),

and for the unary function symbols these are

- **fx**,
- **fy**,
- **xf**,
- **yf**.

The mnemonics **yfy** is not allowed, as it would imply both left and right associativity and would thus permit the interpretation of a term of the form **s f t f u** *both* as **(s f t) f u** and **s f (t f u)**. Consequently, it would not provide a unique interpretation to the term.

The *declaration of an operator* **g** is a statement of the form

```
:- op(pr, mn, g).
```

written in the program before the first use of **g**; **pr** is the priority of **g** and **mn** is the mnemonic of **g**.

(Following our convention of adhering to logic programming notation we should actually use in the above declaration " $\leftarrow$ " instead of ":-". As such declarations do not have a logical interpretation we shall rather use Prolog's ":-".)

Formally, in presence of operator declarations, terms are defined inductively as follows, where with each term we associate a priority in the form of a natural number between 0 and 1200 inclusive and an interpretation in the sense mentioned above:

- a variable is a term with priority 0 and itself as its interpretation,
- if t is a term with interpretation $i(t)$, then (t) is a term with priority 0 and interpretation $i(t)$ (that is, bracketing reduces the priority to 0),
- if f is an n-ary function symbol and $t_1, \ldots, t_n$ are terms with respective interpretations $i(t_1), \ldots, i(t_n)$, then $f(t_1, \ldots, t_n)$ is a term with priority 0 and interpretation $f(i(t_1), \ldots, i(t_n))$,
- if f is a binary operator with priority pr and s and t are terms with respective priorities $pr(s)$ and $pr(t)$ and interpretations $i(s)$ and $i(t)$, then sft is a term with priority pr and interpretation $f(i(s), i(t))$, according to the table below and subject to the corresponding conditions:

mnemonics	conditions
xfx	$pr(s) < pr,\ pr(t) < pr$
xfy	$pr(s) < pr,\ pr(t) \leq pr$
yfx	$pr(s) \leq pr,\ pr(t) < pr$

- if f is a unary operator with priority pr and s is a term with priority $pr(s)$ and interpretation $i(s)$, then the following is a term with priority pr and interpretation $f(i(s))$, according to the table below and subject to the corresponding condition:

term	mnemonics	condition
fs	fx	$pr(s) < pr$
fs	fy	$pr(s) \leq pr$
sf	xf	$pr(s) < pr$
sf	yf	$pr(s) \leq pr$

The arithmetic operators are disambiguated by declaring them internally as follows (the declarations are the ones used in SICStus Prolog):

```
:- op(500, yfx, [+, -]).
:- op(500, fx, -).
:- op(400, yfx, [*, //]).
:- op(300, xfx, mod).
```

Here a list notation is used to group together the declarations of the operators with the same mnemonics and priority.

Returning to our original examples of possibly ambiguous arithmetic terms, we now see that 4+3*5 is a term with priority 500 and interpretation +(4, *(3,5)), -3+4 is a term with priority 500 and interpretation +(-(3), 4) and 12//4//3 is a term with priority 400 and interpretation //(//(12,4), 3). In addition, note that the declaration of negation of a natural number with the mnemonics fx implies that - - 3 is not a (legal) term. In contrast, -(-3) is a (legal) term.

The list of arithmetic operators introduced at the beginning of this section together with infinitely many integer constants: 0, -1, 1, -2, 2, ... determines a language of terms in the sense just defined. We call terms defined in this language *arithmetic expressions* and introduce the abbreviation *gae* for ground arithmetic expressions.

It is worthwhile mentioning that Prolog built-in operators, in particular arithmetic operators, can also be written in the customary prefix notation. (The comma "," though requires a slightly different treatment: in SICStus Prolog it has to be written then as ',', like for instance in ','(A,B).) In particular each arithmetic expression can also be written as a term that is its interpretation in the sense discussed above. In the case of ground arithmetic expressions both forms are equal. For example, we have

```
| ?- 4+3*5 =:= +(4, *(3,5)).

yes
```

Finally, let us mention that Prolog also allows floating point numbers (called *floats*) but we shall not discuss them here.

9.2   Arithmetic Comparison Relations

With each gae we can uniquely associate its *value*, computed in the expected way. Prolog allows us to compare the values of gaes by means of *arithmetic comparison relations* (in short *comparison relations*). The following six comparison relations are provided:

- "less than", written as <,
- "less than or equal" ($\leq$), written as =<,
- "equality", written as =:=,
- "inequality", written as =\=,
- "greater than or equal" ($\geq$), written as >=,
- "greater than", written as >.

As already mentioned in Chapter 5, by definition the built-in relations cannot be redefined, so clauses in which the head refers to the comparison relations are ignored.

Recall that by virtue of the ambivalent syntax, discussed in Section 5.1, in Prolog there is no difference between relation symbols and function symbols. So the above facility of declaring operators can also be used for relation symbols, in particular for the comparison relations, which are written in the infix form.

In the case of SICStus Prolog the comparison relations are declared internally as follows:

```
:- op(700, xfx, [ <, =<, =:= , =\=, >=, > ]).
```

So for example 5*2 > 3+4 is an atom, that by virtue of the ambivalent syntax is also a term with priority 700 and interpretation >(*(5,2), +(3,4)). In turn, the string 5 > 2 > 3+4 is not an atom and *ipso facto* not a (legal) term.

As an aside let us discuss here the status of the other built-in operators in Prolog used so far.

Prolog's ":-" (written in this book as " $\leftarrow$ ") and "," ("and") are pre-declared as infix operators with the following declarations for SICStus Prolog:

```
:- op(1200, xfx, :-).
:- op(1100, xfy, ,).
```

These two declarations imply that H :- A,B is a term with priority 1200 and interpretation :-(H, ,(A,B)). This means that H :- A,B stands for H :- (A,B) and *not* (H:- A), B.

In addition, let us mention that the =/2 built-in defined in Section 5.5 is pre-declared as an infix operator with the following declaration for SICStus Prolog:

```
:- op(700, xfx, =).
```

This ensures for instance that the atom 3+4=5*7 stands for (3+4)=(5*7), because
the priority of =/2 is higher (so its binding power weaker) than that of "+" and
"*".

As another example of the use of infix operators let us introduce a binary relation
<> with the intention of writing X<>Y instead of `diff(X, Y)`. To this end we need
to declare it by, say,

```
:- op(600, xfy, <>).
```

and define it by the rule

```
X<>Y  ←  diff(X, Y).
```

Once `diff` is the relation defined in Exercise 52 of Section 5.3 we can now write
queries like `neighbour(X, guatemala)`, `neighbour(Y, guatemala)`, X<>Y.

Let us return now to the comparison relations. The comparison relations work
on gaes and produce the outcome expected to anyone familiar with the basics of
arithmetic. So for instance, > compares the values of two gaes and succeeds if the
value of the first argument is larger than the value of the second and fails otherwise.
Thus, for example

```
| ?- 5*2 > 3+4.

yes

| ?- 7 > 3+4.

no
```

When one of the arguments of the comparison relations is not a gae, the computation *ends in an error*. For example, we have

```
| ?- [] < 5.

! Error in arithmetic expression: [] is not a number

no
```

Such type of errors are called *run-time errors*, because they happen during the
program execution. The outcome of this form of an error is that the computation
terminates abnormally, without producing any result. Here the error took place
immediately, but it is easy to imagine a situation when it happens only after several
computation steps. So when the built-in comparison relations are used, one has to
be careful when using specific queries.

As a first example of the use of the comparison relations consider the following
program that computes the maximum of two gaes:

```
% max(X, Y, Z)  ←  Z is the maximum of the gaes X and Y.
max(X, Y, X)  ←  X > Y.
max(X, Y, Y)  ←  X ≤ Y.
```

Program: MAXIMUM

Exercise 112 Clarify for which queries of the form max(s, t, u) no error arises.   □

9.3   Complex Domains

Recall from Section 5.6 that by a complex domain we mean a domain built from some constants by means of function symbols. We now discuss an example of a complex domain that involves integers.

To this end let us return here to the problem of representing information about countries (see Section 5.3). Suppose that additionally to the information about the neighbouring countries we also wish to store for each country such items as its capital with its population, surface, population, language(s) used, etc. One possibility is to use a relation, say country of the arity corresponding to the number of items of interest. The neighbours could be stored in the form of a list which would fill one argument of the country relation and similarly with the languages used. Then to ask a question like

"list the countries whose capital has less than 100000 inhabitants"

we could use the query

```
country(Name, _, Cap_Population, _, _, ...), Cap_Population < 100000.
```

There are two disadvantages of such a representation. First, each time a query is formulated, the whole atom country(...) needs to be used. Secondly, when the number of items to be considered grows, it is better to arrange them in a hierarchical way which naturally reflects their logical structure. Such a structuring can easily be done using function symbols. In our case we can envisage the following term structure:

```
country(Name,
        capital(Cap_Name, Cap_Population),
        Surface,
        people(Population, Languages),
        Neighbours
        )
```

Then each entry will be a fact of the form entry(country(...)). To make the interaction with the so stored information more natural, it is useful to define selector relations which select appropriate fields. In particular, using the anonymous variables we can define

```
name(country(Name, _, _, _, _), Name).
surface(country(_, _, Surface, _, _), Surface).
cap_population(country(_, capital(_, Cap_Population), _, _, _),
               Cap_Population).
neighbours(country(_, _, _, _, Neighbours), Neighbours).
```

etc. We can now formalize various questions in a natural way as queries. For
example,

"list the countries whose capital has less than 100000 inhabitants"

```
| ?- entry(Country), cap_population(Country, Cap_Population),
     Cap_Population < 100000,
```

"list the neighbours of Honduras whose surface is larger than 50000 km^2"

```
| ?- entry(Country), name(Country, honduras),
     neighbours(Country, Neighbours),
     member(Name, Neighbours), name(Neighbour, Name),
     surface(Neighbour, Surface), Surface > 50000.
```

where `member` refers to the program MEMBER, etc.

Exercise 113 A disadvantage of this representation is that each time a query is posed,
the values of all local variables, like `Country`, `Neighbours`, `Surface`, in the last example, are printed. Find a way to avoid it.   □

The above representation of the countries could be made more readable using
SICStus Prolog's infix operator ":" and writing each country in the following form:

```
country(name :  Name,
        capital :  (Cap_Name, Cap_Population),
        surface :  Surface,
        people :  (Population, Languages),
        neighbours :  Neighbours
        )
```

Here `name`, `capital`, `surface`, `people` and `neighbours` are constants which
play a role analogous to the field identifiers in Pascal records.

The operator ":" is defined internally in SICStus Prolog as

```
:- op(550, xfy, :).
```

The precedence of ":" implies that its binding power is stronger than "," which
ensures its correct usage in the above representation.

9.4 Lists of Integers

Lists of integers form an often used domain for which a number of important programs exist. In all of them we use the built-in comparison relations on gaes. In fact, all these programs work equally well on lists of gaes.

Ordered List
The following program checks whether a list is an ordered one.

```
% ordered(Xs)  ←  Xs is an ≤-ordered list of integers.
ordered([]).
ordered([X]).
ordered([X, Y | Xs])  ←  X ≤ Y, ordered([Y | Xs]).
```

Program: ORDERED

Note that according to this program any one element list is ordered. To enforce a more limited interpretation we could use in the second clause Prolog's built-in integer which tests whether a term is an integer. For example, we have

```
| ?- integer(-5).
```

```
yes
```

Slowsort
One of the most fundamental operations on the lists is sorting. The task is to sort a list of integers. We begin our presentation with the following naive way of sorting.

```
% ss(Xs, Ys)  ←  Ys is an ordered permutation of the list Xs.
ss(Xs, Ys)  ←  permutation(Xs, Ys), ordered(Ys).
```

augmented by the PERMUTATION program.

augmented by the ORDERED program.

Program: SLOWSORT

Obviously, this program is hopelessly inefficient and, as already explained in Section 1.4, it is often used as a benchmark.

Quicksort
A more efficient way of sorting, called *quicksort* was proposed by Hoare [Hoa62]. According to this sorting procedure, a list is first partitioned into two sublists using an element X of it, one consisting of elements smaller than X and the other consisting of elements larger or equal than X. Then each sublist is quicksorted and the resulting sorted sublists are appended with the element X put in the middle. This can be expressed in Prolog as follows where X is chosen to be the first element of the given list:

```
% qs(Xs, Ys) ← Ys is an ordered permutation of the list Xs.
qs([], []).
qs([X | Xs], Ys) ←
    part(X, Xs, Littles, Bigs),
    qs(Littles, Ls),
    qs(Bigs, Bs),
    app(Ls, [X | Bs], Ys).
```

```
% part(X, Xs, Ls, Bs) ← Ls is a list of elements of Xs which are < X,
                         Bs is a list of elements of Xs which are ≥ X.
part(_, [], [], []).
part(X, [Y | Xs], [Y | Ls], Bs) ← X > Y, part(X, Xs, Ls, Bs).
part(X, [Y | Xs], Ls, [Y | Bs]) ← X ≤ Y, part(X, Xs, Ls, Bs).
```

augmented by the APPEND program.

Program: QUICKSORT

For example,

```
| ?- qs([7,9,8,1,5], Ys).
```

```
Ys = [1,5,7,8,9]
```

Note that because of the use of the built-ins $>$ and $\leq$ an error will be signalled if the arguments are not integers:

```
| ?- qs([3,4,X,7], Ys).
```

```
! Error in arithmetic expression: not a number
```

Exercise 114 Check that, contrary to expectations, for all terms s the query qs([s], Xs) does not end in an error. □

Quicksort with Accumulator

In Section 5.5, while discussing the NAIVE_REVERSE program, we noted its inefficiency and introduced the concept of an accumulator. This led to a more efficient program, REVERSE.

The source of inefficiency of the NAIVE_REVERSE was the unnecessary use of the APPEND program. The use of an accumulator allowed us to eliminate there the unneeded calls to the app relation. A similar improvement can be achieved for the QUICKSORT program:

```
% qs(Xs, Ys) ← Ys is an ordered permutation of the list Xs.
qs(Xs, Ys) ← qs_acc(Xs, [], Ys).
```

```
% qs_acc(Xs, Ys, Zs) ← Zs is the result of concatenating the ordered
                        permutation of the list Xs and the list Ys.
```

```
qs_acc([], Xs, Xs).
qs_acc([X | Xs], Zs, Ys) ←
    part(X, Xs, Littles, Bigs),
    qs_acc(Littles, [X | Y1s], Ys),
    qs_acc(Bigs, Zs, Y1s).

part(_, [], [], []).
part(X, [Y | Xs], [Y | Ls], Bs)  ←  X > Y, part(X, Xs, Ls, Bs).
part(X, [Y | Xs], Ls, [Y | Bs])  ←  X ≤ Y, part(X, Xs, Ls, Bs).
```

Program: QUICKSORT_ACC

Here the middle argument of `qs_acc` is used as an accumulator. This version of the *quicksort* is more efficient than the previous one.

Mergesort

Another way of sorting lists is called *mergesort*. According to this sorting procedure, a list of length at least 2 is first split into two lists of length differing at most by 1 (called below a *fair split*) then each sublist is mergesorted and finally the resulting sorted sublists are merged, preserving the ordering. This leads to the following Prolog program:

```
% ms(Xs, Ys)  ←  Ys is an ordered permutation of the list Xs.
ms([], []).
ms([X], [X]).
ms([X, Y | Xs], Ys) ←
    split([X, Y | Xs], X1s, X2s),
    ms(X1s, Y1s),
    ms(X2s, Y2s),
    merge(Y1s, Y2s, Ys).

% split(Xs, Ys, Zs)  ←  Ys and Zs is a result of a fair split of Xs.
split([], [], []).
split([X | Xs], [X | Ys], Zs)  ←  split(Xs, Zs, Ys).

% merge(Xs, Ys, Zs)  ←  Zs is the result of an order preserving merging of
                        Xs and Ys.
merge([], Xs, Xs).
merge(Xs, [], Xs).
merge([X | Xs], [Y | Ys], [X | Zs]) ←
    X ≤ Y,
    merge(Xs,[Y | Ys], Zs).
merge([X | Xs], [Y | Ys], [Y | Zs]) ←
    X > Y,
    merge([X | Xs], Ys, Zs).
```

Program: MERGESORT

The fair split of a list is achieved here in an elegant way by means of the reversed order of parameters in the recursive call of `split`.

Exercise 115 Write a program which formalizes the following sorting procedure (called *insertion sort*): to sort a list, sort its tail and insert the head in the sorted tail so that the order is preserved.   □

9.5   Difference Lists

When discussing the programs `REVERSE` and `QUICKSORT_ACC` we noted that they rely on the use of accumulators. From accumulators there is only one step to an important alternative representation of lists, called difference lists.

One of the drawbacks of the concatenation of lists performed by the `APPEND` program is that for lists `s,t` the execution of the query `app(s, t, Z)` takes the number of steps that is proportional to the length of the first list. Difference list is a generalization of the concept of a list that allows us to perform concatenation in constant time. The fact that many programs rely explicitly on list concatenation explains importance of difference lists.

In what follows we use the subtraction operator "`-`" written in the infix form. Its use has nothing to do with arithmetic, though intuitively one should read it as the "difference". Formally, a *difference list* is a construct of the form $[a_1, ..., a_m | x] - x$, where x is a variable and where we used the notation introduced in Section 5.5. It *represents* the list $[a_1, ..., a_m]$ in a form amenable to a different definition of concatenation. Namely, consider two difference lists $[a_1, ..., a_m | x] - x$ and $[b_1, ..., b_n | y] - y$. Then their concatenation is the difference list $[a_1, ..., a_m, b_1, ..., b_n | y] - y$.

This concatenation process is achieved by the program that consists of a single clause.

```
% append(Xs, Ys, Zs)  ←   the difference list Zs is the result of concatenating
                          the difference lists Xs and Ys.
append(X-Y, Y-Z, X-Z).
```

Program: APPEND_DL

For example, we have:

```
| ?- append([a,b|X]-X, [c,d|Y]-Y, U).

U = [a,b,c,d|Y]-Y,
X = [c,d|Y]
```

which shows that `U` became instantiated to the difference list representing the list `[a,b,c,d]`. By instantiating appropriately the "output" argument we can actually obtain the outcome list directly, as an instance of a specific variable:

```
| ?- append([a,b|X]-X, [c,d|Y]-Y, V - []).

V = [a,b,c,d],
X = [c,d],
Y = []
```

This instantiation method is also used in two examples below when "linking back" the program that uses difference lists with the program that expects "usual" lists as an outcome.

The use of difference lists instead of lists in programs that use the **app** relation to concatenate the lists (that is in the mode **app(+,+,-)** in the sense of Section 7.3) leads to more efficient programs. In these programs the calls of the **app** relation are replaced by the corresponding calls of the **append** relation. Unfolding these calls of **append** in the sense of Section 7.7 leads to programs that do not use the APPEND_DL program anymore and perform the list concatenation "on the fly".

The resulting programs closely resemble the programs with accumulators. To see this reconsider the programs **REVERSE** and **QUICKSORT**. The version of **REVERSE** that employs the difference lists looks as follows.

```
% reverse(Xs, Ys)  ←   Ys is the reverse of the list Xs.
reverse(X1s, X2s)  ←  reverse(X1s, X2s - []).

% reverse(Xs, Zs - Ys)  ←  Zs is the result of concatenating
                            the reverse of the list Xs and the list Ys.
reverse([], Xs - Xs).
reverse([X | X1s], Ys - X2s)  ←  reverse(X1s, Ys - [X | X2s]).
```

Program: REVERSE_DL

Notice that this program can be obtained from the **REVERSE** program by transposing the last two arguments and by replacing "," (the comma) between them by the "-" function symbol.

A similar transformation yields a version of the **QUICKSORT** program with the difference lists.

```
% qs(Xs, Ys)  ←  Ys is an ordered permutation of the list Xs.
qs(Xs, Ys)  ←  qs_dl(Xs, Ys - []).

% qs_dl(Xs, Y)  ←  Y is a difference list representing the ordered
                   permutation of the list Xs.
qs_dl([], Xs - Xs).
qs_dl([X | Xs], Ys - Zs)  ←
     part(X, Xs, Littles, Bigs),
     qs_dl(Littles, Ys - [X | Y1s]),
     qs_dl(Bigs, Y1s - Zs).
```

```
part(_, [], [], []).
part(X, [Y | Xs], [Y | Ls], Bs) ← X > Y, part(X, Xs, Ls, Bs).
part(X, [Y | Xs], Ls, [Y | Bs]) ← X ≤ Y, part(X, Xs, Ls, Bs).
```

Program: QUICKSORT_DL

Exercise 116 Modify the IN_ORDER and FRONTIER programs so that they employ difference lists. □

As a final example of the use of difference lists, we consider the implementation of a queue. Formally, a *queue* is a data structure to which elements can be added or removed according to the *First-In, First-Out* policy. This policy is ensured by two operations: *enqueue* that adds an element at the tail of the queue and *dequeue* that removes the element from the head of the queue.

In the program below a queue is represented as a difference list of the elements that are present in it, while the operations *enqueue* and *dequeue* take care that this representation is maintained. An additional operation, *setup*, is used to create the empty queue.

```
% setup(Q)  ←  Q is the empty queue.
setup(X-X).
% enqueue(A, Q, Q1)  ←  Q1 is the result of adding the element A
                         to the queue Q.
enqueue(A, X-[A|Y], X-Y).
% enqueue(A, Q, Q1)  ←  Q1 is the result of removing the element A
                         from the queue Q.
dequeue(A, [A|X]-Y, X-Y).
```

Program: QUEUE

The following listing illustrates the use of this program.

```
| ?- setup(X), enqueue(a,X,Y), enqueue(b,Y,Z),
      dequeue(A,Z,U), dequeue(B,U,V).
```

```
A = a,
B = b,
U = [b|_A]-_A,
V = _A-_A,
X = [a,b|_A]-[a,b|_A],
Y = [a,b|_A]-[b|_A],
Z = [a,b|_A]-_A
```

Interestingly, this program also allows us to generate "negative" queues. By this we mean a situation in which at a certain stage the total number of the *dequeue* operations exceeds the total number of the *enqueue* operations. In this case, the variables present in the *dequeue* operations become instantiated to the corresponding values that are enqueued later. For example, we have

```
| ?-   setup(X), dequeue(A,X,U), dequeue(B,U,V),
        enqueue(a,V,Y), enqueue(b,Y,Z).

A = a,
B = b,
U = [b|_A]-[a,b|_A],
V = _A-[a,b|_A],
X = [a,b|_A]-[a,b|_A],
Y = _A-[b|_A],
Z = _A-_A
```

9.6   Binary Search Trees

In Section 5.7 we discussed various algorithms on binary trees. The insertion
and deletion of elements of a tree can be defined in many ways. However, if no
restriction on the form of the tree is imposed, a tree can degenerate into a list
and the advantage of the tree representation — shorter access time for finding
the elements stored — is gone. Therefore it is natural to look for some classes of
binary trees studied in Section 5.7 which remain properly "balanced". One natural
restriction is the following one, where we assume that all the elements stored are
integers.

A tree is called a *binary search tree* (in short, a *search tree*) if in every subtree
of it the root x is greater than all elements in the left subtree and less than all
elements in the right subtree.

Search Tree
We now wish to write a program which tests whether a ground term is a search
tree. To this end we have to redefine them inductively. Note that according to the
definition, a tree is a search tree iff

- it is empty, or
-     — its left subtree is a search tree,

    — if its left subtree is non-empty, then its maximum is less than the root,

    — its right subtree is a search tree, and

    — if its right subtree is non-empty, then its minimum is greater than the
      root.

Thus for each search tree we need to maintain its minimum and maximum. Now
the minimum and maximum of a search tree can be deduced from the minima and
maxima of its left and right subtrees by noticing that

- if the left subtree is empty, then the root is the minimum, otherwise
- the minimum of a search tree equals the minimum of its left subtree,

- if the right subtree is empty, then the root is the maximum, otherwise
- the maximum of a search tree equals the maximum of its right subtree.

This leads to the following program where the minima and maxima are maintained only for non-empty trees:

```
% is_search_tree(Tree)  ←  Tree is a search tree.
is_search_tree(void).
is_search_tree(T)  ←  is_search_tree(T, Min, Max).

% is_search_tree(Tree, Min, Max)  ←  Tree is a search tree with a
                                      minimum element Min and a
                                      maximum element Max.
is_search_tree(tree(X, void, void), X, X).
is_search_tree(tree(X, void, Right), X, Max)  ←
    is_search_tree(Right, Min, Max), X < Min.
is_search_tree(tree(X, Left, void), Min, X)  ←
    is_search_tree(Left, Min, Max), Max < X.
is_search_tree(tree(X, Left, Right), Min1, Max2)  ←
    is_search_tree(Left, Min1, Max1), Max1 < X,
    is_search_tree(Right, Min2, Max2), X < Min2.
```

Program: SEARCH_TREE

Exercise 117 Analyze the behaviour of this program for non-ground terms. □

Various operations can be easily defined and efficiently performed when a search tree is used to represent the data. For example, to sort the elements stored in the search tree it suffices to use the in-order traversal.

Exercise 118 Prove the above statement. □

Search Tree Member
Next, it is not necessary to search through the whole tree to find whether an element is present in it. Instead, the following algorithm can be used. Consider a non-empty search tree t with the root y and an element x.

- If x =:= y, then x is present in t; otherwise,
- if x < y, then search for x in the left subtree of t,
- if x > y, then search for x in the right subtree of t.

This can be expressed by the following program.

```
% in(Element, Tree)  ←  Element is an element of the search tree Tree.
in(X, tree(X, Left, Right)).
in(X, tree(Y, Left, Right))  ←  X < Y, in(X, Left).
in(X, tree(Y, Left, Right))  ←  X > Y, in(X, Right).
```

Program: IN_TREE

This program does not correspond exactly with the mentioned algorithm, because only positive conclusions can be expressed by means of clauses. So the situation when the tree is empty is handled by default — no clause deals with such a case.

Minimum

The program SEARCH_TREE can also be used to find a minimum element of a search tree. Notice however, that a minimum element in a search tree is always its leftmost leaf. Using this observation we can compute the minimum element stored in a search tree in a direct way, without the use of any comparison relation.

```
% minimum(Tree, Element)  ←  Element is the minimum element of the
                                    search tree Tree.
minimum(tree(X, void, _), X).
minimum(tree(Y, Left, _), X)  ←  minimum(Left, X).
```

Program: TREE_MINIMUM

Note that for the empty tree this program fails.

Exercise 119 Write a program TREE_MAXIMUM which computes the maximum element of a search tree.   □

Exercise 120 Write a program which tests whether a ground term is a search tree by translating directly the definition of a search tree into clauses, using the programs TREE_MINIMUM and TREE_MAXIMUM. Why is this program less efficient than the program SEARCH_TREE?   □

Insertion

Next, let us consider operations which change the search tree. In each case one needs to take care that after the operation the tree remains a search tree. It is easy to insert an element x in a search tree t in an appropriate way — it suffices to insert it as a leaf at the right position. The following algorithm does the job.

If t is empty, then create a tree with the root x and empty left and right subtrees. Otherwise compare x with the root y of the search tree t.

- If x =:= y, then output the present search tree; otherwise
- if x < y, then insert x in the left subtree of t,
- if x > y, then insert x in the right subtree of t.

The following program formalizes this algorithm.

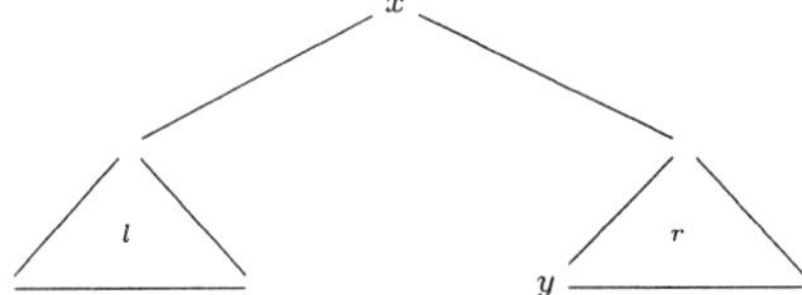

Figure 9.1 A search tree

```
% insert(Element, Tree, Tree1)  ←  Tree1 is the result of inserting
                                    Element in the search tree Tree.
insert(X, void, tree(X, void, void)).
insert(X, tree(X, Left, Right), tree(X, Left, Right)).
insert(X, tree(Y, Left, Right), tree(Y, Left1, Right)) ←
    X < Y, insert(X, Left, Left1).
insert(X, tree(Y, Left, Right), tree(Y, Left, Right1)) ←
    X > Y, insert(X, Right, Right1).
```

Program: INSERT

Deletion

The deletion of an element from a search tree is more complicated, since a literal removal of an element from a tree can create a "hole" in the tree. This hole has then to be filled by an element from the tree in such a way that the tree remains a search tree.

Let x be the element to be deleted. x is the root of a subtree t, with the left subtree l and the right subtree r. Then the right candidate to fill the hole is the leftmost leaf, say y, of r. Indeed, when discussing the program TREE_MINIMUM we already noted that y is the minimum element of r. Thus, all the elements of r are greater than y. Moreover, x < y, so all the elements of l are less than y. This situation is depicted by the diagram in Figure 9.1.

These considerations lead to the program below. The "transfer" of the element y to fill the hole is accomplished here by the procedure delmin which defines inductively the minimum element of a search tree and the result of deleting it from the tree. This procedure is a modification of the program TREE_MINIMUM.

```
% delete(Element, Tree, Tree1)  ←  Tree1 is the result of deleting
                                    Element from the search tree Tree.
delete(X, tree(X, void, Right), Right).
delete(X, tree(X, Left, void), Left).
delete(X, tree(X, Left, Right), tree(Y, Left, Right1)) ←
    delmin(Right, Y, Right1).
delete(X, tree(Y, Left, Right), tree(Y, Left1, Right)) ←
    X < Y, delete(X, Left, Left1).
delete(X, tree(Y, Left, Right), tree(Y, Left, Right1)) ←
```

```
    X > Y, delete(X, Right, Right1).
% delmin(Tree, Element, Tree1)  ←  Element is the minimum element
                                    of Tree and Tree1 is the result of
                                    deletion of Y from Tree.
delmin(tree(Y, void, Right), Y, Right).
delmin(tree(X, Left, _), Y, tree(X, Left1, _))  ←
    delmin(Left, Y, Left1).
```

Program: DELETE

Exercise 121 Why can the program INSERT with the query insert(x, Tree, tree) not be used to delete an element x from a search tree tree?   □

Exercise 122 The DELETE program is nondeterministic in the sense that for a query delete(x, t, T) with x an element and t a tree more than one clause is applicable. As a result different answers can be generated when the clauses are reordered. Investigate possible answers to the query delete(x, tree(x, void, right), T1), where right is a search tree, for different clause orderings.   □

Exercise 123 An alternative solution for filling the "hole" caused by deletion is to use the rightmost leaf of the left subtree of t. Write the corresponding program.   □

Exercise 124 Write a program which sorts a list of integers by first repeatedly inserting them into a search tree and then listing them by means of the in-order traversal.   □

Exercise 125 In general, arbitrary items are stored in a tree, not necessarily integers. In this case it is customary to associate with each item a natural number *key* which is used for all comparison purposes. Propose an appropriate data representation and modify the proposed algorithms on search trees to this case.   □

As in the case of trees, insertions and deletions in a search tree can also degenerate it into a list. This problem can be avoided if trees are used which remain balanced in presence of insertions and deletions. Several proposals were made in the literature — see, e.g. Cormen *et al.* [CLR90]. Some of them were elegantly coded in Prolog — see, e.g. Bratko [Bra86].

9.7   Evaluation of Arithmetic Expressions

So far we have presented programs that use ground arithmetic expressions, but have not yet presented any means of evaluating them. The advantages of evaluating gaes will become clear in a moment. For example, no facilities have been introduced so far to evaluate 3+4. All we can do at this stage is to check that the outcome is 7 by using the comparison relation =:= and the query 7 =:= 3+4. But using the comparison relations it is not possible to *assign* the value of 3+4, that is 7, to a variable, say X. Note that the query X =:= 3+4 ends in an error.

To overcome this problem the *arithmetic evaluator* `is/2` is incorporated into Prolog. `is/2` is defined internally as an infix operator with the following declaration in the case of SICStus Prolog:

```
:- op(700, xfx, is).
```

Consider the call `s is t`. Then `t` has to be a ground arithmetic expression (gae). The call of `s is t` results in the unification of the *value* of the gae `t` with `s`. If `t` is not a gae then a run-time error arises, that is the computation *ends in an error*.

Thus, the following possibilities arise.

- `t` is a gae.
  Let `val(t)` be the value of `t`.

  - `s` is identical to `val(t)`.
    Then the arithmetic evaluator succeeds and the empty computed answer substitution is produced. For example,

    ```
    | ?- 7 is 3+4.
    ```

    ```
    yes
    ```

  - `s` is a variable.
    Then the arithmetic evaluator also succeeds and the computed answer substitution {s/val(t)} is produced. For example,

    ```
    | ?- X is 3+4.
    ```

    ```
    X = 7
    ```

  - `s` is not identical to `val(t)` and is not a variable.
    Then the arithmetic evaluator fails. For example,

    ```
    | ?- 8 is 3+4.
    ```

    ```
    no
    | ?- 3+4 is 3+4.
    ```

    ```
    no
    ```

- `t` is not a gae.
  Then an error arises. For example,

  ```
  | ?- X is Y+1.
  ```

  ```
  ! Error in arithmetic expression: not a number
  ```

Exercise 126 Analyze what are the possible outcomes of the arithmetic evaluator `s is s+1`. □

Let us consider now some uses of the arithmetic evaluator.

Factorial

The proverbial factorial function can be computed as follows in Prolog:

```
% fact(N, F)  ←  F is N!.
fact(0, 1).
fact(N, F)  ←  N > 0, N1 is N-1, fact(N1, F1), F is N*F1.
```

Program: FACTORIAL

Note the use of a local variable `N1` in the arithmetic evaluator `N1 is N-1` to compute the decrement of `N` and the use of a local variable `F1` to compute the value of `N1` factorial. Such uses of local variables are typical for computing using integers in Prolog.

Exercise 127 Write a program computing the exponent X^Y of two natural numbers.

□

Between

The following program has already been defined in Section 1.4.

```
% between(X, Y, Z)  ←  X, Y are gaes and Z is an integer between X and Y,
                       inclusive.
between(X, Y, Z)  ←  X ≤ Y, Z is X.
between(X, Y, Z)  ←  X < Y, X1 is X+1, between(X1, Y, Z).
```

Program: BETWEEN

It allows us to generate all the integer values in a given range. For example:

```
| ?- between(10, 14, Z).

Z = 10 ;

Z = 11 ;

Z = 12 ;

Z = 13 ;

Z = 14 ;

no
```

Exercise 128 Usually the following, slightly simpler program is used to compute the above relation:

```
between(X, Y, X)  ←  X ≤ Y.
between(X, Y, Z)  ←  X < Y, X1 is X+1, between(X1, Y, Z).
```

Find a query for which these two programs yield different results.

Another Length

The `LENGTH` program of Section 5.5 is hardly useful for computing the length of a list, since it computes it in terms of numerals. Here is Prolog's version which yields the arithmetic output:

```
% length(Xs, N)  ←  N is the length of the list Xs.
length([], 0).
length([_ | Ts], N)  ←  length(Ts, M), N is M+1.
```

Program: LENGTH1

Exercise 129 Complete the program below to an alternative definition of the `length` relation:

```
length(Ts, M)  ←  length1(Ts, N), ....
length1([], 0).
length1([_ | Ts], N+1)  ←  length1(Ts, N).
```

□

Exercise 130 The use of the `sequence` relation in the program SEQUENCE is rather awkward. Define a binary relation `length1` such that for a natural number n the query `length1(Ss,n)` generates a list `Ss` of different variables of length n and use it in an alternative version of the program SEQUENCE. Can the relation `length` of the program LENGTH1 be used for this purpose? □

Exercise 131 Write a program that computes the number of nodes in a given binary tree. □

9.8   Concluding Remarks

In this chapter we introduced Prolog facilities dealing with arithmetic. To this end we introduced the comparison relations on ground arithmetic expressions and the arithmetic evaluator `is`. Let us now try to assess these Prolog features.

9.8.1   Comparison Relations

Because of the possibility of errors, the use of arithmetic expressions in Prolog is quite cumbersome and can easily lead to problems. Suppose for example that we wish to consider natural numbers in the range [1,100]. One way to do this is by listing all the relevant facts, so `small_num(1)`, `small_num(2)`, etc. This is hardly a meaningful way of programming. It is more natural to define what constitutes a desired number by means of arithmetic expressions. Thus, we naturally define

```
small_num(X)  ←  1 ≤ X, X ≤ 100.
```

Unfortunately, these two definitions are not equivalent. For example, with the first definition of `small_num` the query `small_num(X), X < 10` produces all numbers smaller than 10 whereas with the second definition an error arises, because of the improper use of the built-in relation $\leq$. In fact, one needs to use here the more complicated program BETWEEN, defined in the previous section.

We conclude that apparently obvious program modifications in the presence of comparison relations can lead to complications.

9.8.2 Arithmetic Evaluator

Ground arithmetic expressions can be evaluated only using the arithmetic evaluator `is`. However, its use can also easily cause a run-time error. Moreover, the appropriate use of `is` in specific programs, like FACTORIAL, is quite subtle because it relies on the introduction of fresh variables for holding intermediate results. This proliferation of local variables makes an understanding of such programs more difficult. In imperative programming languages the reuse of the same variables in computation can be seen in such circumstances as an advantage. In functional programming the corresponding functions can be programmed in a much more natural way.

As an example of these complications reconsider from Section 5.4 the task of producing all pairs X, Y such that $X + Y = s^3(0)$. In Section 5.4 we allowed X and Y to be numerals and the corresponding query was simply `sum(X, Y, s(s(s(0))))`. If we wish to produce all pairs of natural numbers X, Y such that $X + Y = 3$, then the corresponding query `X + Y = 3` is incorrect and we actually need to use a more complicated and artificial query `between(0,3,X), Y is 3-X`.

We conclude that arithmetic facilities in Prolog are quite subtle and require good insights to be properly used.

9.9 Bibliographic Remarks

As in Chapter 5, most of the programs we discussed here were taken from other sources. In particular, Section 9.5 is influenced by the corresponding presentation of difference lists in Sterling and Shapiro [SS86].

The above mentioned complications and shortcomings of Prolog's arithmetic facilities have motivated work on the modifications of Prolog. In several language proposals this problem was addressed by attempting to combine logic and functional programming. A number of first approaches to this subject are presented in De Groot and Lindstrom [GL86] whereas more recent proposals are gathered in Apt *et al.* [ABR93]. The two most recent programming languages based on the logic programming paradigm which address Prolog's problems with arithmetic are LIFE (see Aït-Kaci [Ait93]) and Gödel (see Hill and Lloyd [HL94]). For a recent survey on various methods of integrating functions into logic programming see Hanus [Han94].

Yet another way to deal with the integration of the arithmetic and logic programming is offered by *constraint logic programming*, a generalization of logic programming which combines programming with constraints — an area of artificial intelligence — with logic programming. For a a recent survey on this subject see Jaffar and Maher [JM94].

Finally, it may be of interest for the reader to learn that the signs "+" and "-" were used for the first time by R. Widman in 1486, the sign "=" was invented by R. Recorde in 1557, ">" and "<" were introduced by T. Harriot in 1639 and "*" by J. H. Rahn in 1659 (see Cajori [Caj28] and Ifrah [Ifr85]). It would be interesting to learn the origins of the signs "=:=", " =<" and " >=".

9.10   Summary

In this chapter we introduced a subset of Prolog that extends the one introduced in Chapter 5 by Prolog's facilities that allow us to deal with arithmetic. These involve

- use of operators to determine the binding power,
- arithmetic comparison relations,
- arithmetic evaluator "is".

We followed here the presentation style used in Chapter 5 and presented programs according to the domain over which they computed. These were here

- complex domains that involve integers,
- lists of integers,
- binary search trees.

9.11   References

[Ait93]   H. Aït-Kaci. An introduction to LIFE — programming with logic, inheritance, functions, and equations. In D. Miller, editor, *Proceedings of the International Symposium on Logic Programming*, pages 52–68. MIT Press, Cambridge, MA, 1993.

[ABR93]   K.R. Apt, de Bakker J.W., and J.J.M.M. Rutten, editors. *Current Trends in Logic Programming Languages*. The MIT Press, Cambridge, MA, 1993.

[Bra86]   I. Bratko. *PROLOG Programming for Artificial Intelligence*. International Computer Science Series. Addison-Wesley, Reading, MA, 1986.

[Caj28]   F. Cajori. *A History of Mathematical Notations*. The Open Court Publishing Company, 1928. Republished in 1974 in a paperback edition.

[CLR90] T.H. Cormen, C.E. Leiserson, and R.L. Rivest. *Introduction to Algorithms.* MIT Press, Cambridge, MA, 1990.

[GL86] D. de Groot and G. Lindstrom, editors. *Logic Programming, Functions, Relations and Equations.* Prentice Hall, New York, 1986.

[Han94] M. Hanus. The integration of functions into logic programming: from theory to practise. *Journal of Logic Programming*, 19-20:583–628, 1994.

[HL94] P. M. Hill and J. W. Lloyd. *The Gödel Programming Language.* The MIT Press, Cambridge, MA, 1994.

[Hoa62] C.A.R. Hoare. Quicksort. *BCS Computer Journal*, 5(1):10–15, 1962.

[Ifr85] G. Ifrah. *Les chiffres ou l'histoire d'une grande invention.* Editions Robert Laffont, S.A., Paris, 1985.

[JM94] J. Jaffar and M.J. Maher. Constraint logic programming: a survey. *Journal of Logic Programming*, 19,20:503–581, 1994.

[SS86] L. Sterling and E. Shapiro. *The Art of Prolog.* MIT Press, Cambridge, MA, 1986.

Verification of Pure Prolog Programs with Arithmetic

The aim of this chapter is to study verification of pure Prolog programs with arithmetic. In Chapters 6–8 we developed methods that allowed us to deal with the correctness of pure Prolog programs. Here we show that by a simple modification these methods can also apply to pure Prolog programs with arithmetic. One new aspect of correctness that we shall have to take into account is the possibility of run-time errors due to the presence of arithmetic relations.

In the next section we begin our exposition by explaining what changes are needed to the syntax assumed in Chapters 6–8 in order to deal with programs written in pure Prolog with arithmetic (from now on called *arithmetic programs*). In Section 10.2 we explain why the procedural interpretation of logic programs cannot be used to model the possibility that an LD-derivation ends in an error.

In the subsequent two sections, that is 10.3 and 10.4, we show that both termination and the occur-check freedom of arithmetic programs can be established by the methods originally developed in Chapters 6 and 7.

Then in Section 10.5 we introduce the notions of well-typed queries and programs and use them in Section 10.6 to consider a new aspect of correctness, namely the absence of errors in the presence of arithmetic relations.

Finally, in Section 10.7 we consider partial correctness. We explain there how the methods developed in Chapter 8 naturally extend from the case of pure Prolog programs to arithmetic programs.

10.1 Syntax

In the case of pure Prolog we first dealt with its foundations, that is logic programming, then introduced pure Prolog and subsequently, in Chapters 6–8, adjusted the syntax of logic programs to be able to deal formally with pure Prolog programs.

In the case of pure Prolog with arithmetic we reversed the presentation and first presented programs in pure Prolog with arithmetic. To deal formally with these programs we now need to modify the syntax. To this end we extend the language assumed in Chapters 6–8 by allowing the function symbols $+, -, *$ and the constants $0, -1, 1, -2, 2, \ldots$ We write these function symbols in the infix form. Further, we allow the arithmetic comparison relations $<, \leq, =:=, \neq, \geq, >$ and the arithmetic evaluator is, all of them written in the infix form.

Recall from Chapter 9 that for the comparison relations an error arises when one of the arguments is not a ground arithmetic expression (gae) and for the arithmetic evaluator is an error arises when its second argument is not a gae.

Notice that we did not introduce here the division operation. This simplifies the presentation and limits the possible run-time errors to the ones just mentioned.

10.2   Procedural Interpretation

When studying pure Prolog programs with arithmetic in a formal way we have to decide about the status of the arithmetic built-ins, that is the comparison relations $<, \leq, =:=, \neq, \geq, >$ and the arithmetic evaluator s is t. Are they some further unspecified relation symbols the definitions of which we can ignore? With this choice we face the following problem.

One of the properties of these built-ins is that in some situations the evaluation of atoms containing them results in an error. Now, the procedural interpretation of logic programs does not provide any facilities to deal with such errors. However, one could consider "trading" them for failure, that is to model their occurrence by means of failed LD-derivations. Unfortunately, this is not possible.

Indeed, the query 1>0 succeeds, so by the Lifting Corollary 3.23 the query X>Y succeeds, as well, whereas it was supposed to fail. Hence, it is not possible to model the fact that the query X>Y ends in an error. We conclude that the procedural interpretation of logic programming discussed in Chapter 3 cannot be used to capture the behaviour of the arithmetic relations properly.

To model Prolog's interpretation of arithmetic relations within logic programming we introduce the following notions.

Definition 10.1

- We call an atom *arithmetic* if its relation symbol is either a comparison relation $<, \leq, =:=, \neq, \geq, >$, or the arithmetic evaluator is.
- We say that an arithmetic atom is *correctly instantiated* if either its relation is a comparison relation and both of its arguments are gae or it is of the form s is t and t is a gae.
  We call an arithmetic atom *incorrectly instantiated* if it is not correctly instantiated.
- We say that an LD-derivation *ends in an error* if in some of its query an incorrectly instantiated arithmetic atom is selected. $\qquad\square$

In what follows we assume that an LD-derivation that ends in an error abnormally terminates with the first query in which an incorrectly instantiated arithmetic atom is selected. We could enforce this by redefining the notion of an LD-resolvent in the presence of arithmetic atoms. Thus in the presence of arithmetic a finite LD-derivation can be successful, failed or abnormally terminating. In our considerations the abnormal termination is not studied separately. In fact, we try to identify queries which both terminate in the sense studied in previous chapters and are such that no LD-derivation of them ends in an error.

We now add to each program infinitely many clauses which define the ground instances of the arithmetic relations. Given a gae n we denote by `val(n)` its value. For example, `val(3+4)` equals 7. So for $<$ we add the following set of unit clauses:

$$\{\texttt{m} < \texttt{n} \mid \texttt{m, n} \text{ are gaes and } \texttt{val(m)} < \texttt{val(n)}\},$$

for "`is`" we add the set

$$\{\texttt{val(n) is n} \mid \texttt{n} \text{ is a gae}\},$$

etc. We denote this infinite set of ground unit clauses by $P(Ar)$. (Actually we identify here atoms with unit clauses, but no confusion will result.)

For example, both the clauses `7 is 7` and `7 is 3+4` are in $P(Ar)$, while `3+4 is 7` is not. We also assume that, conforming to the status of built-ins, in the original program arithmetical relations are not used in clauses heads, that is they are defined only by the above ground unit clauses.

From now on, when discussing the behaviour of pure Prolog programs with arithmetic we shall always assume that each such program is automatically augmented by the program $P(Ar)$.

These added clauses allow us to compute resolvents when the selected atom is an arithmetic one. For example, using the leftmost selection rule, the query `X is 3+4, X < 2+3` resolves to only one query, namely `7 < 2+3` (using the clause `7 is 3+4`) and the query `7 < 2+3` fails. Thus all LD-derivations of the query `X is 3+4, X < 2+3` fail, which agrees with Prolog's interpretation.

Now, that the programs consist of infinitely many clauses some properties of them could be affected. For example, in Chapter 6 to study the LD-trees we used the König's Lemma 6.2, which assumes that the considered tree is finitely branching. Note, however, that thanks to the "ending in an error" provision every query with a selected arithmetic atom has at most one descendant in every LD-tree. Consequently, the resulting LD-trees remain finitely branching.

10.3   Termination

The approach to termination of pure Prolog programs presented in Chapter 6 and based on the Finiteness 1 Corollary 6.9 and Finiteness 2 Corollary 6.24 can be readily extended to pure Prolog programs with arithmetic — it suffices to use the level mappings which assign to ground atoms with the arithmetic relation the value 0.

As an illustration we consider here two examples. The first one concerns termination w.r.t. all selection rules.

Length1
Consider the LENGTH1 program:

```
length([], 0).
length([_ | Ts], N) ← length(Ts, M), N is M+1.
```

Take the level mapping defined as follows:

$$|\texttt{length}(s, t)| \; = \; |s|,$$
$$|s \text{ is } t| \; = \; 0.$$

Recall from Section 6.2 that the function $|\;|$ assigns to terms natural numbers in such a way that for a list s, $|s|$ equals its length.

It is clear that LENGTH1 is recurrent w.r.t. $|\;|$. In addition, for a list s and an arbitrary term t, the atom length(s,t) is rigid and hence bounded. By the Finiteness 1 Corollary 6.9 we conclude that all SLD-derivations of LENGTH1 $\cup\{\texttt{length}(s, t)\}$ are finite.

The next example deals with termination w.r.t. the leftmost selection rule.

Quicksort
Consider the QUICKSORT program:

```
qs([], []).
qs([X | Xs], Ys) ←
    part(X, Xs, Littles, Bigs),
    qs(Littles, Ls),
    qs(Bigs, Bs),
    app(Ls, [X | Bs], Ys).

part(_, [], [], []).
part(X, [Y | Xs], [Y | Ls], Bs) ← X > Y, part(X, Xs, Ls, Bs).
part(X, [Y | Xs], Ls, [Y | Bs]) ← X ≤ Y, part(X, Xs, Ls, Bs).

app([], Ys, Ys).
app([X | Xs], Ys, [X | Zs]) ← app(Xs, Ys, Zs).
```

Observe the following.

- QUICKSORT is not recurrent. In fact, consider the second clause instantiated with the substitution {X/a, Xs/b, Ys/c, Littles/[a | b], Ls/c}. Then the ground atom qs([a|b], c) appears both in the head and the body of the resulting ground clause.

- The clauses defining the $\mathtt{part}$ relation are recurrent w.r.t. level mapping $|\mathtt{part}(x, xs, ls, bs)| = |xs|$, $|s > t| = 0$ and $|s \leq t| = 0$.
- Extend now the above level mapping with

$$
\begin{aligned}
|\mathtt{qs}(xs, ys)| &= |xs|, \\
|\mathtt{app}(xs, ys, zs)| &= |xs|.
\end{aligned}
$$

Recall from Section 6.2 that $\mathtt{APPEND}$ is recurrent w.r.t. $|\,|$. Next, define a Herbrand interpretation of $\mathtt{QUICKSORT}$ by putting

$$
\begin{aligned}
I = \quad & \{\mathtt{qs}(xs, ys) \mid |xs| \geq |ys|\} \\
\cup \; & \{\mathtt{part}(x, xs, ls, bs) \mid |xs| \geq |ls| + |bs|\} \\
\cup \; & \{\mathtt{app}(xs, ys, zs) \mid |xs| + |ys| \geq |zs|\} \\
\cup \; & ground(\mathtt{X} > \mathtt{Y}) \\
\cup \; & ground(\mathtt{X} \leq \mathtt{Y}).
\end{aligned}
$$

In Section 6.5 we used proof outlines to present a proof that a program is acceptable. We now use them to show that $\mathtt{QUICKSORT}$ is acceptable w.r.t. $|\,|$ and I. The proof outlines for the unit clauses are obvious and omitted.

$$
\begin{aligned}
&\{1 + |xs| + |ys| \geq 1 + |zs|\} \\
&\mathtt{app}([x|xs], ys, [x|zs]) \qquad \leftarrow \\
&\qquad\qquad\qquad\qquad \mathtt{app}(xs, ys, zs). \\
&\qquad\qquad\qquad\qquad\quad \{|xs| + |ys| \geq |zs|\}
\end{aligned}
$$

$$
\begin{aligned}
&\{1 + |xs| \geq 1 + |ls| + |bs|\} \\
&\mathtt{part}(x, [y|xs], [y|ls], bs) \qquad \leftarrow \\
&\qquad\qquad\qquad \mathtt{X} > \mathtt{Y}, \\
&\qquad\qquad\qquad \mathtt{part}(x, xs, ls, bs). \\
&\qquad\qquad\qquad\quad \{|xs| \geq |ls| + |bs|\}
\end{aligned}
$$

$$
\begin{aligned}
&\{1 + |xs| \geq |ls| + 1 + |bs|\} \\
&\mathtt{part}(x, [y|xs], ls, [y|bs]) \qquad \leftarrow \\
&\qquad\qquad\qquad \mathtt{X} \leq \mathtt{Y}, \\
&\qquad\qquad\qquad \mathtt{part}(x, xs, ls, bs). \\
&\qquad\qquad\qquad\quad \{|xs| \geq |ls| + |bs|\}
\end{aligned}
$$

$$
\begin{aligned}
&\{1 + |xs| \geq |ys|\} \\
&\mathtt{qs}([x|xs], ys) \qquad \leftarrow \\
&\qquad\quad \mathtt{part}(x, xs, \mathtt{littles}, \mathtt{bigs}), \qquad \{1 + |xs|\} \quad \{|xs|\}\\
&\qquad\qquad \{|xs| \geq |\mathtt{littles}| + |\mathtt{bigs}|\} \\
&\qquad\quad \mathtt{qs}(\mathtt{littles}, ls), \qquad\qquad\qquad\quad \{|\mathtt{littles}|\} \\
&\qquad\qquad \{|\mathtt{littles}| \geq |ls|\} \\
&\qquad\quad \mathtt{qs}(\mathtt{bigs}, bs), \qquad\qquad\qquad\qquad \{|\mathtt{bigs}|\} \\
&\qquad\qquad \{|\mathtt{bigs}| \geq |bs|\} \\
&\qquad\quad \mathtt{app}(ls, [x|bs], ys). \qquad\qquad\quad \{|ls|\} \\
&\qquad\qquad \{|ls| + 1 + |bs| \geq |ys|\}
\end{aligned}
$$

Using the Termination 2 Corollary 6.25 we conclude that QUICKSORT is left terminating. Moreover, we obtain that, for a list s and an arbitrary term t, the atom qs(s,t) is rigid and hence bounded. By the Finiteness 2 Corollary 6.24 we obtain that all LD-derivations of QUICKSORT $\cup\{qs(s,t)\}$ are finite.

Exercise 132 Provide a proof outline showing that the QUICKSORT_ACC program

```
% qs(Xs, Ys)  ←  Ys is an ordered permutation of the list Xs.
qs(Xs, Ys)  ←  qs_acc(Xs, [], Ys).

% qs_acc(Xs, Ys, Zs)  ←  Zs is the result of concatenating the ordered
                         permutation of the list Xs and the list Ys.
qs_acc([], Xs, Xs).
qs_acc([X | Xs], Zs, Ys)  ←
    part(X, Xs, Littles, Bigs),
    qs_acc(Littles, [X | Y1s], Ys),
    qs_acc(Bigs, Zs, Y1s).

part(_, [], [], []).
part(X, [Y | Xs], [Y | Ls], Bs)  ←  X > Y, part(X, Xs, Ls, Bs).
part(X, [Y | Xs], Ls, [Y | Bs])  ←  X ≤ Y, part(X, Xs, Ls, Bs).
```

is acceptable. Conclude that for a list s, all LD-derivations of QUICKSORT_ACC $\cup\{qs(s,t)\}$ are finite. □

We conclude that the methods developed in Chapter 6 apply to arithmetic programs, as well. In fact, the base for our approach to termination, the Finiteness 1 Corollary 6.9 and Finiteness 2 Corollary 6.24, remain valid for arithmetic programs, as the same proof carries through.

However, some caution has to be exercised when interpreting the results of Chapter 6 in the presence of arithmetic. Namely, the Acceptability Theorem 6.28 does not hold any more. Indeed, consider the program with only one clause:

```
p  ←  X < Y, p.
```

Because the LD-derivations which end in an error are finite, the above program is left terminating. However, it is easy to see that it is not acceptable — just consider the ground instance p ← 1<2, p and recall from Section 10.2 that the clause $1 < 2$ is added to the program, so it is true in every model of it. (In contrast, the program consisting of the clause

```
p  ←  X < X, p.
```

is acceptable.) This shows that the proposed method of proving termination is somewhat less general in the case of programs with arithmetic.

Exercise 133 Call a program P *error-free* if for all ground non-arithmetic atoms A the LD-derivations of $P \cup \{A\}$ do not end in an error.

Let P be a left terminating, error-free program. Prove that for some level mapping $|\ |$ and an interpretation I of P

(i) P is acceptable w.r.t. $| \, |$ and I,

(ii) for every query Q such that the LD-derivations of $P \cup \{Q\}$ do not end in an error, Q is bounded w.r.t. $| \, |$ and I iff all LD-derivations of $P \cup \{Q\}$ are finite.

Hint. Refine the proof of the Acceptability Theorem 6.28 by noting that the LD-tree Lemma 6.27 remains valid in presence of arithmetic relations provided it is applied to a query Q such that all LD-derivations of $P \cup \{Q\}$ are finite *and* do not end in an error. $\square$

10.4 Occur-check Freedom

Next, we deal with the issue of the occur-check. The approach of Chapter 7 is applicable to pure Prolog programs with arithmetic without any modification. The reason is that the unit clauses which define the arithmetic relations are all ground, so they automatically satisfy the conditions of the Occur-check 1 Corollary 7.18 and the Occur-check 2 Corollary 7.25. To see how these results apply here reconsider the three programs considered in the previous section. The first two examples confirm the usefulness of the methods provided in Chapter 7 while the third one indicates their limitations.

Length1
First, consider the `LENGTH1` program with the moding `length(+,-)`, `is(-,+)`. Then `LENGTH1` is well-moded and the heads of all clauses are output linear. By the Occur-check 1 Corollary 7.18 for s ground, `LENGTH1` $\cup$ `{length(s, t)}` is occur-check free.

Moreover, in this moding `LENGTH1` is also nicely moded and the heads of all clauses are input linear. Thus, the Occur-check 2 Corollary 7.25 applies here, as well and yields that when t is linear and s is an arbitrary term such that $Var(\mathtt{s}) \cap Var(\mathtt{t}) = \emptyset$, `LENGTH1` $\cup$ `{ length(s, t)}` is occur-check free. In particular, this conclusion holds for any list s and a variable t not appearing in s.

Quicksort
Next, consider `QUICKSORT` with the moding reflecting its use, that is
`qs(+,-)`,
`partition(+,+,-,-)`,
`app(+,+,-)`,
`>(+, +)`,
`≤(+, +)`.
It is easy to check that `QUICKSORT` is then well-moded and the heads of all clauses are output linear. The Occur-check 1 Corollary 7.18 applies and yields that for s ground, `QUICKSORT` $\cup$ `{qs(s, t)}` is occur-check free.

Moreover, in this moding `QUICKSORT` is also nicely moded and the head of every clause is input linear. Thus, the Occur-check 2 Corollary 7.25 applies, as well and yields that when t is linear and $Var(\mathtt{s}) \cap Var(\mathtt{t}) = \emptyset$, `QUICKSORT` $\cup$ `{ qs(s, t)}` is occur-check free. However, this conclusion is of hardly any interest, because QUICKSORT is meant to sort ground lists.

Quicksort with Accumulator

Finally, consider the QUICKSORT_ACC program. It is natural to use it with the moding qs(+,-). However, there is no way to complete this moding so that the program is well-moded.

Indeed, the clause which defines the qs relation then enforces that the last position of the qs_acc relation is moded output. Moreover, as the first occurrence of the variable Y1s in the second clause defining the qs_acc relation is within the term [X | Y1s], this position has to be moded output as well. So both the second and third positions of the qs_acc relation are moded output. But then the first clause defining qs_acc is not well-moded.

Exercise 134 Prove that no moding exists for which the program QUICKSORT_ACC is nicely moded, with the heads of all clauses being input linear.   □

We conclude that the proof of the occur-check freedom of the QUICKSORT_ACC program is beyond the scope of the methods introduced in Chapter 7. In Apt and Pellegrini [AP94] a refinement of the methods given in Chapter 7 is proposed which can be used to deal with this program. Finally, note that if we reverse the order of the recursive calls to qs_acc, then the resulting program becomes well-moded and we can prove its occur-check freedom using the Occur-check 1 Corollary 7.18.

10.5   Well-typed Queries and Programs

To deal with the absence of run-time errors we now introduce types. They allow us to ensure that the input positions of the selected atoms remain correctly typed during the program execution.

The following very general definition of a type is sufficient for our purposes.

Definition 10.2 A *type* is a set of terms closed under substitution.   □

Certain types will be of special interest below:

U — the set of all terms,

List — the set of lists,

Gae — the set of of gaes,

ListGae — the set of lists of gaes.

From now on we fix a specific set of types, denoted by *Types*, which includes the above ones.

We now associate types with relation symbols.

Definition 10.3 A *type* for an n-ary relation symbol p is a function t_p from $[1, n]$ to the set *Types*. If $t_p(i) = T$, we call T *the type associated with the position i of p*. Assuming a type t_p for the relation p, we say that an atom $p(s_1, \ldots, s_n)$ is *correctly typed in position i* if $s_i \in t_p(i)$. $\qquad\square$

In the remainder of this section we adopt the following

Assumption *Every considered relation* has a fixed mode and a fixed type associated with it.

This assumption will allow us to talk about modes and types of input positions and of output positions of an atom. An n-ary relation p with a mode m_p and type t_p will be denoted by

$$p(m_p(1) : t_p(1), \ldots, m_p(n) : t_p(n)).$$

We can talk about types of input positions and of output positions of an atom. For example, $\mathbf{part}(+ : Gae, + : ListGae, - : ListGae, - : ListGae)$ denotes a relation **part** with four arguments: the first position is moded as input and typed Gae, the second position is moded as input and typed $ListGae$ and the third and fourth positions are moded as output and typed $ListGae$.

Intuitively, the modes and types indicate how the arguments of a relation should be used: the given, known arguments should be put in the input positions and these arguments should belong to the types of the corresponding input positions. The terms in which the values should be computed should be put in the output positions. The idea is that the computed values should belong to the types of the corresponding output positions. This intuition is not precise because the computation can also instantiate the input positions and the output positions can be filled in by terms which are not instantiated by the computation (for example, ground terms of the appropriate types).

To prove that the modes and types are used in a way conforming to the above intuition we need to impose certain conditions on a program and a query. This brings us to the notion of a well-typed query and a well-typed program. The notion of well-typed queries and programs relies on the concept of a type judgement.

By a *typed term* we mean a construct of the form $s : S$ where s is a term and S is a type. Given a sequence $\mathbf{s} : \mathbf{S} = s_1 : S_1, \ldots, s_n : S_n$ of typed terms we write $\mathbf{s} \in \mathbf{S}$ if for $i \in [1, n]$ we have $s_i \in S_i$.

Definition 10.4

- A *type judgement* is a statement of the form $\mathbf{s} : \mathbf{S} \Rightarrow \mathbf{t} : \mathbf{T}$.
- We say that a type judgement $\mathbf{s} : \mathbf{S} \Rightarrow \mathbf{t} : \mathbf{T}$ *is true* and write

$$\models \mathbf{s} : \mathbf{S} \Rightarrow \mathbf{t} : \mathbf{T},$$

    if for all substitutions θ, $\mathbf{s}\theta \in \mathbf{S}$ implies $\mathbf{t}\theta \in \mathbf{T}$. $\qquad\square$

For example, the type judgements $x : Gae$, $l : ListGae \Rightarrow [x \mid l] : ListGae$ and $[x \mid l] : ListGae \Rightarrow l : ListGae$ are both true.

Exercise 135 Prove the following properties of type judgements.

(i) Let $\phi, \phi_1, \phi_2, \phi_2', \phi_3$ and ψ be sequences of typed terms. Suppose that $s \in S$ and $\models s : S, \phi \Rightarrow \psi$. Then $\models \phi \Rightarrow \psi$.

(ii) Suppose that $\models \phi_2 \Rightarrow \phi_2'$ and $\models \phi_1, \phi_2', \phi_3 \Rightarrow \psi$. Then $\models \phi_1, \phi_2, \phi_3 \Rightarrow \psi$.

(iii) Call a typed term $\mathbf{t} : \mathbf{T}$ *realizable* if $\mathbf{t}\eta \in \mathbf{T}$ for some η. Suppose that $\mathbf{t} : \mathbf{T}$ is realizable, $\models \mathbf{s} : \mathbf{S}, \mathbf{t} : \mathbf{T} \Rightarrow \mathbf{u} : \mathbf{U}$ and $Var(\mathbf{t}) \cap Var(\mathbf{s}, \mathbf{u}) = \emptyset$. Then $\models \mathbf{s} : \mathbf{S} \Rightarrow \mathbf{u} : \mathbf{U}$.

□

To simplify the notation, when writing an atom as $p(\mathbf{u} : \mathbf{S}, \mathbf{v} : \mathbf{T})$ we now assume that $\mathbf{u} : \mathbf{S}$ is a sequence of typed terms filling in the input positions of p and $\mathbf{v} : \mathbf{T}$ is a sequence of typed terms filling in the output positions of p. In other words, $p(\mathbf{u}, \mathbf{v})$ is an atom in which $\mathbf{u}$ fill in the input positions, $\mathbf{v}$ fill in the output positions and p is moded and typed $p(+ : \mathbf{S}, - : \mathbf{T})$.

Definition 10.5

- A query $p_1(\mathbf{i_1} : \mathbf{I_1}, \mathbf{o_1} : \mathbf{O_1}), \ldots, p_n(\mathbf{i_n} : \mathbf{I_n}, \mathbf{o_n} : \mathbf{O_n})$ is called *well-typed* if for $j \in [1, n]$

$$\models \mathbf{o_1} : \mathbf{O_1}, \ldots, \mathbf{o_{j-1}} : \mathbf{O_{j-1}} \Rightarrow \mathbf{i_j} : \mathbf{I_j}.$$

- A clause

$$p_0(\mathbf{o_0} : \mathbf{O_0}, \mathbf{i_{n+1}} : \mathbf{I_{n+1}}) \leftarrow p_1(\mathbf{i_1} : \mathbf{I_1}, \mathbf{o_1} : \mathbf{O_1}), \ldots, p_n(\mathbf{i_n} : \mathbf{I_n}, \mathbf{o_n} : \mathbf{O_n})$$

  is called *well-typed* if for $j \in [1, n+1]$

$$\models \mathbf{o_0} : \mathbf{O_0}, \ldots, \mathbf{o_{j-1}} : \mathbf{O_{j-1}} \Rightarrow \mathbf{i_j} : \mathbf{I_j}.$$

- A program is called *well-typed* if every clause of it is. □

Thus, a query is well-typed if

- the types of the terms filling in the *input* positions of an atom can be deduced from the types of the terms filling in the *output* positions of the previous atoms.

And a clause is well-typed if

- ($j \in [1, n]$) the types of the terms filling the *input* positions of a body atom can be deduced from the types of the terms filling in the *input* positions of the head and the *output* positions of the previous body atoms,

- $(j = n + 1)$ the types of the terms filling in the *output* positions of the head can be deduced from the types of the terms filling in the *input* positions of the head and the types of the terms filling in the *output* positions of the body atoms.

Note that a query with only one atom is well-typed iff this atom is correctly typed in its input positions and a unit clause $p(\mathbf{s} : \mathbf{S}, \mathbf{t} : \mathbf{T}) \leftarrow$ is well-typed if $\models \mathbf{s} : \mathbf{S} \Rightarrow \mathbf{t} : \mathbf{T}$.

We now prove that the notion of well-typedness is a special case of the notion of well-assertedness introduced in Chapter 8 in Definition 8.5. Below we use the assumption made on page 265 which states that every considered relation has a fixed mode and a fixed type associated with it.

Theorem 10.6 (Reduction) For every relation symbol there exists a specification in the sense of Definition 8.2 such that for every clause c and every query Q

  (i) c is well-typed iff c is well-asserted,
  (ii) Q is well-typed iff Q is well-asserted.

Proof. For every relation symbol p let

$$pre_p = \{p(\mathbf{s} : \mathbf{S}, \mathbf{t} : \mathbf{T}) \mid \mathbf{s} \in \mathbf{S}\},$$

$$post_p = \{p(\mathbf{s} : \mathbf{S}, \mathbf{t} : \mathbf{T}) \mid \mathbf{t} \in \mathbf{T}\}.$$

That is, pre_p consists of all the p-atoms that are correctly typed in their input positions while $post_p$ consists of all the p-atoms that are correctly typed in their output positions.

This implies the claim. $\qquad\square$

Exercise 136 Prove that the notion of a well-moded clause (respectively query) is a special case of the notion of a well-typed clause (respectively query). $\qquad\square$

The result just proved allows us to draw conclusions analogous to those made in Section 8.2, now reformulated for the notion of well-typedness. We list them below.

Lemma 10.7 (Well-typedness) An SLD-resolvent of a well-typed query and a well-typed clause is well-typed. $\qquad\square$

Corollary 10.8 (Well-typedness) Let P and Q be well-typed. Then all queries in all SLD-derivations of $P \cup \{Q\}$ are well-typed. $\qquad\square$

Corollary 10.9 (Well-typed Computed Answer) Let P and Q be well-typed. Then for every computed answer substitution θ for $P \cup \{Q\}$, each atom in $Q\theta$ is well-typed in its output positions. $\qquad\square$

Exercise 137 Prove the above corollary directly, using the Well-typedness Corollary 10.8. □

Finally, we obtain the following conclusion.

Corollary 10.10 (Correct Typing) Let P and Q be well-typed, and let ξ be an LD-derivation of $P \cup \{Q\}$. All atoms selected in ξ are correctly typed in their input positions. □

10.5.1 Examples

The above results allow us to draw some conclusions about the program behaviour. Let us see now to what extent these results can be applied to specific programs. We concentrate here on our three running examples and analyze the use of Well-typed Computed Answer Corollary 10.9. Note that this corollary refers to an arbitrary selection rule. In the next section we shall analyze the use of the Correct Typing Corollary 10.10.

Length1
We use the following modes and types:
length$(+ : U, - : Gae)$,
is$(- : Gae, + : Gae)$.
It is easy to check that LENGTH1 is then well-typed. Indeed, its first clause is well-typed because 0 is a gae and the second clause is well-typed because if m is a gae, then m+1 is a gae. Note that the above moding and typing imposes no type restrictions on the input position of the length relation and consequently every length-atom is well-typed.

By the Well-typed Computed Answer Corollary 10.9 we conclude that for arbitrary terms s,t every computed answer substitution θ of length(s,t) is such that tθ is a gae.

Quicksort
The following moding and typing of the qs relation reflects the natural use of QUICKSORT:
qs$(+ : ListGae, - : ListGae)$.
We now complete the moding and typing in such a way that QUICKSORT is well-typed:
$> (+ : Gae, + : Gae)$,
$\leq (+ : Gae, + : Gae)$,
part$(+ : Gae, + : ListGae, - : ListGae, - : ListGae)$,
app$(+ : ListGae, + : ListGae, - : ListGae)$.
By way of example, notice that the clauses of the APPEND program are well-typed since that following implications clearly hold:

$\models$ Ys $: ListGae \Rightarrow$ Ys $: ListGae$,

$$\models [\mathtt{X}|\mathtt{Xs}] : ListGae \;\Rightarrow\; \mathtt{Xs} : ListGae,$$

$$\models \mathtt{Zs} : ListGae \;\Rightarrow\; [\mathtt{X}|\mathtt{Zs}] : ListGae.$$

A similar reasoning shows that other clauses of QUICKSORT are well-typed, as well.

Assume now that $\mathtt{s}$ is a list of gaes and $\mathtt{t}$ an arbitrary term. The query $\mathtt{qs(s,t)}$ is then well-typed and by the Well-typed Computed Answer Corollary 10.9 we conclude that every computed answer substitution θ of $\mathtt{qs(s,t)}$ is such that $\mathtt{t}\theta$ is a list of gaes.

Exercise 138 Prove that for lists $\mathtt{s}$ and $\mathtt{t}$, all c.a.s.s θ for APPEND $\cup$ $\{\mathtt{app(s,t,u)}\}$ are such that $u\theta$ is a list. $\qquad\square$

Exercise 139 Prove that for a list $\mathtt{s}$ all c.a.s.s θ for PERMUTATION $\cup$ $\{\mathtt{perm(s,t)}\}$ are such that $t\theta$ is a list.
Hint. Use the following moding and typing:
$\mathtt{perm}(+ : List, - : List)$,
$\mathtt{app}(- : List, - : List, + : List)$ for the first call to APPEND,
$\mathtt{app}(+ : List, + : List, - : List)$ for the second call to APPEND. $\qquad\square$

Quicksort with Accumulator
To deal with the QUICKSORT_ACC program we would like to use the same moding and typing for the $\mathtt{qs}$ relation as in QUICKSORT, that is
$\mathtt{qs}(+ : ListGae, - : ListGae)$.
Unfortunately, this moding and typing cannot be completed so that QUICKSORT_ACC is well-typed. Suppose otherwise. Then on account of the clause defining the $\mathtt{qs}$ relation, we have to mode and type the last position of $\mathtt{qs\_acc}$ as $- : T_1$, where $T_1 \subseteq ListGae$. This in turn, on account of the first clause defining the $\mathtt{qs\_acc}$ relation, forces us to mode the second position $\mathtt{qs\_acc}$ as $+ : T_2$, where $T_2 \subseteq T_1$. But then

$$\models [\mathtt{X}|\mathtt{Xs}] : ListGae,\ \mathtt{Zs} : ListGae,\ \mathbf{o} : \mathbf{O} \;\Rightarrow\; [\mathtt{X}|\mathtt{Y1s}] : T2,$$

where $\mathbf{o} : \mathbf{O}$ is the sequence of typed terms filling in the output positions of the atom $\mathtt{part(X, Xs, Littles, Bigs)}$, is a part of the statement that the second clause defining $\mathtt{qs\_acc}$ is well-typed. Hence,

$$\models [\mathtt{X}|\mathtt{Xs}] : ListGae,\ \mathtt{Zs} : ListGae,\ \mathbf{o} : \mathbf{O} \;\Rightarrow\; [\mathtt{X}|\mathtt{Y1s}] : ListGae.$$

Contradiction, since this type judgement is not true.

We conclude that, given a query $\mathtt{qs(s,t)}$ with $\mathtt{s}$ a list of gaes, we can prove using the Well-typed Computed Answer Corollary 10.9 that for QUICKSORT every computed answer substitution θ is such that $\mathtt{t}\theta$ is a list of gaes, but that the same conclusion cannot be established for QUICKSORT_ACC using only this corollary. This shows the limitations of the notion of well-typedness.

In Section 10.7 we shall prove (a strengthening of) the above conclusion for QUICKSORT_ACC using the notions of well-asserted queries and programs. This shows that the notion of well-assertedness is more powerful than the notion of well-typedness.

Note however, that it is easy to establish the just discussed conclusion concerning QUICKSORT_ACC using the Well-typed Computed Answer Corollary 10.9 *together* with the Independence Theorem 3.33. Indeed, consider a modification of the QUICKSORT_ACC program obtained by the transposition of the recursive calls to the qs_acc relation, that is by replacing the second clause defining this relation by

```
qs_acc([X | Xs], Zs, Ys)  ←
    part(X, Xs, Littles, Bigs),
    qs_acc(Bigs, Zs, Y1s),
    qs_acc(Littles, [X | Y1s], Ys).
```

Call the resulting program QUICKSORT_ACC1. Use now the following moding and typing for the qs_acc relation:
$qs\_acc(+ : ListGae, + : ListGae, - : ListGae)$,
and adopt for other relations the same moding and typing as in the case of QUICKSORT.

Exercise 140 Prove that QUICKSORT_ACC1 is then well-typed. □

By the Well-typed Computed Answer Corollary 10.9 we now conclude that for a query qs(s,t) with s a list of gaes, every computed answer substitution θ for the QUICKSORT_ACC1 program is such that $t\theta$ is also a list of gaes. Now by the Independence Theorem 3.33 the same conclusion can be drawn for the QUICKSORT_ACC program.

Exercise 141 Show that the moding $qs(+, -)$ can be extended so that QUICKSORT_ACC1 is well-moded. □

Exercise 142 Call a query Q *properly typed* if a query obtained by a permutation of the atoms of Q is well-typed and call a clause $H \leftarrow \mathbf{B}$ *properly typed* if for a query $\mathbf{C}$ obtained by a permutation of the atoms of $\mathbf{B}$ the clause $H \leftarrow \mathbf{C}$ is well-typed. Prove that an SLD-resolvent of a properly typed query and a properly typed clause is properly typed. □

10.6 Absence of Run-time Errors

We now show how the notion of well-typedness allows us to establish the absence of run-time errors. Due to the introduced syntax limitations these errors can arise only due to the use of arithmetic operations. To prove the absence of errors we thus need to show that for a program and a query of interest, no LD-derivation ends in an error. This requires an analysis of the form of the arguments of the selected atoms. Now, the Correct Typing Corollary 10.10 does allow us to carry out such an analysis. More precisely, the following conclusion of it will now be of use for us.

Corollary 10.11 (Absence of Errors) Consider a program with arithmetic P and a query Q such that

- P and Q are well-typed,
- each arithmetic comparison relation p is moded and typed $p(+ : Gae, + : Gae)$,
- the arithmetic evaluator is is moded and typed $is(- : Gae, + : Gae)$ or $is(+ : Gae, + : Gae)$.

Then the LD-derivations of $P \cup \{Q\}$ do not end in an error.

Proof. It suffices to note that by virtue of the Correct Typing Corollary 10.10 all selected arithmetic atoms in all LD-derivations of $P \cup \{Q\}$ are correctly instantiated. $\qquad\square$

This result can be used to prove the absence of errors, both for the arithmetic comparison relations and for the arithmetic evaluator is. To see its usefulness we now show how it can be applied to the three running examples of this chapter.

Length1

We use the modes and types used in the previous section, that is
$length(+ : U, - : Gae)$,
$is(- : Gae, + : Gae)$.
We noticed that LENGTH1 is then well-typed. By the Absence of Errors Corollary 10.11 we conclude that for arbitrary terms s,t the LD-derivations of LENGTH1 $\cup$ $\{length(s, t)\}$ do not end in an error.

Quicksort

Again, we use the modes and types used in the previous section, that is
$qs(+ : ListGae, - : ListGae)$,
$> (+ : Gae, + : Gae)$,
$\leq (+ : Gae, + : Gae)$,
$part(+ : Gae, + : ListGae, - : ListGae, - : ListGae)$,
$app(+ : ListGae, + : ListGae, - : ListGae)$.
We noted that QUICKSORT is then well-typed. Assume now that s is a list of gaes and t an arbitrary term. The query qs(s,t) is then well-typed and by the Absence of Errors Corollary 10.11 we conclude that the LD-derivations of QUICKSORT $\cup$ $\{qs(s,t)\}$ do not end in an error.

Exercise 143 Prove that the Absence of Errors Corollary 10.11 can also be applied to the query qs(s,t), with s a list of gaes, when the moding and typing for the relation qs is $qs(+ : ListGae, - : U)$. $\square$

Exercise 144 Let s be a list of gaes and t an arbitrary term. Prove that the LD-derivations of MERGESORT $\cup$ {ms(s,t)} do not end in an error. $\square$

Quicksort with Accumulator
To deal with the QUICKSORT_ACC program we use the following moding and typing:
$qs(+ : ListGae, - : U)$,
$qs\_acc(+ : ListGae, - : U, - : U)$,
with the same moding and typing for the $>, \le$ and **part** relations as those used for QUICKSORT.

Exercise 145 Prove that QUICKSORT_ACC is then well-typed. $\square$

Again by the Absence of Errors Corollary 10.11 we conclude that, for a list of gaes s and an arbitrary term t, the LD-derivations of QUICKSORT_ACC $\cup$ {qs(s, t)} do not end in an error.

Note that we used here quite a "weak" typing in the sense that no type information about the output positions of the qs and qs_acc relations was used. Yet it was sufficient to establish the desired conclusion.

Exercise 146 Let s be a list of gaes and t an arbitrary term. Prove that all the selected qs_acc-atoms in all LD-derivations of QUICKSORT_ACC $\cup$ {qs(s, t)} are of the form qs_acc(s,t,u) where s is a list of gaes and t is not a variable. $\square$

Exercise 147 Prove that for a binary tree t built from integers, the LD-derivations of SEARCH TREE $\cup$ {search_tree(t, min, max)} do not end in an error irrespectively of the choice of the terms min and max. $\square$

10.7   Partial Correctness

Next, we discuss partial correctness of (pure Prolog) programs with arithmetic. In Chapter 8 we introduced two notions of partial correctness and provided for each of them a method to establish it. We now review what modifications of these methods are needed to deal with programs with arithmetic.

10.7.1   Well-asserted Queries and Programs

The first notion of partial correctness was dealt with using the well-asserted queries and well-asserted programs. When dealing with programs with arithmetic we need to remember (see Section 10.2) that to each such program we added infinitely many clauses which define the arithmetic relations. It is natural to assume a fixed specification for all these relations. The specifications given below reflect the use of these relations and closely correspond with the information contained in the unit clauses that were added to each program with arithmetic. For $<$ we define

$$pre_< = \{\, \mathtt{s} < \mathtt{t} \mid \mathtt{s}, \mathtt{t} \text{ are gaes}\,\},$$

$$post_< = \{\, \mathtt{s} < \mathtt{t} \mid \mathtt{s}, \mathtt{t} \text{ are gaes and } \mathtt{val(m)} < \mathtt{val(n)}\,\},$$

and similarly for other comparison relations. For the arithmetic evaluator is we define

$$pre_{\mathtt{is}} = \{\, \mathtt{s}\ \mathtt{is}\ \mathtt{t} \mid \mathtt{t} \text{ is a gae}\,\},$$

$$post_{\mathtt{is}} = \{\, \mathtt{s}\ \mathtt{is}\ \mathtt{t} \mid \mathtt{t} \text{ is a gae and } \mathtt{s} = \mathtt{val(t)}\,\}.$$

The use of the above "pre-declared" specifications forms the only difference between the notion of well-assertedness considered here and in Section 10.2.

The following observation shows that these "pre-declared" specifications are correct.

Note 10.12 (Arithmetic Relations) The program $P(Ar)$ is well-asserted w.r.t. to the above specifications.

Proof. It is sufficient to note that for each $A \in P(Ar)$ we have $\models post(A)$. $\square$

Let us consider now the running examples of this chapter.

Length1
We use the following specification:

$$pre_{\mathtt{length}} = \{\, \mathtt{length(s,t)} \mid \mathtt{s} \text{ is a list}\,\},$$

$$post_{\mathtt{length}} = \{\, \mathtt{length(s,|s|)} \mid \mathtt{s} \text{ is a list}\,\}.$$

Exercise 148 Prove that LENGTH1 is well-asserted w.r.t. the above specification. $\square$

By the Partial Correctness Corollary 8.10 we conclude that for a ground list $\mathtt{s}$

$$\{\mathtt{length(s,N)}\}\ \mathtt{LENGTH1}\ inst(\mathtt{length(s,N)}) \cap post_{\mathtt{length}}.$$

But the set $inst(\mathtt{length(s,N)}) \cap post_{\mathtt{length}}$ has just one element, $\mathtt{length(s,|s|)}$, so every successful LD-derivation of $\mathtt{LENGTH1} \cup \{\mathtt{length(s,N)}\}$ yields the computed instance $\mathtt{length(s,|s|)}$.

Quicksort

We now prove partial correctness of QUICKSORT. Below we use the following terminology. We say that an element a *splits a list of gaes* s *into* ls *and* bs if

- a is a gae,
- ls is a list of elements of s which are $< $ a,
- bs is a list of elements of s which are $\geq$ a.

Consider the following specifications:

$$pre_{\mathbf{qs}} = \{qs(s, t) \mid s \text{ is a list of gaes}\},$$

$$post_{\mathbf{qs}} = \{qs(s, t) \mid s, t \text{ are lists of gaes and } t \text{ is a sorted permutation of } s\},$$

$$pre_{\mathbf{part}} = \{part(a, s, ls, bs) \mid s \text{ is a list}\},$$

$$post_{\mathbf{part}} = \{part(a, s, ls, bs) \mid \quad s, ls, bs \text{ are lists of gaes and } \\ a \text{ splits } s \text{ into } ls \text{ and } bs\},$$

$$pre_{\mathbf{app}} = \{app(s, t, u) \mid s, t \text{ are lists of gaes}\},$$

$$post_{\mathbf{app}} = \{app(s, t, u) \mid s, t, u \text{ are lists of gaes and } s * t = u\},$$

Here "$*$" stands for the list concatenation, defined in Section 8.3.

The first clause defining the qs relation is obviously well-asserted, since [] is a list of gaes. To prove that the second clause defining the qs relation is well-asserted it suffices to notice the following implication:

> if x splits a list of gaes xs into littles and bigs, and ls is a sorted permutation of littles and bs is a sorted permutation of bigs, then ls * [x|bs] is a sorted permutation of [x|xs].

The proof that the other clauses of QUICKSORT are well-asserted is left to the reader.

By the Partial Correctness Corollary 8.10 we conclude that for a list of gaes s

$$\{qs(s, Ys)\} \text{ QUICKSORT } inst(qs(s, Ys)) \cap post_{\mathbf{qs}}.$$

But the set $inst(qs(s, Ys)) \cap post_{\mathbf{qs}}$ consists of one element, qs(s, t), where t is a sorted permutation of s.

We conclude that every successful LD-derivation of QUICKSORT $\cup \{qs(s, Ys)\}$ yields a computed instance qs(s, t) such that t is a sorted permutation of s.

Quicksort with Accumulator

Finally, to prove partial correctness of QUICKSORT_ACC we define

$$pre_{\mathsf{qs\_acc}} = \{\mathsf{qs\_acc(s,t,u)} \mid \mathsf{s} \text{ is a list of gaes}\},$$

$$post_{\mathsf{qs\_acc}} = \{\mathsf{qs\_acc(s,t,u)} \mid \quad \mathsf{s} \text{ is a list of gaes and}$$
$$\text{if } \mathsf{t} \text{ is a list of gaes then } \mathsf{sort(s)*t = u}\},$$

where, for s a list of gaes, sort(s) denotes a sorted permutation of s. Adopt for the other relations the same specifications as those used for the QUICKSORT program.

The reasoning that QUICKSORT_ACC is then well-asserted is somewhat elaborate due to the second clause defining the qs relation. The crucial step is the proof that the post-assertion of the head is implied by the conjunction of the pre-assertion of the head and of the post-assertions of the body atoms.

So assume that

(i) [x|xs] is a *ListGae*,
(ii) x splits xs into littles and bigs,
(iii) littles $\in$ *ListGae* and if [x|y1s] $\in$ *ListGae* then sort(littles)*[x|y1s]
    = ys,
(iv) bigs $\in$ *ListGae* and if zs $\in$ *ListGae* then sort(bigs)*zs = y1s.

Now if zs $\in$ *ListGae* then by (iv) y1s $\in$ *ListGae* and sort(bigs)*zs = y1s, so by (iii) ys $\in$ *ListGae* and sort(littles)*[x|sort(bigs)*zs] = ys and, consequently, by (ii) sort([x|xs])*zs = ys. Thus, we established the post-assertion of the head.

We conclude that QUICKSORT_ACC is well-asserted.

As the specification for the qs relation is the same as in the case of QUICKSORT, we conclude now by the Partial Correctness Corollary 8.10 that, for a list of gaes s and an arbitrary term t, every successful LD-derivation of QUICKSORT_ACC $\cup$ $\{\mathsf{qs(s,Ys)}\}$ yields a computed instance qs(s, t) such that t is a sorted permutation of s.

10.7.2 Computing Strongest Postconditions

To compute the strongest postconditions, in Section 8.5 we used the Intersection 1 Corollary 8.12 and its refinement, the Intersection 2 Corollary 8.17. The following two modifications of these results hold for programs with arithmetic.

Corollary 10.13 (Intersection 3) Assume that the Herbrand universe of $\mathcal{L}$ is infinite. Consider an arithmetic program P and an atom A. Suppose that the LD-derivations of $P \cup \{A\}$ do not end in an error and that the set $ground(A) \cap \mathcal{M}(P)$ is finite. Then $sp(A, P) = ground(A) \cap \mathcal{M}(P)$.

Proof. First, observe that the proof of the Intersection 1 Corollary 8.12 remains valid for infinite programs. The reason is that both the Soundness Theorem 4.4 and the Strong Completeness Theorem 4.13 remain valid for the SLD-resolution with infinite logic programs. Checking this claim is routine is left to the reader.

This allows us to draw the desired conclusion in the case when we ignore the introduced proviso that for programs with arithmetic, LD-derivations can end in an error. Now, the assumption that the LD-derivations of $P \cup \{A\}$ do not end in an error allows us to draw the same conclusion when the proviso about the errors is used. $\qquad\square$

Note that the additional assumption used in the above corollary is needed. Indeed, consider the query X < 2. Then the set $ground(\text{X} < 2) \cap \mathcal{M}(P(Ar))$ is finite, while $sp(\text{X} < 2, P(Ar)) = \emptyset$.

Corollary 10.14 (Intersection 4) Assume that the Herbrand universe of $\mathcal{L}$ is infinite. Consider a well-asserted arithmetic program P and a well-asserted atomic query A. Suppose that the LD-derivations of $P \cup \{A\}$ do not end in an error and that the set $ground(A) \cap \mathcal{M}_{(pre,post)}(P)$ is finite. Then $sp(A, P) = ground(A) \cap \mathcal{M}_{(pre,post)}(P)$. $\qquad\square$

Exercise 149 Prove the above corollary. $\qquad\square$

To use these corollaries we use the following modifications of the Unique Fixed Point Theorems 1 8.13 and 2 8.18.

Theorem 10.15 (Unique Fixed Point 3) Let P be an acceptable arithmetic program. Then $\mathcal{M}(P)$ is a unique fixpoint of T_P. $\qquad\square$

Theorem 10.16 (Unique Fixed Point 4) Let P be an acceptable arithmetic program. Then $\mathcal{M}_{(pre,post)}(P)$ is a unique fixpoint of $T_{pre(P)}$. $\qquad\square$

Exercise 150 Prove the above two theorems. $\qquad\square$

Note that in both theorems we have now replaced left termination by acceptability. The reason is that, as noticed in Section 10.3, for arithmetic programs these notions do not coincide. The result indicated in Exercise 133 is hardly of use here because many natural programs, for example `QUICKSORT`, are not error-free (just consider the query `qs([a,b],c)`).

We now illustrate the use of these results on our three running examples.

Length1

In the case of the `LENGTH1` program we can use the Unique Fixed Point Theorem 3 10.15 to check that

$$\mathcal{M}(\text{LENGTH1}) \quad = \quad \begin{aligned} &P(Ar) \\ \cup \quad &\{\text{length}(s, |s|) \mid s \text{ is a ground list}\}. \end{aligned}$$

This theorem is applicable here, since we proved in Section 10.3 that the program
LENGTH1 is recurrent, that is acceptable.

So for a ground list s the set $ground(\texttt{length(s,N)}) \cap \mathcal{M}(\texttt{LENGTH1})$ consists of
just one element: $\texttt{length(s,|s|)}$. In Section 10.6 we proved that for all terms
s,t the LD-derivations of length(s,t) do not end in an error. So the Intersection
3 Corollary 10.13 applies here and yields

$$sp(\texttt{length(s,N)}, \texttt{LENGTH1}) = \{\texttt{length(s,|s|)}\}.$$

Quicksort

To deal with the QUICKSORT program we rather use the $\mathcal{M}_{(pre,post)}(\texttt{QUICKSORT})$
interpretation, where we refer to the specifications for QUICKSORT given in the
previous subsection. We proved in Section 10.3 that QUICKSORT is acceptable and
in the previous subsection that it is well-asserted, so we can use the Unique Fixed
Point 4 Theorem 10.16 to determine the interpretation $\mathcal{M}_{(pre,post)}(\texttt{QUICKSORT})$.

Exercise 151 Prove that

$$
\begin{aligned}
\mathcal{M}_{(pre,post)}(\texttt{QUICKSORT}) \quad = \quad & P(Ar) \\
\cup \quad & \mathcal{M}_{(pre,post)}(\texttt{APPEND}) \\
\cup \quad & \{\texttt{part(a,s,ls,bs)} \mid \texttt{s,ls,bs} \text{ are lists of gaes and} \\
& \qquad \texttt{a} \text{ splits s into ls and bs}\} \\
\cup \quad & \{\texttt{qs(s,t)} \mid \texttt{s,t} \text{ are lists of gaes and} \\
& \qquad \texttt{t} \text{ is a sorted permutation of s}\}.
\end{aligned}
$$

by checking that the set on the right-hand side is indeed a fixpoint of the program
$T_{pre(\texttt{QUICKSORT})}$. $\square$

So for a list of gaes s the set $ground(\texttt{qs(s,Ys)}) \cap \mathcal{M}_{(pre,post)}(\texttt{QUICKSORT})$ consists
of just one element: qs(s,t), where t is a sorted permutation of s. In Section
10.6 we proved that the LD-derivations of QUICKSORT $\cup$ {qs(s,Ys)} do not end in
an error. Consequently, by the Intersection 4 Corollary 10.14 we have

$$sp(\texttt{qs(s,Ys)}, \texttt{QUICKSORT}) = \{\texttt{qs(s,t)}\}.$$

Quicksort with Accumulator

Finally, we consider the QUICKSORT_ACC program with the specifications given in
the previous subsection.

Exercise 152 Prove that

$$
\begin{aligned}
\mathcal{M}_{(pre,post)}(\texttt{QUICKSORT\_ACC}) \quad = \quad & P(Ar) \\
\cup \quad & \{\texttt{part(a,s,ls,bs)} \mid \texttt{s,ls,bs} \text{ are lists of gaes and} \\
& \qquad \texttt{a} \text{ splits s into ls and bs}\} \\
\cup \quad & \{\texttt{qs(s,t)} \mid \texttt{s,t} \text{ are lists of gaes and} \\
& \qquad \texttt{t} \text{ is a sorted permutation of s}\} \\
\cup \quad & \{\texttt{qs\_acc(s,t,u)} \mid \texttt{s} \text{ is a list of gaes and if t is} \\
& \qquad \text{a list of gaes then } \texttt{sort(s)*t = u}\},
\end{aligned}
$$

using the Unique Fixed Point 4 Theorem 10.16.   □

By the same reasoning as above we thus conclude that for a list of gaes s

$$sp(\mathrm{qs}(\mathrm{s},\mathrm{Ys}),\mathtt{QUICKSORT\_ACC}) = \{\mathrm{qs}(\mathrm{s},\mathrm{t})\}.$$

10.7.3   Absence of Failures

Finally, we consider the absence of failures. For pure Prolog programs we used the Absence of Failures Corollary 8.19. For programs with arithmetic the following modification of it can be used.

Corollary 10.17 (Absence of Failures 1) Assume that the language $\mathcal{L}$ has infinitely many constants. Consider a program P and an atom A. Suppose that the LD-derivations of $P\cup\{A\}$ do not end in an error and that the set $ground(A)\cap\mathcal{M}(P)$ is non-empty. Then there exists a successful LD-derivation of $P \cup \{A\}$.   □

Exercise 153 Prove the above corollary.   □

As a simple application of this corollary note that for a list s' there exists a successful LD-derivation of $\mathtt{LENGTH1} \cup\{\mathtt{length}(\mathrm{s'},\mathrm{N})\}$ because the set

$$ground(\mathtt{length}(\mathrm{s'},\mathrm{N})) \cap \{\mathtt{length}(\mathrm{s},|\mathrm{s}|) \mid \mathrm{s} \text{ is a ground list}\}$$

is non-empty.

As for a non-ground list s' this set is infinite, this result cannot be established using the Intersection 3 Corollary 10.13.

10.8   Concluding Remarks

In the conclusions of Chapter 8 we assessed the scope and applicability of the methods that we introduced to deal with correctness of pure Prolog programs. These comments apply equally well to programs with arithmetic. For example, the proof of partial correctness of the $\mathtt{LENGTH1}$ program given in Section 10.7 does not carry through to a non-ground input list s because then the set $ground(\mathtt{length}(\mathrm{s},\mathrm{N})) \cap \mathcal{M}(\mathtt{LENGTH1})$ is infinite, so the Intersection 3 Corollary 10.13 cannot be applied.

To indicate further limitations of these methods we used the $\mathtt{QUICKSORT\_ACC}$ program. We noted in Section 10.4 that the proof of its occur-check freedom for natural queries cannot be established using the methods developed in Chapter 7. Then, in Section 10.5, we noticed that the desired information about the form of its computed instances cannot be established using the notion of well-typedness whereas this notion is adequate to deal satisfactorily with most of the other programs here considered.

QUICKSORT_ACC is of course just an example of a program for which more elaborate techniques are needed to deal with its correctness. In general, programs that use accumulators and difference lists often (but not always — see, e.g. the PALINDROME program) fall into this category.

In this chapter we also dealt with a new problem, namely the absence of runtime errors due to the presence of arithmetic relations. To this end we modified the notion of an LD-derivation and introduced the notion of well-typedness. In Section 10.5 we showed that this notion is a special case of the notion of well-assertedness. So we could have carried out the considerations of Section 10.6 without introducing the notion of well-typedness.

However, this notion is notationally simpler in that the modes and types can be defined in a more compact and intuitive form. Moreover, Aiken and Lakshman [AL93] showed that the problem of whether a program or query is well-typed w.r.t. a given moding and typing is decidable for a large class of types which includes the ones studied here. So, for this class of types, the modes and types can be declared and checked at the compile time. This makes it possible to turn pure Prolog with arithmetic into a typed language.

The remark at the end of Section 10.5 shows that the notions of well-modedness and well-typedness depend in a crucial way on the ordering of the atoms in the clause bodies. The same holds for the notion of well-assertedness. On the other hand, as already observed in Section 8.1, the notion of the computed instance does not depend on this ordering. So when studying the properties of computed instances it would be natural to introduce more flexible versions of these notions which abstract from the ordering of the atoms in the clause bodies. Exercise 142 offers one such a possibility.

10.9 Bibliographic Remarks

The modelling of Prolog's interpretation of arithmetic relations within logic programming given in Section 10.2 is due to Kunen [Kun88].

The notions of well-typed query and well-typed program are due to Bronsard *et al.* [BLR92]. (Unfortunately, a well-typed query (respectively program) is called there a well-moded query (respectively program).) In this paper a language allowing us to define in a concise way recursive (i.e., inductively defined) and polymorphic (i.e., parametric) is introduced.

The definition of these notions given here follows Apt and Etalle [AE93] in that it abstracts from the concrete syntax for types and from the way the type judgements are proved. In this paper modes and types were used to identify a large class of pure Prolog programs for which unification can be replaced by (iterated) matching, a computing mechanism used in functional programming.

The Well-typedness Lemma 10.7 is from Apt and Luitjes [AL95]. It strengthens the original lemma of Bronsard *et al.* [BLR92] from LD-resolvents to SLD-resolvents.

The Reduction Theorem 10.6 and Exercise 136 are from Apt and Marchiori [AM94], where the notions of well-modedness, well-typedness and well-assertedness are formally compared.

In Pedreschi [Ped94] and Boye and Małuszyński [BM95] alternative definitions of well-typed queries and programs were proposed which for certain programs, including QUICKSORT_ACC, allow us to draw such stronger conclusions about the form of the computed instances.

The method of Apt *et al.* [AGP96] mentioned in Section 8.7 which allows us to compute the strongest postconditions of arbitrary queries for certain programs, is also applicable to arithmetic programs.

10.10   Summary

In this chapter we discussed the verification of pure Prolog programs with arithmetic. We noted that all the correctness aspects studied for pure Prolog programs, that is

- termination,
- occur-check freedom,
- partial correctness and
- absence of failures

can be established by a small refinement of the techniques developed in Chapters 6–8. A new aspect of correctness we had to take into account was

- absence of run-time errors due to the presence of arithmetic relations.

To this end we introduced the notions of

- well-asserted queries and programs.

10.11   References

[AE93]   K. R. Apt and S. Etalle.   On the unification free Prolog programs.   In A. Borzyszkowski and S. Sokołowski, editors, *Proceedings of the Conference on Mathematical Foundations of Computer Science (MFCS 93)*, Lecture Notes in Computer Science, pages 1–19. Springer-Verlag, Berlin, 1993. Invited Lecture.

[AGP96] K.R. Apt, M. Gabbrielli, and D. Pedreschi. A closer look at declarative interpretations. *Journal of Logic Programming*, 28(2): 147–180, 1996.

[AL93] A. Aiken and T. K. Lakshman. Automatic type checking for logic programs. Technical report, Department of Computer Science, University of Illinois at Urbana Champaign, 1993.

[AL95] K. R. Apt and I. Luitjes. Verification of logic programs with delay declarations. In V.S. Alagar and M. Nivat, editors, *Proceedings of the Fourth International Conference on Algebraic Methodology and Software Technology, (AMAST'95)*, Lecture Notes in Computer Science 936, pages 66–90. Springer-Verlag, Berlin, 1995. Invited Lecture.

[AM94] K. R. Apt and E. Marchiori. Reasoning about Prolog programs: from modes through types to assertions. *Formal Aspects of Computing*, 6(6A):743–765, 1994.

[AP94] K. R. Apt and A. Pellegrini. On the occur-check free Prolog programs. *ACM Toplas*, 16(3):687–726, 1994.

[BLR92] F. Bronsard, T.K. Lakshman, and U. Reddy. A framework of directionality for proving termination of logic programs. In K. R. Apt, editor, *Proceedings of the Joint International Conference and Symposium on Logic Programming*, pages 321–335. MIT Press, Cambridge, MA, 1992.

[BM95] J. Boye and J. Małuszyński. Two aspects of directional types. In Leon Sterling, editor, *Proceedings of the International Conference on Logic Programming 95*, pages 747–764. MIT Press, Cambridge, MA, 1995.

[Kun88] K. Kunen. Some remarks on the completed database. In R. A. Kowalski and K. A. Bowen, editors, *Proceedings of the Fifth International Conference on Logic Programming*, pages 978–992. The MIT Press, Cambridge, MA, 1988.

[Ped94] D. Pedreschi. A proof method for run-time properties of Prolog programs. In P. van Hentenryck, editor, *Proceedings of the 1994 International Conference on Logic Programming*, pages 584–598. MIT Press, Cambridge, MA, 1994.

Chapter 11

Towards Full Prolog

So far we have dealt only with a small fragment of Prolog which is hardly adequate for programming. In this chapter we discuss various other features of Prolog and explain their meaning and use.

Some of these features have also been studied from the program correctness point of view. This study has always taken place by considering appropriate extensions of logic programming. The exposition of these developments and of the application of the resulting theories to verification of Prolog programs would require another hundred or so pages and thus would make this book inappropriate for a one semester course. Moreover, the correctness aspects of these Prolog programs have not been studied in a systematic fashion. Therefore we limit ourselves to providing necessary pointers to the literature.

We begin our presentation by discussing in the next section the cut operator. In Section 11.2 we explain its use by presenting programs that deal with sets. Next, in Section 11.3 we discuss Prolog facilities that allow us to collect all solutions to a query. In Section 11.4, we introduce an interesting feature of Prolog — meta-variables and explain their use. We also explain there how these two features — cut and meta-variables — allow us to define some other control facilities in Prolog.

In Section 11.5 we introduce negation in Prolog and illustrate its use by means of simple programs. Negation is an important facility because it allows us to write simpler and shorter programs and because it provides a readily available computational interpretation of non-monotonic reasoning, an important branch of common-sense reasoning, an area of artificial intelligence. We illustrate these uses of negation in Section 11.6, where we present a number of programs that deal with directed graphs and in Section 11.7, where we explain the modelling of non-monotonic reasoning.

In the subsequent two sections we study various meta-level built-ins. These are built-ins that allow us to access, compare or modify the syntactic entities out of which the programs are built. In particular, in Section 11.8 we deal with the built-ins that allow us to inspect, compare and decompose terms and in Section 11.9 we consider the built-ins that allow us to inspect and modify the programs.

Then, in Section 11.10, we discuss Prolog's input/output facilities. We conclude the chapter by discussing in Section 11.11 the issue of program verification in the presence of the features here discussed and the literature on related extensions of the theory of logic programming.

11.1   Cut

One of the sources of inefficiency in Prolog is the generation of a too large search space. This problem has been addressed in the language by providing a built-in nullary relation, denoted as "!" and called *cut*, which allows us to prune the search space during the program execution. In this section, we define the meaning of cut.

Informally, cut is defined as follows. Consider the following definition of a relation p:

$$p(s_1) \leftarrow A_1.$$
$$\ldots$$
$$p(s_i) \leftarrow B, !, C.$$
$$\ldots$$
$$p(s_k) \leftarrow A_k.$$

Here, the i-th clause contains a cut atom (there could be others, either in the same clause or in other clauses). Now, suppose that during the execution of a query, some atom $p(t)$ is resolved using the i-th clause and that later on, the cut atom thus introduced becomes the leftmost atom. Then the indicated occurrence of ! succeeds immediately, but additionally

1. all other ways of resolving B are discarded and
2. all derivations of $p(t)$ using the $i+1$-th to k-th clause for p are discarded.

In other words, let Q be a node in T with the cut atom as the selected atom and let Q' be the node that introduced this cut atom. Then, the execution of this cut atom succeeds immediately and additionally results in pruning all the branches that originate in Q' and are to the right of Q. This effect of pruning is illustrated in Figure 11.1.

Note that this operational definition of the behaviour of the cut operator depends on the leftmost selection rule and on viewing the program as a sequence of clauses, instead of a set of clauses.

The following example illustrates Prolog computation in presence of cut.

Example 11.1 Consider the following Prolog program:

$$p \leftarrow r, !, t.$$
$$p.$$

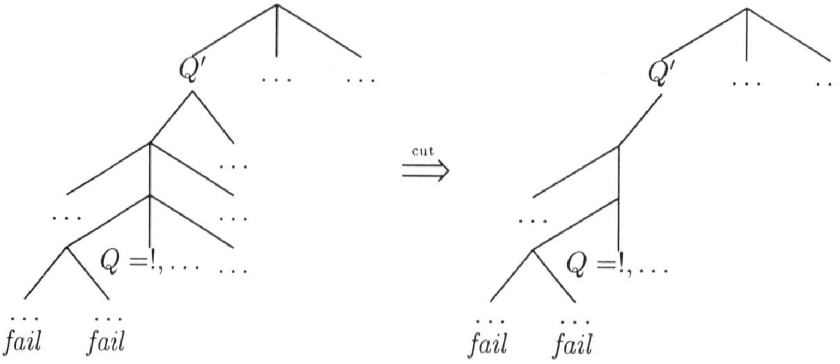

Figure 11.1 The effect of pruning by cut

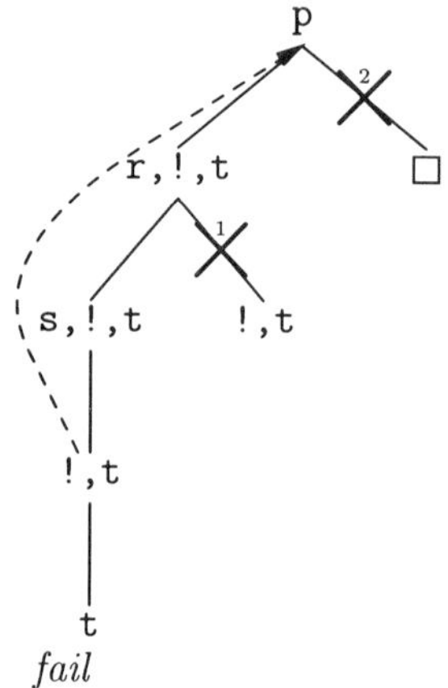

Figure 11.2 A computation tree for the query p

```
r ← s.
r.
s.
```

An LD-tree for the query **p** and the program augmented by the fact **! .** is shown in Figure 11.2. This tree is augmented with a dashed arrow. In the node at the source of this arrow the selected atom is the cut atom. This cut atom is introduced by resolving the query **p**. We say that this query **p** is the *origin* of the considered cut atom. We use here a dashed arrow to point from the selected cut atom to its origin. Execution of this cut atom leads to pruning: the middle branch is pruned according to rule 1 and the rightmost branch is pruned following rule 2. Additionally, the only direct descendant, **t**, is generated.

In the figure, the pruned branches are marked using a cross. The label on the cross refers to the rule that was responsible for the pruning of this branch. Here, the computation ends in a failure. □

To define formally the computation process of Prolog in presence of cut we need to be more precise about the notion of origin.

Definition 11.2 Let $\mathcal{B}$ be a branch in an initial fragment of an LD-tree and let Q be a node in this branch with the cut atom as the leftmost atom. Then, the *origin* of this cut atom is the first predecessor of Q in $\mathcal{B}$ (counting from Q upward) that contains less cut atoms than Q. □

To see that this definition properly captures the informal meaning of the origin note that, when following a branch from top to bottom, the cut atoms are introduced and removed in a First-In Last-Out manner.

Definition 11.3 We now extend the notion of a Prolog tree introduced in Definition 5.1 to pure Prolog with cut. To this end we simply add a new case to the definition of the *expand* operator given in Definition 5.1:

- **prune**: the leftmost atom of Q is the cut atom;
  let $Q =!, \mathbf{B}$ and let Q' be the origin of this cut atom. Remove from $\mathcal{T}$ all the nodes that are descendants of Q' and lie to the right of the path connecting Q' with Q and add $\mathbf{B}$ as the only direct descendant of Q.

As before we define the Prolog tree for a query Q as the limit of the repeated application of the *expand* operator to the leftmost unmarked query. □

In Figure 11.3, we show the successive stages of the construction of a Prolog tree for for the query p and the following program P:

```
p  ←  s, r.
q.
s  ←  q,!, t.
s.
```

Note that in this figure, the result of the "cut step" (that is, the fifth tree) is not itself part of the sequence of expansions; it was added to clarify the effect of the **prune** step.

The above definition of a Prolog tree is less obvious than the one given in Chapter 5 because now the intermediate trees can both "grow" (in the case of the **expand** step) and "shrink" (in the case of the **prune** step). If these steps alternate then it is not clear what is the limit of such an expansion process. To prove the correctness of this definition we define the notions of *inclusion* between the initial fragments of the LD-trees and of the *limit* of a growing sequence of initial fragments of the LD-trees. For the initial fragments of the LD-trees considered in Chapter 5 these notions were obvious.

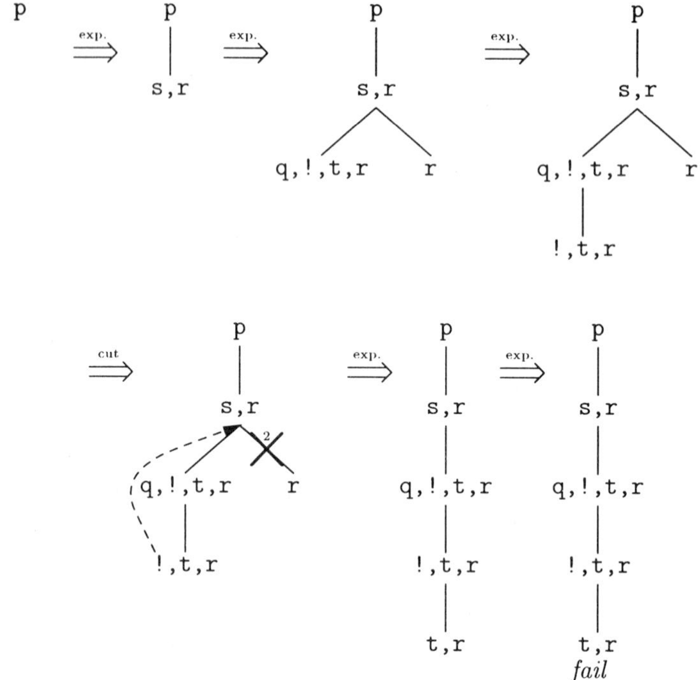

Figure 11.3 Step-by-step construction of a Prolog tree

Definition 11.4 Let $\mathcal{T}$ and $\mathcal{T}'$ be initial fragments of LD-trees. We say that $\mathcal{T}$ *is expanded to* $\mathcal{T}'$ if $\mathcal{T}'$ is constructed from $\mathcal{T}$ by means of one of the following two operations:

  (i) adding some direct descendants to a leaf of $\mathcal{T}$ or marking an unmarked leaf;
  (ii) removing a single subtree from $\mathcal{T}$, provided its root is not a single direct descendant in $\mathcal{T}$.

We denote by $\sqsubset$ the transitive closure of the relation "$\mathcal{T}$ is expanded to $\mathcal{T}'$". □

Lemma 11.5 (Expansion) The relation $\sqsubset$ is an irreflexive partial ordering.

Proof. The transitive closure of a relation is a transitive relation, so we only need to prove irreflexivity. Suppose by contradiction that for some $\mathcal{T}$ we have $\mathcal{T} \sqsubset \mathcal{T}$. Operation (ii) diminishes the number of nodes in the tree. So in the sequence of expansions leading from $\mathcal{T}$ to $\mathcal{T}$ eventually operation (i) is applied. But operation (i) turns an unmarked leaf to an internal node or to a marked leaf, whereas neither operation (i) nor operation (ii) turns an internal node to a leaf or a marked leaf to an unmarked one. Thus, operation (i) is applied to an unmarked leaf of $\mathcal{T}$ and is "irreversible". Contradiction. □

Corollary 11.6 (Expansion) The relation $\sqsubseteq$ defined by

$$\mathcal{T} \sqsubseteq \mathcal{T}' \text{ iff } \mathcal{T} \sqsubset \mathcal{T}' \text{ or } \mathcal{T} = \mathcal{T}',$$

is a partial ordering. $\qquad\qquad\square$

Exercise 154 Prove the Expansion Corollary 11.6. $\qquad\qquad\square$

Now the Expansion Corollary 11.6 justifies Definition 11.3. More formally, this definition is justified by the fact that every countable partial ordering with the least element (here the relation $\sqsubseteq$, with the one node tree as the least element) can be canonically extended to a cpo (see e.g. Gierz *et al.* [GHK$^+$80]), so the limits of growing countable chains always exist.

Member1
We have already observed that the definition of the meaning of the cut operator depends on the leftmost selection rule and on the clause ordering. This excludes any declarative interpretation of it and forces one to rely solely on the procedural interpretation when arguing about the correctness of programs that use cut. This is an obvious drawback and in fact the cut operator is the main source of errors in Prolog programs. In general, it is preferable to use constructs that are defined by means of cut *internally*, like the ones we shall discuss in Sections 11.4 and 11.5.

In the subsequent presentation of programs that use cut we shall indicate some of the subtleties involved in its use. We begin with a simple example. Let us modify the `MEMBER` program of Section 5.5 so that it generates only one solution:

```
% member1(Element, List)  ←  Element is an element of the list List.
member1(X, [X | _])  ←  !.
member1(X, [_ | Xs])  ←  member1(X, Xs).
```

Program: MEMBER1

Here the cut takes place as soon as an element is found and its execution prevents backtracking. The behaviour of the query below should now be compared with that of `member(X, [tom, dick, harry])` on page 126:

```
| ?- member1(X,  [tom, dick, harry]).

X = tom ;

no
```

Note also that we still have

```
| ?- member1(harry, [tom, dick, harry]).

yes
```

etc.

Exercise 155 Draw the Prolog tree for the program MEMBER1 and the above queries
member1(X, [tom, dick, harry]) and member1(harry, [tom, dick, harry]).   □

To illustrate further uses of cut, we now retake the thread of Chapters 5 and 9
and discuss programs computing over a specific domain.

11.2   Sets

Finite sets form a fundamental data structure. Prolog programs that implement
operations on sets typically rely on the use of cut. Sets are not supported in Prolog
by any built-in facilities though, as we shall see in the next section, Prolog provides
some features that allow us to construct the set of all solutions to a query. In what
follows we represent finite sets as ground lists without repetition, so the set $\{1, 3, 7\}$
is simply represented by *any* of the following lists: [1,3,7], [1,7,3], [3,1,7], [3,7,1],
[7,1,3], [7,3,1]. In the sequel by a *set* we mean a list without a repetition. To avoid
various complications we consider here only sets of ground terms. We now present
a couple of programs dealing with sets.

Set
First, let us transform a ground list into a set by removing the duplicate elements.
The following program performs this task:

```
% set(Xs, Ys)  ←   the ground list Ys is the result of removing duplicates
                    from the ground list Xs.
set([], []).
set([X | Xs], Ys)  ←  member(X, Xs), !, set(Xs, Ys).
set([X | Xs], [X | Ys])  ←  set(Xs, Ys).
```

augmented by the MEMBER program.

Program: SET

Here, the purpose of the cut is to ensure that the third clause is used only when
the test member(X, Xs) of the second clause fails. We now have

```
| ?- set([1,2,1,2,3], Ys).

Ys = [1,2,3] ;

no
| ?- set([1,2,1,2,3], [1,2,3]).

yes
```

but also

```
yes
| ?-  set([1,2,1,2,3], [1,3,2]).
```

no

Exercise 156 Modify the above program so that it can also be used to test whether
the second argument is a set representation of the first one. In particular the last query
should then succeed. □

We now present three programs which implement basic operations on sets.

Add
First, we consider the problem of adding an element to a set.

```
% add(X, Xs, Ys)  ←  the set Ys is the result of adding the element X to
                      the set Xs.
add(X, Xs, Ys)  ←  member(X, Xs), !, Xs = Ys.
add(X, Xs, [X | Xs]).
```
augmented by the MEMBER program.

Program: ADD

This program illustrates a subtlety in using cut. The apparently more natural
form of the first clause, namely

```
add(X, Xs, Xs)  ←  member(X, Xs), !.
```

would restrict the use of the program to the queries of the form add(s,t, Z),
where s,t are sets. Indeed, we would then have

```
| ?- add(a, [a], [a,a]).
```

yes

In general, the atoms appearing before the cut, should be viewed as the *only*
tests to be performed before the execution of the atoms appearing after the cut. If
these tests are not satisfied, the next clause is attempted. Now, the above clause
introduces an additional, implicit test that the second and third arguments of **add**
are the same. This test is absent in the original formulation of the program ADD
for which we obtain, as desired,

```
| ?- add(a, [a], [a,a])
```

no

Union

Next, we deal with the union.

```
% union(Xs, Ys, Zs)  ←  the set Zs is the union of the sets Xs and Ys.
union([], Ys, Ys).
union([X | Xs], Ys, Zs)  ←  member(X, Ys), !, union(Xs, Ys, Zs).
union([X | Xs], Ys, [X | Zs])  ←  union(Xs, Ys, Zs).
```

augmented by the MEMBER program.

Program: UNION

We now have

```
| ?- union([1,3,5], [2,4,6], Zs).

Zs = [1,3,5,2,4,6] ;

no

etc.
```

Exercise 157 Write an alternative program which defines the union relation using the SET program.   □

Intersection

Finally, we deal with the intersection.

```
% inter(Xs, Ys, Zs)  ←  the set Zs is the intersection of the sets Xs and Ys.
inter([], _, []).
inter([X | Xs], Ys, Zs)  ←
    member(X,Ys), !,
    Zs = [X | Z1s], inter(Xs,Ys,Z1s).
inter([X | Xs], Ys, Zs)  ←  inter(Xs, Ys, Zs).
```

augmented by the MEMBER program.

Program: INTERSECTION

Exercise 158 Investigate the behaviour of the above program with the second clause replaced by

```
inter([X | Xs], Ys, [X | Zs])  ←  member(X,Ys), !, inter(Xs,Ys,Zs).
```

for the query `inter([a], [a], [a])`.   □

Exercise 159

(i) Write a program that computes the set difference.

(ii) The symmetric difference of two sets A and B is defined as $(A - B) \cup (B - A)$, where $A - B$ denotes the set difference. Write a program that computes the symmetric difference of two finite sets.   □

Other natural relations on sets include the set equality, membership and the subset relation. To define them, respectively, the programs PERMUTATION, MEMBER and SUBSET can be used.

Exercise 160 Write a program that defines a binary relation subset1 such that for a set ys the query subset1(Xs, ys) generates all subsets of ys.   □

Exercise 161 Write a program that computes the number of different elements in a list without the use of the program SET.   □

Exercise 162 Modify the programs QUICKSORT, QUICKSORT_ACC and MERGESORT using cut in such a way that the size of the Prolog trees is reduced for the usual queries. Provide examples that illustrate the achieved reduction in size.   □

11.3   Collecting All Solutions

When discussing in Section 5.1 the interaction with a Prolog system we explained that all solutions to a query can be obtained by the repeated typing of ";". This can be both time consuming and unsatisfactory for certain purposes. In some applications it is natural to collect all solutions to a query in a list or a set. Prolog offers some built-ins that make such constructions possible. These built-ins heavily rely on the fact that Prolog assumes ambivalent syntax, so that a query can be used as a term. In particular, SICStus Prolog provides the following built-ins that allow us to collect all solutions to a query.

11.3.1   findall/3

Consider a call findall(term, query, bag). Then query has to be a non-variable term. It is treated as a query and the call findall(term, query, bag) finds values of term as instantiated by all the c.a.s. of query, collects them in a list in the order of generated solutions and unifies this list with bag.

The call findall(term, query, bag) does not instantiate any variables that appear in query (assuming that bag and query do not share a variable).

In a typical use of findall both term and bag are different variables. Then the call of findall(term, query, bag) instantiates bag to the list of all instances of term which are found in all successive successful Prolog derivations of the query query.

For example, assuming that the MEMBER program is part of the considered program, we have

```
| ?- findall(X, member(X, [tom, dick, tom, harry]), Ls).

Ls = [tom,dick,tom,harry] ;
```

```
no
```

and, assuming that the program used on page 3 is part of the considered program we have

```
| ?- findall(X, direct(X,Y), Ls).

Ls = [amsterdam,amsterdam,seattle,anchorage] ;

no
```

11.3.2   bagof/3

Consider a call `bagof(term, query, bag)`. The difference between `findall/3` and `bagof/3` is that the latter may backtrack in case `query` contains some local variables, that is variables that do not appear in `term`. In this case the successive calls of `bagof(term, query, bag)` generate different solutions, each with different values for the local variables of `query`. In contrast to `findall/3`, the local variables of `query` can become bound during the calls of `bagof(term, query, bag)`.

To illustrate the simple use of `bagof/3` consider the following query:

```
| ?- bagof(X, member(X, [tom, dick, tom, harry]), Ls).

Ls = [tom,dick,tom,harry] ;

no
```

and to see the difference between `bagof/3` and `findall/3` consider the following query:

```
| ?- bagof(X, direct(X,Y), Ls).

Ls = [seattle],
Y = anchorage ;

Ls = [anchorage],
Y = fairbanks ;

Ls = [amsterdam],
Y = paramaribo ;

Ls = [amsterdam],
Y = seattle ;

no
```

11.3.3 setof/3

The only difference between this built-in and `bagof/3` is that the last argument now becomes a set and not a list of all solutions, so duplicates are removed; additionally the elements are sorted according to some standard ordering. In particular, we now have

```
| ?- setof(X, member(X, [tom, dick, tom, harry]), Ls).


Ls = [dick,harry,tom] ;


no
```

To prevent the binding of local variables and the resulting "case distinction" in the successive calls of the `setof/3`, SICStus Prolog provides a syntactic means to bind the (local) variables of the query by means of an existential quantifier. For a query `Q` with a variable `X`, the query `X^Q` denotes `Q` preceded by an existential quantification over `X`. In the call `setof(term, X^query, set)` the variable `X` does not get bound and no backtracking takes place in case different values for `X` exist in successful computations of the query `query`.

In such a way a call of `setof/3` can be used to generate a single *set* of all solutions to a query. For example, we now have

```
| ?- setof(X, Y^direct(X,Y), Ls).


Ls = [amsterdam,anchorage,seattle] ;


no
```

Formally, `^` is an infix operator declared in SICStus Prolog by

```
:- op(200, xfy, ^).
```

The construct `X^Q` "on its own" is a legal query; during its execution the quantification "`X^`" is ignored.

Exercise 163 The `findall/3` built-in is similar to `bagof/3` in that the computed output list does not have to be a set. Suggest an implementation of a variant of the `findall/3` built-in that makes it similar to the `setof/3` built-in. □

11.4 Meta-variables

One of the unusual features of Prolog is that it permits the use of variables in the positions of atoms, both in the queries and in the clause bodies. Such a use of a variable is called a *meta-variable*. Computation in the presence of the meta-variables is defined as for pure Prolog programs with the exception that the mgus employed can now also bind the meta-variables. So, for example, for the program

```
p(a).
a.
```

the query `p(X), X` resolves to `a` and subsequently to the empty query. In other words, the Prolog computation of the query `p(X), X` ends in a success.

Prolog requires that the meta-variables become instantiated before they are selected. In other words, the selection of a meta-variable by the leftmost selection rule leads to a run-time error. For example, for the above program and the query `p(X), X, Y` the Prolog computation ends up in an error.

Meta-variables are useful in a number of ways. For example, when added to pure Prolog programs, they allow us to define disjunction by means of the following simple program:

```
or(X,Y)  ←  X.
or(X,Y)  ←  Y.
```

Actually, in SICStus Prolog disjunction is a built-in pre-declared as an infix operator ";" using the declaration

```
:- op(1100, xfy, ;).
```

and defined internally by the above two clauses, with "or" replaced by ";". The use of disjunction in Prolog sometimes leads to a more elegant program formulation.

Tree Isomorphism

As an example consider the program which tests whether two binary trees are isomorphic. We consider two such trees isomorphic if one of them can be obtained from the other by reordering some of its branches. This relation can be defined as follows:

- two empty trees are isomorphic,
- two non-empty trees are isomorphic if they have identical root and either
    - both the left subtrees and the right subtrees are isomorphic or
    - the left subtree of the first one is isomorphic with the right subtree of the other and the right subtree of the first one is isomorphic with the left subtree of the other.

This leads to the following program.

```
% iso(Tree1, Tree2)  ←  Trees Tree1 and Tree2 are isomorphic.
iso(void, void).
iso(tree(X,Left1,Right1), tree(X,Left2,Right2))  ←
    iso(Left1,Left2),iso(Right1,Right2) ;
    iso(Left1,Right2),iso(Right1,Left2).
```

Program: TREE_ISOMORPHISM

As the precedence of "," is lower than that of ";", the atom of the form A,B ; C,D stands for ;((A,B), (C,D)).

Exercise 164 Rewrite the program FRONTIER using disjunction, without a reference to the relation nel_tree.   □

11.4.1   Control Facilities

Using meta-variables some other extensions of pure Prolog can be defined. In particular, using the cut operator and the meta-variables we can introduce some control facilities. For example the if_then_else relation, well-known in the imperative and functional languages, can be defined by means of the program

```
if_then_else(P, Q, R)  ←  P,!,Q.
if_then_else(P, Q, R)  ←  R.
```

In SICStus Prolog if_then_else is a built-in defined internally by the above two clauses. if_then_else(P, Q, R) is actually written as P → Q;R. No cuts are allowed in P.

Here → is a built-in pre-declared as an infix operator using the declaration

```
:- op(1050, xfy, → ).
```

As the precedence of " → " is lower than that of ";", the atom P → Q;R stands for ;(→ (P,Q), R). "On its own" the atom → (P,Q) is a legal construct and stands for ;(→ (P,Q), fail), that is P → Q;fail.

We conclude this section by mentioning that Prolog also provides an indirect way of using meta-variables by means of a built-in relation call/1. call/1 is defined internally by the clause

```
call(X)  ←  X.
```

Using call/1 it is possible to "mask" the explicit use of meta-variables, but the outcome is the same.

11.5   Negation

The if_then_else construct can in turn be used to define negation by the single clause

```
¬(X)  ←  (X → fail;true).
```

Recall from Section 5.2 that the query fail always fails and the query true always succeeds. So, procedurally, ¬(Q) is executed as follows. If Q succeeds, then ¬(Q) fails and if Q fails, then ¬(Q) succeeds.

By unfolding the if_then_else relation we obtain the alternative, equivalent, but less intuitive definition

```
¬(X) ← X, !, fail.
¬(_).
```

In fact, in SICStus Prolog negation is a built-in pre-declared as a unary prefix operator "\+" using the declaration

```
:- op(900, fy, \+).
```

and defined internally by the above two clauses with "¬(X)" replaced by "\+ X". No cuts are allowed in X.

In the subsequent programs and queries we shall continue to use the logical symbol "¬" instead of "\+". This allows us to look at the clauses and queries that use negation from the logical point of view.

Negation is a powerful device. It often allows us to write simpler and shorter programs. However, it is also a subtle operation and its improper use can easily lead to complications. For example, a and b are different constants, so we have as expected

```
| ?- ¬(a = b).
```

yes

(Recall from Section 5.5 that "=/2" is internally defined by the single fact X = X.) However, we also have

```
| ?- ¬(X = b).
```

no

even though there exists an instance of X that is different from b, namely a.

A theoretical work (see Section 11.11 for a more extensive discussion) shows that it is safe to use negation when it is applied to ground queries and that so limited a use of negation admits a declarative interpretation. To illustrate the use of negation we now present a number of example programs.

Not_equal
Probably the most common such program is the following one:

```
% X ≠ Y ← ground term X differs from the ground term Y.
X ≠ Y ← ¬ (X = Y).
```

Program: NOT_EQUAL

We now can define the `diff` relation referred to in Exercise 52 in Chapter 5, by simply identifying it with the "≠" relation, that is by using the clause

```
diff(X, Y) ← ¬ (X = Y).
```

Note that this simplification is quite significant. The definition of `diff` does not now need to be modified each time more countries are considered. Moreover, it consists of just two clauses (counting X = X.) This is a significant gain; in fact, the previous definition had no less than 42 clauses. However, as the example above shows, its use should be limited to ground queries.

Remove

As an example of the use of "$\neq$" consider now the problem of deleting from a list all occurrences of a given element. The following program does the job.

```
% remove(Xs, X, Ys)  ←  Ys is the result of removing all occurrences of the
                         element X from the ground list Xs.
remove([ ], _, [ ]).
remove([X | Xs], X, Ys)  ←  remove(Xs, X, Ys).
remove([Y | Xs], X, [Y | Ys])  ←  X ≠ Y, remove(Xs, X, Ys).
```

augmented by the NOT_EQUAL program.

Program: REMOVE

This program is meant to be used for the queries of the form `remove(xs, x, s)`, where `xs` and `x` are ground. For example, we have

```
| ?- remove([1,3,3,5], 3, Ys).
```

```
Ys = [1,5]
```

Exercise 165 Write a program that computes the result of removing the first occurrence of an element from the list.   □

Set/1

The following program tests whether a ground list represents a set. This is tantamount to checking that the list has no duplicates.

```
% set(Xs)  ←  Xs is a ground list without duplicates.
set([]).
set([X | Xs])  ←  ¬ member(X, Xs), set(Xs).
```

augmented by the MEMBER program.

Program: SET/1

In the already presented programs that dealt with sets we could "enforce" checking that the arguments are indeed sets by using the above relation `set/1`.

Disjoint

We call two ground lists *disjoint* if no element is a member of both of them. This statement, when translated into first-order logic, yields

```
disjoint(Xs, Ys)  ←  ¬ ∃Z(member(Z, Xs), member(Z, Ys)).
```

Unfortunately, due to the presence of the existential quantifier this is not a legal clause. Defining an auxiliary relation `overlap` solves the problem and yields the following program which allows us to test whether two ground lists are disjoint:

```
% disjoint(Xs, Ys)  ←  Xs and Ys are ground lists with no common element.
disjoint(Xs, Ys)  ←  ¬ overlap(Xs, Ys).

% overlap(Xs, Ys)  ←  the lists Xs and Ys have a common element.
overlap(Xs, Ys)  ←  member(Z, Xs), member(Z, Ys).
```

augmented by the MEMBER program.

Program: DISJOINT

Exercise 166 Write an alternative program that uses the programs given in Section 11.2. $\qquad\square$

11.6   Directed Graphs

As further illustration of the use of negation we now consider pure Prolog programs with negation which deal with finite directed graphs. Formally, a *directed graph* G is a pair $(\mathcal{N}, \mathcal{E})$, where $\mathcal{N}$ is a set and $\mathcal{E}$ is a relation on $\mathcal{N}$, that is $\mathcal{E} \subseteq \mathcal{N} \times \mathcal{N}$. The elements of $\mathcal{N}$ are called the *nodes* of G and the pairs which belong to $\mathcal{E}$ are called the *edges* of G. If the set $\mathcal{N}$ is finite, the directed graph is called *finite*.

Prolog does not have any built-in facilities that deal with graphs. We represent here a finite directed graph (in short: a *graph*) by a (ground) list of its edges. In turn, we represent an edge from node a to node b by the term $e(a,b)$. In this representation the isolated nodes of the graph are omitted. However, we consider here only algorithms dealing with paths in graphs and, consequently, such a (mis)representation is adequate for our purposes.

Formally, given a graph g, by a *path in g from a to b* we mean a sequence $a_1, \ldots, a_n$ $(n > 1)$ such that
- $e(a_i, a_{i+1}) \in g$ for $i \in [1, n-1]$,
- $a_1 = a$,
- $a_n = b$.

A path is called *acyclic* if its elements are distinct and is called *cyclic* (or a *cycle*) otherwise. A path $a_1, \ldots, a_n$ is called a *simple cycle* if $a_1 = a_n$ and $a_1, \ldots, a_{n-1}$ are distinct. In what follows we present paths as lists.

Finally, recall that a graph is called *acyclic* if no cyclic path exists in it. We use the customary abbreviation *dag* for "directed acyclic graph".

Exercise 167 Write a program which tests whether a path is a simple cycle. $\qquad\square$

Transitive Closure of a Dag
A *transitive closure of a graph* $(\mathcal{N}, \mathcal{E})$ is the graph $(\mathcal{N}, \mathcal{E}^*)$ where $\mathcal{E}^*$ is the transitive closure of $\mathcal{E}$. Consider now the problem of computing the transitive closure of a graph. This problem is much simpler to solve when the graph is acyclic, so we handle this special case first. The following pure Prolog program computes the transitive closure of a dag:

```
% trans(X, Y, Graph)  ←  the edge e(X,Y) is in the
                          transitive closure of the dag Graph.
trans(X, Y, Graph)  ←  member(e(X,Y), Graph).
trans(X, Z, Graph)  ←
    member(e(X,Y), Graph),
    trans(Y, Z, Graph).
```

augmented by the `MEMBER` program.

Program: TRANS_DAG

Transitive Closure

Unfortunately, the above program cannot be used for arbitrary graphs. Indeed, consider the query `trans(a, b, [e(a,a)])`. Then, using the second clause, it eventually resolves to itself, so a divergence arises.

A solution is obtained by adding an additional argument to the `trans` relation in which the list of nodes is maintained which should be avoided when searching for a path from the first node to the second one. The following comments can help to understand this program better.

In general, it cannot be claimed that a path from the first node to the second is acyclic, because the edges of the form `e(a,a)` can belong to the considered graphs. However, for each pair of nodes we can always find a connecting path $a_1, \ldots, a_n$ $(n > 1)$, the *interior* of which $a_2, \ldots, a_{n-1}$ is acyclic. (In particular, for $n = 2$ the interior of $a_1, \ldots, a_n$ is empty and hence acyclic.) We call such a path *semi-acyclic*. Finally, we say that a path $a_1, \ldots, a_n$ $(n > 1)$ *avoids* a list `s` if no element of its interior is a member of `s`.

```
% trans(X, Y, Graph)  ←  the edge e(X,Y) is in the
                          transitive closure of the graph Graph.
trans(X, Y, Graph)  ←  trans(X, Y, Graph, []).

% trans(X, Y, Graph, Avoids)  ←  there is a semi-acyclic path in Graph
                                  from X to Y which avoids Avoids.
trans(X, Y, Graph, _)  ←  member(e(X,Y), Graph).
trans(X, Z, Graph, Avoids)  ←
    member(e(X,Y), Graph),
    ¬ member(Y, Avoids),
    trans(Y, Z, Graph, [Y | Avoids]).
```

augmented by the `MEMBER` program.

Program: TRANS

This program can be used in a number of ways. First, we can check whether there exists in a graph g a path connecting two nodes, say a and b — by using the query `trans(a, b, g)`. Next, we can generate all nodes reachable in a graph g from a given node, say a — by using the query `trans(a, X, g)`. Finally, we can generate all pairs of nodes which form the transitive closure of a graph g — by using the query `trans(X, Y, g)`. Of course, the program TRANS_DAG can be used in the same ways.

Path

Let us extend now the above program by generating for each pair of nodes belonging to the transitive closure a path which connects them. This is easily done by maintaining an extra argument in the `trans` relation:

```
% path(X, Y, Graph, Path)  ←  Path is a semi-acyclic path which
                                 connects X and Y in the graph Graph.
path(X, Y, Graph, Path)  ←  trans(X, Y, Graph, [], Path).

trans(X, Y, Graph, _, [X, Y])  ←  member(e(X,Y), Graph).
trans(X, Z, Graph, Avoids, [X | Path])  ←
    member(e(X,Y), Graph),
    ¬ member(Y, Avoids),
    trans(Y, Z, Graph, [Y | Avoids], Path).
```

augmented by the MEMBER program.

Program: PATH

It is interesting to note that this program can be used for several seemingly unrelated purposes.

- To compute all the queries mentioned in the case of the program TRANS.
  To this end for a graph g it just suffices to use the query `path(s, t, g, _)` instead of `trans(s, t, g)`.
- To compute for each pair of nodes in the transitive closure of a graph a semi-acyclic path that connects them.
  For a given pair of nodes a and b in the graph g the appropriate query is `path(a, b, g, Path)`.
- To generate all acyclic paths in a graph.
  To this end for a graph g it suffices to use the query `path(_, _, g, Path)`, `set(Path)`, where the `set` relation is defined by the program SET/1.
- To generate all simple cycles in a graph.
  To this end for a graph g it suffices to use the query `path(_, _, g, Path)`, `simple_cycle(Path)`, where `simple_cycle` is the relation defined in Exercise 167.

As an example, consider the directed graph

$$g := [e(a, b), e(b, c), e(c, a), e(c, d), e(d, a), e(d, b)],$$

depicted in Figure 11.4.

Now, to compute an acyclic path connecting two nodes, say c,b, we can use the query

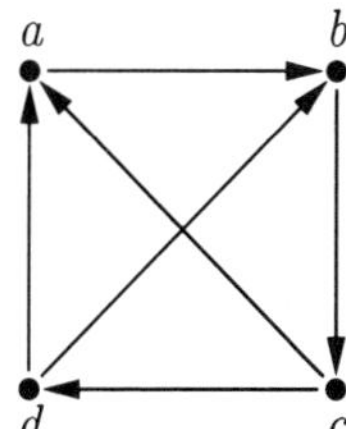

Figure 11.4 A directed graph

```
| ?- path(c,b,[e(a,b),e(b,c),e(c,a),e(c,d),e(d,a),e(d,b)], Path),
     set(Path).
```

```
Path = [c,a,b]
```

To generate all acyclic paths in g which start in a given node, say b we pose the query

```
| ?- path(b,_,[e(a,b),e(b,c),e(c,a),e(c,d),e(d,a),e(d,b)], Path),
     set(Path).
```

```
Path = [b,c]  ;
```

```
Path = [b,c,a]  ;
```

```
Path = [b,c,d]  ;
```

```
Path = [b,c,d,a]  ;
```

```
no
```

And to generate all simple cycles in g of length 5 we use the query

```
| ?- path(_, _,[e(a,b),e(b,c),e(c,a),e(c,d),e(d,a),e(d,b)], Path),
     simple_cycle(Path), length(Path,5).
```

```
Path = [a,b,c,d,a]  ;
```

```
Path = [b,c,d,a,b]  ;
```

```
Path = [c,d,a,b,c]  ;
```

```
Path = [d,a,b,c,d] ;
```

```
no
```

Exercise 168 Write a program which tests whether a graph is a dag.   □

Win

Finally, consider the problem of determining a winner in a two-person finite game in which winning and losing are the only possible outcomes. We represent the game by a graph the nodes of which are positions in the game and the edges of which are the moves in the game. This graph is acyclic, since the game is assumed to be finite. The program to solve the above problem is remarkably concise. Its only clause just defines when a position is a winning one, namely when a move exists which leads to a losing, that is non-winning, position:

```
% win(X, Graph)  ←  X is a winning position in the game
                       represented by the graph Graph.
win(X, Graph)  ← member(e(X,Y), Graph), ¬ win(Y, Graph).
```

augmented by the `MEMBER` program.

Program: WIN

This program assumes that the graph is acyclic, so for a graph g and a node a representing the beginning position in the game, the query `acyclic(g)`, `win(a, g)`, where `acyclic` is the relation defined in Exercise 168 ensures its proper use.

Exercise 169 Use this program to write a program for playing a simple game, like tic tac toe.   □

11.7   Non-monotonic Reasoning

A reasoning method is called *monotonic* if the addition of new assumptions leads to a (possibly not strict) increase of conclusions (or, in other words, if the addition of new assumptions does not invalidate the already obtained conclusions). SLD-resolution can be viewed as a reasoning method where we consider the program clauses as assumptions and the computed instances as conclusions. Clearly, SLD-resolution is in this sense a monotonic reasoning method and so are most logics considered in mathematical logic.

Non-monotonic reasoning methods naturally arise when dealing with incomplete information. Suppose, for example, that using available information we concluded that all English writers have been native English speakers. However, this conclusion turns out to be false if we add the additional information that Joseph Conrad was a native Polish speaker.

One of the striking features of Prolog is that it can naturally support non-monotonic reasoning — by means of negation. In this section we show solutions to two well-known problems in the non-monotonic reasoning by means of pure Prolog programs with negation.

The Birds Program

As the first example consider the proverbial problem concerning the birds. The problem is to reason in the presence of default assumptions. In the natural language they are often expressed by means of the qualification "usually". In what follows the "usual" situations are identified with those which are not "abnormal".

We stipulate the following assumptions.

- The birds which are not abnormal fly (i.e., birds usually fly).
- The penguins are abnormal.
- Penguins and eagles are birds.
- Tweety is a penguin and Toto is an eagle.

The problem is to deduce which of these two birds flies. The solution in Prolog is immediate. We simply translate the above statements into the following rules.

```
fly(X)  ←  ¬ ab(X), bird(X).
ab(X)  ←  penguin(X).
bird(X)  ←  penguin(X).
bird(X)  ←  eagle(X).
penguin(tweety).
eagle(toto).
```

Program: BIRDS

We now obtain the desired conclusions:

```
| ?- fly(toto).

yes
| ?- fly(tweety).

no
```

The Yale Shooting Problem

In this example we assume from the reader an elementary knowledge of first-order logic. In Hanks and McDermott [HM87] a simple problem in temporal reasoning, a branch of non-monotonic reasoning, was discussed. It became known in the literature as the "Yale Shooting Problem". Hanks and McDermott's interest in this problem arose from the fact that apparently all known theories of non-monotonic reasoning, when used to formalize this problem, led to too weak conclusions. The

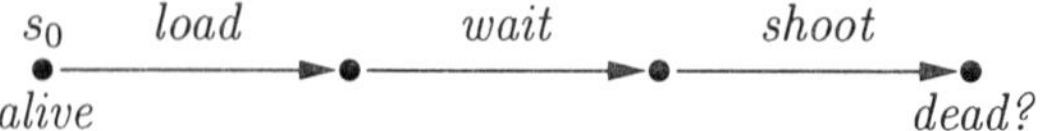

Figure 11.5 The Yale Shooting Problem

problem has been in the meantime extensively discussed in the literature and several solutions to it have been proposed.

Let us now explain the problem. We closely follow Hanks and McDermott [HM87] here. Consider a single individual who in any situation can be either `alive` or `dead` and a gun that can be either `loaded` or `unloaded`. The following statements are stipulated:

- At some specific situation s_0 the person is alive.
- The gun becomes loaded any time a `load` event happens.
- Any time the person is shot with a loaded gun, he becomes dead. Moreover, the fact of staying alive is abnormal with respect to the event of being shot with a loaded gun.
- Facts which are not abnormal with respect to an event remain true.

To formalize these statements Hanks and McDermott [HM87] used the *situation calculus* of McCarthy and Hayes [MH69] in which one distinguishes three entities: facts, events and situations, denoted respectively by the letters f, e and s, and the function *result* such that for an event e and a situation s the term $result(e, s)$ denotes the situation resulting from the occurrence of e in s.

The above four statements lead to the following four formulas of first-order logic:

$$holds(alive, s_0),$$

$$\forall s\ holds(loaded, results(load, s)),$$

$$\forall s\ (holds(loaded, s) \rightarrow (ab(alive, shoot, s) \land holds(dead, result(shoot, s)))),$$

$$\forall f \forall e \forall s\ ((holds(f, s) \land \neg ab(f, e, s)) \rightarrow holds(f, result(e, s))).$$

The problem was to find a way of interpreting these formulas so that statements like

$$holds(dead,\ result(shoot,\ result(wait,\ result(load,\ s_0))))$$

could be proved. Here *wait* is a new event whose occurrence is supposed to have no effect on the truth of the considered facts. Figure 11.5 informally depicts the situation to which the above statement refers.

The solution to the Yale Shooting Problem in Prolog is completely straightforward.

```
holds(alive, []).
holds(loaded, [load | Xs]).
holds(dead, [shoot | Xs]) ← holds(loaded, Xs).
ab(alive, shoot, Xs) ← holds(loaded, Xs).
holds(Xf, [Xe | Xs]) ← ¬ ab(Xf, Xe, Xs),  holds(Xf, Xs).
```

Program: YSP

Note that this program is an almost literal translation of the above formulas to Prolog syntax. To enhance readability we used here the list notation [e | s] instead of *result*(*e, s*) and denoted the initial situation by the empty list [ ].

In contrast to the solutions in other formalisms, Prolog solution can be used not only to model the problem but also to compute answers to the relevant queries. For example, we have

```
| ?- holds(dead, [shoot, wait, load]).
```

```
yes
```

```
| ?- holds(dead, [wait, load]).
```

```
no
```

11.8   Term Inspection Facilities

Prolog offers a number of built-in relations that allow us to inspect, compare and decompose terms. In particular, the following built-ins belong to the first category:

- `var/1`, which tests whether the term is a variable,
- `nonvar/1`, which test whether the term is not a variable,
- `ground/1`, which tests whether the term is ground,
- `compound/1`, which tests whether the term is a compound term,
- the already mentioned in Section 9.4 `integer/1` which tests whether the term is an integer,
- `atom/1`, which tests whether the term is a non-integer constant (an *atom* in Prolog's terminology),
- `atomic/1`, internally defined by the following two rules:

```
atomic(X) ← atom(X).
atomic(X) ← integer(X).
```

So it tests whether the term is a constant.

As a simple example of the use of the `nonvar/1` built-in consider the following modification of the LIST program:

```
% list(Xs)  ←  Xs is a list.
list([]).
list([H | Ts])  ←  nonvar(Ts), list(Ts).
```

Program: LIST1

Now the test `nonvar(Ts)` prevents divergence. In fact, it turns out that for the program LIST1 every query universally terminates. This was not the case for the LIST program.

The built-ins in the second category allow us to compare terms. In particular,

- `==/2` tests whether two terms are literally identical:

```
| ?- f(X) == f(X).


yes
| ?- f(X) == f(Y).


no
```

- `\==/2` tests whether two terms are not literally identical; internally it is defined by the clause

$$X \mathrel{\backslash\!=\!=} Y \;\leftarrow\; \neg(X == Y).$$

So these two built-ins are used as infix operators. In SICStus Prolog they are defined internally as follows:

```
:- op(700, xfx, [ ==, \== ]).
```

Finally, the built-ins in the third category allow us to decompose the terms. To explain their meaning we use the following terminology. Given a term $f(s_1, \ldots, s_n)$ we say that f is its *leading symbol*, n is its *arity*, $s_1, \ldots, s_n$ are its *arguments* and s_i is its *i-th argument* $(i \in [1..n])$. In addition, we call a term of the form $f(x_1, \ldots, x_n)$, where $x_1, \ldots, x_n$ are different variables, a *most general term of arity n*.

In this category there are three built-ins.

11.8.1   functor/3

`functor/3` either extracts from a term the leading symbol and its arity or constructs a most general term of the given arity with the given function symbol as the leading symbol.

More precisely, consider a call `functor(t, f, n)`. There are two cases.

- `t` is a non-variable term.
  Let `f'` be the leading symbol of `t` and `n'` the arity of `t`. Then the call of `functor(t, f, n)` unifies the pair `(f',n')` with `(f',n')`. For example,

```
| ?- functor(f(a,b), F, N).
```

```
F = f,
N = 2
```

In the presence of arithmetic operators `functor/3` deals correctly with the infix notation:

```
| ?- functor(3*4+5, F, N).
```

```
F = +,
N = 2
```

- t is a variable.
  Then f has to be a non-numeric constant ("atom" in Prolog's terminology) and n a natural number. Then the call of `functor(t, f, n)` instantiates t to a pure variable term of arity n the leading symbol of which is f.
  For example

```
| ?- functor(T, f, 3).
```

```
T = f(_C,_B,_A)
```

Any other uses of `functor/3` lead to a run-time error.

11.8.2   arg/3

`arg/3` extracts a specific argument from a term.

Consider a call `arg(n, t, a)`. Then n has to be a natural number and t a compound term. The call `arg(n, t, a)` then unifies the n-th argument of t with a. For example,

```
| ?- arg(3, f(a,b,c), A).
```

```
A = c
```


11.8.3   ../2

`=..` (pronounced "univ") either creates a list which consists of the leading symbol of the term followed by its arguments or constructs a term from a list that starts with a function symbol and the tail of which is a list of term arguments.

It is internally defined as an infix operator with the following declaration in the case of SICStus Prolog:

```
:- op(700, xfx, =..).
```

More precisely, consider a call s = ..t. Two cases arise.

- s is a non-variable term, say $f(s_1, \ldots, s_n)$. Then the call s = ..t unifies the list $[f, s_1, \ldots, s_n]$ with t. For example,

```
| ?- f(a,g(X)) =.. L.
```

```
L = [f,a,g(X)]
```

- s is a variable.
  Then t has to be a list, say $[f, s_1, \ldots, s_n]$, the head of which (so f) is a non-numeric constant. Then the call s = ..t instantiates s to the term $f(s_1, \ldots, s_n)$. For example,

```
| ?- T =.. [app, a, b, X].
```

```
T = app(a,b,X)
```

Any other uses of =.. lead to a run-time error.

As an example of the use of several built-ins introduced in this section consider the following program which tests whether two terms can be unified and in case they do produces an mgu of them. We assume here that =/2 is implemented by means of unification without the occur-check.

```
% unify(X,Y)  ←  the terms X and Y unify.
unify(X,Y)  ←  var(X), var(Y), X = Y.
unify(X,Y)  ←  var(X), nonvar(Y), not_occ(X, Y), X = Y.
unify(X,Y)  ←  var(Y), nonvar(X), not_occ(Y, X), Y = X .
unify(X,Y)  ←  nonvar(X), nonvar(Y), atomic(X), atomic(Y), X = Y.
unify(X,Y)  ←  nonvar(X), nonvar(Y),
               compound(X), compound(Y), term_unify(X,Y).

term_unify(X,Y)  ←  functor(X,F,N), functor(Y,F,N), unify_args(N,X,Y).

unify_args(N,X,Y)  ←  N > 0,unify_arg(N,X,Y),
                      N1 is N-1, unify_args(N1,X,Y),
unify_args(0,X,Y).

unify_arg(N,X,Y)  ←  arg(N,X,ArgX), arg(N,Y,ArgY),
                     unify(ArgX,ArgY).

not_occ(X,Y)  ←  var(Y), X \== Y.
not_occ(X,Y)  ←  nonvar(Y), atomic(Y).
```

```
not_occ(X,Y)  ←  nonvar(Y), compound(Y),
                 functor(Y,F,N), not_occ(N,X,Y).

not_occ(N,X,Y)  ←  N > 0, arg(N,Y,Arg), not_occ(X,Arg),
                   N1 is N-1, not_occ(N1,X,Y).
not_occ(0,X,Y).
```

Program: UNIFICATION

The query unify(s,t) yields an mgu of s and t as a computed answer substitution if s and t unify and otherwise fails. The computation implements a unification algorithm and proceeds as follows. If both s and t are variables, then one is substituted by the other by means of the =/2 built-in. If one of them is a variable and the other not, then it is checked by means of the not_occ/2 relation that the variable term does not occur in the other term (the occur-check). If so, then the variable term is substituted by the other term, again by means of =/2.

If neither s nor t is a variable, but both are constants, then it is tested, by means of =/2, whether they are identical. The case when both s and t are compound terms is handled by calling the relation term_unify.

The query term_unify(s,t) is evaluated by first identifying the form of s and t by means of the built-in functor/3. If for some function symbol f and $n \geq 0$, s is of the form $f(s_1,\ldots,s_n)$ and t is of the form $f(t_1,\ldots,t_n)$, then the relation unify-args is called. Note that the values of F and N are computed here by the first call of functor/3 and then used for testing in the second call of functor/3.

The query unify_args(n,s,t) succeeds if the sequence of the first n arguments of s can be unified with the sequence of the first n arguments of t. When $n > 0$, the first clause is used and these arguments are unified pairwise starting with the last pair. Each pair is dealt with by calling the relation unify_arg.

The query unify_arg(n,s,t) is executed by first extracting the n-th arguments of s and t by means of the built-in relation arg and then calling unify recursively on these arguments. If this call succeeds, the c.a.s. produced modifies s and t and the recursive call of unify_args operates on this modified pair of s and t. Finally, when $n = 0$, unify_args(n,s,t) succeeds immediately.

It is clear from this description what is the intended meaning of the relations term-unify, unify_args and unify_arg. We leave the explanation of the operation of the relations not_occ/2 and not_occ/3 to the reader.

Exercise 170 Write a program that computes the list of all variables of a term.   □

11.9   Program Manipulation Facilities

Another unusual feature of Prolog is that it allows us to access and modify the program during its execution. In this section we consider Prolog built-ins that support these operations.

Just as in the case of the built-ins discussed in Section 11.3, the ambivalent syntax of Prolog is crucial here, because in the built-ins considered here atoms and queries are treated as terms.

To understand the programs discussed below recall from Section 9.3 that "," is right associative, so the query A,B,C,D stands for (A,(B,(C,D))), etc.

11.9.1   clause/2

To access the definitions of the relations present in the considered program, Prolog provides the clause/2 built-in. This built-in assumes that true is the body of a unit clause. In its call the first argument has to be a non-variable. This determines the relation to which the call refers to. Given a call clause(head, body), first the term head is unified with a head of a clause present in the considered program. If no such clause exists, the call of clause(head, body) fails. Otherwise, the first such clause is picked and the term head $\leftarrow$ body is unified with this clause. Upon backtracking successive choices for head are considered and the corresponding alternative solutions are generated.

If at the moment of the call the first argument is a variable, a run-time error arises. So, assuming that MEMBER is part of the considered program we have

```
| ?- clause(member(X,Y), Z).

Y = [X|_A],
Z = true ;

Y = [_A|_B],
Z = member(X,_B) ;

no
```

Once the program clauses can be accessed, by means of the clause/2 built-in, we can construct programs that take other programs as data. Such programs are usually called meta-programs. As a typical example consider the problem of writing in Prolog an interpreter for pure Prolog. The required program is remarkably concise and intuitive.

```
% solve(X)  ←  the query X succeeds for the
                program accessible by clause/2.
solve(true)  ← !.
solve((A,B))  ←  !, solve(A), solve(B).
solve(A)  ←  clause(A, B), solve(B).
```

Program: META_INTERPRETER

The first clause states that the built-in **true** succeeds immediately. The second clause states that a query of the form $A, \mathbf{B}$ is provable if A is provable and $\mathbf{B}$ is provable. Finally, the last clause states that an atomic query A is provable if there exists a clause of the form $A \leftarrow \mathbf{B}$ such that the query $\mathbf{B}$ is provable.

The cuts are used here to enforce the distinction "by cases": either the argument of **solve** is **true** or a non-atomic query or else an atomic one. The cuts also prevent that upon backtracking queries of the form **clause(true, B)** are considered.

To illustrate the behaviour of the program **META_INTERPRETER** assume again that **MEMBER** is a part of the considered program. We then have

```
| ?- solve(member(X, [tom,dick,harry])).


X = tom ;


X = dick ;


X = harry ;


no
```

This program forms a basis for building various types of interpreters for larger fragments of Prolog or for its extensions. For example, using meta-variables the program **META_INTERPRETER** can be easily extended to the case of pure Prolog with arithmetic, by adding to it the following clauses:

```
arithmetic(_ < _).
arithmetic(_ =< _).
arithmetic(_ =:= _).
arithmetic(_ =\= _).
arithmetic(_ >= _).
arithmetic(_ > _).
arithmetic(_ is _).
solve(A) :- arithmetic(A), !, A.
```

The last clause "shifts" the calls of arithmetic atoms to the "system level". In other words, these calls are executed *directly* by the underlying Prolog system.

Exercise 171 The last clause has to be inserted at the right place in the program **META_INTERPRETER** in order to prevent that upon backtracking queries **clause(A, B)**, where **A** is an arithmetic atom, are considered. Determine this place. □

For example, assuming now that the program **QUICKSORT** is a part of the program considered we now have

```
| ?- solve(qs([7,9,8,1,5], Ys)).


Ys = [1,5,7,8,9]
```

11.9.2 assert/1

Additionally, Prolog provides facilities for adding and removing clauses from the underlying program.

The `assert/1` built-in adds its argument as the clause to the program at some place in the program. Its argument has to be a syntactically correct clause. The actions of adding the clauses to the program through the calls of `assert/1` are not "undone" during backtracking.

There are two more specific versions of `assert/1`; `asserta/1` adds its argument at the beginning of the program and `assertz/1` adds its argument at the end of the program.

11.9.3 retract/1

The `retract/1` built-in is in some sense a reverse of `assert/1`. It allows one to remove a clause from the program.

Consider the call `retract(clause)`. The argument `clause` has to be sufficiently instantiated so that the relation whose clause is to be removed can be uniquely determined. The call `retract(clause)` then results in unifying the term `clause` with a clause of the program. If no such clause exists the call fails. Otherwise the first such clause is removed from the program. Upon backtracking successive choices for `clause` are considered and the corresponding clauses are removed from the program. The actions of removing the clauses of the program by means of the calls of `retract/1` are not "undone" during the backtracking.

`assert/1` and `retract/1` are particularly useful for database applications written in Prolog. They are also useful for implementing various system routines and built-ins like the ones considered in Section 11.3.

Finally, let us remark that in SICStus Prolog the relations which are accessed by the built-ins explained in this section have to be declared as *dynamic*. For example, to be able to execute the query `solve(member(X, [tom,dick,harry]))` we need to insert at the beginning of the source program that contains the definition of `member` the declaration

```
:- dynamic member/2.
```

11.10 Input/Output Facilities

Finally, we discuss the input/output facilities of Prolog. We only mention here the most important built-ins provided by the Prolog systems. They can be divided into two categories — those concerned with reading and writing and those concerned with file manipulation.

Below we refer to an "input stream" and "output stream". These are two files, which by default are the terminal screen. Both input stream and output stream can be temporarily changed by commands which we shall explain shortly.

In particular, the following built-ins belong to the first category:

- `get0/1`, which unifies its argument with the ASCII code of the next character of the output stream,
- `get/1`, which unifies its argument with the ASCII code of the next printable character of the output stream,
- `put/1`, which prints the character with the ASCII code equal to the value of its argument,
- `read/1`, which unifies its argument with the next term of the current input stream. The period "." marks the end of this term. If the sequence of characters until the period is not a term, a run-time error arises,
- `write/1`, which writes its argument on the current output stream,
- the already mentioned in Section 5.2 `nl/0`, which produces a new line.

For example, we have

```
| ?-  get(X), put(X), nl, put(X+1).
|: a
a
b
X = 97
```

Here "|:" is the SICStus Prolog prompt for the input. Recall that 97 is the ASCII code of the character a.

Strings are written in Prolog by surrounding them with double quotes. A string is internally identified with the list of the ASCII codes of its characters. `name/2` is a built-in that provides conversion between these two forms of representing strings, as the following two representative examples show:

```
| ?- name(X, [97, 98]).

X = ab

| ?- name(ab, Y).

Y = [97,98]
```

Using `name/2` and the built-in list facilities we can easily manipulate strings. For example, we have

```
| ?- "Alma" = [X, Y | Z], name(New, [Y, X | Z]).

New = lAma,
```

```
X = 65,
Y = 108,
Z = [109,97]
```

Recall that 65 is the ASCII code of the character A, etc.

The following built-ins belong to the second category:

- `seeing/1`, which unifies its argument with the name of the current input stream; in SICStus Prolog "user" is the the name for the terminal screen,
- `see/1`, which makes its argument the current input stream,
- `seen/0`, which closes the current input stream,
- `telling/1`, which unifies its argument with the name of the current output stream,
- `tell/1`, which makes its argument the current output stream,
- `told/0`, which closes the current output stream.

`seeing/1` and `telling/1` built-ins are used to retrieve the name of the previously used file, such as in the sequence `seeing(File)`, `see(newfile)`, `...`, `seen`, `see(File)` in which after processing the file `newfile` the current input stream becomes the previous one.

11.11 Concluding Remarks

In this chapter we introduced a number of important features of Prolog, explained their meaning and presented various Prolog programs that use them.

It should be stressed here that precise meaning of many of the built-ins introduced here is not at all obvious. We tried to be precise but in some cases we just explained their typical use. Moreover, we did not say much about their interaction. For example, we said nothing about the nested uses of `findall`, `bagof` or `setof`, did not explain the effect of cut on the disjunction ";", etc.

The desire to clarify these subtle points motivated research for a precise semantics of full Prolog and prompted the efforts to standardize the language. In Deransart and Ferrand [DF87] and Börger and Rosenzweig [BR94] rigorous semantics of large fragments of the language are provided. By now Prolog is standardized — see ISO [ISO95] and Deransart *et al.* [DEC96].

Returning to program correctness, it should come as no surprise that verification of Prolog programs that use the features discussed here is by no means trivial. The additional complication is that, apart from some limited cases, most of these facilities do not have a declarative interpretation. In other words, the verification of such programs has to rely solely on their procedural interpretation which is pretty complex. A good example is the cut operator. We have noted already in Section 11.1 that its meaning does not admit declarative interpretation and illustrated by means of the program ADD in Section 11.2 that it is easy to come up with wrong uses of it.

As another example of the difficulties in the presence of cut note that by the Unfolding 1 Theorem 7.28 and the Independence Theorem 3.33, a pure Prolog non-recursive program and its unfolding yield for every query the same computed answer substitutions. This property, however, does not hold any more in the presence of cut. Indeed, take the program

```
p  ←  !, q.
p.
```

and the query p. Then the Prolog computation ends in a failure. However, by unfolding q the first clause gets deleted, so the computation for the query p and the resulting program ends in a success.

It is interesting to note that the meta-variables do admit a declarative interpretation. In fact, Apt and Ben-Eliyahu [ABE96] showed that there exists a well-defined declarative interpretation of logic programs with meta-variables and that the soundness and completeness of SLD-resolution can be extended to logic programs with meta-variables. The declarative interpretation can be used to reason about the correctness of pure Prolog programs with meta-variables.

We have already noted in Section 11.5 that in general negation in Prolog does not admit a declarative interpretation and mentioned that when it is applied to ground queries a declarative interpretation of it is possible. In fact, there is a whole area of the theory of logic programming that is concerned with the procedural and declarative interpretation of logic programs augmented with negation. For further discussion we introduce the following terminology. By a *literal* we mean an atom or a negation of an atom. By a *general query* we mean a finite sequence of literals and by a *general clause* a construct of the form $H \leftarrow \mathbf{L}$, where H is an atom and $\mathbf{L}$ a general query. Finally, a *general program* is a finite set of general queries.

The procedural interpretation of general programs is an extension of the SLD-resolution that allows us to deal with negative literals. It is called SLDNF-resolution and was proposed by Clark [Cla78]. Negation is interpreted in it using the "negation as finite failure" rule. Intuitively, this rule works as follows: for a ground atom A,

$$\neg A \text{ succeeds iff } A \text{ finitely fails},$$
$$\neg A \text{ finitely fails iff } A \text{ succeeds},$$

where "finitely fails" means that the corresponding evaluation tree is finite and all its leaves are marked with *fail*.

The correct formal definition is more subtle than it seems. In particular, the original definition does not properly capture the computational process involved and is not adequate for reasoning about termination. The reader is referred to Martelli and Tricomi [MT92] and Apt and Doets [AD94] for a precise definition of the SLDNF-resolution.

There are several "competing" declarative interpretations of general programs. They can be divided into two categories. The first one involves restriction to all (possibly three valued) models of a program extension, called *completion*. This approach was originated by Clark [Cla78], where the notion of completion was introduced. The three valued approach was introduced in Kunen [Kun89]. The second one, in some cases considered for a limited class of general programs, involves restriction to a single (possibly three valued) Herbrand model. This approach was pursued in Fitting [Fit85], Apt *et al.* [ABW88], van Gelder [vG88], van Gelder *et al.* [vGRS88] and various other publications.

The soundness and completeness results for SLDNF-resolution and its modifications relate the procedural and declarative interpretation, usually for a selected class of general programs and queries. In contrast to the case of the customary logic programs no simple clear cut completeness result has been established. For a systematic study of all these issues an interested reader can consult the survey article of Apt and Bol [AB94].

The theory of general programs can be used for verification of pure Prolog programs with (arithmetic and) negation. Among various aspects of program verification the most often studied one has been termination. In fact, in the references Apt and Pedreschi [AP93] and Bal Wang and Shyamasundar [BS94] and Baudinet [Bau88], already mentioned in Chapter 6, termination of general programs w.r.t. the leftmost selection rule is also considered.

To summarize, certain Prolog features discussed in this chapter, like meta-variables and negation, do admit a declarative interpretation under some restrictions. This makes it possible to verify Prolog programs that use them without having to refer to the procedural interpretation. For other features, like cut, the recourse to the procedural interpretation is in general necessary. For yet other features, like the term inspection facilities and program manipulation built-ins, more work needs to be done to clarify the situation. See also the next section.

11.12   Bibliographic Remarks

The problem of formalizing the meaning of cut has been studied in a number of publications starting from Jones and Mycroft [JM84], where various semantics for Prolog with cut were defined. This work was pursued by Arbab and Berry [AB87], Debray and Mishra [DM88] and, more recently, by Lilly and Bryant [LB92]. The approach presented here is due to Apt and Teusink [AT95].

The WIN program appeared first in Gelfond and Lifschitz [GL88]. Termination of the programs TRANS and WIN is considered in Apt and Pedreschi [AP93] and various other aspects of their correctness are dealt with in Apt [Apt95].

The Yale Shooting Problem was extensively discussed in the literature and its formalizations in various formalisms for non-monotonic reasoning were given. The solution in Prolog presented here was found independently by Apt and Bezem [AB91], Elkan [Elk89] and Evans [Eva89] where its declarative and procedural interpretation were also studied.

The formal aspects of the term inspection facilities have been considered in Apt *et al.* [AMP94], where procedural and declarative interpretation of logic programs with arithmetic and the term inspection facilities has been proposed. This declarative interpretation has been used there to prove universal termination of the programs LIST1 and UNIFICATION for all queries.

Finally, the program (scheme) META_INTERPRETER appeared first in Pereira *et al.* [PPW78]. Sterling and Shapiro [SS86] discussed in detail various extensions of it. There is by now an extensive body of work concerning the procedural and declarative interpretation of the logic programming counterpart of this program, that is the program without cuts. The early references include Kowalski [Kow79], Bowen and Kowalski [BK82] and Hill and Lloyd [HL88]. The more recent references are Levi and Ramundo [LR93], Martens and de Schreye [MS95b, MS95a] and Kalsbeek [Kal95]. Pedreschi and Ruggieri [PR96] studied various correctness aspects of the META_INTERPRETER program and of its extensions.

Most of the other programs presented here are taken from the books of Bratko [Bra86], Clocksin and Mellish [CM84] and Sterling and Shapiro [SS86].

11.13 Summary

In this chapter we discussed various features of Prolog so far left out of consideration. These included

- the cut operator,
- facilities for collecting all solutions,
- meta-variables,
- negation,
- facilities for term manipulation,
- facilities for program manipulation,
- input/output facilities.

We illustrated the use of these features by presenting a number of Prolog programs which dealt with

- sets,
- directed graphs,
- game trees

and showed how these features can be used to implement

- non-monotonic reasoning,
- logical operations, like unification,
- meta-interpreters, that is interpreters of (fragments of) Prolog written in Prolog.

For the convenience of the reader we conclude by listing the declarations of all the operators that were discussed in this book.

```
:- op(1200, xfx, :-).
:- op(1100, xfy, [;, ,]).
:- op(1050, xfy, → ).
:- op(900, fy, \+).
:- op(700, xfx, [ =, <, =<, =:= , =\=, >=, >, is, =.., ==, \== ]).
:- op(550, xfy, :).
:- op(500, yfx, [+, -]).
:- op(500, fx, -).
:- op(400, yfx, [*, //]).
:- op(300, xfx, mod).
:- op(200, xfy, ^).
```

11.14   References

[AB87]   B. Arbab and D.M. Berry. Operational and denotational semantics of Prolog. *Journal of Logic Programming*, 4:309–330, 1987.

[AB91]   K. R. Apt and M. A. Bezem. Acyclic programs. *New Generation Computing*, 29(3):335–363, 1991.

[AB94]   K. R. Apt and R. Bol. Logic programming and negation: a survey. *Journal of Logic Programming*, 19-20:9–71, 1994.

[ABE96]   K.R. Apt and R. Ben-Eliyahu. Meta-variables in logic programming, or in praise of ambivalent syntax. *Fundamenta Informaticae*, 1996. To appear in a special issue devoted to the memory of Prof. H. Rasiowa.

[ABW88]   K. R. Apt, H. A. Blair, and A. Walker. Towards a theory of declarative knowledge. In J. Minker, editor, *Foundations of Deductive Databases and Logic Programming*, pages 89–148. Morgan Kaufmann, Los Altos, CA, 1988.

[AD94]   K. R. Apt and H. C. Doets. A new definition of SLDNF-resolution. *Journal of Logic Programming*, 18(2):177–190, 1994.

[AMP94]   K. R. Apt, E. Marchiori, and C. Palamidessi. A declarative approach for first-order built-in's of Prolog. *Applicable Algebra in Engineering, Communication and Computation*, 5(3/4):159–191, 1994.

[AP93]   K. R. Apt and D. Pedreschi. Reasoning about termination of pure Prolog programs. *Information and Computation*, 106(1):109–157, 1993.

[Apt95]   K. R. Apt. Program verification and Prolog. In E. Börger, editor, *Specification and Validation Methods for Programming Languages and Systems*, pages 55–95. Oxford University Press, Oxford, 1995.

[AT95]   K.R. Apt and F. Teusink. Comparing negation in logic programming and in Prolog. In K.R. Apt and F. Turini, editors, *Meta-logics and Logic Programming*, pages 111–133. The MIT Press, Cambridge, MA, 1995.

[Bau88]   M. Baudinet. Proving termination properties of Prolog programs. In *Proceedings of the 3rd Annual Symposium on Logic in Computer Science (LICS)*, pages 336–347. IEEE Computer Society, Edinburgh, 1988.

[BK82]   K. A. Bowen and R. A. Kowalski. Amalgamating language and metalanguage in logic programming. In K. L. Clark and S.-Å. Tärnlund, editors, *Logic Programming*, pages 153–72. Academic Press, London, 1982.

[BR94]   E. Börger and D. Rosenzweig. A mathematical definition of full Prolog. *Science of Computer Programming*, 24:249–286, 1994.

[Bra86]   I. Bratko. *PROLOG Programming for Artificial Intelligence*. International Computer Science Series. Addison-Wesley, Reading, MA, 1986.

[BS94]   Bal Wang and R.K. Shyamasundar. A methodology for proving termination of logic programs. *Journal of Logic Programming*, 21(1):1–30, 1994.

[Cla78]   K. L. Clark. Negation as failure. In H. Gallaire and J. Minker, editors, *Logic and Databases*, pages 293–322. Plenum Press, New York, 1978.

[CM84]   W.F. Clocksin and C.S. Mellish. *Programming in Prolog*. Springer-Verlag, Berlin, second edition, 1984.

[DEC96]   P. Deransart, A. Ed-Dbali, and L. Cervoni. *Prolog: The Standard*. Springer-Verlag, Berlin, 1996.

[DF87]   P. Deransart and G. Ferrand. An operational formal definition of Prolog. In *International Symposium on Logic Programming*, pages 162–172. IEEE Computer Society, San Francisco, CA, August 1987.

[DM88]   S. Debray and P. Mishra. Denotational and operational semantics for Prolog. *Journal of Logic Programming*, 5(1):61–91, 1988.

[Elk89]   C. Elkan. A perfect logic for reasoning about action, 1989. Manuscript. University of Toronto.

[Eva89]   C. Evans. Negation-as-failure as an approach to the Hanks and McDermott problem. In *Proceedings of the Second International Symposium on Artificial Intelligence, Monterrey, Mexico*, 1989.

[Fit85]   M. Fitting. A Kripke-Kleene semantics for general logic programs. *Journal of Logic Programming*, 2:295–312, 1985.

[GHK+80]   G. Gierz, K.H. Hofmann, K. Keimel, J.D. Lawson, M.W. Mislove, and D.S. Scott. *A Compendium of Continuous Lattices*. Springer-Verlag, Berlin, 1980.

[GL88]   M. Gelfond and V. Lifschitz. The stable model semantics for logic programming. In R.A. Kowalski and K.A. Bowen, editors, *Proceedings of the Fifth International Conference on Logic Programming*, pages 1070–1080. The MIT Press, Cambridge, MA, 1988.

[HL88]   P. M. Hill and J. W. Lloyd. Analysis of meta-programs. In H.D. Abramson and M.H. Rogers, editors, *Proceedings of the Meta88 Workshop*, pages 23–52. MIT Press, Cambridge, MA, 1988.

[HM87]   S. Hanks and D. McDermott. Nonmonotonic logic and temporal projection. *Artificial Intelligence*, 33:379–412, 1987.

[ISO95]   ISO. Information Technology — Programming Language — Prolog, Part 1: General Core, 1995. ISO/IEC DIS 13211-1:1995(E).

[JM84]   N. D. Jones and A. Mycroft. Stepwise development of operational and denotational semantics for Prolog. In Sten-Åke Tärnlund, editor, *Proceedings of the Second International Conference on Logic Programming*, pages 281–288, Uppsala, 1984.

[Kal95]   M. Kalsbeek. Correctness of the vanilla meta-interpreter and ambivalent syntax. In K.R. Apt and F. Turini, editors, *Meta-logics and Logic Programming*, pages 3–26. The MIT Press, Cambridge, MA, 1995.

[Kow79]   R.A. Kowalski. *Logic for Problem Solving*. North-Holland, New York, 1979.

[Kun89]   K. Kunen. Signed data dependencies in logic programs. *Journal of Logic Programming*, 7:231–246, 1989.

[LB92]   A. Lilly and B.R. Bryant. A prescribed cut for Prolog that ensures soundness. *Journal of Logic Programming*, 14(4):287–339, 1992.

[LR93]   G. Levi and D. Ramundo. A formalization of metaprogramming for real. In D. S. Warren, editor, *Proceedings ICLP'93*, pages 354–373. The MIT Press, Cambridge, MA, 1993.

[MH69]   J. McCarthy and P.J. Hayes. Some philosophical problems from the standpoint of artificial intelligence. In B. Meltzer and D. Mitchie, editors, *Machine Intelligence 4*, pages 463–502. Edinburgh University Press, Edinburgh, 1969.

[MS95a]   B. Martens and D. De Schreye. Two semantics for definite meta-programs, using non-ground representation. In K.R. Apt and F. Turini, editors, *Meta-logics and Logic Programming*, pages 57–81. The MIT Press, Cambridge, MA, 1995.

[MS95b]   B. Martens and D. De Schreye. Why untyped non-ground meta-programming is not (much of) a problem. *Journal of Logic Programming*, 22(1):47–99, 1995.

[MT92]   M. Martelli and C. Tricomi. A new SLDNF-tree. *Information Processing Letters*, 43(2):57–62, 1992.

[PPW78]   L.M. Pereira, F.C.N. Pereira, and D.H.D. Warren. *User's Guide to DECsystem-10 Prolog*. Department of Artificial Intelligence, University of Edinburgh, 1978.

[PR96]   D. Pedreschi and S. Ruggieri. Verification of metainterpreters, 1996. *Journal of Logic and Computation*. To appear.

[SS86]   L. Sterling and E. Shapiro. *The Art of Prolog*. MIT Press, Cambridge, MA, 1986.

[vG88]   A. van Gelder. Negation as failure using tight derivations for general logic programs. In J. Minker, editor, *Foundations of Deductive Databases and Logic Programming*, pages 149–176. Morgan Kaufmann, Los Altos, CA, 1988.

[vGRS88]   A. van Gelder, K. Ross, and J.S. Schlipf. Unfounded sets and well-founded semantics for general logic programs. In *Proceedings of the Seventh Symposium on Principles of Database Systems, ACM-SIGACT-SIGCOM*, pages 221–230. ACM Press, New York, NY, 1988.

Index

Prentice Hall International Series in Computer Science (*continued*)

PEYTON JONES, S.L. and LESTER, D., *Implementing Functional Languages*
POMBERGER, G., *Software Engineering and Modula 2*
POTTER, B., SINCLAIR, J., and TILL, D., *An Introduction to Formal Specification and Z*
ROSCOE, A.W. (ed.), *A Classical Mind: Essays in honour of C.A.R. Hoare*
ROZENBERG, G. and SALOMAA, A., *Cornerstones of Undecidability*
RYDEHEARD, D.E. and BURSTALL, R.M., *Computational Category Theory*
SHARP, R., *Principles of Protocol Design*
SLOMAN, M. and KRAMER, J., *Distributed Systems and Computer Networks*
SPIVEY, J.M., *An Introduction to Logic Programming through Prolog*
SPIVEY, J.M., *The Z Notation: A reference manual* (2nd edn)
TENNENT, R.D., *Principles of Programming Languages*
TENNENT, R.D., *Semantics of Programming Languages*
WATT, D.A., *Programming Language Concepts and Paradigms*
WATT, D.A., *Programming Language Processors*
WATT, D.A., WICHMANN, B.A. and FINDLAY, W., *ADA: Language and methodology*
WATT, D.A., *Programming Language Syntax and Semantics*
WELSH, J. and ELDER, J., *Introduction to Modula 2*
WELSH, J. and ELDER, J., *Introduction to Pascal* (3rd edn)
WELSH, J. and HAY, A., *A Model Implementation of Standard Pascal*
WIKSTRÖM, A., *Functional Programming Using Standard ML*
WOODCOCK, J. and DAVIES, J., *Using Z: Specification, refinement, and proof*